THE AGE OF THE CATHEDRALS

GEORGES DUBY

THE AGE OF THE CATHEDRALS

ART AND SOCIETY 980-1420

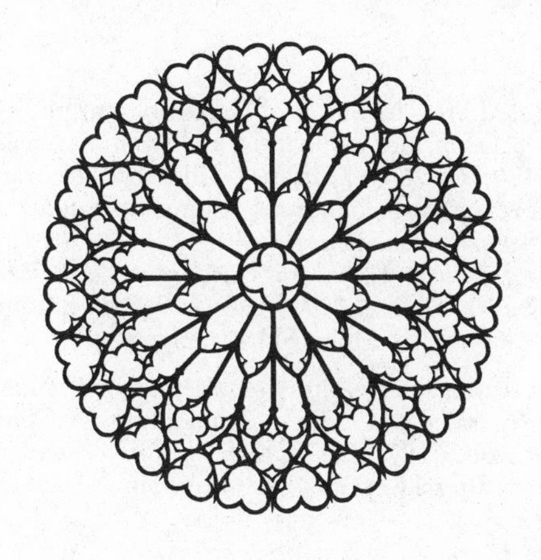

Translated by

Eleanor Levieux and Barbara Thompson

THE UNIVERSITY OF CHICAGO PRESS

THE UNIVERSITY OF CHICAGO PRESS, CHICAGO 60637
CROOM HELM LIMITED, LONDON

Printed in the United States of America
85 84 4 5

The revised French edition of this work was published as *Le Temps des cathédrales: L'art et la société 980–1420,* ©1976 by Editions Gallimard. The original version was published in three volumes as *Adolescence de la chrétienité occidentale 980–1140, L'Europe des cathédrales 1140–1280,* and *Fondements d'un nouvel humanisme 1280–1420,* ©1966–1967 by Editions d'Art Albert Skira, Geneva.

All quotations from Dante are taken from *The Divine Comedy,* translated, with a commentary, by Charles Singleton, ©1970, 1973, and 1975 by Princeton University Press. Reprinted by permission of Princeton University Press.

Library of Congress Cataloging in Publication Data

Duby, Georges.
The age of the cathedrals.

Translation of Le temps des cathédrales.
Includes index.
1. Art, Medieval. 2. Art and society. 3. Civilization, Medieval. I. Title.
N5970.D8313 701'.03 80–22769
ISBN 0–226–16769–0

CONTENTS

PART ONE

THE MONASTERY

980-1130

A mere handful of men—unending emptiness stretching so far west, north, and east that it covers everything—fallow land, fens and wandering rivers, heaths, woods and pastureland, every conceivable type of erstwhile forest leaving behind it brush fires and the woodburners' furtive sowing—clearings here and there, wrested from the forest but still only half-tamed; shallow pitiful furrows that wooden implements drawn by scrawny oxen have scratched on the unyielding soil; within this food-producing area, large still-empty blotches—fields left fallow for one year, or two or three, sometimes even ten years, so that the soil can rest and recover its fertility in nature's own way—huts of stone, mud, or branches, clustered in hamlets surrounded by thorn hedges and a belt of gardens; sometimes, inside the palisade that shields it, a chieftain's dwelling, a wooden hangar, granaries, the slaves' sheds and the cooking hearth some ways off to the side; sparsely scattered towns, the mere whitened skeletons of Roman cities invaded by rural nature, streets in ruins that ploughs swing wide of, fortifications haphazardly repaired, stone structures dating back to the Roman Empire that have been turned into churches or strongholds; near them a few dozen huts that house the vinegrowers, weavers, and blacksmiths, all the domestic craftsmen who make ornaments and arms for the garrison and the local bishop; two or three Jewish families who lend a little money on pledge; trails, the long lines of men toiling at portage, flotillas of small boats on every waterway . . .

Such is the Western world in the year 1000. Compared with Byzantium, compared with Córdoba, it seems rustic, very poor and defenseless. A wild world, ringed round by hunger. Its meager population is in fact too large. The people struggle almost barehanded, slaves to intractable nature and to a soil that is unproductive because it is poorly worked. No peasant, when he sows one grain of wheat, expects to harvest much more than three—if it is not too bad a year; that means bread to eat until Easter time. Then he will have to manage on herbs, roots, the makeshift food that can be gleaned from forest and riverbank and, on an empty belly, he will do the heavy summer tasks and wither with fatigue while he awaits the harvest. When—as more often happens—the weather is not good, the grain supply runs out even earlier and the bishops must waive prohibitions and upset ritual to permit the eating of meat during Lent. Sometimes, when too heavy rains have soaked into the ground and hampered the autumn ploughing, when storms have pummeled and spoiled the crops, the customary food shortage becomes a famine, a great death-dealing wave of starvation. The chroniclers of the times all described such famines, not without a certain satisfaction. "People pursued one another in order to eat each other up, and many cut the throats of their fellow men so as to feed on human flesh, just like wolves."

Were they exaggerating when they described the cadavers heaped high in charnel houses and the roving bands of famished creatures who ate earth and sometimes dug up the dead? All of these writers were men of the Church. They were so meticulous in telling about such distress, or about the endemic illnesses that slowly drained away frail lives and sometimes turned epidemics into appalling mortality rates, because they believed that these calamities were indicative of both mankind's misery and the enigma of God's ways to man. Having enough to eat all year long seemed, at that time, an enormous privilege, reserved for a few noblemen, a few priests, a few monks. All other people were slaves to hunger. They believed that hunger was inherent in the human condition, that it was natural for man to suffer, to feel naked, stripped of everything, helpless in the face of death and evil and indefinable dread. Because man was a sinner. Ever since Adam's fall, hunger had racked him, and no man could claim to be free of hunger any more than he could of original sin. The world of the year 1000 was terrified. What it was most afraid of was its own weaknesses.

For some time, however, imperceptible movements had little by little been raising this wretched population out of its abject poverty. Gradually, in the eleventh century, the peoples of western Europe began to emerge from their barbaric condition. Shaking off famine, they took their place in history one by one. The reason for such an awakening—the infancy of progress—was that precisely at this point in time, and forever after, this region of the world ceased to be a prey to invasions. Henceforth this was to be its outstanding privilege over all other regions, and the guarantee of its steady ascendency. For centuries wave after wave of migrant peoples had rolled almost uninterruptedly over the Western world, disturbing the order of things, rushing the course of history, spoiling and despoiling. For a time the Carolingian conquests had managed to restore a semblance of discipline and peace in continental Europe; but hardly had Charlemagne passed away when the elusive invaders were back again. From Scandinavia, the eastern steppes, and the Mediterranean islands that had fallen under Moslem sway, they swooped down on Latin Christendom to pillage it. Now, the first seeds of what we call Romanesque art began to germinate just at the very time when such raids ceased. The Norsemen settled down and grew tame, the king of Hungary was converted, and the count of Arles chased from their lairs the Saracen strongmen who controlled the passes through the Alps and had just held the Abbot of Cluny for ransom. After the year 980, no more abbeys were sacked, no more flocks of frightened monks fled along the roads with their relics and their ornaments. From then on, whenever flames were visible near the woods on the horizon, they indicated a fire set by some peasant to clear the land, and not by ransacking raiders.

Apparently, during the obscure tenth century, very timid progress in agriculture had begun to radiate outward from the great monastic estates. It was able to develop unhampered, and gradually equipped the peasantry with more effective implements—better ploughs, better methods of harnessing, iron ploughshares that could turn over the earth, fertilize it better, make headway in the heavy soil that had been allowed to lie fallow until then. So it became possible to make more scrub give way to permanent fields, extend clearings and open up new ones, achieve greater yields everywhere and make the harvesters' sheaves more abundant. Although the documents that history has left us do not bear any direct traces of this rural expansion, countless clues confirm its development, and on it rests all of the cultural progress made in the eleventh century. The famine of 1033 described by a monk of Cluny, Raoul Glaber, in his *Histories,* was actually one of Europe's last, for just at that time the recurrent periods of starvation grew shorter and the intervals between them longer. As the rural areas acquired better equipment, they had room for more people, and the population was less at the mercy of every epidemic. Amid the distress of the year 1000 were new tensions as the proportion of younger people grew; for three long centuries this trend was instrumental in Europe's ascension. As Bishop Thietmar of Merseberg wrote in his chronicle, "the thousandth year since the sinless Virgin gave birth to Christ the Savior having arrived, a radiant day dawned over the world."

Only a handful of men, it is true, were able to glimpse that dawn. All the others continued to huddle for a very long time in gloom and wretched anxiety. Regardless of whether they were free or snared in the remaining bonds of slavery, the peasants were still devoid of everything—not so ravenously hungry but harried, without the slightest hope of ever knowing anything better than their pigsty existence, of rising above their condition, even when they succeeded, after ten or twenty years of privations, in putting aside enough money, one coin at a time, to buy a scrap of land. The nobility crushed them. The nobility was the framework of society. And society, on the basis of the powers to protect and exploit which its chiefs were acknowledged to have, was organized like a many-storied edifice; each story was completely cut off from the others, and the top floor was reserved for a small group of very powerful people. A few families—the kings' relatives or friends—held everything in their hands: the land, the enclaves of cultivated soil, and the vast empty spaces that surrounded them, the troops of slaves, the rents due from their tenant farmers and the obligations those tenants had to carry out, the ability to fight, the right to sit in judgment, the right to punish, all of the positions of authority that the Church—and the times—had to offer. Covered with jewels and swathed in fabrics of many colors, noblemen roamed over this wild country with their mounted escorts, appropriating the few things of value that its poverty concealed. They alone benefited from the increased wealth that better methods of working the land were slowly secreting. Only these factors—the profoundly hierarchical arrangement of relationships within society, the powers held by the nobility, and the might of the aristocracy—can account for the fact that the extremely slow growth of such primitive material structures led so rapidly to the signs of expansion that became so abundant in the last quarter of the eleventh century. These included the launching of trade in luxury items, the lust for conquest that drove the warriors of the West to every corner of the world, and finally, the rebirth of a lofty culture. If the unmitigated authority of a very tight-knit class of noblemen and men of the Church had not weighed so heavily on the masses of laborers whom they dominated, the art forms whose development this book proposes to follow would not have been able to emerge in those vast waste lands, amid so rustic and brutish a people, still so poor and so coarse.

The striking thing about these works of art is actually many things at once: their diversity, the exuberant inventiveness they reveal, and their very profound and very substantial unity. There is nothing surprising about their variety. Latin Christendom covered an enormous area; it took months to travel from one end to the other because untamed nature put up countless obstacles and because of the large gaps which still riddled the fabric of the population. Each virtually impenetrable province cultivated its own ethnic features. Throughout the centuries when migrating peoples were on the move and empires were being built up and collapsing, widely varying layers of cultural deposit were being laid down here and there throughout Europe. Some of them, still fresh, spread over given clusters of regions, whose fringes mingled with and interpenetrated others. Also, the tenth-century invaders had ravaged some parts of the Western world more than others. For all of these reasons, there were very considerable local disparities within that world in the year 1000.

Nowhere were they more pronounced than along the edges of the Latin world. To the north, west, and east, the Christian countries were surrounded by a broad, semicircular, more barbarian zone where paganism still survived. This was where in earlier times the Scandinavian expansion—that of the Norse and Danish sea-dogs and the Gotland merchants—had developed. It had left behind a sturdy tradition of boats plying back and forth in the estuaries and sailing upriver. This area was still frequently plagued by spells of banditry, but intertribal rivalry was wearing off and giving way to peaceful trading. From the Saxon strongholds in England, from the banks of the Elbe, the forests of Thuringia and Bohemia, from Lower Austria, missionaries set out to destroy the last idols and erect the cross. Many of them were still martyred. But the princes of these regions, where little by little itinerant peoples had settled, building villages and working the land, were more inclined to lead their subjects to baptism. In welcoming the Gospel they also welcomed a little civilization.

A vigorous contrast to these unpolished outlying regions were the southern marches, those of Italy and the Iberian peninsula, for that is where the Western world encountered two other worlds—Islam and Byzantine Christendom—that were far more refined. At numerous points—in the county of Barcelona, in the tiny kingdoms clinging to the mountains of Aragon, Navarre, Leon, and Galicia, at the outposts of the Po delta (Ferrara, Comacchio, Venice), above all in Rome, the crossroads of Hellenism and Latin influences, fascinated and dazzled by Constantinople, jealous of it—the ferments of progress entered in the form of ideas, techniques, very beautiful objects, and the wondrous gold coins that embodied the material superiority of the cultures to the south which touched Latin Christendom.

The heart of the large continental body that Charlemagne had succeeded in unifying within the empire was also full of diversity. The sharpest contrasts, the ones that showed up in even the most common day-to-day actions, bore the imprint of Rome, still more or less fresh and distinct depending on the area. In northern Germania, for instance, Rome's imprint was altogether nonexistent; in Bavarian Flanders it had been almost wiped out by the waves of barbarians. It was still very vivid, on the contrary, in Auvergne, in the area around Poitiers and in the regions south of the Alps, where the cities were less dilapidated and the language was heavily tinged with Latin. Still other contrasts stemmed from the souvenirs left here and there by the various peoples who had come to settle in the West during the early Middle Ages; Lombardy, Burgundy, Gascony, and Saxony all bore their names. Among the provincial aristocracy, the memory of the earlier conquerors sustained an awareness of nationhood and the type of xenophobic prejudice that made Raoul Glaber of Burgundy so scornful of the inhabitants of Aquitaine: one day he had seen a group of them go by, their garb and their joyousness equally scandalous, escorting a betrothed princess to some northern king. The most important points in this geographical blur were those where cultural zones came together, for this meant confrontations, borrowing, enriching experience. These outstandingly fertile sites were Catalonia, Normandy, and the region around Poitiers, Burgundy, Saxony, and the great plain stretching from Ravenna to Pavia.

What is more surprising is the profound unity which marked this civilization even though it spread far and wide over an area so difficult to tame. For such close kinship, observable at every cultural level, particularly where artistic creativity was concerned, we can make out several reasons. First of all, people were extremely mobile. Much of the Western world's population at that time was still largely nomadic; this was especially true of its leaders. The kings, princes, lords, and bishops, and the numerous attendants who always escorted them traveled constantly. In the course of the year they rode from one to another of their estates to eat the local products on the spot, holding court here or there, and leaving again immediately to visit a church or lead a military expedition. They lived on the road, always on horseback, and interrupted their peregrinations only during the worst of the rainy seasons. Possibly the hardest privation for a monk was to shut himself away forever in a cloister. Since many monks could not bear to do so, they too had to be allowed to wander about, going from abbey to abbey. The fact that the small group of privileged persons on whom the creation of works of art depended moved about so much fostered contacts and encounters.

In this splintered world there were no genuine boundaries. Every man knew that as soon as he ventured beyond the village of his forefathers, no matter where he went he would be a foreigner, hence a suspicious element, and therefore in danger. He might be robbed of everything. The risk began at his very doorstep, but regardless of whether he stayed close to home or went off to the remotest corners of the earth, the degree of risk did not change. Was there any borderline between Latin Christendom and the rest of the universe? In Spain no barrier ever separated the regions overtaken by the hosts of Islam from the zone that was subject to the Christian kings, and in fact that zone varied considerably with the outcome of each military expedition. In 996 Al Mansur ravaged Santiago de Compostela, but fifteen years later the count of Barcelona entered Córdoba. Many of the petty Moslem princes were subjects of the sovereigns of Aragon or Castile by virtue of contracts that guaranteed them protection and required them to pay tribute. Conversely, very vigorous Christian communities thrived and prospered under the power of the caliphs; indeed, a chain of such communities stretched from Toledo to Carthage, Alexandria and Antioch, linking the Western Empire to the Byzantine Empire by the south, all along the "Arabized" shores of the Mediterranean. Had it not been for these many conjunctions, we would be at a loss to explain how the Coptic themes managed to make such enormous inroads in Romanesque iconography, or to account for the pictorial "idiom" found in the illuminations of the *Apocalypse of Saint-Sever*. Eleventh-century Europe was actually very permeable; it lent itself to aesthetic intersection and coalescence.

One factor in cohesion—and very powerful it was too, at the higher levels of culture—was still the bond of the Carolingian era. For several decades virtually the entire Western world had been brought together under a single political domination, governed by a homogeneous group of bishops and judges who all came from the same families and had all received similar education in the royal house; they met periodically as they gathered around the sovereign, their one master, and were united by the multiple ties of kinship, shared memories, and collective work. Distances and natural obstacles notwithstanding, the eleventh-century aristocracy was brought together not only by the same faith but also by the same rites, the same language, the same cultural heritage, the memory of one man: Charlemagne. In other words, by the prestige of Rome and prestige of the Empire.

But the innermost similarities, the ones that linked the diverse types of artistic creation most coherently, stemmed chiefly from art's unique destination. At this period, the sole function of what we call art—or at least, of what remains of it after a thousand years, the least fragile, most sturdily built portion of it—was to offer unto God the riches of the visible world, to enable man, by making such presents, to appease the wrath of the Almighty and win his favors. All great art at the time was sacrificial. It had less to do with aesthetics than with magic. Here we touch on the most deep-seated characteristics of the act of artistic creation in the West between 980 and 1130. During that century and a half, the vitality that propelled Latin Christendom on toward progress had already begun to provide the material means with which to fashion works that were less rough-hewn and far more amplified than before. Yet this development had not yet reached the point where it would overcome established thought patterns and primitive types of conduct. The eleventh-century Christians still felt utterly crushed by mystery, overwhelmed by the unknown world their eyes could not see, the tireless, admirable, disturbing world whose reign went beyond mere appearances. Even the most enlightened thinkers moved in the spheres of the irrational, alive with phantasms. That is why the greatest and possibly the only sacred art in Europe was born at this particular point in history, in the brief interval when man, although he had not yet shaken off his age-old dreads, had access to very effective instruments of creativity.

Now, since the purpose of this art was sacrificial, it was entirely dependent on the elements of society that were responsible for parleying with the unseen powers which governed life and death. Since time immemorial tradition assigned this role to the kings. But at this time feudalism was overtaking Europe; monarchical powers were beginning to be dispersed and grasped in several hands. Little by little, in the new-patterned world, the sovereigns lost control over works of art, and the monks appropriated it instead because the cultural context made them the essential mediators between the human and the sacred. This transfer from rulers to monks shaped most of the features of Western art at that time.

I

IMPERIAL ART

"In the kingdom of heaven, there is but one who reigns and that is he who hurls the thunderbolts. It is only natural that on earth as well there be only one who reigns, under him." Human society in the eleventh century was conceived as an image, a reflection of the city of God, which was a kingdom. The fact was that feudal Europe could not do without a monarch. When the groups of crusaders, whose own indiscipline was glaringly obvious, founded a state in the Holy Land, they promptly made it a kingdom. As the models of earthly perfections, the kings were at the summit of all mental images intended to represent the orderly arrangement of the visible universe. In a culture based on chivalry, all of the heroes—Arthur, Charlemagne, Alexander, David—were kings, and it was the king whom every man of the times, whether priest, warrior, or even peasant, strove to resemble. The birth of the concept "work of art," of the major, overwhelming works to which all others referred, depended particularly closely on royalty, its functions and resources. Accordingly, anyone who wishes to grasp the relationship between social system and artistic creativity must start by closely analyzing the elements on which monarchical authority was based at this time and how that authority expressed itself.

The tradition of royalty, harking back to the Germanic past, had been introduced by peoples whom Rome had taken perforce into its fold. Rome had not detracted in any way from the powers of their chiefs, whose main function was to make war. They led their men of arms into battle. Every spring the young warriors gathered around them, eager for the adventuresome military life. Throughout the Middle Ages the unsheathed sword was the outstanding emblem of sovereignty. But the barbarian kings enjoyed another privilege, at once more mysterious and more vital to the general welfare: the magic power to intercede between their people and the gods. The happiness of all hinged on their mediation. This power came to them from the gods themselves in a direct line, for the blood of the gods flowed in their veins. Hence "it was ever the custom of the Franks, when their king died, to choose another from among the persons of royal blood."

The mid-eighth century was a turning point in the history of the aesthetic missions assumed by Europe's royalty. From that time on, the king of the Franks—the mightiest sovereign in the western world, the one who seemed to loom above all of Latin Christendom—was anointed, as was already the practice with the petty kings of northern Spain. This meant that the Frankish king no longer owed his charisma to his mythical kinship with the powers of the pagan pantheon. Instead, he now received his charisma directly from the biblical God, by sacrament: priests anointed him with the holy oil, and the oil, as it impregnated his body, filled it with the strength of the Lord and all the powers of the next world. Such ritual authorized dynastic transfers of power and at the same time brought the sovereign into the Church. There he took his place among the bishops who, like himself, were consecrated. *Rex et sacerdos:* he received the ring and the staff, the insignia of a pastoral mission. With the hymns of praise intoned during the solemn coronation, the Church established his rank within the celestial hierarchies and defined his role. Now he was concerned not only with combat but with peace and justice as well.

Most important of all, the king naturally took his place at the source of the greatest artistic enterprises. There were several reasons for this. It was only within the Christian Church that the artistic traditions handed down from the glories of Rome lived on in the eighth-century Western world; all of the building and decorating which had formerly aimed to exalt the temporal power of the cities now celebrated the power of the Almighty; great art had become entirely liturgical; and the Christianization of the king's powers now made him the focal point of all Church ceremonial. So, the practice of anointing the king had made art an inherently royal affair.

The art forms born of monarchical initiative became more specific after the year 800, once the restoration of the Empire had increased the scope of royalty in western Europe. Imperial authority, another divine institution, ranked slightly higher in the hierarchy of powers, between the earthly kings and the rulers of heaven. The pope had prostrated himself before Charlemagne and, on Saint Peter's tomb, had hailed him as Augustus. The emperor of the Western world was the new Constantine, the new David; henceforth he, and he alone, had the mission of guiding Latin Christendom to its salvation. Even more than the kings who bowed before them, the new emperors had to comport themselves as godly heroes. But at the same time they knew they were Caesar's successors. In carrying out the dedicatory acts incumbent on them, acts that gave rise to works of art, they were mindful of their predecessors, whose lavish gifts had adorned the cities of antiquity. They wished the objects that were offered to God at their behest to bear the imprint of a certain aesthetic concept—that of the Empire; in other words, of Rome. Accordingly, the artists who carried out their commissions and those of the other Western sovereigns relied chiefly on the works of ancient Rome for their inspiration. In the year 1000, everything that linked the art of the Western world to the art of classical Rome stemmed very directly from the rebirth of the Empire.

Indeed, two centuries after Charlemagne was crowned emperor artistic creativity still depended on the convergence of all temporal power on a sovereign known to be the Lord's anointed. His authority flowed from a supernatural source, and the principal meaning of his ministry was, as in the *Laudes regiae,* the reconciliation of two worlds, the visible and the invisible, and the cosmic harmony of heaven and earth. In the year 1001, at the same time as the movement which was going to feudalize Europe was slowly developing, Europe always relied chiefly on its emperor and its kings—the guides who laid the homage of their entire people at God's feet and distributed heaven's favors among them—for the decoration of its major offerings, that is, the churches, the altar adornments, the reliquaries, and the illustrated books which enclosed the word of God. In the Europe of that time, this mission was deemed to be inherent in their office. The dignity of the royal function was conceived as supreme authority based on liberality, generosity, and magnificence. The sovereign was he-who-gives—who gives to God and who gives to men—and it was fitting that beautiful works should flow from his open hands. The act of giving was intended to overwhelm the person who accepted the gift, to bring him into subjection. Thus it was through the presents he gave that a monarch reigned, through presents that he attracted the benevolence of the supernatural powers to his people, through presents that he won the love of those who served him. When two kings came together, they vied to see which one would give the more superb presents and so affirm his superiority over the other. This was why the best artists of the eleventh century clustered around the sovereigns as long as the latter retained their power. The art of this period was conceived as aulic art, because it was sacred art. The workshops in which it was produced were linked to the kings' courts. The geography of eleventh-century art is therefore an accurate indication of the brilliance of the respective powers on Europe's various thrones.

In the year 1000, in the Western world just as in Byzantium and in the Islamic countries, the most active of these creative centers gravitated around the emperor, sole leader of the faithful. The Empire was still the myth in which Roman Christendom, then being dismembered by the feudal system, found the fundamental unity it dreamed of, and believed to be in accordance with God's plan. Obstinately, Roman Christendom clung to this myth for, under the emperor's authority, it felt united in brotherhood behind Christ, prepared to march in unison toward the perfections of the celestial city. This symbol was related to the eschatological expectation that informed all of Christian thinking: the end of the world and "the consummation of the Roman and Christian Empire" would occur simultaneously when an emperor, the last monarch of the century, went up on to Golgotha to offer his insignia of rank to God, thus opening the reign of the Antichrist.

The *imperium* was a blend of three concepts. In its deepest acceptation it was a divine election, whereby the Almighty chose a leader. The Almighty granted him victory and at the same time filled him with his grace, with that magic power—*felicitas* or *Königsheil*—which placed him above all other sovereigns as the sole guide of God's people. This explains the renewed vigor of imperial power in Saxony in the tenth century. It had been weakened, reduced to the status of a mere idea as Charlemagne's descendants themselves rapidly weakened. But the idea remained clearer in Germania, a region that the Carolingians had shaped with their own hands and had endowed with its only civilization. Of all the German provinces, Saxony was the wildest, but it was there that Christianity, more recently introduced, was more stalwart. The plunderers who raided all Europe spared Saxony, partly because it was very poor and chiefly because its inhabitants defended themselves boldly. To this heaven-sent haven, seemingly blessed by God, thronged fugitive monks with their relics and their knowledge. At the foot of the Harz mountains the Saxon princes had built fortresses that proved effective. They managed to defeat the Hungarian hordes—a plague sent by God—in battles in the open countryside. It was on the battlefield itself that first Duke Henry, then his son Otto, received the *imperium* from their warriors by acclamation.

But immediately they acted as Charlemagne's successors. Remembrance of the Carolingian achievements, the aura that surrounded Aachen constituted in fact the second pillar supporting the idea of empire and directly implied the third: it was the *imperium romanorum* that had been revived in the Western world. The mystique surrounding "empire" was inseparable from the mystique surrounding "Rome." Hailed as the savior of Christianity, Otto I, king of Germany, felt bound to protect and purify the Church of Rome. He journeyed to the Eternal City, for there and only there could the rites of the imperial coronation be carried out, by the pope's own hands, over Saint Peter's tomb.

The resuscitated, Germanized Empire was more Roman than the Carolingian Empire had been. In the year 998, Otto III, the grandson, decided to transfer his residence to the Aventine, and although the bulla with which he sealed his edicts still bore Charlemagne's effigy on one side, on the other it showed a picture of the imperial city, *Roma Aurea.* Although the emperor appointed himself, although he recited the long list of his attributes, he considered the title "Roman" the most important of them. *Renovatio im-*

perii romani: "We have proclaimed Rome capital of the world." The renascent Empire affirmed its universality, and its masters claimed, far more consciously than their Carolingian predecessors had, that they were the lords of the lords of the universe. They no longer clashed with Byzantium. Their own mothers and wives were Greek princesses. They were filled with admiration for the Constantinople of the year 1000, itself in the midst of a rebirth. They took over from the *basileüs* the conception of his authority, and borrowed all of the emblems of his powers—the golden cope, the sphere perfectly held in the right hand, symbolizing a sovereignty embracing the entire world. For the most solemn ceremonies, Emperor Henry II draped himself in a mantel covered with constellations and the signs of the zodiac (embroidered in Italy possibly in about 1020 and still on view today in Bamberg) so that he would seem to be enveloped in the firmament itself. The crown in the Vienna Museum, which may have been that of Otto I, has eight sides, like the eight walls of the palatine chapels, signifying eternity. They are a symbolic evocation of the heavenly Jerusalem, i.e., the flawless realm which is to be revealed on Judgment Day. Did not Caesar's reign prefigure that of Christ returning at the end of time to preside in glory? As "Saint Peter's servant" the emperor-apostle was the leading evangelist, and through the missionaries, who had the benefit of his support, he strove to increase the number of the faithful. He was preceded by the holy lance, which contained a nail from the true cross. He led God's people toward the ultimate triumph, the triumph of good over evil, of resurrection over death. The power of the Ottonian emperors was meant to be total, like God's own power, and when they ordered liturgical books from their court painters they liked the illustrations to show tall women with bowed heads who represented the nations of the Western world, a submissive escort gathered at the base of their throne.

One symbol summed up all the others. It was properly imperial because it signified victory and because in it the emperor identified with Christ the Savior. This symbol was the cross—all of the crosses which the eleventh-century emperors had embellished by their goldsmiths and distributed among the churches within their realm as a sign of their invincible power. On a page from a gospel book decorated some time between 1002 and 1014 in Ratisbon, a painter depicted the then emperor in the center of a cruciform composition, at the crossroads of the universe. Angels come down to him from heaven to drape him with the emblems of his power. Saint Ulrich and Saint Emmeram support his arms, just as Aaron and Hur had supported those of Moses when he fought the Amalecites. And Christ himself, enthroned in the glory of the apocalyptic visions, places the diadem on the emperor's head.

Yet the emperor was actually unable to keep his footing in Rome, where the real rulers were the great families of the local nobility who dwelt among the ancient ruins. Although he was king of Italy and soon became king of

Burgundy and Provence, he did not really reign except over the Germanic lands and over Lotharingia, where Charlemagne's lineage originated. In the year 1000, Otto III had gone to Aachen. "As he did not know exactly where the bones of the caesar Charlemagne lay, he secretly had the stone floor of the church taken up at the place where he believed them to be and then had his men dig until the bones were indeed found, in a royal sarcophagus. Then the emperor took the gold cross that hung about the dead man's throat and part of his clothes that had not yet rotted away; after which he had everything put back in place with the greatest respect." Another chronicle goes on to say that the remains of the first restorer of the Western Empire were disinterred and displayed to the people like the relics of the saints and, once they had been put back in the crypt, "began to demonstrate their powers by various signs and dazzling miracles." The imperial authority, restored but flawed, sought to establish a link between itself and the Carolingian nucleus, already haloed with legends and prodigious feats. It claimed to be Roman and universal, but in fact it was taking on a definite Germanic cast: the most influential centers of artistic creativity in the eleventh century were situated in Saxony, in the valley of the Meuse and on the shores of the Boden See. The Germanic regions nurtured the transplanted Frankish traditions of monarchical art, of a certain architecture, and of pictorial and plastic forms; they incorporated the heritage from the craftsmen of the year 800, invigorated by Byzantine art and the evocation of ancient Rome. But since the emperor's real power was confined to a few provinces and he was not the only reigning authority, imperial art was no longer centered around a single focal point as it had been in Carolingian times. It enhanced other monarchies, far from the seat of empire.

The Empire had not done away with royalty, which predated it and was equally sacred. The kings too considered themselves Christs. Like the bishops—pastors of the people and successors to the apostles—the kings were chosen by the intervention of the Holy Ghost and acclaimed in a cathedral by the assembled clerics and warriors.

> The same day and in the same church, the chosen bishop of Münster was consecrated by the same prelates as had anointed the king, in order that the presence of the king and highest priest at this solemn occasion might be considered a happy omen for the future, since the same church and the same hour had witnessed the unction of two persons who, according to the institution of the Old and the New Testament, are the only ones to be anointed sacramentally and are both called Christ the Lord.

The king led his people in time of war; as soon as age or illness prevented him from riding horseback, he lost all authority. But he was also the minister of the invisible, and this he remained up to his death. Helgaud of Saint-

Benoît-sur-Loire, in his life of King Robert of France, written in about 1040, spoke of the king as of a sort of monk whose first duty was to pray for his people. "He had so much taste for the Scriptures that not a day went by but that he read the Psalms and prayed to God on high in the manner of Saint David." The vow he took on the day of his anointment bound him to shield the priests and the poor people, especially, from the kingdom of darkness. Whenever the members of his court sat at his feet, he was sitting in the very place where Jesus sat, for during this period Jesus was most often depicted as a crowned judge. Helgaud continued:

> God's might conferred on this perfect man such power to heal bodily ailments that it sufficed that his pious hand should touch the crippled at the place where they suffered, and make the sign of the cross, for them to be cured of their illnesses, whatever they might be.

King Henry IV was excommunicated; yet when he traveled through Tuscany, the peasants rushed to touch his garments so that their harvests would be more abundant. Therefore the "king must be considered differently from the throng of laymen, for he has been anointed with the holy oil, and, as such, he shares in the sacerdotal function." He stands before God as the supreme sacrificer. His role in artistic creativity is no different from that of the emperors.

Some of the Western kings in fact vied with the Roman and Germanic sovereigns for the title of emperor. This was especially true in the regions that Charlemagne had never subdued. The English kings called themselves "august emperors of all Albion." By the beginning of the eleventh century Canute had brought all of the shores of the North Sea under his control. "Having overcome five kingdoms—Denmark, Anglia, Brittany, Scotland, and Norway—he became emperor." And the kings of Leon, anointed protectors of Santiago de Compostela when they triumphed repeatedly over the weakened Córdoban princes, likewise spoke of their *imperium* by virtue of which the other Iberian kings should be subject to them. Within the confines of Charlemagne's own realm there was still one king, but only one, whom his biographers thought fit to invest with the rank of *imperator francorum;* this was not the king of Germany, but instead the king of the land of the western Franks, the king of France. In the year 1000 this king was universally considered the rival of the Teutonic emperor. His bishops reminded him that "the Empire itself had had to bow before his predecessors." The king of Germania in fact treated him as his equal. In 1023, when Emperor Henry II and King Robert of France arranged a meeting in the middle of the river Meuse, on the border between their respective states, in order to discuss "the state of the Empire," they treated each other like brothers. Most thinking men of the times considered that the Western world was divided into two great kingdoms: one under Caesar, the other over which reigned the true descendant of Clovis, the king who was crowned in Reims near the baptismal font where the convenant between God and the Franks had earlier been sealed. "We see that most of the Roman Empire has been destroyed, but as long as there are Frankish kings determined to perpetuate it, its dignity will not vanish altogether, for it shall be upheld by kings." In fact, the transfer of the *imperium* actually worked to the benefit of the Franks, and the Ile-de-France region was the true Frankland. The Capetian king who reigned in the year 1000 held conclaves amid bishops and counts, as Charlemagne had. He enriched the churches with his donations. In the abbeys under his protection—at Saint-Germain-des-Près and Saint-Denis—he had the sacred books adorned and illustrated. And since he held himself to be heir to the Empire, the artists who worked for him used the imperial works of the ninth century as their models, just like the artists in Germany.

This is how in the Western world of the year 1000 the power to dispense peace and justice and the powers to intercede which the people's leaders were acknowledged to have were apportioned, along with the related prerogatives. One look at this apportionment shows that there were two Europes. Southern Europe had no king, for beyond the Loire as far as Catalonia the king of France had no more authority. Similarly, in Lyons and in Provence, the emperor had only illusory rights, and throughout Italy his authority tended to become purely fictitious. As a result, there was room in these southern provinces for art to develop untrammeled by any monarch's whims. Europe's kings were all in the north; the exceptions were a few mountain strongholds around Leon and Jaca where the power of the Christian sovereigns of Spain was taking root. At the outermost reaches of the European kingdoms, in the remote Scandanavian hinterland, and in those swamp-encircled parcels of land where the first cathedrals of Poland, Bohemia, and Moravia were being erected close to the princes' residences, slave-artisans continued to use prehistoric artistic resources as they adorned the chiefs of tribes who had hardly heard of Christ's name. But even here, and even while evangelization was progressing, the prestige attaching to kings consecrated by the Church made those artists take their inspiration from the recollection of Carolingian aesthetics, the type that predominated at Winchester, in the entourage of the Anglo-Saxon sovereigns, among clerics and monks whose knowledge came straight from the libraries across the Channel, in Laon, Saint-Miquier, and Corbie. The Capetians' opulent reign preserved it more brilliantly in the old Francia between Reims, Orléans, and Chartres. But these forms of royal art, harking back to the spirit of antiquity, flourished chiefly in Germania, taking root in the forests of Saxony and, more vigorously still, in the areas around Aachen and Liège and along the Rhine, in the Carolingian heartland. At one point the determination of King Henry II made Bamberg, in Franconia, their most thriving center. The seeds were propagated by the many relay points—bishoprics and monasteries—on German soil, and were carried by the Teutonic emperor on his occasional progresses as far as Rome. Such were the most propitious sites, close to the various thrones. There, north of Tours, north of Besançon and the Alpine passes, which had been converted to Christianity, the tradition of augustan patronage and handsome reflections of classicism were preserved.

Eleventh-century man looked upon his king as a knight who, sword in hand, guaranteed his people justice and peace. But he considered him a wise man as well and insisted that he know how to read. As soon as the Western world began to take the institution of monarchy for a *renovatio,* a rebirth of imperial power, its sovereigns were no longer allowed to remain illiterate, as their barbarian ancestors had been. The ideal image which Rome had conceived of the good emperor, the fount of wisdom and knowledge, was resurrected, so that Europe's rulers would strive to resemble it. One chronicler in Limoges, writing at the very beginning of the eleventh century and anxious to prove that the duke of Aquitaine was the equal of kings, attributed these exemplary practices to him:

> He keeps in his palace a great number of books and if war chances to leave him some leisure time, he devotes it to reading them himself, and spends long nights among his books until sleep overcomes him.

But even before that, Eginhard had shown his hero, Charlemagne, spending his vigils learning to write, while King Alfred had had Latin works available in the monastic libraries translated into Anglo-Saxon so that the noblemen at his court could understand them. And Otto III, emperor in the year 1000, who presided over the learned men's discussions, was able to conduct a dialogue with Gerbert, the most famous of them.

But it was the coronation ceremony which had really welded the alliance between the dignity of monarchs and written culture. The sovereign had been integrated into the Church, and the priests of that Church had to be able to handle books since the word of their God was laid down in the texts. So the anointed king had to be a man of letters, and the son who would be called upon to succeed him in his lofty position had to be given a bishop's education. Hugh Capet, who was not yet king but aimed to be, had sent his eldest son, Robert, to study with Gerbert, the best pedagogue of his day, "so that he would inculcate into him enough knowledge of the liberal arts to make him pleasing in the eyes of the Lord by the way he practiced all of the holy virtues."

It was also incumbent on the sovereign, who was responsible for his people's salvation, to make sure that the ecclesiastical body of which he had become a member was of good quality, that is, learned. As a result, in a society whose aristocracy had an entirely military conception of culture and spurned any form of learning, it was his duty to support institutions which would train the clerics to carry out their calling. Even now twentieth-century French children picture Charlemagne as the founder and protector of schools, scolding the bad pupils and placing a fatherly hand on the best pupils' heads; this is simply because he, more than any other king, strove to carry out the obligations implicit in his coronation by ordering that a place of study be instituted near every bishop's palace and abbey. And all of the sovereigns in the year 1000 imitated him. They insisted that the monasteries and cathedral churches be well supplied with books and teachers. They were anxious to establish the best scholastic centers in their palaces, for among the sons of the aristocracy who spent their youth at court, those who were not destined to bear arms and would be installed in the highest ecclesiastical offices had to find the requisite intellectual nourishment without being far from their king. This was one of the most vital and pressing tasks included in the powers that God delegated to each sovereign. As a result, the notion of schooling remained closely linked to the royalty of the eleventh century.

For two reasons—because the monarch considered himself the successor of the Caesars, and, more important, because God himself, in the Scriptures as translated by Saint Jerome, expressed himself in the language of Augustus—the culture disseminated by the royal schools was neither indigenous nor the culture of the times. It passed on a heritage that preceding generations had reverently, jealously safeguarded throughout the obscurity and decay of the Dark Ages—the heritage of a golden age, of the Roman Empire. It was a classical heritage, and it kept the memory of Rome alive.

How many men benefited from this education? A few hundred, a few thousand perhaps, out of every generation—and to the highest level of learning only a few dozen privileged men ever had access. Though they were scattered throughout Europe, with huge distances between them, they knew one another, corresponded, and exchanged manuscripts. Their "school" consisted of themselves, the few books they had copied or had received from their friends, and a tiny cluster of listeners, men of all ages who had traveled the world over and faced the gravest dangers in order to frequent these scholars and listen to them read. All were churchmen and all were motivated by a wish to better serve their God and hear his word.

Now even in Italy and Spain they all had as their mother tongue a dialect which was quite distinct from the text of the Bible and the liturgy. Therefore teaching was based on the study of Latin words, of their meaning and their sequential arrangements—in short, on vocabulary and grammar. The pedagogues of late antiquity had decreed that the way to scholarly learning followed along seven roads to knowledge, the seven "liberal arts." Of these, the eleventh-century masters really cultivated only the first and most elementary: an initiation into the language of the Vulgate. Above all, wrote Abbo of Fleury in the year 1000, pupils must be able to swim in the deep, stormy, cunning ocean of Priscian's grammar; then, so that they would be able to grasp the meaning of Genesis and the Prophets, they would be made to read, or would listen while someone read aloud to them, certain models of proper language by Virgil, Statius, Juvenal, Horace, Lucian, or Terence. Though they were pagan authors, they had used the purest forms of linguistic expression; and for the sake of their pedagogical value their works were rescued from the tidal wave that engulfed Roman culture, and the debris from them that floated on the surface were painstakingly gathered together. Researchers hunted for them in the libraries of Italy, where they had suffered the least. Then the fragments were carefully collated in the scriptoria that flanked every center of learning at that time. The young priests and monks copied out whole passages from them and committed them to memory. Until their dying day they never ceased to quote from classical poems, intermingled with verses from the Psalms. Such principles of education made humanists out of the Church's highest dignitaries, encouraging them to imitate these models—to plagiarize them with all due respect. The German abbess Hrotswith decided to adapt the plays of Terence so that the nuns would not be plunged abruptly into a text too free for them. The Emperor Otto III, born to the purple, was given the schooling of a cleric. He sent copyists to Reims and to the abbey of Bobbio; he ordered copies of the works of Caesar, Suetonius, Cicero, and Livy brought back to him—that is, their recital of all the glories of imperial and republican Rome, the city of which he called himself the master; in Pavia, he meditated on Boethius' *The Consolation of Philosophy*. And all this because he was king. Thus several factors—the methods of ecclesiastical teaching, the type of culture dispensed in the schools, and its deliberate aim of serving the interests of Latin letters—strengthened the ties between monarchy and the resurrected forms of Roman antiquity. That part of artistic creativity which was inspired by the king in person was more resolutely turned toward classicism by the schools.

The artistic tradition of antiquity was passed on by the art of books more than by anything else. Books were considered accessories to the liturgical rites at least as much as instruments of knowledge. They were part of the divine service, and for that reason they had to be as ornate as the altar, the sacred vessels, or the walls of the church. The juncture of written culture and images appeared, more intimately than anywhere else, in books. A great many sacramentaries, lectionaries, and bibles that had been illustrated in the days of Louis the Pious or Charles the Bald still formed the basis of all monastic and episcopal libraries in the eleventh century, and the quality of the workmanship in them could not but arouse admiration. Almost all of the paintings which decorated them imitated early Christian models. The vigorous postures of the evangelists, the semblance of architecture that served as a backdrop for them, all of the ornaments laid out so as to frame the canons and the calendars, and the embellishments of the initials were consonant with the lessons in humanism embodied in the writings of the Latin poets and historians. The images in the Carolingian books were haloed with the same respect as the *auctores* because they were believed to bear the message of Augustan Rome and because, like the grammarians' teachings, they resuscitated pure, undefiled latinity, free of barbaric corruption. These images were copied just as Virgil, Suetonius, or Terence were copied.

On orders given by the emperor at Reichenau or Echternach—and by the kings of France at Saint-Denis—artists covered the parchment pages of the evangelistaries with paintings, borrowing from the ninth-century illustrators in order to edify a décor they deemed worthy of the monarchy. But they were actually inventing, and their creations differed appreciably from Carolingian types. Standing out against the gold background that established them inside the eternity of the liturgical rites, the new forms were profoundly faithful to the aesthetics of the later Empire. Resolutely figurative, linked to the concrete and visible world, they situated the human body in space without deliberately altering its proportions.

The resurrection of relief as a technique was more daring. The Carolingian artists had drawn on the Roman conception of plastic art but had been almost secretive about it, for in the ninth century paganism was still a threatening presence. If people were shown statues of the Lord and—more dangerous still—statues of the saints, might they not be tempted into idolatry once again? To avoid this danger, figures carved out of ivory or wrought by goldsmiths were never taken far from the altar. The only persons who ever came near them were initiates—those who celebrated Mass, men of unshakeable faith and considerable culture. In the year 1000 all this changed. The schools dispelled errors. They recognized and adopted the beauties of the pagan world and dedicated them to God. In the provinces subject to the kings, the wooden divinities which the tribes had worshiped had been destroyed long since, replaced by another symbol: the cross; and the heads of the Church were less afraid of the old gods. So they dared to place images of the divine presence at the church doors, in all the convincing potency that volume conferred on them.

The initiative was doubtless taken in Saxony, the heart of the imperial renascence. Bernward, bishop of Hildesheim, was a learned man. The emperor had chosen him to teach his son. His biographers also portray him as an architect, an illustrator of manuscripts, and a goldsmith. At that time all of those things went together. In 1015 he had two bronze doors cast, piece by piece, for his church. In so doing he was following the example set by Charlemagne and the high dignitaries of the Church in Charlemagne's day. But whereas until then no bronze portals had ever had images carved on them, the Hildesheim doors were covered with images: sixteen scenes juxtaposed in two parallel columns that explained to the people the mystic bonds linking heaven and earth. On the left, the Old Testament figures, "reading" from top to bottom—from the creation of the world to the murder of Abel—illustrate the fall from grace. On the right, figures from the Gospel "read" upward from the annunciation to Christ's resurrection, demonstrating the redemptory movement that elevates mankind, once saved, to eternal glory. At the most untamed, remotest reaches of the Empire, this monument restored the great art of modeling. It was imitated in the Rhineland and in the Meuse valley, and each such imitation was another step along the way that led from the golden altar in Basel to the perfectly classical shapes which a metal-founder, Renier de Huy, cast on the flanks of a baptismal font in Liège between 1107 and 1118. This renascence may have provided the impetus for the great Cluny sculpture. It certainly prepared for the renovation of monumental statuary that was to take place in the mid-twelfth century, first in Saint-Denis, then in Chartres.

What else but a taste for fine Latin verse and the related veneration in which antiquity was held can have induced Bernward to have a replica of Trajan's column carved as well? The masters of the schools which the sovereigns placed under their protection tried to save not only texts but also whatever remained of Rome. Its monuments were falling into ruins, but they worshipfully salvaged cameos, ivories, and remnants of statues. On one occasion, abbot Hugh of Cluny received a poem extolling the discovery of a Roman bust in Meaux. The aesthetics associated with monarchy leaned so far toward antiquity because its craftsmen worked in the vicinity of a given church and on the basis of its collection of relics and ornaments.

The kings were lavish. Each one, in his great generosity, distributed precious fabrics and jewels among the churches under his protection. Furthermore, when he appeared before the people, he had to be surrounded by splendid ornaments. Was he not the very image of God? It was fitting that he bedeck his own person, that gold and gems should envelop his body with glory and make clear to onlookers the miraculous influx that filled him. His strength lay in these precious objects, the visible image of his power. They dazzled his rivals, and he could use them to reward his friends. By displaying all these riches, the sovereign kept the love of the faithful alive. There could be no king without a collection of invaluable ornaments, and as soon as its luster dimmed, the power of the man on the throne began to wane. Such collections were slowly acquired by inheritance, by accretion. Many of the finest items in those collections had come down through the dynasty as heirlooms. Others, gifts from this monarch or that, came from the Orient.

Almost all bore the imprint of Rome (ancient Rome, whose splendors the barbarian kings had pillaged in order to add to their own ostentation), of the new rejuvenated Rome, and of Byzantium, where the style of antiquity was alive again at that very time.

These collections were not dead things, not impersonal museums. Each piece in them had its specific use in a culture where ceremonial was so important, where everything was expressed through rites and symbols, and therefore raiment and settings were especially significant. Moreover, new items were constantly being added to the established basic collection through the practice of mutual gift-giving. One of the first duties of the artists whom the king maintained close to him was to keep the royal treasure in good condition, to renovate ancient ornaments so that they would be more appropriate among the accessories of the secular or sacred liturgy, to set cameos in the binding on a Gospel book or to transform an ancient cup, making a chalice of it. They also altered recently acquired objects so that they would harmonize better with the other items in the collection. Examples of classicism predominated in this accumulation of gold and other items, and the royal palaces were the main repositories of the tradition of classical beauty. So it was only natural for the king's artists, reverently engaged in renovation and adaptation, to try to equal the technical perfection of the ancient objects and, above all, to assimilate their stylistic principles.

Like the art associated with the royal treasures, and for the same reasons, sacred architecture—*le grand oeuvre*—in Europe's kingdoms deliberately hewed closely to the imperial tradition. The churches were in fact royal buildings par excellence, for God revealed himself to mankind as sovereign of the world, crowned and seated on a throne, there to judge the living and the dead. Moreover, every place of worship was supposed to enjoy the protection of the king himself, Christ's lieutenant on earth, and the king's offerings had helped to build it. These kings claimed to be continuing what Charlemagne—and Rome itself—had begun. So they built two types of edifices, in the Roman manner.

It had been Charlemagne's wish that his oratory in Aachen resemble the imperial chapels of which he had seen examples in Ravenna, with their circular floor-plan. This design was meant to express the king's specific mission, which was to intercede for his people with God. It established the connection between the square shape, symbolizing the earth, and the circle, symbolizing heaven. The transition from one to the other was achieved via the octagon, which also, in terms of the symbology attaching to numbers, stood for eternity. In early Christian Rome, the baptisteries were built according to the same plan, since the rites of transfer which released man from his earthly shackles and prepared him to rise to the heights where the angels celebrated the divine glory took place in the baptisteries. The circular two-level layout was of course suited to edifices in which the sovereign, placed above his family and servants as they made obeisance below, interceded with God through prayer.

This layout also fitted into another tradition: the martyrium, or reliquary-tomb, as passed on by the builders of crypts. When the pilgrims to the Holy Land arrived at their journey's end and entered the Holy Sepulcher, the structure they entered was round, like the emperor's chapel. Hence the popularity of this type of architecture. In the eleventh century it spread through the Empire as far as the Slavic borders where Christianity, upheld by the might of empire, was gaining ground. Yet ever since the Church had triumphed—since the Gospel had ceased to be a clandestine affair and had taken over the ancient city and its most official monuments—virtually all of the places of worship in Rome, particularly the ones that had the most prestige because they were built over the sepulchers of Saints Peter and Paul, were basilicas. Each one was like a king's court: a vast, plain rectangle, designed for judicial proceedings; rows of blind arcades resembling the outer doors, which held up a light wooden roof over three parallel aisles; an apse sheltering the seat of the magistrate who handed down the sentence; ample lighting distributed by the lofty windows of the central aisle—in short, an enclosed volume open to the daylight, like a forum. The house of God's people. Liturgical changes in the Carolingian era had resulted in changes in these edifices: the entrance was altered, the atrium was roofed over and turned into a vestibule or antechurch on two levels. On the ground level was a sheltered porch; above it was a prayer room. Were these elements added in order to contain the throngs of pilgrims in the fore of the church so that they would not disturb the service? Was the change intended to create a special place for worship of Christ the Savior, who shared patronage of the church with some local saint? Or did it reflect the recent extension of the ceremonial surrounding funerals? At any rate, this was the origin of the Western additions which, in the countries covered by the Empire, gave basilicas a second apse at the west end, and of the belfry porches put up at the entrance to churches in the Ile-de-France.

In the eleventh century these two types of royal architecture predominated throughout the area where the powers of monarchy best resisted the disintegrating force of feudalism. In Saxony both the basilica of Gernrode, on which work began three years after Otto I was crowned emperor, and Saint Michael's of Hildesheim (whose founder, Bishop Bernward, died there in a coarse homespun robe, in the chapel of the Cross), were totally faithful to the Carolingian models. They were copied in the Champagne region—at Vignory and Montier-en-Der—and the link between the art of the Ottos and that of the Capetians was established through the region around Reims. But little construction was going on at this time in the Ile-de-France, except, immediately after the year 1000, in those churches specially venerated by King Robert: Orléans, Saint-Benoît-sur-Loire, and Saint-Martin-de-Tours.

The same spirit reigned everywhere: in the libraries adjoining the study centers that enjoyed the sovereign's patronage, in the ornaments that were the most visible expression of his authority during the coronation festivities, and within the oratories that he protected. Here and there motifs borrowed from antiquity, meticulously preserved or faithfully reproduced because they were considered examples of perfect beauty, were used to create the backdrop to Christian religious services. The craftsmen who carried out the king's orders in the eleventh century must have copied less closely than their predecessors had done in the time of Charlemagne or the first renascence of imperial culture. After all, antiquity was now two centuries further away. These craftsmen knew of it only through Carolingian copies. Memories of it became blurred, leaving more of a margin in which an artist's inventiveness could develop. But—and this is what counts—the scholars' attitude of reverence and respectful submissiveness set the tone for all culture at this time. A strong feeling that the contemporary world was barbarian and all perfection was to be found in the past repressed initiative and modernistic impulses. Like the future prelates, and like the kings who spent their nights learning to read, the court goldsmiths, painters, metal-founders, and the builders of churches all considered themselves pupils. They dreamed of reproducing the classical models as accurately as possible and scrupulously followed the way mapped out by tradition. But at least, thanks to these craftsmen's docility, the memory of Rome still hung about the kings, amid the herds of swine and the vast empty forests of this peasant world. Rome meant an aesthetic ideal attuned to the verses of the *Aeneid* and the *Pharsalia,* a type of art which refused to let dreams intrude, or spirals, or the geometrical abstractness of Germanic jewelry, or any of the distortions of human and animal shapes found in barbarian finery. It was an art of words, speeches, dialogue, not of phantasms; monumental art, not linear or chiseled art; the aesthetics of architects and sculptors. The art of the *Pericopes* which the painters of Reichenau adorned for the emperors. The art of the scriptorium at Saint-Denis. The art of the baptismal fonts in Liège.

Reichenau, Saint-Denis, and Liège were not capitals; the kings of this time did not have any. They moved about from place to place. Their military function compelled them to ride horseback incessantly. But at times their religious function required them to halt and take their rightful seats among the bishops, in the churches, at the major Christian feasts. In this way the places where their authority gave impetus to cultural creativity became fixed points. Schools and craftsmen's workshops were established in the royal churches, in the great abbeys whose patron was the sovereign himself, and in the bishoprics which supported his power. A map pinpointing the centers of scholarly knowledge and of the related art based on antiquity would not coincide exactly with a map showing the king's respective realms. But taken together, both maps would situate the area where the classical spirit continued to dominate in the eleventh century.

Its principal axis, running from the Loire to the Main, was none other than the axis of the Carolingian renascence. The efforts of Alcuin and all of the patient pedagogues who had sought to restore the use of pure Latin within the Church bore fruit in the Frankish provinces, near the old royal palaces, while the soil of Germania, further east, was too new; in fact, within the German sovereigns' sphere of influence, Saxony was a daring exception. As in the time of Charlemagne, the really active centers of study were still the monasteries of Franconia and along the shores of the Rhine, in Echternach, Cologne, Saint-Gall, and lastly, in the churches of the Meuse valley. At the edges of the provinces which the invasions during the Dark Ages had completely barbarized and of those where the Roman imprint was still fairly clear, the masters and artists of Liège were outstanding. Similarly, in the kingdom of France, there were no flourishing schools anywhere in the south, i.e., the regions the Carolingians had always considered as conquered lands, ripe for exploitation. The centers of monarchical culture were concentrated in the old Frankish country. In the year 1000, the best masters were in three places: Reims, where the oil of the Holy Ampulla, which people were beginning to call miraculous, anointed the kings; the monastery at Fleury-sur-Loire, near Orléans, where the relics of Saint Benedict were preserved, the panegyric of Robert the Pious was written, and Philip I was to be buried; and in Chartres. One hundred years later they were still teaching in Chartres, as well as in Laon, Tournai, Angers, Orléans, and Tours.

Outside the regions watered by the Rhine, the Meuse, and the Seine, there were only two noteworthy spearheads. One came from Neustria and thrust little by little into the lands conquered by the Normans: Fécamp first of all, then the abbey of Bec Hellouin and soon Canterbury, York, and Winchester when, in 1066, a vigorous monarchy was established on both sides of the English Channel and gathered together all the scattered vitality that the Vikings had earlier sown throughout this part of Europe. The other was much bolder; it developed in Catalonia. On this outermost fringe of Christendom, endangered but powerful, and strengthened by all of the gold coins brought back from Moslem lands, the bishops and the abbots of the year 1000 welcomed the exotic types of knowledge that filtered back from those countries. Their minds embraced new objects of curiosity—the science of numbers, algebra, astronomy. Here the young Gerbert came to learn how to make astrolabes. Yet this province, like Germany, had been shaped by the Carolingians, and the memory of Charlemagne was possibly more vivid here than anywhere else, sustained by the persistent infidel peril. He was venerated as the hero of the adventures of the true faith, the precursor of the Crusades—and also the protector of classical literature. In the cathedral at Vich and the abbeys of Ripoli and Cuxa, the pedagogical tradition of Alcuin and Theodulphus lived on. Pupils marveled while their masters read aloud from the poets of antiquity.

The masters and their schools were poor, and their knowledge was very limited. But at least they were faithful and so, amid such an impoverished civilization, capable of keeping art above the level of total savagery. It may seem ridiculous to think that, close by the churches where kings received holy unction, where chroniclers recorded the memory of their exploits and showed them as both men of God and heirs of Augustus, the flourishes of Ciceronian rhetoric were applied to tribal chiefs who boasted glass beads and wore themselves out on pointless mounted excursions. But at least these study centers and libraries, and collections of precious objects whose finest cameos bore the profiles of Trajan and Tiberius, constituted an unbroken chain of naïve and fervent rebirths perpetrating a certain idea of man. Suger's aesthetics, Saint Thomas Aquinas's science, the whole Gothic flowering and the liberating determination that it embodied sent out roots that reached those remote islands of literacy awash in the rusticity and brutishness of the first millenium.

But after the year 1000—and this partly determined the evolution of Western art throughout the eleventh century—the brilliance of these centers of classical culture dimmed, at the same time as the kings' power became more shaky. In 980 their authority was really felt in only a small part of their kingdoms, and in the decades that followed it began to crumble even more. This was a general tendency, but it was more precocious and more pronounced in the kingdom of France; its sovereigns retained their spiritual prestige but the prelates and the leaders of the different provinces ceased to appear at their court. By 1100 only the lesser noblemen from the vicinity of Paris and a few household officers came to sit by their king's side. The feudal system had proliferated all about the throne; and royalty, while still a vital support for feudalism, had been stifled by it little by little. The crown was now nothing but a sign, one figure in a symbolic speech. The real powers, the *regalia,* were now scattered and held in many lands. Among the attributes of sovereignty were the patronage of the churches and the wish to embellish them; in short, the overall direction of artistic creativity. By the middle of the eleventh century the great church-builder in northern France was no longer the king but instead the duke of Normandy—his vassal.

The king of Germany's authority did not disintegrate so rapidly; it cannot be said that Germania had been feudalized before 1130. But gradually the emperor saw his remaining rights in Italy fall away. And, worst of all, his authority began to be challenged by the pretensions of another power whose star was in the ascendant: the bishop of Rome. Already in the year 1000 Abbot William of Volpiano had been able to write: "The power of the Roman emperor, to which monarchs throughout the world were formerly subject, is now divided among several scepters in the various provinces, while the power to bind and to unbind, both in heaven and on earth, has been bestowed upon the doctrinal authority of Peter and is inseparable from it." One hundred years later, when the pope had brought most of the churches of the Western world under his sole authority, he was determined to castigate the kings. He fought bitterly in Germany itself to wrest Caesar's prerogatives from him. Thus between 980 and 1130 a combination of two very vigorous trends deprived the kings everywhere of their true means of action: the trend toward disintegration of monarchical authority in the Western world, and another trend, found more uniformly throughout Latin Christendom, which fostered reform in the Church by transfering the *auctoritas* to the prelates and grouping them around the Holy See.

This was the beginning of the gap in the history of Western art, occurring between the reign of Emperor Henry II and that of King Louis IX (Saint Louis) of France, that interrupted the continuity of the great artistic undertakings carried out in the sovereign's name. The weakening of monarchy constituted a setback to the royal influence over aesthetics, first felt in Europe's southern provinces where, as early as 980, the royalty ceased to have any real existence. Because the schools in those regions were less vigorous or, at any rate, followed curriculums that were oriented differently, the ever-fertile background of Roman tradition was able to produce cultural patterns that developed unhindered.

For as the authority of the kings receded in Provence, Aquitaine, and Tuscany, it revealed another of the many faces of Rome—but with a difference. Not the face that had fascinated Charlemagne and still fascinated Otto III or Abbo of Fleury with features that were pure but frozen in the stiffness of archaistic restorations, as elegant, and as dead, as a line of Virgil's poetry. Not the face of classicism. Instead a face enlivened by whatever was still modern about Rome in this part of the Western world. Among the temples and amphitheaters that were still upright, in cities where the usages of urban living were still vivid, the Roman tradition had never died. It had been enriched by the various types of Christendom—Byzantine, Coptic, or Mozarab—to which it had adapted. As royalty faded away and the cultural patterns artificially revived by the emperor's whims became atrophied, long-standing obstacles to the development of new art forms were overcome. In the eleventh century the same vitality that gave birth to the feudal system let the new art forms spring up out of the old Latin background and bear fruit. The classical traditions of the monarchical schools were countered by everything Roman that continued to penetrate the cultural texture of daily life, rather than lying inert in the libraries and collections of valuables. Similarly, royal art was countered by Romanesque art as such, which flourished after the year 1000, in the new springtime of the world.

2

THE WORLD OF FEUDALISM

In the eyes of God—in the eyes of his servants, the prelates of the ninth century—men formed but a single people. Of course their race, their condition, their sex, their high or low birth, and their function distinguished among them. Yet as Agobard, archbishop of Lyons, wrote in the time of the emperor Louis the Pious, "they all asked for but one kingdom." In the king's own person the sacerdotal and military functions were combined; he held power within the temporal order and bore the community's responsibilities with regard to the supernatural forces, and behind him a unified human society continued on its way toward the light. In point of fact it was divided: there were barriers separating the clerics and the monks, the laymen and the churchmen, and above all, in this slave-owning society, freemen and people who were treated like animals. But during the early Middle Ages the small elite caste formed by heads of the Church—the only people capable of thinking in abstract terms and the only ones whose opinion has come down to us in written texts—had pictured God's people as homogeneous; and this prevailing feeling of oneness, based on the institution of monarchy, was related to another guiding notion: the stability of the social edifice. A Latin word, *ordo,* expressed the immutability of the several groups making up society; each individual belonged to one of them as he marched, at his own pace, toward resurrection and salvation. When God created the world, he put each man in his proper place, in a situation which gave him certain rights and assigned a certain function to him in the gradual construction of the kingdom of God. Let no man step out of his place. Any disturbance in this orderly arrangement would be sacrilegious. On the day of his anointment, the king solemnly guaranteed to uphold the customary prerogatives of each body composing society.

Indeed, the very primitive universe of the ninth century might seem to have been motionless, frozen in the cycles of rural life: the seasons followed one another unchangingly and time moved in a circle like that which the stars described in the heavens. No one in that world could cherish the hope of acquiring enough wealth to rise above his rank and attain the higher echelons of the temporal hierarchy. The rich were all heirs; their fortune and their glory came from time immemorial, handed down, generation after generation, from the remotest ancestors. And the poor all labored on the same land that their fathers had made fertile through their toil. Any change seemed accidental, even scandalous. Like the kings and the emperors, God sat securely at the hub of the universe, master of the immutable.

Yet in fact the world was changing, though imperceptibly, and at a rate which speeded up only very gradually. As the year 1000 drew near, new social structures began to appear, starting in the most advanced of the Western provinces: the kingdom of France. What makes the eleventh century modern is precisely this upsetting of the established order. It went so deep that it affected every aspect of civilization, particularly the way in which power and wealth were distributed, and the way in which man's relationship to God was conceived. As a result it affected the mechanisms of artistic creativity. We cannot possibly understand the emergence of Romanesque art or its specific features without referring to this change: the establishment of what we call the feudal system.

The impetus for the mutation had nothing to do with the economy; its growth was very slow and did not yet alter the conduct of life in any significant way. The impetus was a fact of political life: the kings' gradual loss of power. In the hands of the great Carolingians, the unity of imperial power seems somewhat miraculous. How did those heads of warrior bands manage to hold together and actually govern the unbelievably far-flung, dense, and impenetrable Empire of the year 800? How did they manage to reign simultaneously over Friesland and Friuli, over Barcelona and the banks of the river Elbe? To be genuinely obeyed in all of these roadless, cityless provinces where even horses were few and royal messengers went on foot? Their authority was based on a permanent state of war, an uninterrupted spurt of conquest. Charlemagne's ancestors had come out of Austrasia at the head of a small group of kinsmen, friends, and faithful servants who followed and obeyed them because they were victorious and because they distributed the booty from every campaign and let them loot the conquered regions to their hearts' content. The Carolingians had succeeded in keeping these earliest companions, their sons and nephews, faithful through arranged marriages and through the ties of kinship and of vassals' vows. Every spring, when the grass began to grow again and it became possible to launch mounted expeditions, they gathered all these friends about them—the counts, the bishops, and the abbots of the great monasteries. And for this reunited troupe it was the start of the great annual festival of destruction, killing, rape, and depredation; and the king, at the head of his carefree escort, marched off once more to savor the joys of offensive warfare.

Yet even as early as the ninth century, in the interval between these seasonal adventures—in the autumn, when each one of the sovereign's friends went home to his own land and was once again surrounded by the men of his lineage, his concubines, his slaves, and his protégés, he was immediately beyond the grasp of the king's authority. There was no way to keep an eye on these local princes: the roads were impracticable. So each one of them was free to reign unchecked over the lands around his residence. He was the lord of a peasantry that kneeled before him; they dimly knew that a king existed but revered the bearer of that title as some distant master, invisible like God himself. As far as the rustics were concerned, peace and prosperity depended on their local lords. In times of famine, the poor could always count on a few handfuls of grain from the lord's granaries. If he used his powers unfairly, there was no one to whom they could complain.

There came a time, shortly after the Empire was resurrected, when the kings ceased to be conquerors; no more military expeditions, no more booty, no more rewards. Why should the grandees of each kingdom brave the fatigues and dangers of endless rides just to join a sovereign who no longer distributed any bounty? Their visits became more infrequent. Little by little, the number of people at the kings' courts dwindled, and the state imperceptibly fell apart. Its break-up was hastened just at that time by invasions from various quarters—Norsemen, Saracens, and Hungarians. Unforeseen enemies appeared on the European continent and on the islands as well. The fighting was no longer some remote business, beyond the frontiers of Christianity; it was now a local matter, in Christianity's very bosom. It was a sad matter as well. The pagan bands would appear all of a sudden, looting and burning, then would slip away maddeningly by boat or on horseback. The king's army was made for premeditated aggression; slow and clumsy, it took a long time to gather its men together and start them moving, and proved entirely incapable of resisting, repulsing, or preventing the invaders' incursions. Given the state of permanent danger to which the entire Western world was soon exposed, the only war chiefs capable of restoring peace were the petty princes in each region. Only they could withstand surprise attacks and call up all able men at the very first alert. Only they could maintain castles on their lands and equip them with a standing garrison; these were the defensive landmarks, the great earthen bulwarks within which all the peasants and their animals could take refuge. No doubt about it: safety no longer depended on the king but instead on the local lords. The king's authority lost ground to a crucial extent, living on in men's minds only as a sort of myth. In the reality of day-to-day existence, all prestige and power shifted to the local chiefs, the dukes and counts, who became the real heroes of Christian resistance. Armed with miraculous swords, aided by God's angels, they forced the invaders to retreat empty-handed. Warriors at their gatherings intoned long sing-song chants mocking the powerless sovereigns and lauding the local lords' feats.

From the regions south and west of Latin Christendom, regions over which the Carolingians had only shaky control and which had just suffered more at the looters' hands, stemmed two parallel changes that affected the two main sectors of society: the laity and the Church. In each province men who had once raised contingents under their banners, on behalf of their kinsman and sovereign, the king, now broke away from him completely. It is true that they still proclaimed their loyalty to him and on occasion still placed their hands in his, as a sign of homage. But henceforth they considered that the powers of coercion which had been delegated to them were rightfully theirs as an element of their family heritage. They exercised those powers freely and handed them down to their eldest sons.

The dukes, who were the greatest princes, those responsible for defending a whole slice of the kingdom, were the first to make themselves autonomous at the beginning of the tenth century. The parceling out of political power that followed from this nonobedience went no further in the northern and eastern portions of the old Carolingian empire, for there the kings retained more authority and the tribal structures more vitality. But elsewhere it continued. Soon the counts in turn shook off the authority of the dukes. Then, not long before the year 1000, the counts' principalities also fell apart. Each chief who was responsible for one fortified castle, within a canton composed of forests and clearings, pieced together around that fortress a small independent state. Kingdoms were still to be found everywhere at the start of the eleventh century; sovereigns were still anointed, and no man doubted that they were God's own delegates. But at the same time military strength and the power to judge and punish were scattered among a multitude of political cells of all sizes.

Each of them had its master called "sire," "lord" (in Latin *dominus,* he who genuinely rules over others), and this title which he boasted was the word used to designate God in the vocabulary of Christian rites. Nothing, in fact, could withstand or check his power. He held the prerogatives which had been the king's monopoly. Like the sovereign, he felt himself a member of a dynasty. His ancestors had rooted it in the country he governed, in the fortified castle where he gathered his vassals together, and the offshoots of his family would flourish on the same soil century after century—a tree with but a single trunk for, like the king's crown, the local lord's authority was passed on, whole and indivisible, from father to son. Like the king, each sire felt bound to maintain peace and justice in the name of God, and the whole network of rights that enabled him to carry out that mission converged on his castle. Towers had once been the symbols of the sovereigns' cities, then of kingly majesty in its military personification; now a tower seemed the nucleus of an embodiment of personal power. It was the seat of the prestige and authority attaching to a given lineage. "The men of great fortune and noble birth spent most of their time fighting and making war," wrote one chronicler early in the twelfth century. "In order to shield themselves from their enemies, vanquish their equals, and oppress the weak, it is their wont to throw up earthworks as high as possible, and to dig a broad, deep ditch all about them. Around the top run ramparts made of tree trunks, squared and sturdily put together." Such was the castle of those days. It was a very primitive type of construction, yet effective, given the very primitive state of military technique. Secure behind such stockades, each separate chief defied his rivals. He defied the king himself. But in any case the structures of political power and the entire new social system radiated out from the castle.

That system corresponded to the changes that had recently occurred in the art of making war. When it came to fighting the ninth- and tenth-century invaders, the old-style royal army—a troupe of foot soldiers with motley trappings—was powerless. Only well-equipped riders protected by breastplates could hold their own, reach the endangered positions, and pursue the aggressors. Accordingly, the ragtail throng of free peasants was no longer pressed into service; they had no weapons other than sticks and stones, nor did they have time to train for combat. Service in wartime became the exclusive privilege of a limited number of professional fighters. The population in the vicinity of the castle, which took refuge there in time of danger and for that reason was willing to obey a chief, was divided henceforth into two distinct categories on the basis of this new military specialization.

The lord of the castle treated these categories differently. All of these men were his men. But the "poor," the "rustics," who did not directly defend the land, constituted, as far as he was concerned, a homogeneous mass that he protected but also exploited as he liked. All of these people belonged to him. There were no more freemen, no more enslaved men. Each man bore an equal burden of requisitions and mandatory unpaid labor services—*corvées*—the price he paid for the peace of which the lord of the manor was the guarantor.

At the opposite extreme were the few village youths who, because they still had the privilege of bearing arms and knew how to use them well, were considered truly free. Since they came, on a rotating basis, to serve as the garrison within the castle, since the general peace depended henceforth on the action of their aggressive little squad, and since they gave all their blood and strength to maintaining that peace, they were able to avoid being exploited and subject to the local nobleman's orders. Their duty toward the master of the tower amounted to a few honorable obligations that stemmed from their vow as vassals, the homage they had sworn to the lord of the manor. They were warriors and horsemen [*chevaliers*]: knights. Their squadron gathered under the banner of the local chief just like the great escorts which the eighth-century kings had swept off with them to pillage and plunder. Grouped about each lord, they surrounded him with a faithful replica of the king's court. This new pattern of political and social relations actually expressed the necessary adaptations of the forms of state to concrete realities that had been momentarily overcome or concealed by the conquering strength of the Carolingian sovereigns, but that continued, several steps below the level of monarchy itself, to determine the interplay of man-to-man relations. Those realities were the vigor of the aristocracy, the outstanding importance of the great rural estates, and the impossibility of governing from afar. The feudal break-up of power corresponded to the reality of an inward-turned rural world, imprisoned within countless invincible partitions. Master of all, upheld by the loyalty of his knights, each chief of a fortified castle seemed like a little king. Yet he lacked the essential attribute of a sovereign: he was not anointed. And this fact led to the other movement, which was a reaction on the part of the Church.

As a matter of principle, the power of the kings in the early Middle Ages did not oppress what was God's share of the world—that is, his churches and the men responsible for serving him. The sovereigns protected the Church, or at least refrained from exploiting it in too obvious a way. All the bishoprics and all the great monasteries held charters of privilege from them forbidding the representatives of the temporal authority to collect taxes within the estates of those religious establishments or to requisition their men there. The fact that the kings had grown weaker and all of the local powers had acquired their independence was a challenge to such franchises. The dukes, counts, and manor lords were defending a given territory as a whole. They were determined to judge, punish, and exploit all of its inhabitants who were not knights, regardless of whether or not they depended on the Church. This was the beginning of encroachment. Furthermore, as these princes resided far away from the king, the strongest of them had taken over another of the sovereign's prerogatives: they claimed to be the guardians and patrons of the cathedrals and monasteries, and as such they were determined to name the bishops and abbots themselves. The Church had been tolerant when the sovereigns chose the ecclesiastical dignitaries because the monarchs had been consecrated by the Church, and that had endowed them with celestial power. But the Church could not tolerate such interference from a duke or a count, whose only qualification was his strength. The Church fought back.

But the Church was lacking in kingly support. Because royalty as an institution was faltering, the ecclesiastical leaders claimed for themselves what had been the monarchs' chief function: the mission of keeping the peace. Through the coronation ceremony, God delegated powers to the kings that the kings were no longer capable of using. God was entitled to take back those powers and use them directly himself, that is, through his servants. This trend first appeared in the area which was more deprived of a sovereign than any other—southern Gaul, Aquitaine, and the region around Narbonne—where it was solemnly endorsed in the closing years of the tenth century at the great outdoor assemblies presided over by the bishops. Then the idea worked its way northward along the valley of the Rhône and the Saône. By 1020 it had spread as far as the northern boundaries of the kingdom of France, but it did not cross them, for beyond those boundaries the emperor ruled, and his stature still sufficed to keep peace and order. But in all the rest of France,

> the bishops, the abbots, and the other men devoted to holy religion began to gather the people together in synods. There they brought a goodly number of saints' skeletons and countless reliquaries filled with relics. Prelates and princes from every part of the country met to protect the peace and maintain the holy faith. In an account divided into chapters, they listed the acts that were forbidden and those that one's oath to God Almighty committed one to carrying out. The most important of these was to observe an inviolable peace.

God's peace. Like its predecessor, the kings' peace, it guaranteed special protection to the frailest, most vulnerable portions of Christianity. God himself now guaranteed that the poor, the men of prayer, and the buildings set aside for religious worship and the area around them were to be immune. Whosoever violated these places of asylum and attacked the weak would be declared anathema and excluded from the community of the faithful until he had repented. He would be exposed to the wrath of God, the invisible Master, who dwelled in the very heart of anxiety and was capable of unleashing all the forces of horror in this world and the next.

> I shall not invade a church in any manner, because of the safeguard under which it is placed, nor shall I invade the storerooms within the precincts of the church. I shall not attack a cleric or a monk when he is not carrying a secular weapon, nor a man of their squad if he has neither lance nor shield. I shall not take away any ox, cow, pig, sheep, lamb, or goat, nor shall I take a donkey or the bundle that it carries, or the mare or her unweaned foal. I shall not seize any peasant, man or woman, any sergeant-at-arms or merchant. I shall neither take their deniers, nor force them to pay ransom. I shall not ruin them by extorting all that they possess on the pretext that their lord is at war.

These were some of the promises that knights at one such gathering in 1024 had to make. To break them would have meant throwing themselves head first into the demons' grasp.

The first effect of this legislation was to single out a clearly defined group within society—a group which, in the eyes of the Church leaders, appeared to be in a state of permanent aggression and responsible for all the disorder in the world. This group represented a danger to be warded off; its destructive powers were to be contained with the help of spiritual sanctions and the terrifying threat of divine wrath. Who were these men who, in terms of the elementary duality embodied in Christian beliefs, seemed to constitute the army of evil? None other than the knighthood. It was the knights of his own diocese whom bishop Jordan of Limoges excommunicated, cursing their weapons and their horses—that is, the instruments of their turbulence and the insignia of their social position. The stipulations of the Lord's peace were like a finger pointing to one group: the men who waged war. This was the class that the disintegration of kingly authority and the new assignment of powers to command and of seigneurial profits to be reaped had just singled out from among the other laymen, by attributing a specific vocation to it and acknowledging that it had privileges. That vocation was none other than the temporal—military—vocation of kings; and the privileges were those of princes.

As for the rest, the enslaved masses, the faceless crowd bent over its food-producing drudgery, the Church intended to keep them under its especial protection. That is, under its thumb. The assemblies held in the name of God's peace were actually the scene of bitter rivalry, played out before an uncomprehending audience, for power and the advantages that power brought with it. The bishops and abbots, who were either hostile to the peace movement—like Adalbero of Laon and Gerard of Cambrai—or in favor of it, appeared as deputies for the enfeebled kings. No more mingling of spiritual and temporal, as personified by the Carolingian sovereigns; this was what the monarchs of the year 1000 harked back to when they distributed crosses, carried reliquaries about on their backs, and founded new basilicas. The upsurge of feudalizing trends wrenched apart two layers of power perceivable in practical reality: power in the realm of worldly things and power in the realm of the sacred. Within the ruling class, a split widened between the warriors, who had no more spiritual function, no more magical power, and the churchmen, who took over all of the charismatic missions that had belonged to royalty.

This is what matters, particularly for anyone interested in the conditions with which social structures surround the birth of works of art. In the course of the eleventh century the local lords seized most of the royal prerogatives that authorized them to exploit the people. They thus deprived the kings of the benefits hitherto conferred by their position of supremacy and stripped them of part of the resources that had sustained their splendor. In so doing they limited the extent to which the sovereigns could play a role in artistic creativity, fostered instead by the muted yet decisive emergence of the new class of lords. The peasantry felt their power as a closer, heavier pressure, exacting more relentless taxes from them and goading them into greater productivity. Unpaid labor services owed to the nobility increased. Part of the resulting profit was lost in the tumult of war, squandered on ostentation, drained off into the collective feasts at which the more prominent knights showed off their power by periodically destroying wealth.

Nonetheless, even in southern Europe, where the forces of political dissolution waxed most vigorous and the power of the monarchy was most violently repulsed, the resources that enabled great art to flourish did not diminish. They increased. The fact was that most of the lords' revenues were not dissipated in worldly expenditure. It continued to be set aside, devoted to sacred things. It gave impetus to artistic creativity. For the feudal lords feared God, and sought to win his favors. Therefore, just as the kings had done, they divested themselves of their wealth and bestowed it on the clerics and monks. The generosity of the higher nobility replaced that of royalty. Pious donations now gave their beneficiaries less restricted means with which to build, carve, and paint.

Unlike the sovereigns, however, the knightly donators did not guide the artists of their time directly, for they were not men of letters, as the kings had to be. They did not assume liturgical tasks as much as the kings did. They were not personally invested with dedicatory functions. So it was that royalty's aesthetic responsibilities reverted to the Church itself, along with that other royal attribute, the duty of protecting the poor. But—and this was still another effect of the upheaval in political and social conditions—ecclesiastical art was forged in a world which the warriors' brutality crushed with all its weight. It clearly bore the imprint of a culture that was violent, irrational, unable to write, attuned to exploits, rites, and symbols: the culture of knighthood.

Gradually during the eleventh century one word came into widespread use. In France, first of all, it became the distinctive title of the entire aristocracy. In its Latin form the term referred only to the military vocation. But the vulgar dialect was more accurate. It termed *chevaliers* [horsemen, knights] all men who sat high up on their war horses, looking down on the poor masses and terrorizing the monks. Arms and an ability to fight—these are what brought them together. Some of them descended from the old nobility, directly related, through kinship and services rendered, to the kings of the early Middle Ages. Others were big village landowners, rich enough not to work with their hands and to be able to keep effectively equipped as soldiers. In addition there were all of the *valets d'armes;* less wealthy, they were fed by their lords in their castles, slept near the master in the great wood-paneled halls, lived on his gifts. In short, they were adventurers come from heaven knew where, to cluster together under the banner of some young chief and follow him wherever battles and expeditions might lead them, to spoils and glory. The knightly class had been a disparate body; now it was more and more closely bound together by its privileges and its position at the peak of the political and social system. Its cohesion was due even more to a single type of behavior, a single hope, a single set of virtues—those of the specialists in war.

All of them were men and boys. The highest expression of eleventh-century culture ignored women. There was virtually no room for them in its art. No depictions of female saints; at most golden idols with wasp eyes placed at the doorway to darkness, and no one dared face their unseeing gaze. The few feminine images with any grace to them in the context of ecclesiastical decoration were crowned allegorical figures representing the months and the seasons; they were suited to Latin verses and, like them, were the wrecked survivors of classical aesthetics, as unreal and untimely as the flowers of rhetoric. The Mother of God could sometimes be seen as a remote and hieratic figure in the midst of transpositions of the Gospel, but in fact she was only a supernumerary. Her face remained in the background, like that of the lord's wife at gatherings of the men who made war with him. Usually woman was shown as a sinuous winding vine, the weed that mingles with the grain to spoil it. A lascivious creature, the germ of corruption denounced by the Church's moralists, Eve the temptress, responsible for man's fall and all the sin in the world.

As a masculine society, knighthood was a society of heirs. The ties of kinship built its framework. The power of the living lords sprang from the glory of those who were dead, from the fortune and renown that the ancestors had bequeathed to their descendants like a sacred trust passed on from each generation to the next. The dukes, the counts, and the masters of the castles maintained that it was because their lineage was linked to that of royalty by a tangled netword of blood relationships that they had been able to take the kings' place and seize their prerogatives. "What a man acquires by birth, no man's will can deny," Bishop Adalbero wrote; "the ancestors of the nobility had kings' blood in their veins." That was why the evocation of one's ancestors played such a great role in this social group. Even the most insignificant adventure-seeker claimed to have a valiant ancestor, and every knight felt himself drawn into action by the cohorts of the dead who had once made famous the name he bore and would demand a reckoning from him. Although the deceased were lost in the shadows beyond the reach of memory, each nobleman knew the names of the founding fathers of his lineage. The troubadours' ballads perpetuated the memory of these eponymous heroes; through those songs they passed into legend, and lived on, among the timeless myths. Their bodies had been brought together and laid to rest in the burial place chosen long before by the first ancestor to leave the king's household and set himself up as an independent power. The most vivid elements in the religious rites of this time converged on those tombs. The Christianity of the year 1000, attuned to the mental patterns of the military aristocracy, seems at first glance to have been a religion of the dead. So strong was the solidarity among the living members of the lineage, making them all rush to aid any one of their number who was attacked and, if he died, affront the aggressor's kinsmen in order to avenge him, that the Church was obliged to acknowledge that the living relatives could still help their deceased to achieve salvation and could acquire indulgences for them. Almost all of the knighthood's acts of charity—and they constituted at the time one of the most substantial sources of support for artistic creativity—were motivated by the wish to succor the deceased members of one's lineage from beyond the tomb.

In this social group it was the "youths"—mature men—who set the tone. They had finished their apprenticehsip. They had proven their strength and ability in public in the course of the collective initiation ceremony which marked their formal introduction into the warrior caste. Yet for a long time to come, as long as their fathers were still alive and they could not take control over their estates, they would have to put up with the state of dependency, each in his father's house, to which the agrarian economy of the times would reduce them. So they escaped, roaming the world with friends their own age in search of prey and pleasure. This is why the outstanding qualities of the knighthood were courage and strength, adding up to aggressive valor. The hero whom all youths tried to emulate, whose praises were sung by the newborn literature in the vulgar tongue to which the assembled soldiers listened, was an athlete built for combat on horseback. He was broad, thick-chested, and heavy; his physical capacities were exalted above all others. Only the body counted, along with the heart—but not the mind. Future knights did not learn to read, for studying would spoil their souls. The knighthood was deliberately illiterate. It made of war, whether real or fictitious, the crucial act, the one that gave life its savor, the game in which a man risked everything, his honor and his very existence, but from which the best came back rich and triumphant, wreathed in glory worthy of their ancestors. The echo of it would resound from one age to the next. Eleventh-century culture, so deeply influenced by the warriors' vocation, was almost entirely based on the joy of capture, kidnapping, and attack.

A knight fought only when the weather was clement, and the qualities admired in a fighter were not the only pillars supporting his concept of ethics. A complex hierarchy of loyalties and honorable obligations was able, when the kings' authority wavered, to maintain a discipline of sorts within the aristocracy of the Western world. The chivalrous hero, enclosed in that hierarchy, was both lord and vassal. Accordingly, he learned to be as lavish as the best of lords and as loyal as the best of vassals. Like his model, the king, lord of lords, a good knight was supposed to distribute everything he had to those he loved. One duke of Normandy said he no longer held on to land in order to give it to his men but instead "all of the moveable goods I possess I will give entirely to you: arm-bands and swordbelts, breastplates, helmets and leg armor, horses, battle-axes, and these very handsome embellished swords. Under my roof, and at all times, you shall enjoy the benefits of my bounty and of the glory attendant on knighthood, if you willingly take the oath to serve me." Generosity above all: that was the cardinal virtue. Of equal importance was another quality: loyalty. A knight who broke his sworn faith lost his right to hold his head high at assemblies of fellow warriors. At this level of the body social, the entire edifice of peace rested on a fabric of individual and collective oaths and the ties of solidarity that wove them tightly together. Boldness, vigor, generosity, fealty—these were the several aspects of honor, and honor in turn was the quintessential value, the most coveted stakes in that code of permanent emulation which was life at war and at court.

An analysis of these types of behavior and the thought patterns behind them is useful to anyone trying to understand the specific harmonies that characterized the works of art of this period. Art was not created under the warriors' auspices nor for their own use. It is true that they adorned their bodies with jewelry, that craftsmen decorated the hilts of their swords, that their wives and daughters embroidered the state robes and the lengths of cloth used to drape the great halls or the walls of the lords' private chapels. But these were only small or fragile objects—only the fringes, as it were, of an empire over which architecture, sculpture, and painting reigned supreme. A work of art meant, at this period, a church. There was no such thing as great art that was not sacred art. As they had been before, only the kings and the men of prayer were in charge of all arrangements. Yet the spirit of knight-errantry seeped into this domain, invading and penetrating it through and through. The kings of France, the kings of England, and soon the emperor himself began, little by little, to feel like knights themselves as their power gradually crumbled away and dissolved within the feudal system that besieged it. Who, then, could still distinguish between their function and that of an individual lord? Their conduct was forced to pattern itself on the warrior ethic. The Church, meanwhile, fell under the sway of the laymen—in other words, of the knights.

Every church, in fact, came into being in the center of a lordship or dominion that provided its priests with enough to live on. Consequently, every bishop, abbot, and canon had a throng of peasants about him and sat in judgment on them. Surrounded by vassals, every bishop, abbot, and canon became a builder, and brought a tumultuous personal escort of fighting men into the cloister itself. Knights came to kneel before the ecclesiastic; bare-headed, they placed their hands in his and so became his liege men, swearing on the relics to be faithful to him, and were invested with a fief. Theoretically, God's servants were forbidden to wage war, for the Church never shed blood; yet many of them could not resist the joy of fighting. Were they not supposed to defend the wealth of their churches' patron saints against all aggressors? To expose their bodies to danger so that Christ's kingdom would spread? One bishop came to see the Cid Campeador and told him, "Today I said the mass of the Holy Trinity for you, then I left my village and came looking for you, for I would like to kill some Moors. I should like to do honor to my rank and to my own hands; and I want to be in the vanguard so as to strike all the harder." When these prelates rode out on an expedition, helmets on their heads and lances in their hands, leading the armed band of young clerics from their church, the virtues of honor, loyalty, and valor were no less essential to them than they were to the knights they were about to face. Though they believed themselves responsible for God's peace, it did not mean they must refuse to fight. Peace had to be achieved through effort and action. Its other name was victory.

What about the spirit of poverty? It had deserted the Church of the year 1000. The highest echelons of the clergy were comfortably installed within the feudal system; their wealth placed them on the same level as the crowned heads, and as the prestige of royalty declined they aspired to take precedence over it. They were confident that it was God's wish for them to be glorious and that the riches they possessed were the necessary support for their eminent position. The ecclesiastics vituperated against the knights and called them instruments of evil because they looked on them as rivals and challenged them for the possibility of wielding authority and reaping the profits to be had from exploiting the working people. The Church of this period was seized by a taste for combat and a thirst for power.

Furthermore, all of its dignitaries and virtually all of its monks came from noble families. When the right to appoint bishops and abbots still belonged to the king, he always chose them from among men of high birth, as his Carolingian predecessors had done. In a society based on kinship ties, all virtues, and particularly the ability to command men, could stem from only one source: blood relationship. If the functions of authority attaching to all the high ecclesiastical offices had been assigned to anyone other than men of noble blood, this would have seemed contrary to the divine plan, by which power itself and all lordly prerogatives were reserved for certain categories. The feudal lords who had succeeded in wrestling patronage of any given church from the sovereign considered it part of their heritage and exploited it as part of their personal fortune. Sometimes they kept the abbacy for themselves, or assigned it to one of their sons, or gave it to some vassal as a reward for faithful service. In assigning functions within the Church, the emperors, kings, and barons used the very rites of feudal investiture wherein some symbolic object was passed from the patron's hand to that of his beneficiary.

At this time ritual gestures were of such importance that it gradually became customary to look upon pastoral functions as fiefs that turned their incumbents into vassals and bound them to serve. In this way the body of the Church sank deeper into the feudal system, even becoming incorporated into it, and the invasion of the spiritual realm by the temporal went deeper as well. Service to one's lords tended to take precedence over service to the Lord, and priests became still less distinct from laymen. In fact it would have been difficult not to confuse the two groups. The distance between the canons and the knights, their brothers or their cousins, had become nil. The canons no longer lived the communal life prescribed by the old rules. They could be seen managing their landed estates—their prebends—just like other lords. They went hunting; they were fond of fine horses and handsome armor. Many of them lived with women. The only appreciable distinction would have been the difference stemming from a fundamentally different upbringing, from the veneer of scholastic culture that all the members of the Church's higher echelons possessed and all knights rejected. But even that distinction was fading away. The schools, as an institution, were vegetating under the influence of the feudal prelates. Both the overall decline of all the centers of learning that the Carolingians had determinedly set up in the cathedrals and monasteries, and the way the values of classicism gradually faded out of all works of art as the eleventh century wore on, were caused chiefly by the irresistible intrusion of the spirit of knighthood into the heart of the clergy.

Because that intrusion affected every aspect of religion, it also affected the development of sacred art. Because the clerics and monks mingled closely with the feudal courts where the nobility harshly asserted its superiority by flaunting its wealth in ostentatious display, the clerics and monks in turn placed greatest emphasis on adornment, on the most conspicuous ornaments, on everything that glittered and incorporated the most precious substances. So the eleventh-century Church draped itself in gold and precious stones, just like the feudal lords, in order to demonstrate—just as they did—its paramount position in the hierarchy of the powers instituted by God's will. The Church persuaded the lords that they must devote part of their treasure to the celestial powers, that before they died they must take all the gems and jewelry their greed had accumulated and lay them before the altars and hang them about the necks of idols-cum-reliquaries. The kings set the example. Henry II of Germany bequeathed to Cluny "his gold scepter, his gold orb, his imperial robe of gold, his gold crown, and his gold crucifix, all of these together weighing one hundred pounds." The monk of Saint-Benoît-sur-Loire who told the story of King Robert's life meticulously described—and even weighed—all of the valuable objects which the churches of Orléans had received from that sovereign: here, sixty pounds of silver; there, one hundred sous' worth of gold; elsewhere, an onyx vase purchased for sixty pounds. "And as for the altar to Saint Peter, to whom the church is dedicated, he had it entirely covered over with pure gold. His wife, Queen Constance, had seven pounds' worth of that same gold removed, after her sainted husband had died, and gave it to God and to Saint-Aignan so as to embellish the roofs of the monastery she had built."

All the less important lords were eager to equal the kings in generosity. The duke of Aquitaine gave to Saint-Cybard d'Angoulême "a cross of gold decorated with stones weighing seven pounds, and silver candelabra fashioned by the Saracens and weighing fifteen pounds." When some knights had overcome a band of Moslems at an outlying point of Christendom, "[and] the booty had been brought together, the weight of all that metal was enormous—for it was the Saracens' custom when going into battle to adorn themselves with many plaques of silver and gold. The knights did not forget their promise to God and sent it straightaway to the monastery of Cluny, and Saint Odilo, abbot of that place, had it made into a splendid ciborium for the altar of Saint Peter." All of the glittering jewelry that the pagan kings of former times had borne with them to their graves was now heaped up in the house of God, and made it more dazzling than the thrones of the greatest princes. While the masses starved, the knighthood lightheartedly destroyed wealth, but the Church made lavish, fascinating use of it, determined, through its rites, to outdo the knights in ostentation. Should not God appear in the most dazzling glory, in that halo of light which the sculptors of Romanesque apocalypses depicted as an almond-shaped sheath about his body? Did he not deserve to possess a more magnificent collection of treasures than all the mightiest men on earth could boast?

For he was the Lord. Men pictured his authority in feudal terms. When Saint Anselm tried to describe its all-powerful existence in the invisible world, he placed it at the pinnacle of a hierarchy of homage. The angels held fiefs granted by God; their conduct with regard to him was that of vassals—his thanes, says the Anglo-Saxon poem *Cynewulf*. Every monk felt he was doing valiant battle for the Lord in exactly the same way as the domestic warriors who, in every castle, awaited their reward. The monks hoped one day to recover man's lost heritage, the fief confiscated long ago as punishment for their fathers' disobedience. Meanwhile, the theologians reduced laymen—where divine grace was concerned—to the rank of enslaved peasants. Bishop Eberhart went so far as to make Christ his father's vassal. Men's submission to the Lord their God fit into the context of earthly day-to-day relationships by which all of a feudal lord's subjects submitted to him. The true Christian's aim was to be God's faithful follower, and that was why the position in which the vassal paid homage—kneeling, bareheaded, hands clasped—became at this time the posture associated with prayer. Such faithfulness made loyalty and service an obligation. But since the contract of vassalhood bound the two persons who were parties to it to help each other mutually; since a feudal lord was bound to help his liege man when that man had done his duty; since the masters of the great rural estates were duty-bound to distribute food to their peasant tenants in times of famine, and since generosity was seen as the greatest virtue of great men, so each Christian, the vassal of his God, hoped similarly for his protection against all dangers in this world. Above all he awaited a share in Paradise—the everlasting fief.

Meanwhile, the lords of this life on earth reserved their best gifts for the most valiant warriors as rewards for their exploits. This meant that it was through exploits that man would win God's favors. Eleventh-century Christianity, infused with knightly values, took on a heroic dimension. Its greatest saints were fighting men. Like Saint Alexis, whose ascetic exploits were celebrated by a poem in the vulgar tongue composed in about 1040 for a princely court in Normandy, they were depicted as model knights—brawny youths dedicating their tenacity and their physical suffering to their lord. It was difficult, obviously, for a society dominated by the activity of turbulent mounted fighters to assimilate the message of mercy and humility contained in the Gospel. In order to have some impact on the young warriors and bring them back to God, the priests, who had grown up with them within the castle precincts and who, like them, were servants in a master's house, described the Church to them as a militia whose chief, Jesus, trained them for battle and brandished his cross like a banner. They told them the lives of the military saints—Maurice or Demetrius—and exhorted them to show like valor in the struggle that every man must put up against an invisible but ever-present and formidable enemy, the evil cohort of the demon's vassal spirits. The institution of chivalry had so great a hold on patterns of thought that the alternatives of military action were central to them all.

The entire universe was one continuous combat. The very stars did battle. One night a monk named Adémar of Chabannes saw "two stars in the Lion fighting together; the smaller raced, furious and at the same time affrighted, toward the larger, and the latter repulsed it toward the west, with its mane of rays." In other words, the Christians of this period, at grips with mystery, behaved no differently than in a feudal war. Piety was understood as a state of perpetual vigilance, a series of attacks and adventures, resistance to perfidious assaults. Every man looked upon his earthly life as a province he must defend against infiltrators and return, intact, to his Lord; his honor depended on his doing this. On Judgment Day, his courage and his weaknesses would be weighed in the balance. Certain Romanesque frescoes show fierce Christs holding the sword of justice and victory tightly between their teeth.

How could a man carry out the actions that this God-lord, this terrifying, sword-bearing God expected, and thereby enter into his good graces? By abiding by his laws? Could one grasp what those laws were? No one will ever know how much of the Gospels' light was glimpsed by the peasant masses huddled in their dens, held back at the threshold of the church. From there they saw only snatches of the priest's gestures and dimly heard songs chanted in Latin of which they understood not a single word. What could the poor hope for from a rural clergy recruited in the rustic context of the manor estates—parish priests who plowed their fields themselves so as to feed their children and their wives, and quickly forgot whatever little they may have learned. How did Jesus appear to those very priests? What did they understand of his teachings? We actually know little more about the knights' religion, except that it boiled down to a matter of rites, gestures, and formulas, for the written word was banished from their culture, which was based on spoken words and images—that is, on formalism. When a warrior made a vow, what he considered most important was not the commitment his soul had made but a matter of physical posture, the fact that his hand placed on the cross, on the Bible, or on a bag of relics was making contact with the realm of the sacred. Or when he stepped forward to become a lord's liege man, it was again a matter of posture—a certain position of the hands, a sequence of ritually arranged words, and the mere fact of uttering them made the contract binding. Or again, when he entered into possession of a fief, the need for a ritual gesture made him take a lump of earth, or a banner, or some symbolic object, in his hand. Crushed by the unknown powers of nature and trembling at the idea of death and of what comes after it, the knight clutched at certain rites, believing they would induce God to be lenient with him. In the *Song of Roland,* for instance, Roland is about to die. He confesses his sins, he remembers the story of the resurrection of Lazarus; he thinks of Daniel in the lion's den. But what saves him is—a gesture. As a sign of final homage, he holds out his right gauntlet toward God, and the archangel Gabriel comes down from heaven to carry this symbol of allegiance to the Lord.

Similarly, the biographer of King Robert the Pious gives him the highest praise for having devoted so much effort to ceremonial, especially the communion rites. "He arranged them with such particular care that it scarcely seemed that God was being received there through another's pomp and ceremony; rather, he appeared in the very glory of his own majesty." Following the monks' example, this sovereign intoned psalm after psalm when on his death bed and, when his time drew near, "he continually made the sign of the cross on his forehead, his eyes, his eyelids, his lips, his throat and his ears."

All of these rites gave physical shape to mental images and stemmed from a certain concept of God. It was a twofold concept, just as every man's image of the king and the lords who took over the attributes of monarchy was twofold, embracing both war and justice, the sword and the scepter. The eleventh-century God was not very different from the leaders of the men who hid in the marshes to ambush the last marauding Norsemen of the year 1000. It was vital that every man should join the troop that God led and, together with him, attack the shadowy forces whose existence was only dimly perceived—in premonitory visions of death, in the rustlings and murmurings that filled the night; no one doubted that terrifying and irresistible forces reigned supreme over a mysterious universe of which the human senses could discern only the outermost layer. In order to determine which of two men was innocent and which guilty, one needed only to burn them both with a red-hot iron and then compare how their burns healed in order to see which man had sinned. Or one plunged them both into water: it would reject the man who was impure. People put their trust in the magic powers of natural elements, relying on them to arbitrate, through ordeals of this sort, between good and evil, God and Satan. The Lord needed men to help him in his arduous struggle against sin; the faithful, prostrate and expectant, must have looked on its outcome as uncertain.

Yet the eleventh-century Christian perceived the strength of the Almighty through an act of justice, just as the peasant perceived that of the master of the land he worked, and the knight that of the master of his fief. God meted out justice; he punished. By the end of that century, the most familiar image of him was the one the sculptors had placed majestically above the monastery entrances: the Almighty seated on the judge's throne and surrounded by his vassals, assessor-barons who were not so much the Apostles as the elders of the apocalyptic visions, and especially, the archangels, the dukes of the celestial army. One of them is Saint Michael, standing before the throne like a seneschal; he is organizing the session of the court. For God's tribunal issues its decrees just as do the courts of the earthly lords.

When a defendant appeared before any of the numerous assemblies responsible, in this world, for reconciling the knights and calming the vengeful urges of feuding clans, he never appeared alone. Friends assisted him. They always took the oath and bore witness to his innocence. Among the members of the court the defendant could always see men who had blood ties to him or ties of mutual loyalty. He counted on them; they would speak up for him. Possibly they could make the sentence more lenient. That was why the men of this period, living as they did in dread of the Last Judgment, were so anxious to secure the saints' goodwill. The saints—the heroes of the faith—were the members of God's court. He would listen to their opinions. They would soften his wrath. Any man could win them over and make sure they would intercede for him; he could do this in the same way as he would gain indulgence on earth: by giving presents. "Win friends in heaven with the fruits of iniquity"—this admonition appeared again and again in the preambles to the charters which were put away for safekeeping in the monasteries and there perpetuated the memory of noblemen's offerings. Saints were everywhere. They peopled invisible space, but it was also possible to enter into communication with them on earth at certain places: the churches that were dedicated to them; some churches even contained the remains of their earthly bodies. And so, through the men of prayer who were attached to all such churches, the saints received alms, the gifts that were supposed to secure their good will and bind them to their donors. The knights of the eleventh century were incapable of restraining their violent instincts or even discerning what the Master expected of them; no matter what they did, they all felt guilty and in danger of being punished. Therefore, by distributing offerings among countless religious institutions, they hoped that when the time came, they would appear in a better light before the celestial court.

Where justice on earth was concerned, a money gift was the way to win over the local lord as well. The knightly courts rarely sentenced defendants to bodily punishment. When the court had finished sitting, one always talked money; giving a few coins meant restoring the harmony that the misdeed had destroyed and quenching the thirst for revenge that any aggressive act aroused not only in its victims but also in their kinsmen and in the prince on whom law and order depended. The prince felt insulted by anyone who, through an act of violence, had shattered the peace he was supposed to guarantee. Therefore a man who was found guilty was sentenced to pay. He paid the monetary compensations that the opposing family expected and also a fine, as reparations for the damages that the king, the count, or the lord of the manor—all the persons responsible for the security of the community at large—suffered because of his action. God's pardon was purchased in the same way. "Alms wash away sin just as water puts out fire." The gesture of almsgiving sprang from the basic piety of a Christian population crushed by a feeling of unavoidable guilt.

Giving to God did not mean giving to the poor. In such a thankless rural setting, who, besides the nobility, did not seem poor? Indigence was the common lot. Its remedies lay in the formal functioning of the seignorial institutions and the natural generosity of the great of this earth. It is true that Robert the Pious lived surrounded by poor people. On Holy Thursday, "he knelt and with his own blessed hand placed vegetables, fish, bread, and a denier in the hands of each one of them." Twelve of them accompanied him wherever he went, and "he had a considerable number of them in reserve, to replace those who died, and in this way their number never declined." But we would be misinterpreting such gestures if we neglected their symbolic side. In fact the king-cum-Christ was ritually miming a scene from the Scriptures when, in commemoration of the Last Supper, he distributed sacred nourishment, with twelve supernumeraries by his side playing the role of the apostles. Every offering which could appease God's wrath went to the churches. Every man and every woman who had not made his or her way into the militia of God's servants and lived a slave to the forces of evil gave his or her most precious belongings to the churches. Some of them gave their own bodies and their offspring; especially within the territorial limits of the Empire there was a growing number of "altar dependents" who came in single file every year, on the day that was dedicated to the patron saint of their particular church, and deposited on the sacrificial stone a basket made of wax and a symbolic denier as signs of their willing serfdom. But everyone gave of his own possessions—either the most valuable of his valuables or, far more often, land, which was the one true wealth. Although such offerings were made at all times so as to cancel out a given misdeed as soon as it was committed, the giving of alms took on its full value when the donor was on death's doorstep.

Early in the twelfth century there was a renascence of monumental sculpture; images of hell were carved at the entrance to many a church. They stemmed from a type of propaganda whose various elements became common about 1040; the fear it instilled in laymen helped to increase the number of donations *in articulo mortis*. Such gifts did not benefit only their individual donors, for each donor had in mind not only his own salvation but also that of his entire lineage. When he drew on the fortune that his ancestors had bequeathed to him, he did it partly so that the souls of his deceased relatives would benefit from it. He hoped to mingle with them unnoticed when the Last Judgment came, in the reconstituted oneness of his race, forming a single immortal person who would collectively bear the responsibility of each member of that race. The ceaseless flow of pious donations sparked the most vigorous economic movement of a period that was barely emerging from complete sluggishness. Along with the dividing up of legacies among their heirs, it led to the only notable transfers of wealth that occurred at that time. Such gifts stripped the lay aristocracy for the benefit of the Church's aristocracy. They amply offset all of the pilfering done by marauding knights, and slowly, and at their expense, placed ecclesiastical power on a sturdier foundation. Had it not been for this enormous influx of material goods which continually swelled the saints' heritage and provided the clerics devoted to them with superabundant resources, there would be no explaining the vigor of artistic development in Europe between 980 and 1130. Although it was agricultural progress that caused Romanesque art to flourish, it could not have made that art so robust if the dominant caste—the knighthood—had not devoted so large a share of its wealth to the glory of God.

There was another way of securing the friendship fo God and of the powers that sat at his court, another way of shedding worldly goods and sins, but it placed greater demands on body and soul. That was by going on pilgrimages. By leaving behind the haven of one's family group and one's house, facing the insecurity that began as soon as one crossed the threshold, going away for months at a time, passing through hostile villages. Could there be any more valiant offering to the Lord and his saints, whose tomb one set out to visit? A pilgrimage was the most thorough and most acceptable form of asceticism that the hero-conscious Christianity of the eleventh century could offer to knights fearing for their salvation.

A pilgrimage was three things at once. First of all, it was an act of penance. The bishop imposed it, as an instrument of purification, on individuals who publicly confessed to exceptional misdeeds. Next, it was a symbol. By traveling, a pilgrim acted out the procession of God's people toward the promised land and drew nearer to God's Kingdom. And finally, a pilgrimage was a pleasure. At this period there was considered to be no more attractive type of amusement than traveling—particularly when one traveled with friends, as pilgrims generally did. The groups of pious travelers that sailed down rivers and moved along trails in fact differed very little from the wandering adventure-seeking bands of youths, and still less from the cohorts of vassals who did their duty as counselors by answering their lord's summons to gather about him for a few days. The pilgrims, too, were doing a form of service at court. On the prescribed day they gathered about the gold-plated jewel-studded chests in which relics were housed; invisible forces that could heal the body and purify the soul emanated from these reliquaries, containing scattered fragments of holy men's bones, reminders of their presence in this world. No one believed for a minute that the mysterious saints would withhold their benevolence from people who had walked so far in order to draw closer to them. Monks recorded in volumes such as the *Miracles of Saint Foy* or *Miracles of Saint Benedict* the many marvels that proved the effectiveness of such peregrinations.

They were undertaken by stages, and their milestones were churches possessing relics. When King Robert wished to prepare himself to face death, he set out with his court during Lent to pay homage to the saints that were "one with himself in serving God." His lengthy itinerary took him to Bourges, Souvigny, Brioude, Saint-Gilles du Gard, Castres, Toulouse, Sainte-Foy de Conques, and Saint-Gérard d'Aurillac. Would any admirer of Romanesque art not choose the same itinerary today? For in the eleventh century, and particularly in the southern provinces, where the power of kings was dwindling, it was in the vicinity of the miraculous tombs that the boldest architectural experiments were made and the inventive powers were nurtured that were to create the new shapes and boldness of monumental sculpture.

This creativity was sustained by the wealth which the pilgrims heaped up about the reliquaries. Here is a description of one such accumulation of valuables used to adorn altars and renovate places of worship:

> What further contributed to its increase was the tomb of Saint Trond which sparkled each day with new miracles. Indeed, for nearly half a mile round about the town, on all the public ways that converged on it and even in the fields and meadows, a throng of pilgrims—noblemen, freemen, and ordinary people—streamed in every day, and particularly on feast days. Those who could not find lodging in the houses because there were so many people slept in tents or in makeshift shelters made of branches draped with cloth. You would have thought they had posted themselves round about the town in order to besiege it. In addition there were numerous merchants who, with their horses, carts, wagons, and beasts of burden, struggled to provide the pilgrims with food. And what of the offerings placed on the altar? We will not even mention the incredible quantities of animals brought there—horses, oxen, cows, hogs, sheep, and ewes. It was impossible to estimate the amount of linen and wax, the number of loaves and cheeses, or the value of all those goods. As for the silver thread and the coins that heaped up steadily until nightfall, several sacristans were employed at gathering them together, and this task took up all of their time.

In the eleventh century all devout Christians who sought to win divine mercy for themselves through pilgrimages dreamed of praying at one time or another before three tombs: Saint Peter's, Saint James's (Santiago de Compostela), and the tomb of Christ. William, the duke of Aquitaine who was living in the year 1000, "had formed the habit in his youth of going every year to Rome, seat of the apostles; and in the years when he did not go there, he compensated for it by going on a journey of piety to Compostela." The count of Angoulême, shortly before his death in October 1026, joined a group of several hundred knights who were starting out for Jerusalem in the hope of arriving by Lent the following year. Other feudal lords had preceded him. Raoul Glaber noted in his *Histories,* when he came to the year 1033, that

> an immense throng began to converge, from every corner of the world, on the sepulcher of Jesus in Jerusalem: first of all common people; then men of medium station; then all of the greatest men—kings, counts, bishops, and prelates. And finally—a sight never seen before—very noble ladies likewise traveled toward that place along with the poorest people. Many of them wished to die before returning to their own country.

And many of them did die, for two reasons. Because they had decided to undertake that tremendous trip at the most propitious time for great offerings—i.e., as the moment of death drew near—so that it would be of immediate benefit to them. But also because in order to reach the Holy Sepulcher they had to journey through huge provinces where Western Christians, considered savages, were not always made welcome. Perhaps it was the increasing danger that surrounded such travel that induced the knights-errant, toward the middle of the eleventh century, to come together and form armed bands, determined to fight if need be. More likely this aggressive preparedness reflected the youthful vigor of a country that was beginning to flex its new muscles. At any rate, this was a decisive moment in the religious history of the knighthood.

Until then, the Church had tried to shield itself from the warriors' turbulence. It had placed protective enclosures around certain holy places and also around certain categories of society—clerics, monks, and the poor—for which it assumed patronage. Now it was thinking of converting the knights themselves, tearing them out of the clutches of evil, channeling all of their energy and mettle into the service of God. It became customary to choose Pentecost, commemorating the manifestation of the Holy Spirit, for the initiation ceremonies—thoroughly pagan and family affairs—by which warriors' sons were accepted into the ranks of fighting men. Priests came for the occasion to bless their swords, and the magic formulas they recited over those sanctified weapons entrusted them with the erstwhile royal missions of protecting the weak and fighting the infidel.

The first synods devoted to preserving God's peace had never denied the warriors' right to fight; God, it was considered, had placed them at the top of the social hierarchy so that they could fulfill their military function. But in about 1020 certain clerics began to declare that the joys of making war were guilty pleasures, and that any man who decided to deny himself those pleasures would find grace in the eyes of the Almighty. The obligations of observing a truce were added to the dictates of God's peace. During the period of penance a man was supposed to give up war along with the other physical pleasures: "from [the beginning of] Lent until Easter, I shall not attack any horseman who is unarmed." By mid-century, when the pilgrimages to Santiago de Compostela and Jerusalem were gradually coming to resemble acts of aggression in Moslem territory, the assemblies convened by the bishops condemned all violence among Christians. "Let no Christian kill another, for without doubt, whoever kills a Christian spills the blood of Christ."

But in that case, what about the knights? In the divine plan they were designated for combat; but now where would they be able to wield their weapons? The answer was: outside the confines of God's people, against the enemies of the faith. Holy war, and holy war alone, was legitimate. In 1063, when the knights of Champagne and Burgundy were preparing to go on a pilgrimage to Spain, the pope enrolled them in a holy war, ordering them to attack the unbelievers. As the successor to Peter, who held the keys to paradise, he promised indulgence to those who happened to die in the process. In the name of Christ, then, these men took Barbastro, a Saracen city full of women and gold. Thirty-two years later, another pope designated a more exalted outlet for knightly excesses: they were to deliver the tomb of Jesus himself. He offered an emblem, the symbol of victory, to all the armed pilgrims who answered his summons. That emblem was the cross, Christ's own banner. What were the crusades, after all, if not the final outcome of the pressure which the feudal mentality had so long brought to bear on Christianity? And what were the first crusaders, if not the faithful vassals of a jealous God who led the war into his enemies' camp and used sword and fire to bend them to his will? The sculpture of holy subjects in this period included chain mail, helmets, armor, shields, and a whole army of lances among the attributes of divine strength, aimed at the forces of darkness.

3

THE MONKS

Covered with armor and bristling with weapons, the Western world of the eleventh century lived in fear. How could it help but tremble before unfathomable, forbidding nature? The texts that have come down to us do not clearly show a wave of terror suddenly breaking over the year 1000, but they do at least indicate that some Christians anxiously awaited the year 1033, the thousandth anniversary of Christ's Passion, the anniversary of God's death. It counted more than the anniversary of his birth in a culture that placed so much importance on remembering the deceased and visiting tombs. In his history, Raoul Glaber shows that date preceded by a whole host of supernatural events. "People believed that the orderly pattern of the seasons and the elements which had reigned since the beginning of time had reverted to chaos once and for all and that the end of mankind had come." At all events, we know that ripples of fear ran through the suggestible populace from time to time, affecting now this place and now that, touching off incoherent migrations that sometimes drew entire villages into hopeless ventures.

At the origin of this shuddering and dread was the expectation that the end of time was near. "The world is growing older" was a common phrase in the preambles to charters marking donations. But everyone wanted to foresee the exact moment when the world would sink down into torment. To that end, the scholars pored over the Scriptures. In chapter 20 of Revelation they read that Satan would be freed of his chains and that horsemen bringing chaos with them would swoop out of the corners of the earth "when the thousand years have been completed." On the basis of that prediction, certain priests, in the middle of the tenth century, preached "to the people, in a church at Paris, that the Antichrist would appear at the end of the year 1000 and that the Last Judgment would follow shortly thereafter." Many churchmen, however, opposed that statement, maintaining, on the contrary, that it was blameworthy to try to pry out God's secret and that it was not up to man to guess the day and the hour. The Gospel mentions no specific date but instead points out the premonitory signs:

> The nations shall rise up against one another and the kingdoms likewise against one another; here and there plagues, famines, and earthquakes shall occur, and this shall be the beginning of the suffering.

That is the moment when each man would have to be prepared to look upon the dazzling face of Christ, coming down from heaven to judge the living and the dead. Anxiously, the Western world at the time of the millennium watched for these first symptoms.

What did that world know of the structures of the Creation? The stars were seen to revolve regularly; dawn followed dawn and spring followed spring; every creature was born and eventually died. Men were aware of an orderly pattern established by God; the walls of the Romanesque churches were in harmony with it, and their builders strove to convey it. But it sometimes happened that these recurrent patterns skipped a beat. Meteors were seen, and comets whose trajectory did not coincide with the circular motion of the stars. Monsters rose up out of the sea, such as the whale "which appeared one November morning at dawn, like unto an island, and could be seen continuing on its way until the third hour of the day." What were men to think of calamities, violent storms, volcanic eruptions? Of the dragon that, one Saturday evening before Christmas, many terrified witnesses saw in the sky over Gaul, "darting sheaves of lightning as it moved south"? Descriptions of disturbing anomalies in fire, in water, in the heavens, and in the bowels of earth constituted the main topic of the chronicles written by the monks of the time. They carefully noted these occurrences because they were convinced that such events formed a network of clues which might, one day, shed light on man's destiny. They were considered omens. During the eclipse of 1033 people saw one another as pale as death. "Then a terrible fright seized their souls, as they realized what this sight portended: a frightful catastrophe was to strike mankind." When a certain comet appeared, Raoul the monk wondered:

> Who can say whether it was some new star that God was sending or simply a heavenly body which he had made to shine more brightly, as an omen? Only he can say whose wisdom governs all things better than any man. One thing however is certain: whenever men see a marvel of that sort occur, then shortly thereafter some terrible and surprising event overwhelms them.

For even the most scholarly minds pictured the universe as a sort of mysterious forest which no man could measure. Anyone wishing to plunge deeper into it and defend himself against the dangers it encompassed must use the same tactics as a hunter—follow twisting paths, rely on imprints and tracks, and let himself be guided by a set of illogical coincidences. The order that held the world together was based on a fabric of tenuous links that embodied magic influences. Every word, every sound, every gesture, every flash of lightning which the senses perceived was a sign, and it was by patiently unraveling the complex skein of such symbols that man could gradually move forward in the dense undergrowth where nature held him prisoner.

At the heart of mystery, supernatural wonders occurred. What mattered was to determine who or what, among the ambiguous powers crouching behind appearances, brought them forth. Was it the satanic powers that every man could feel swarming under the ground and ready to leap out from the bushes? In Romanesque art they were shown as bestial creatures, part woman and part reptile. "Does not every man know that the wars and hurricanes and deaths—in faith, all the evils that plague the human race—are brought about by demons?" Although the process of Christianization had clothed the deep-seated beliefs of the eleventh century in a number of images and formulas, it had not entirely eradicated the ways in which the people's instinctive faith pictured the inscrutable in an attempt to understand it. In terms of these myths, based on the contrast between night and day, life and death, the flesh and the spirit, the universe was the scene of a tournament, a duel between good and evil, between God and the rebel armies that denied and disturbed his prescribed order. Through such myths the people understood that natural calamities—interruptions in nature's customary rhythm—signified the defeat of the forces of good and the victory of Satan, the Enemy whom an angel had held prisoner "until the thousand years had past" but who now was breaking loose, attacking and leaving chaos everywhere, like the marauding horsemen who galloped over fields and ruined the anticipated crops.

But why not take the opposite view? Why not believe that it was God himself who placed such signs before men's eyes? A violent God, quick to fly into a rage, like the earthly kings when they felt betrayed or challenged, yet a God who never ceased to love his sons and wished to forewarn them, to put them on their guard, who refused to strike them unexpectedly and was determined to leave them a respite in which to prepare themselves for the heaviest blows he dealt. Though man lived under the crushing weight of the divine power, yet he must continue to be confident. His creator had given him eyes with which to see and ears with which to hear. He spoke to man in parables, as Jesus had spoken to his disciples, and it was up to every Christian to discover the hidden meaning of the obscure metaphors he used. By means of the changes he carefully contrived in the cosmic order of things, God was doing mankind the favor of alerting it. Such rumblings had the effect of a first remonstrance. In the year 1000, so many of the plagues that descended on the rural world—flood, war, disease, or famine—were natural occurrences in a civilization that was helpless before extremes of climate and the various forms of biological aggression and altogether incapable of restraining its own bursts of passion. Inexplicable otherwise, they were considered harbingers of the day of wrath, the warnings mentioned in the Gospel according to Saint Matthew. Hence, inducements to do penance.

It is true that everything that enables us to know something of the spirit of the eleventh century comes from texts that were written in monasteries. Their testimony was influenced by a specific code of ethics, for they came from men whose vocation made them lean toward pessimism and pattern their behavior on models of renunciation. The monks naturally exhorted men to accept privations to which they had consented themselves, and the wonders they observed gave support to their words. God showed that he was irritated. Predictions of the avenging Christ's imminent return became more frequent. The One King would soon summon mankind to his banquet hall; all men must quickly make ready. Woe to anyone who had not donned his purest robes. Let every man therefore attend to washing himself of his sins and, by voluntarily giving up the pleasures of this world, disarming the wrath of the Almighty. We may be certain that the great mass meetings in southern Gaul whose aim was to establish God's peace urged the faithful to achieve collective purification through repentance. In Aquitaine, cases of erysipelas raged everywhere—God's impatience inflicting disease on his creatures. In Limoges "the bodies and relics of the saints were solemnly brought forth from all sides; the body of Saint Martial, the patron saint of Gaul, was pulled from its sepulcher. Then the world swelled with immense joy, and everywhere evil ceased its ravages while the duke and the great men together concluded a pact that provided for peace and justice."

The reestablishment of the peace played a role in the ascetic movement that was stimulated by omens announcing the Last Judgment. After all, the sermons urging observance of God's peace enjoined men to give up the joys of battle. At the very time when the Church was urging the knighthood to observe truces—a form of periodic abstinence—as the types of penance best suited to their condition, it made the rules about fasting more stringent. It began to take the position that its priests, as models of Christian living, should set the example with regard to poverty and chastity, give up knightly luxury and send their concubines away—in other words, live like monks. In order to appease God's wrath and prepare for the Second Coming, which was felt to be imminent, the ferments of sin had to be cast out and, consequently, the basic prohibitions had to be more strictly observed. Satan held his slaves prisoners by making them covet four things: meat and drink, war, gold, and women. Let men resist those temptations in preparation for the Day of Judgment. For centuries the monks had been doing just that: renouncing wealth, laying down their arms, fasting, observing continence.

The Church now recommended that all Christians imitate the members of the religious orders, impose the same rules of poverty, chastity, peace, and abstinence on themselves and like monks, turn their backs on all that was fleshly in the world. Then the entire human race, at last converted, would be able to march confidently toward Jerusalem.

Since the clergy assured all who would listen that the end of time was near, the eleventh century took as its ideal—the one that works of art were supposed to convey—the very principles of monasticism. Amid the vast stretches of barely reclaimed land, amid tribes bowed down under the weight of their poverty and shaken by spasms of latent anxiety, and alongside the castles where soldiers stood watch, fortresses of a different sort arose, places of asylum and hope. They were the monasteries, and attacks by the demonic armies shattered against their defenses. The earthly city was supported, it was believed, by two columns, and defended by two associated types of militia: the men who bore arms and the men who prayed to God. But what better place in which to pray than within the havens of purity protected by the cloister walls? In all the abbeys of the Western world, a host of Abels offered to the Lord the only sacrifices that were truly pleasing to him. They had more power to disarm the Lord's wrath than the fallen kings of Europe or the bishops and priests. They were the masters of what was sacred. Although the knighthood camped in the midst of Latin Christendom and held it firmly in its grip, it was the monks who reigned supreme in the enormous spiritual realm of mental anguish and religious fear and trembling. In other words, the realm of artistic creativity.

A society that put so much store in formulas and gestures and trembled before invisible forces needed rites by which to repulse its fears and establish its relationships with the supernatural powers. It needed sacraments, and that meant it needed priests. More necessarily still, no doubt, in the eyes of this society, were the continuously chanted prayers which rose toward God's throne along with the smoke of burning incense, like a permanent offering, praising him and imploring his mercy. Therefore, this society needed the monks.

Their most important mission was to pray for it. At this period, the individual did not count. He was lost to sight, part of a group wherein each man's initiatives were immediately blended into common actions and a common responsibility. Just as a family feud concerned every member of the clan and its retorts were aimed not only at the original aggressor but at all his kinsmen, similarly all of Christendom felt jointly liable before evil and before God, sullied by a crime committed by any of its members, purified by the abstinence of a few among them. Most men believed themselves too weak and too ignorant to achieve their own salvation. They relied on its coming about through other members of society agreeing to a sacrifice which would be of benefit to the entire community and reflect on all of its members. Those few, the agents of redemption, were the monks. The monastery stepped in as an instrument of spiritual compensation, attracting divine forgiveness and distributing it to the people roundabout.

Of course the monks were the first to benefit from their own merit; it was for themselves, first of all, that they earned the invisible fief which, in heaven, would reward them for their services. But others received their share of such grace, and the closer they were to the monastic community, the larger was their share. The monks' first task was to work for the salvation of their own flesh and blood; this is why it was such a widespread custom in noble families to make an offering of their very young children, who were placed in abbeys so that all their lives long they would pray for their brothers who continued to live in the world. Next, the monks worked for the salvation of their spiritual brothers. To this end many laymen bound themselves to a monastery, either through making a donation of their bodies, through the homage of vassalhood, or through joining one of the prayer associations which spread like a network about each church. And lastly, the monks worked for their benefactors' salvation—which meant that alms came pouring into their hands. Such were the reasons that caused monasteries to spring up everywhere and made them so prosperous. (These monasteries were for men only; in this masculine culture, still at the stage of questioning whether women had souls, there were few nunneries.)

The monks' main function as salvation-seekers also justified the fact that a sizeable share of monastic revenue was earmarked for decorative undertakings. For the Lord was to be praised not only through prayer but also through offerings of beauty, in the form of ornaments and the architectural arrangement that was best suited to conveying the omnipotence of an eternal God. So it was that the withdrawal of monarchical power and other social trends shifted the erstwhile royal missions of consecration and all of the impetus for artistic creativity to the abbeys. It was the liturgical functions that the monks performed on behalf of the people as a whole that led to the blossoming of sacred art in the eleventh century.

In the second place, the monasteries had become repositories for relics. No layman would as yet have dared to keep in his own possession the remains of the holy bodies. Through those bones, endowed with such tremendous powers, mystery established its presence in the midst of the visible universe. Only the king and men of great purity were entitled to keep them. The communities of priests had watched over the relics for centuries, but they gradually gave way to the morals of their times and were slowly replaced by communities of monks. Every monastery was the property of a saint who would allow no one to touch it and would turn the flames of God's wrath against anyone who violated his rights. The saint resided there bodily through the vestiges of his earthly existence. Any person wishing to pay homage to him, to beseech his help in times of trial, in illness (whose outcome he decided), or in the expectation of death, must do so at the place where his relics were. Most abbeys stood on the burial place of some martyr or evangelizer, a hero in the struggle against evil and darkness. They might even stand on several tombs. "In the small church [at Saint-Germain d'Auxerre] there were twenty-two altars"; and Raoul Glaber, who arranged the saints' epitaphs properly, "adorned in the same way the sepulchers of certain religious figures." The monks, who organized the relic worship that took place close by the sarcophagi, were the necessary intermediaries between the subterranean world of the dead and that of life on earth. This was their other function, an essential one that profoundly influenced art, for it was felt necessary to arrange all about the relics ornaments that were worthy of their virtues. It was also because each monastic church had become a reliquary itself that it was covered with splendid objects. And this decor, applied to the remains of the saints, was naturally related to funerary art.

The attention which eleventh-century Christendom paid to death reflected the victory of beliefs that came from the people's deepest roots, beliefs that the triumphs of the feudal system reinvigorated, imposed on the ecclesiastics, and thereby elevated to the highest levels of culture, where they once again found ample expression. All of the legends that form the texture of the *chansons de geste* germinated in the vicinity of burial places—at the Alyscamps in Arles or at the tomb of Girart of Roussillon in Vézelay—at a time when Christian funeral rites were undergoing change. Formerly the sinner's remains had merely been entrusted to the Lord's mercy. Now the knighthood demanded of its priests that they intervene so as to impart sanctity to the corpse. Funeral rites began to incorporate the gestures of censing and the formulas of intercession for the deceased, by which the priesthood affirmed its power to remit sins itself. Until such time as the dead body should be resurrected, it could not remain in any place more propitious for its salvation than close to the reliquaries and the choir from which prayers rose throughout the day toward God the judge. The greatest lords even managed to have themselves buried inside the monastic churches themselves. Round about them huge cemeteries spread; the best and most costly grave sites were situated next to the church wall. The community lavished on those burial places the benefits of a funeral service which expanded to the point of invading the liturgy. Day after day the necrology showed the names of more and more people for whose special benefit the mass would be sung. And lastly, the monasteries received the dying. In the eleventh century it became common for the knights of the West to be "converted," to change their way of life on their deathbeds and don the habit of Saint Benedict. When the time of death was come, they joined the great monastic family, the spiritual lineage which would never die out; like all kinship networks, it was concerned for the salvation of its deceased and would pray for them throughout time without end. Perhaps, when Judgment Day came and the resurrected person stood among his brothers the monks, the Eternal God would not notice that his robe was less white than theirs. Because the abbeys were looked upon as collective tombs, as an intermediate stage between the dullness of the earth and the splendor of heaven, they were decked with all the beauty in the world.

The monasteries were necessary in so many ways—as depositories of relics, as burial places, as sources of indulgences—that there were countless numbers of them. But they had to be very pure if their action was to appear entirely efficacious. Now the institution of monasticism had been seriously damaged during the troubled ninth and tenth centuries. It had been the first to suffer from the marauding bands of Norsemen, Saracens, and Magyars that invaded Europe. They sacked and burned the nearly defenseless abbeys filled with valuables, and the monks fled in disorder. Breaking the barrier in spite of themselves, they were suddenly plunged into the midst of the empire of the Evil One and left defenseless, at the mercy of worldly temptations. Most of them came together in safer provinces less exposed to pagan attacks. The monks of Noirmoutier, fleeing ever farther from the Vikings, wandered for a long time; ultimately they transferred the relics of Philibert, their patron saint, to Tournus on the river Saône. In that peaceful place they were then able to build one of the most beautiful edifices to be born out of the new art.

But then the monasteries bowed under another yoke: the weight of the feudal system. The kings who in former times had protected them let them slip out of their grasp. In the year 1000, in the diocese of Noyon, near though it was to the residences of the Capetian kings, the king of France kept only one of the seven abbeys under his protection. All of the others had gradually come under the protection of the lords, who dispensed justice locally, on a private basis. Moreover, many noble families, not only princes but also lesser manor lords, founded monasteries at this time, for several reasons: to have the benefit of their prayers, to send some of their sons there to take up the monastic life, and to bury their dead there. Each of them looked upon the monastery as his own property, and it soon became the common lot of the religious to be part of a family heritage, just like the tenant farmers and household slaves. They were subjects of a master who sometimes harassed and exploited them shamelessly. Only the master made a profit from the adoration shown by the faithful and from the offerings placed near the reliquaries. He often misappropriated the wealth intended for the altars, using it to feed his hounds and his women, and reduced the friars to barely making do with what he deigned to leave them. At best, the monks had to consent to giving up a large share of their estate as a fief to their patron's knights. Every abbot or prior, no matter how independent he might be, was compelled to plead against the noblemen in the vicinity who challenged the saint's rights. He had to make war on them, and this position, amid the turbulent feudal context, gave rise to disorder and laxity. How could the rule of an order be applied? How could the enclosing wall continue to separate two worlds? How could the monks help but be sullied by the blood spilled in combat, by gold and the works of the flesh? How could they remain educated?

As soon as the West had emerged free of such tumult and disaster, its masters had bent their energies to restoring the instruments of collective prayer as the most urgent task. Certain aging princes had taken the initiative. Anxious to secure allies in heaven, they strove to make the monasteries that their ancestors had founded or that they had taken away from royal patronage revert to the way of life of regular clergy. This reform movement had started very early, at the beginning of the tenth century. By 980 it was very rigorous; by about 1130 it faded away, having accomplished all of its goals. The basic functions which the monastic communities took over during this period of Christian history explain why the reform mentality developed in the abbeys first of all. Until the beginning of the twelfth century, the secular Church continued to be imprisoned in temporal considerations; as a result, the abbots had precedence over the bishops, and the monks triumphed everywhere, for they were holier, and the services they rendered to God were of distinctly higher quality. Thus, prior to 1130, it was the monasteries, and not the cathedrals, that were the Western world's greatest cultural centers, the great crucibles of the new art. The monasteries, established in rural areas at the centers of estates invigorated by the steady progress made in agricultural techniques, were better suited to the requirements and structures of an essentially rural society. But their primacy stemmed above all from the fact that the monastic institutions were renovated much earlier, purged of the infections that had momentarily corrupted them. In the medieval West, abbots attained to holiness before bishops did, reorganized the system of schools earlier than they did, and were quicker to stop squandering income. The abbots used the ever more generous donations they received to rebuild and adorn their churches for the greater glory of God.

Generally speaking, it was through the efforts of some especially gifted man, known for his energy and the strictness of his morals, that monasteries were reformed; for those reasons, the feudal princes who wanted to be able to count on docile monks would ask him to wipe out disobedience wherever it occurred. His mission made him travel from one place to another. But since he did not want the improvements he had just brought about to be only fleeting, he usually strove to remain in charge of the many reformed establishments. Together they formed a body of which he was the head; because all of its parts were united, they were better protected against any return of the forces of dispersion, particularly interference by lay powers. Reform led spontaneously to the formation of congregations, whose structure determined certain features of sacred art. Art historians, when discussing Romanesque art, used to divide it into provinces: the Poitiers school, the Provençal school. Yet the relationship that we can make out between eleventh-century religious edifices actually depended far less on geographical proximity than on spiritual ties. From one end of Christendom to the other they united the monasteries that had been purified by the same reformer and so continued to feel the close bonds of brotherhood. The men who headed them deliberately built the same type of churches and adorned them in similar ways, so as to show that such an alliance existed.

There were many of these congregations—for instance, the one in Lorraine which stemmed from the efforts of Richard of Saint-Vanne, or the group in the Mediterranean region that brought a number of Catalonian, Sardinian, and Tuscan monasteries together under the auspices of Saint-Victor-de-Marseille. Take the example of William of Volpiano, abbot of Saint-Bénigne-de-Dijon. In 1001 the duke of Normandy summoned him to bring the monks of Fécamp back into the paths of righteousness. Then in 1003 he founded Fruttuaria in Lombardy. He was successful because the requirements he laid down were exacting to the point of being *super regula,* above and beyond the rule. Demanding "mortification of the flesh, abasement of the body, lowly garments, of nourishment very little," he imposed on the friars the strict asceticism which would keep them entirely pure.

All along a line stretching between his earliest initiatives in northern Italy and on the shores of the English Channel, the reform spread from Fécamp to Saint-Ouen-de-Rouen, Bernay, Jumièges, Saint-Michel-au-péril-de-la-mer [Saint Michael of the dangers of the sea]—the latter invoked by Roland when he was about to die, because it was the archangel's task to weigh the souls of the dead before the Judgment Seat. These were the abbeys that William the Conqueror and Lanfranc drew on, after 1066, to supply England with good bishops; here too the greatest scholars of 1100, including Saint Anselm, were trained. The influence of Dijon spread as far as Bèze, Septfontaines, Saint-Michel-de-Tonnerre, and Saint-Germain-d'Auxerre, where Raoul Glaber was a monk, and the influence of Fruttuaria over Sant'Ambrogio in Milan and Sant'Apollinario in Ravenna. When William of Volpiano died in 1031, he was the sole abbot of forty monasteries in which over twelve hundred religious prayed.

The Cluniac order stood sovereign above all the other congregations of the eleventh century. Instituted in 910, the abbey of Cluny had been conceived as totally independent. No intrusion by the temporal powers or even by the bishops was allowed. Its founder had deliberately linked it directly with the Church of Rome; the same patron saints, Peter and Paul, protected it. The Cluniac order was successful because of this thorough segregation;

its monks maintained the privilege of designating their abbot themselves, free of any pressure from outside the order. In 980 Cluny was highly respected, but its influence was still somewhat limited, for its abbot, Maieul, had refused to reform Fécamp and Saint-Maur-des-Fossés, allowing his disciple, William of Volpiano, to carry out that task in his stead. It was Saint Odilo who built up the Cluniac empire after the year 1000. Bringing together a number of small establishments, he united them around a single abbot, around a certain conception of the monastic life, the *ordo cluniaciensis,* and lastly, around special liberties which, with the aid of the Holy See, guaranteed to all of the member convents immunity from the decisions of the manor lords and exemption from those of the bishops. The order spread on both sides of the border that separated the kingdom of France and the Empire, into Burgundy, Provence, and Aquitaine. In other words, into regions of the West that most completely escaped the sovereigns' control, into the area most favorable to the feudal dispersion of power and the peace of God, into provinces where Latin was used not because court archaeologists had artificially revived it but because the language had roots that went deep into the soil of local history. Into the true home of Romanesque art.

Cluny's influence gradually spread to Spain along the road to Santiago de Compostela, and pervaded the great royal monastery of San Juan de la Peña, through which the Iberian Church adopted the rites of the Church of Rome. In 1077 the king of England entrusted the monastery at Lewes to the order of Cluny, and two years later the king of France did the same with the Parisian monastery of Saint-Martin-des-Champs. In this way the Cluniac order implanted itself in regions where the impetus for art came from the kings. It also secured the favors of the West's greatest sovereigns; from the king of Castile it received Moslem pieces of gold, and from the king of England silver coins. This precious metal was used to rebuild the abbey church, to clothe it in ornaments worthy of the immense body of which that church was the head. Yet the Cluniac version of the Church was neither imperial nor royal. It was autonomous. And although the Cluniac monks honored Alfonso of Castile and Henry of England as the movement's true founders, the entire enterprise was actually led by the abbot Hugh, friend to the emperor, adviser to the pope, and the unchallenged guide of the Christian world in his day.

The reformed monks in Lorraine accepted the authority of their bishops who, thanks to the emperor's determination, were the best—rather, the least bad—of Europe's prelates at that time. But in the provinces where the Cluniac order was established, the intrusions of the feudal system had so corrupted the central functioning of the secular Church that the Cluniac movement took a resolutely antiepiscopal position. It broke up the dioceses at the very time when the independence of the manor lords was breaking up the countries. In terms of the history of institutions, the triumph of Cluny meant that the influence of the episcopacy began to ebb, and the Carolingian system—in which the state was based on the joint authority of the bishops and the counts, both of whom were under the sovereign's control—crumbled still further. And in terms of the history of culture and cultural activity, this triumph meant the decline of the cathedral schools and the weakening of the humanistic strivings channeled into the reading of Latin classics. In other words, the aesthetics attached to the imperial system regressed. In terms of mental and religious attitudes and artistic creativity, Cluny's conquests corresponded to the conquests made by the feudal system. The effects of both types of conquest combined to wipe out the old foundations. The area in which Cluny triumphed grew wider and wider—and coincided exactly with the regions where the art forms we call Romanesque flourished. Within that area, the Carolingian traditions dissolved and faded away, giving free rein to the indigenous forces that sprang from the Roman substratum.

Along with the improvements brought about in the rural economy and the installation of the feudal system, the rise of the Cluniac order, which was a response to those two developments, was the most important fact in the history of eleventh-century Europe. It was a total success. Bishop Adalbero wrote a poem whose sole purpose was to convince the king of France that the victories of that black-garbed, all-invading militia, posted everywhere, were actually undermining the king's power. Success of this magnitude was due to the exceptional stature of the four abbots who, one after the other, guided the great monastery's destiny for two centuries. It was based on the strictness of the order's rules and on clever propaganda, and even more on the fact that this religious institution was perfectly adapted to the functions that the lay world expected it to perform. Raoul Glaber wrote

> Let every man know that this convent has not its equal anywhere in the Roman world, particularly when it comes to delivering souls that have fallen under the demon's sway. Communion is taken there so frequently that virtually not one day passes but that this never-ending link [between man and God] makes it possible to wrest some soul from the power of the evil spirits. I myself am witness that in this monastery it is a custom, made possible by the very great number of monks, that masses be celebrated constantly from the earliest hour of the day until the hour assigned for rest; and they go about it with so much dignity and piety and veneration that one would think they were angels rather than men.

The monks of Cluny had taken over the functions of the priesthood; the eucharistic consecration became associated with the acts of abstinence proper to monastic vows. By the same token, the unworthiness and, in fact, the insubordination of the secular priests became more obvious. Cluny's triumph aimed at that universality of monasticism which the bishops of

Aquitaine had dreamed of, amid epidemics and anguish, while the millennium of the Passion drew near. Moreover—and this may have been the decisive factor in the order's success—Cluny satisfied the desires of a Christendom that was still in the savage state and whose religious practices all converged on adoration of the dead. Never anywhere except in the great Burgundian abbey of Cluny were the funeral rites held so well—and the same was true of the Mass, the intoning of music, and the anniversary repasts in which the entire community of monks gathered, to share with a dead man whose psalmody had evoked the sorrows of life the bread, the wine and the very choice dishes that were served at princely tables. It was the abbots of the Cluniac order who conceived the idea of combining the services commemorating all of the dead in a single liturgical rite, held on November 2. They asserted that souls in Purgatory could be more quickly freed from their otherworldly torments if it was arranged to have prescribed prayers said for them. Relying on the hundreds of priories placed under their spiritual control, they undertook to Christianize the popular religion, but this time in depth, by reconciling the promise of final resurrection contained in the Scriptures with beliefs in the survival of the dead. As a result, the greatest lords in Europe expressed their desire to be laid to rest in the cemetery attached to the monastery. The Cluny basilica—the culmination of eleventh-century art—grew out of soil made fertile by a multitude of tombs. Both structurally and by its ornamentation, it was meant to signify the resurrection of all the dead, to the sound of trumpets, and amid the dazzling of the Second Coming.

In making their way toward God, the monks of eleventh-century Europe followed two separate paths. One of them retraced an itinerary laid down earlier by Byzantine Christendom, and as a result the area in which it was most successful was located near the blurred line that stretched across central Italy and separated the Latin-speaking world from the Hellenic. Naturally it overflowed to the south as far as Sicily and the tip of the peninsula, where at this time the sons of the Norman lords went to seek adventure; little by little they wrested that region from Byzantium and Islam, annexing it to the Western world. Soon they erected a Romanesque cathedral in Bari. In these regions monks literally turned their backs on the world and went into the desert. Just as they did in the Sinai and in Cappodocio, individual monks went to dwell in caves and there, naked and covered with lice, utterly heedless of their bodies, they lived on nothing, on what God in his goodness granted to the lilies of the field and the birds of the air.

The mountains of Lazio, Tuscany, and Calabria were peopled with anchorites during this period. In scattered small groups of hermitages, disciples clustered about a master and subjected themselves to the mortifications on which salvation depended. Little by little, these colonies of solitary men came together in federations such as the order of the Camaldolese founded by Saint Romuald. Many men who were not Italian became fascinated by this unsociable form of repentance. The emperor, Otto III, went to see Saint Nil, another champion of mortification. Along with Franco, bishop of Worms, and "in great secrecy, barefooted and wearing a hair shirt, he went to live in a cave close by the church of Christ, and there they remained concealed for fourteen days, employing their time in prayer and fasting and vigils."

Of course this monastic way of life, an attempt to reject the world forever in favor of total poverty, silence, and confinement to a cell, ruled out all artistic creativity—at least as long as it was not glossed over by success in the temporal world, as at Pomposa. Throughout the eleventh century the idea of a hermit's existence grew increasingly popular as certain aspects of it—the physical heroism and self-control it presupposed—appealed to the world of chivalry and its penchant for great feats. It gradually spread, reaching the very heart of the West when Bruno founded the Carthusian order, and Stephen of Muret, that of Grandmont. The yearning for austerity that it embodied began to protest against the Romanesque school of aesthetics, paving the way for the advent of Cistercian art. But the height of its success came after 1130. Until then, Western monasticism as a whole had followed the other direction, the one to which Benedict of Nursia had led the way in the sixth century. The Benedictine rule had spread from Monte Cassino and from the abbey at Fleury-sur-Loire which claimed to possess the master's remains. In particular, it spread through and from England, which had been evangelized by monks of that order. The Carolingian reformers had imposed it on most of the monasteries in Europe.

This approach was somewhat similar to the other, for both expressed the will to be isolated, to renounce the world, and both were indifferent to the sending of missionaries. But two principles—moderation and the spirit of communal living—separated them. Each Benedictine monastery harbored a society of the family type firmly led by a father—the abbot—invested with all of the powers and bearing all of the responsibilities of the pater familias of ancient Rome. The monks were brothers, and the disciplinary rules which shattered any personal initiative they might feel were even more stringent than the ties that bound groups of blood relations into one tight clan. Saint Benedict based all of his injunctions on the virtue of obedience:

> Obedience without delay is the first degree of our state of humility. Give up your own will and take up the strong and noble arms of obedience in order to fight under the banner of Christ, our true King.

"Arms," "combat," "banner"—the monastic family considered itself a *scola,* that is to say, a squad, respecting the military authority of a superior.

The religious committed themselves, in the fullest sense of the word, by a written vow analogous to the one which the soldiers of the declining Roman Empire used to take. There was such team spirit, they lived in such close quarters that no concession was made to individuality, not even for the abbot, who ate and slept and prayed in the midst of his sons, true militiamen, bound to him by a tie closer than the vassal's devotion, and unable to loosen it.

Stability was another cardinal virtue in the Benedictine code of ethics; it condemned vagabondage and any lingering impulse toward independence. Therefore, like all feudal families, the community would set itself up on the strength of a heritage, a landed estate that gave it roots. None of its members owned anything as individuals; nothing belonged to any one of them. Without the slightest hesitation a Benedictine monk could say that he was poor; but in fact his poverty was no different from that of a knight's sons—their father was rich but they had no income of their own. It bore an even closer resemblance to the poverty of the domestic warriors whom the most powerful noblemen fed and housed in their castles and who owned nothing but their arms. Like those members of the secular world—the world's militia—each monk shared in what belonged to the community; from it he drew his subsistence and the hardy, well-off existence enjoyed by the rural nobility of that time. Because each Benedictine monastery seemed to be a house similar to the family networks within the aristocracy, it easily managed to fit into the social framework of the early Middle Ages, attracting many young noblemen and all of those aged lords who wished to end their days in the shadow of the Lord. In harmony with this temporal situation was the spirit of moderation that infused Saint Benedict's precepts—an emphasis on equilibrium, reserve, a sense of restraint, a reasonable amount of wisdom, and they in turn made this "very modest rule, for beginners" a great success in the Western world. The master had said, "We hope not to establish anything that is too harsh or demanding," and in so saying he deliberately turned his back on the heroes of asceticism. He had limited the periods of fasting and proposed a simple moral code, in place of the excesses of mysticism, for he believed that if Christ's soldiers were to be able to fight effectively, they had to be adequately fed, clothed, and rested. A monk should forget his body rather than insist on overcoming it. He should work the land about his house diligently so as to reap more bountiful harvests from it and so offer more lavish sacrifices to God.

Cluny followed the Benedictine rule but interpreted it in its own way. The variations which the Cluniac practices imposed on Saint Benedict's teaching stemmed from the most deeply-rooted features of the new art. First of all, Cluny unhesitatingly took its place in the hierarchy which, ever since the earliest centuries of Latin Christendom, installed God's servants on the highest rung of the social ladder. Cluny had no qualms about accepting the wealth, the opulence sustained by the steady flow of alms into each one of the order's priories, for it deemed that no one could use that wealth to better purpose than it did. After all, did not Cluny devote its wealth entirely to the service of the Lord? Why then should Cluny refuse it? And since Cluny constituted the foremost of the Almighty's armies, why shouldn't it let its sons, as knights of the times, live like lords and be maintained by the peasants' labor? It was God's wish that that labor should feed the warriors and the men who spent their lives in prayer. Saint Benedict had decided that the monks themselves would take part in the work to be done, plowing their fields and harvesting their crops, for two reasons: as self-punishment and because idleness opened the door to temptations. But the nobiliary prejudices triumphed in the Cluniac order—those prejudices that deemed it unsuitable for a truly free man to toil like a peasant, that considered physical labor a punishment, a blemish on a man's honor, at the very least an indignity, and maintained that for that very reason God had created slaves. The monks of Cluny carried out only symbolic tasks. They were served, as manor lords were, by the tenants who cultivated their estates and the servants who did the menial chores. Although these monks were men of leisure, they did not lead a studious life, for Saint Benedict had neglected intellectual activities as such. He was concerned with spiritual nourishment, not with the conquests of the mind. His Rule provided that illiterates could join the monastery's ranks. The Benedictine monks in England, however, whose exemplary life led to the reform of the Frankish Church in the eighth century, had filled in that void, making the schools one of the pillars of monastic life. Because Latin was an altogether foreign tongue for them, they read Virgil. Thus, in the Carolingian era, the monasteries of Gaul and Germania had become brilliant centers of imperial culture. By the year 1000 many of them still were, in Bavaria, Swabia, and Catalonia—the regions most faithful to the tradition of monarchy. In the eleventh century the best libraries and the boldest masters were at Saint-Gall or Reichenau, at Monte Cassino, at the abbey of le Bec Hellouin or at Ripoll, but not at Cluny.

The Cluniac order was still in the grip of the reaction against intellectual work which, for austerity's sake, had swept through certain abbeys in the Empire early in the ninth century. Things had not gone so far as to close the schools or the bookcases, but the trend was to have exercises focus on the reading of the Church Fathers, particularly Gregory the Great. After the year 1000, the abbeys of the Cluniac order continued to discourage their sons from familiarity with the pagan classics and to warn them that any monk who enjoyed the poems of ancient Rome ran the risk of incurring spiritual infection. The fact that such mistrust with regard to the *auctores* of antiquity was the dominant influence in the circles where Romanesque concepts were forged may make it easier to understand what distinguished Romanesque art from imperial art and from all the "renaissances" and their humanistic aims. Of the three arts making up the *trivium,* two appeared unnecessary from the monk's standpoint: rhetoric—what use would eloquence be to a man who lived in silence and almost always expressed himself by means of gestures?—and dialectics, the science of reasoning, utterly useless in a cloistral retreat where there was no one to talk to or persuade. Only grammar was suitable for his training. But did this mean that a monk must expose himself to the insidious attractions of profane letters? In order to know the meaning of Latin words, was it not enough for him to use such repositories of learning as the *Etymologies* of Isidore of Seville? With the aid of such compilations, which took works of literature apart and stripped their content of its charms, let the spiritual son of Saint Benedict sit in the cloister bays and carry on his solitary rumination over a handful of passages from Scripture; let him gradually commit them to memory. For it was not through subtle reasoning nor by giving in to the charms of fine language that a man could approach true knowledge. A monk was dedicated to silence, striving to attain unto heaven and the divine light. He would perceive its gleam more quickly if a given word or image could bob up to the surface of his consciousness through the spontaneous workings of memory. Intuition would spring of its own accord from the association of these words and the illumination of the symbols.

This was the frame of mind which surrounded the birth of monastic painting, sculpture, and architecture in the eleventh century. It included no reasons, no method, and very little reference to the classic texts. Instead, it consisted of the Scriptures, learned entirely by heart, each word in them considered a sign from God and therefore treasured like a priceless object, weighed, examined, and tested until it was accidentally brought into contact with another word and light gleamed forth from the encounter. The underlying thought pattern shifted with the various facets of reminiscence but was at all times orderly, under the cohesive influence of liturgical symbolism. Indeed—and this was the basic feature of the Cluniac style of monastic life—everything in it converged on the service of the Lord, the *opus Dei,* the ceremonies embodied in divine service. All of the modifications made by the *ordo cluniaciensis* in the text of the Benedictine Rule combined to magnify that function. Saint Benedict himself had looked upon it as essential. He had singled out the singing of God's praises as every monk's specific mission, and devoted twelve chapters of his Rule to the arrangement of the liturgical rites. In his eyes, the purpose of the monastic profession was to hold public prayer as a community and for the benefit of all the people. If the monastery housed a school, it was solely in order to prepare its pupils for that action, in which the vocations of obedience and humility were fulfilled to the highest degree. Public prayer also furthered the experience of collective living, since nothing could better create cohesion among the friars than the ceremonial of divine service, and the liturgy gathered together all the wealth of insight gleaned during the reading and solitary meditation.

The Cluniac order, however, was more demanding on this score. First of all, it lengthened the duration of the service. According to the text of the Rule, the monks should have devoted less time to reciting the psalter each week and to the rhythmic reading of excerpts from the Bible and more to other, temporal occupations. But in the Cluniac adaptation of the Rule, divine service took up as many as seven hours on an ordinary day and still more on each high holy day. It became an exhausting task to sing so long, and this justified the monks' abandoning manual labor and living in the comfortable conditions which the order decreed for its religious. In order to make God's glory more resplendent, Cluny determined to deflect toward divine service the taste for adornment and inclination toward luxury that were implicit in the spirit of knighthood. The best-managed domains yielded riches in greater abundance each day and the faithful from every corner of Christendom devotedly sent them to the abbey in a steady stream. What was to be done with the gold coins and silver ingots that Christ's knights, victorious over Islam, dedicated to the monastery? They should be used to make the ceremonies more sumptuous. All of the houses of the Cluniac order formed, as it were, one huge workshop where artist-monks set about adorning the Lord's mansion. Raoul Glaber marveled at the "veritable emulation that made each Christian community determined to possess a more sumptuous church than that of its neighbors," that "roused the world itself to shake off its decrepitude and drape itself everywhere in a white cloak of churches."

But these new edifices, as well as the decorations that covered them and the profusion of precious objects that surrounded their altars were actually no more than a perfectly fitting envelope containing a far more extensive work of art, reborn each day in the disciplined splendors of the liturgy.

They developed throughout the year, like a sort of very slow ballet whose role was to mime human destiny and the progression of time, from the Creation to Judgment Day. The monk's communal and bodily participation in this ballet was expressed, first of all, by a procession similar to the procession of God's chosen people whom Moses guided to the Promised Land and Christ led toward the heavenly Jerusalem. In Carolingian times, this basic rite had determined the layout of the new complexes of abbey churches. It induced the builders of Saint-Riqiuer, for instance, to erect three churches, some distance apart from one another; the family of monks, in procession, visited them one after the other, just as the human soul, moved by the desire for God, and encouraged by its intuition of analogical symbols, was conveyed from one to another of the three divine persons. Similarly, the requirements of processional liturgy made it necessary to add new side aisles to the plan of a basilica, to develop ambulatories around the choir and provide a number of exits, and suggested that the nave be lengthened. In the third church that Saint Hugh built, at Cluny, he wished to depict more clearly the enormous amount of ground man must cover before reaching his salvation. So he placed the porch—where the first intimation of the Light occurred—at an impressive distance from the choir, the point at the center where space was stretched vertically by the stretching of pillars and arches, where the sacrifice took place and the collective prayer rose upward to God.

Liturgy meant music. Eleventh-century spirituality bloomed in the form of full-voiced chanting, in unison, by a chorus of men's voices. It was pleasing to God to find such unanimity when his creatures sang his praises. Seven times each day the choir of Cluniac monks went in procession to the church, there to sing the Psalms, and their singing embodied the features that distinguished the Benedictine style from Eastern monachism: restraint, modesty, an interpretation quelling any incipient tendency toward individual fantasy. At Cluny, the principles of humility and obedience exalted the functions of the precentor; to him the abbot delegated his full authority so that he might lead and discipline the choir.

In the monasteries of the West, inventiveness was doubtless not excluded from the act of musical creation. The great eleventh-century abbeys, such as Saint-Gall or Saint-Martial in Limoges, were the astonishingly long-lived, questing centers of liturgical art—which, when all is said and done, was the major art form of the time. It associated poem with melody. In the technical language used by those centers "finding" actually meant arranging new texts to fit the modulations of plainsong. The men who devoted themselves to this were fully aware that they were conferring a sacred character on grammar. Ingeniously, they bent the vocabulary of prayer to fit the simple rhythms of Gregorian melody; these in turn corresponded perfectly to the rhythms of the entire cosmos and hence to divine thought. To the angels' eternal praise they added the words of human language. As a result, the *quadrivium*, or second cycle of the liberal arts in the eleventh-century schools, consisted almost entirely of music. Arithmetic, geometry, astronomy were only secondary sciences, the mere servants of music. Music was the culmination of the teaching of grammar, on which the *trivium* focused. Since no one ever read silently, since any true reading borrowed the vocalizations used in chanting, and since, if psalms were to be chanted perfectly, each of the celebrants had to know the sacred text by heart, meditation on the meaning of the Latin words and meditation on the musical tones went hand in hand. The only logic that was acknowledged in this cultural context was the inherent logic of musical harmony. When Gerbert strove to "make the different notes perfectly distinct by arranging them on the monochord, by dividing their consonances and symphonies into tones, half-tones, and sharps and methodically apportioning them," he undoubtedly recognized the beginnings of what was to become scholastic analysis two centuries later; but what he was aiming at was to grasp the concealed order of the universe.

Music—and through it the liturgy—were the most effective instruments of knowledge available to the culture of the eleventh century. Words made it possible, both through their symbolic meaning and through the thought associations brought about by an encounter with them, to probe the world's mysteries intuitively. Words led to God. Melody led to him still more directly because it afforded glimpses of the harmonic chords of the divine creation and because it gave the human heart a way to mold itself to the perfection of the divine intentions. In chapter 19 of his Rule, Saint Benedict quoted Psalm 138: "before the gods will I sing praise unto thee." In his view, the choir of monks prefigured the heavenly choir, did away with the partitions separating heaven and earth, and was in itself an introduction into the ineffable and the realm of uncreated light. "When we sing psalms," he said, "we stand before the Godhead and his angels." Through choral singing, man in his entirety—body, soul, and mind—moved toward illumination. He attained unto the *stupor* or *admiratio,* the motionless contemplation of eternal splendor, that Beaudoin of Ford, a Cistercian, spoke of in the twelfth century. The monastic world did not seek to rationalize its faith; instead, it strove to stimulate that faith through the collective wonderment that filled the persons who celebrated mass. It was not concerned with causes, effects, or proofs, only with communicating with the invisible, and believed that nothing led to that goal more directly than the experience of choral liturgy. When the same melodies and the same verses recurred week after week, always at the same hour of the day, surely each monk must be in a position, through the very act of musical utterance, to share profoundly in inexpressible virtues that the human mind could not otherwise encompass.

> The rites which are carried out during the divine service, according to a yearly cycle, are signs of the loftiest realities; they contain the greatest sacraments and the full majesty of the celestial mysteries. They were instituted for the glory of the head of the Church, our Lord Jesus Christ, by men who grasped the sublimity of those mysteries to the fullest extent and proclaimed it through the spoken and the written word and the rites. Among the spiritual treasures with which the Holy Ghost enriches its Church, we should lovingly cultivate the gift of fully understanding what we are actually saying when we pray and sing psalms.

Rupert of Deutz added, "It is nothing other than a way of prophesying."

In eleventh-century society, the monks were the officiants in a ceremony of perpetual praise; and in them came together all the creative powers of a work of art, closely bound up with the liturgy, and still more deeply related to music. On the capitals of the choir, in the center of the new basilica, Hugh of Cluny decided to represent the musical tones. For him they constituted the elements of a cosmogony because of the secret correspondences which, according to Boethius, linked the seven notes of the musical scale to the seven planets and so provided a key to the harmony of the entire universe. But above all, Abbot Hugh wished the friars to meditate on those images, as a sort of diagram of the divine mystery. *"Tertius impingit Christumque resurgere fingit"* [The third tone sounds forth and represents the resurrection of Christ]: this inscription, accompanying the depiction of the third tone, defined its function. Through the emotion it aroused, this tone prepared the soul, better than words, reading, or demonstrations, to feel what the resurrection of the Lord truly was.

4

THE THRESHOLD

God cannot be seen directly. The contemplative life that begins on earth will only be perfect once God has been seen face to face. When a gentle, simple soul has been elevated to speculative heights and when, breaking the ties of the flesh, it has contemplated what lies in heaven, it cannot long remain above itself, for the weight of the flesh pulls it back down to earth. Though it is struck by the immensity of the light on high, it is quickly reminded of its own nature; yet the little it has been able to taste of the divine sweetness is of utmost benefit to it, and soon thereafter, inspired by great love, it hastens to resume its upward flight.

These were the tensions in monastic spirituality. Eleventh-century man was confined within close limits by his senses and the pitiable means available to him. The spiritual life aspired, through experiencing perfect brotherhood, through the liturgy, through music, and lastly through works of art, to transcend those limits. It was one continuous effort to outreach sense perception and intellectual understanding, to glimpse what would be revealed to mankind, entire and resurrected, when the world's last day came, to fathom that other part of the universe whose attractions and powers could be guessed but not seen. A yearning for God—in other words, a yearning for mystery.

No matter how scholarly they were, the men of the Church could not intellectualize their faith. Their equipment for reasoning proved to be as inadequate as the wooden plows that farmers dragged over parcels of cleared land. They did not read Greek, and the wisdom of the antique philosophers was lost to them once and for all. The handful of scientific treatises that a moribund Rome, indifferent to any genuine science, had bequeathed to them were not enough to liberate their thinking from the patterns that governed peasant wisdom. Like their worldly brothers, the terrified hunters and knights who ventured into unknown thickets and the ambushes of war, the men of God were on the alert. Gerbert, whose culture was universally admired in the year 1000, was considered not a philosopher but a magician. He too set traps for the invisible. Through tricks and charms he tried to win over the forces of destiny. Man, at this point in history, felt as if surrounded by thick bushes; somewhere in them God was concealed. Yet on the basis of certain imprints, man could discern his presence; the works of his hand could be glimpsed. This made it possible to follow his trail, and, by dint of much patience and love, catch up with him or, at least drive him out into the open and see him flash by.

By means of collective rites, of participation—through gestures—in the mysteries, men could rise above their own natures and, as Rupert of Deutz expressed it, become prophets themselves, that is, heralds of God. Among the instruments used to grasp the ungraspable, music and liturgy were foremost. No one as yet included reasoning among them. The tool universally used was exegesis, encompassing all the types of mental inquiry. Signs issued from the invisible God; they were as mysterious as he was himself. It was vital to decipher those messages, and all teaching methods had aimed for that goal ever since the rebirth of study in the Carolingian monasteries.

The Benedictine monk Raban Maur, "preceptor of Germania" and abbot of Fulda in the second quarter of the ninth century, was one of the first to define the approach. "It has occurred to me," he said, "to compose a short treatise which would deal not only with the nature of things and the property of words but also with their mystical meaning." Words and nature were the two fields accessible to the human mind in which God consented to appear. Accordingly, every monk pored over the Scriptures, and the teaching of grammar prepared him to progress from the oral to the spiritual and so, by degrees, to penetrate the meaning of every syllable. He also pored over the created world in search of analogies whose interlinking might lead him toward the truth. "Through the countless differences which God, Creator of all things, established between the faces and forms of his creatures, he intended to enable the soul of a scholarly man to rise, by means of what the eyes see and the mind grasps, to a simple knowledge of divinity." And Raoul Glaber added: "These indubitable connections between things preach God to us in a way that is evident, beautiful, and silent all at the same time; for whereas each thing, with an immutable movement, presents the other in itself by proclaiming the principle from which it proceeds, it needs to rest on that principle anew."

Such was the methodological itinerary. Since God created the universe that the human sense perceived, there remained a substantive identity between the Almighty and his creature—or at least a very close union, the *universitas* mentioned by Johannes Scotus Erigena. Thus it was possible to discern God by, in the words of Saint Paul, gradually moving ahead *per visibilia ad invisibilia.* Creation, as a mute and motionless predication, embodied the richest lesson in the divine pedagogy. But just as one acquired greater understanding of the Scriptures by bringing out the correspondences between the words, the verses, and the various passages of the Old Testament and the New, just so it was important to discover relationships, harmonies—in short, a certain order amid the diversity of shapes and faces to be found in the visible universe. As William of Conches and Geroh of Reichersberg were later to put it, the world was "an orderly collection of creatures." It was *quasi magnum citaram,* "like a great zither." What man called art existed for one purpose: to make the harmonic structure of the world visible, to arrange a certain number of signs in exactly the right places. Art gave substance to the fruits of the contemplative life and transposed them into simple forms so as to make them perceivable by persons having just begun their initiation. Art was a discourse on God, as were liturgy and music. Like them, art aimed to prune and thin out the undergrowth and abstract the fundamental values buried in the dense core of nature and the Scriptures. Art revealed the inner framework of the orderly edifice called creation. To that end, art relied on certain texts containing the divine words, on the images which those words aroused, and on the numbers that marked off the cadences of the universe. Like both music and the liturgy, art used several means. Symbolism was one; the unexpected juxtaposition of conflicting values was also a means because, by striking one another, they caused truth to leap forth; and the rhythms through which the world breathed in unison with the divine respiration were yet another means. A monument, an example of the goldsmith's art, or a piece of sculpture constituted a gloss of the world, an explanation of it by virtue of their structures, the relative positions of the various elements composing them, the numerical relations maintained between those elements, and the patterns they made visible. Under the effects of its gradual action, which, between 980 and 1130, accompanied the emergence of polyphonal music and scholastic meditation, art offered a clue to the mystery. Art enabled man to grasp the substantive reality of the universe instantaneously, more perfectly than through reading and the mere seeing of things, more profoundly than through reasoning.

Thus in the architecture and the figurative arts of the eleventh century, as well as in its music and liturgy, we should recognize an initiatory process. For this reason there was nothing "popular" about the forms they used. They were not meant for the masses but only for the restricted elite that had begun to rise in the echelons of perfection. Works of art could of course play a certain role in the teaching of the faithful—the very role that kept the first forms of theater, tried out by the Benedictines of Fleury-sur-Loire and Saint-Martial in Limoges, on the outer edges of the liturgy. In 1025 the synod of Arras, in arguing against the heretics who rejected the hierarchy, the sacraments, the liturgy, and doubtless all figurative art as well, stated that "through the intervention of certain painted images, the illiterate contemplate what they would be unable to grasp through the written word." The new representational type of sculpture on a monumental scale that appeared after 1100 was available to the gathering throngs of believers as a teaching instrument. Some of the greatest examples of Romanesque sculpture, placed at the threshold of abbey churches or the crossroads of the principal pilgrimage itineraries, were very obviously designed for the edification of the masses and therefore used a visual terminology that would be understandable by all. The tympanum of Conques is one example. Nonetheless, educational intentions were of only marginal importance in the artistic creations of this period. The aesthetics that underlay monastic art were closed and inward-looking, devised for the initiate, for those pure men who refused the corrupted world and its temptations, and so preceded the main body of Christians in their march toward truth.

For the universe did not stand still. It moved with God's own movement. Every spiritual experience was lived as a forward thrust, a progress, wed and guided at the same time by music and liturgy; and although architecture, sculpture, and painting were immobile by nature, they too had a mission to convey the universal movement, which in fact appeared twofold. To begin with, it was circular. The rhythms of the cosmos, the stars in their courses, the turning of day into night and season into season, and all types of biological growth followed cyclical patterns, and their periodic repetitions had to be taken as signs of eternity.

That was why in the Benedictine monasteries divine service—to which, according to the Rule, "nothing should be preferred"—took place in accordance with two concentric circles. The first was the one described each day by the singing of psalms. While it was still dark, the bell awoke the monks for the nocturnal rites. Then came lauds, a celebration of God offered at the first light of dawn, followed by prime, simultaneous with the rising sun. During the daytime hours, when the monks had to go about various occupations, just like other men, the offices of terce, sext, and nones were briefer; but prayer came into its own again as the night hours approached. At compline the brethern were reunited and, as they sang together, found courage to face the dark.

The other cycle was the yearly one centered on Easter. One of the main tasks of both the sacristan and the cantor, who were responsible for the liturgical arrangements, was to work out the calendar each year, assign the various texts to be read, and plan the service so as to take exceptional celebrations into account. Hence a life of prayer implied the uninterrupted experience of cosmic time. By submitting to its circular rhythms and avoiding any accident that might upset them, the monastic community was already living eternity. It had genuinely overcome death, for the reiteration of daily and yearly prayers wiped out all trace of personal destiny, all awareness of growth and decline. Hence the symbol of the sidereal rhythms was the most important of the figures placed in the cloister and in books for purposes of guiding their beholders' meditation. Yet from the very instant when God created the world, he had stepped outside the eternal in order to establish his creature—and himself—in time and in a destiny that was a straight line. And from that instant everything—man's progress, the progress of history itself—was oriented, and religious monuments also had to be oriented, turned towards a specific point in space, if they were to interpret the divine intentions faithfully.

Obviously, the commotion that took hold of Western civilization in this century—this feeling of a necessary forward thrust—helped to infuse new life into it. At the heart of knightly behavior was the imperious desire for adventure, a joyous impulse that swept all young men away to the ends of the earth. The first impression left by accounts of Europe in the year 1000 is that of one overwhelming departure—departure of pilgrims, departure of the boatmen hastening to sell wine or dyed cloth at the fairs, departure of pioneer peasants clearing the land, and soon the departure of the crusaders and the migration of the prostitutes whom Robert of Arbrissel and other visionary preachers summoned to redemption in 1100. Monks, on the other hand, tooks vows of stability. While the will to reform ecclesiastical manners and morals grew stronger, monks were less often to be seen on the roads. Shut up in their cloisters, they were striving to interpret history.

Writing history was one of their specific functions. The monks chronicled their own times and recorded past events. They did so for several reasons. First of all, out of respect for a tradition that the authors of antiquity had made illustrious. The teaching of classical Latin in the cloisters was based more on commentaries on the pagan historians than on commentaries on the poets. Sallust was considered less of a threat to the faith than was Virgil. Livy's works were among the Lenten readings proposed to the monks of Cluny in 1049. But in addition the taste for historic accounts was in harmony with the ultimate purpose of monastic culture. After all, what was history if not one way of taking inventory of creation? History offered an image of man; in other words, an image of God. Orderic Vital, a Benedictine monk who was one of the best historians of his day, proclaimed: "History must be sung like a hymn in praise of the Creator, the just Governor of all things." Since history was a song of glory, it too fitted into the liturgy. And finally, history made it easier to follow mankind as it moved through the web of time, toward salvation, to recognize the several stages of its progress and discern how it was oriented. History opened out onto a prospect. It helped men to choose the right path, swim in the mainstream, and more surely reach port. From the origins of the world up to its end, one continuous procession appeared. The Scriptures, which were no different from a history, described it as a gradual ascension in three phases. The New Testament—the second phase—had smoothed out the rough spots that remained in humankind during the first phase, prior to the Incarnation. But compared to what he would become after the Second Coming, man was in exactly the same situation as the just men had been in, under the old law, in relation to the apostles. The world was growing older; the end of time could not be far away. Eleventh-century man lived in expectation of it. His sense of human history had to prepare him for that transition. It was the duty of all men who prayed, particularly the monks, to show—and smooth—the way. The processions to and within the abbey churches were symbolic realizations of history. They completed the last phase as they mimed the entry into the Kingdom of Heaven. The goal of all monastic meditation and all monastic art was to rend the veil and contemplate what lay beyond the open sky.

Since this was so, it became less essential to observe visible nature. In fact, man had to leave it behind, for it was in the Scriptures that he could discover what prefigured the Revelation. Because eleventh-century Christianity, guided by its monks, insisted on depicting what would soon take place before its eyes, and because it considered human history an accidental, subordinate development, it did not scrutinize the Synoptic Gospels or the Acts of the Apostles as closely as it did the Old Testament or the Book of Revelation. Scenes from the life of Jesus did not often appear in the figurative art of the times. Scenes from his childhood or from the Passion did decorate the capitals of certain cloisters, and sometimes appeared in the nave of the church as well. Christ's existence was indeed a form of history, and each episode in it also constituted a landmark on the road leading to salvation. Despite this, the Gospel narratives were earthly; they involved a cavern, fish, kings following a star as they traveled, robbers and inns, asses and fig trees, lances, thorns, a storm-tossed lake—scenes from everyday life. The story was sometimes traversed by messages from the invisible, but only as brief flashes. To people oppressed by their own everyday existence, groping for cracks in it by which to escape from hunger, fear, and dangers of all sorts, people trying to rise above their poverty through dreams of light, the text of the Synoptic Gospels surely seemed too modest, too colorless. Indigent themselves, they did not want to hear about more poverty but instead about glory. They found sustenance in mirages. Accordingly, eleventh-century sacred art concentrated on condensing the teachings of the Gospel into a handful of signs. It turned them into pillars of fire, like the one Jehovah used to guide his people toward the Promised Land. None of these images showed Jesus as a brother. Instead he was the master, the one who judges from on high, the Lord. Against the golden background of the pericopes the painters installed the apostles—outside of time, remote from unpredictable nature, far from mankind. Who in those days could have imagined Saint James or Saint Paul— those overwhelmingly powerful beings whose tombs were the site of so many miracles, and who hurled lightning and intolerable skin inflammations at those who contemned their rights—as fishermen and paupers? How could the Christianity of the year 1000, prostrate before its reliquaries, have dared to emphasize Christ's human traits? The Roman apostles lived in an invisible universe—that of the Christ resurrected at Easter, who forbade the holy women to touch his body, that of Jesus rising from the earth on Ascension day, that of the Almighty enthroned in the apse at Cluny or Tahull.

Neither the Christ of Cluny nor the Christ of Tahull was derived from the Gospels. They came straight from the Book of Revelation—from the dazzling heart of light. No other portion of the Scriptures offers more details about the structures of the world to come or any more exalting description of "the holy Jerusalem [whose] light was like unto a stone most precious, even like a jasper stone, clear as crystal. . . . And the city had no need of the sun, neither of the moon, to shine in it: for the glory of God did lighten it, and the Lamb is the light thereof" [Rev. 21:11, 23]. In the cloisters, the religious meditated constantly on these strange words; they were commented upon, repeated, illustrated. What Saint John's vision showed was a magnificent, transfigured universe, but one that was not really different from the visible universe. For heaven and earth were arranged in very similar ways and closely related, at the bosom of the divine harmony. As bishop Adalbero noted:

> This mighty Jerusalem is simply, it seems to me, a vision of peace. The King of Kings does govern it, the Lord does reign over it. Though it be divided into parts, nonetheless it is a whole. Not one of its gleaming gates is divided by the slightest length of metal. Its walls have no stones; its stones, no walls. Its stones are living stones; the gold paving its courtyards is living gold. It sparkles and gleams, more resplendent than molten gold. It is constituted at one and the same time by a citizenry of angels, who reign over the city, and the throng of men, who aspire to do so.

The city of God and the earthly City communicated.

As a result, although man's eyes would be dazzled, when heaven opened its gates he would not find the surroundings unfamiliar. It was even possible for man, during his life on earth, to picture his future place of residence. This is what all of the painters did who, for the benefit of the Ottonian emperors, or in Mozarabic Christian states, or in the monasteries of Aquitaine where the Cluniac movement was gaining ground, illustrated the Book of Revelation or its commentary by Beatus of Liebana. None of those painters could have wished for a sharper stimulus for his inventive powers;

none of the monks of the Western world, afire with love for God, could have wished for a more reliable foothold as he strained toward the invisible.

The art of the eleventh century reflected men's hopes. The visible universe was narrow, restive, transitory, and decaying. The type of Christianity preached and practiced by the medieval Church sought to free the people from it. It followed that its art did not attempt to render palpable reality. But at the same time it was not abstract art, for the essential concordances made nature a faithful reflection of what was beyond nature. While an artist drew his inspiration from the forms found in nature, he also refined them and sifted through them so as to make them worthy of the glory of the Second Coming. He strove to find equivalents for the gleams of light glimpsed through mystic contemplation, to depict the absolute. And this aim fit in neatly with the monasteries' missions. It was there that works of art as such had begun to appear. The function of a monastery was not only to offer up to God the public and unceasing praises that were due him, but also to prepare men as a whole for the Resurrection. The monks were in the vanguard. They had already left the temporal world behind; an enclosing wall separated them from it. As abstinence of various kinds had already purified them, they had covered half the distance, and were toiling up the mountain whence one could see, through the mist, the marvels of the land of Canaan. It was as if the monks' desire for God sucked up every aspect of their art.

> Who shall give us wings like those of the dove so that we may then fly through all the kingdoms of the world and enter within the southern sky? Who shall lead us into the city of the great King, so that what we now read on the written page, what we perceive as riddles and as if in a mirror, we shall then see by the grace of God, close by God in his presence, and shall rejoice over it?

Perhaps study would make this possible; surely music and liturgy would, and art along with them.

> Let us lift up our hearts to them as well as our hands, let us transcend all transitory things. Let our eyes shed tears without end amid the joys that are promised to us. Let us rejoice over what has already been wrought among the faithful, for but yesterday they were fighting for Christ, and today they reign with him. Let us rejoice over what we have been told, in truth: we shall enter the land of the living.

This lyrical passage by an anonymous disciple of John of Fécamp indicates the vocation of sacred art: it must do all in its power to break the chains. The door to the monks' church opens onto the mystery of God.

At the entrance to each place of worship heaven did in fact open up. As a result of liturgical innovations, certain funerary ceremonies took place in the narthex, as did the special rites devoted to the Savior. This was where scenes illustrating the Apocalypse were placed so as to initiate the people into the mysteries. At Saint-Benoît-sur-Loire they decorated the capitals of the bell tower. At Saint-Savin, in the forechurch, the painters depicted Christ, his arms widespread, inside a circle. Near him two angels hold up the instruments of the Passion, and he is surrounded by the strange figures that peopled John's vision.

But before the light could stream out from the Lamb, the four angels that guard the four winds of the earth would blow their trumpets and everything would be destroyed. Therefore any man, living or dead, who entered the church must first wipe out the germs of corruption within himself and strip himself of everything—weapons, wealth, relatives, even his will power—just as the monks did when they took their vows. Then he would be fit to fall in with the great procession.

> And the nations of them which are saved shall walk in the light of it: and the kings of the earth do bring their glory and honor into it. And the gates of it shall not be shut at all by day: for there shall be no night there. And they shall bring the glory and honor of the nations into it. And there shall in no wise enter into it anything that defileth, neither whatsoever worketh abomination, or maketh a lie: but they which are written in the Lamb's book of life.
>
> [Revelation 21:24–27]

Romanesque art was created by a handful of men whose spiritual ascension carried them toward this mirage. For the sake of creating its image they gathered together the most marvelous things they could find: gold and lapis lazuli and the strange perfumes which the merchant caravans brought back in tiny quantities from the East. One day they decided to carve their vision in stone.

Of all the experiments, all the innovations, all the surpassings of limits that the growth of the West occasioned in the field of artistic creativity, was any more overwhelming than the deliberate return to monumental sculpture? For centuries imperial art, nourished by memories of classicism, had been asserting the qualities of the human figure established in the three dimensions conferred on it by space. Gradually that art had pushed aside the features of barbarian art: its fine tooling and recurrent tendency to use abstract geometrical or vegetal motifs. The revolution occurred after 1100, in the Romance part of Christendom, the provinces where latinity had never died away, where the Cluniac monks and their ally, the pope, had come to feel that they were the masters of the world and begun to demand the *imperium*—and the prestige and functions it carried with it—for themselves. The first bold decisions by the prelates of the Ottonian renascence—who had statues of Christ on the cross carved in stone and biblical scenes cast in bronze—and the intiatives of the goldsmiths of Aquitaine, fashioning the metal of reliquaries into the shape of a body—had paved the way. The revolutionary act itself consisted of erecting divine figures which had the plasticity of Roman statues. No longer hidden away near the altar in the secrecy of liturgical rites or in the darkness of the crypt, they were daringly, publicly placed at the very church door, windswept and conspicuous.

In which monastery does such boldness succeed in overcoming the last scrap of reticence? Which is the oldest Romanesque tympanum, the one at Moissac, or the one at Cluny, which is now gone? Although archaeologists may debate the question, no one will ever know, for the chronology of works of art from this period is altogether shaky. These sculptures were offerings to the Eternal. They were situated outside of time; no one thought of dating them. In order to decorate the edifice he had undertaken to build—and he was determined to adorn every element of it as soon as it was begun—Hugh of Cluny had gathered together the most capable artists in all Christendom in the main abbey church. When they arranged the scheme of ornamentation for the capitals of its choir, and later, in 1115, when they put the scene of the Ascension in place on the threshold of the world's largest basilica, these artists found inspiration in the forms used by the Meuse valley goldsmiths in their work. Through their creations, Southern art—the Romanesque art of arches, carved demons, and sirens—came together with the classic traditions of imperial art in the narthexes of monastic churches.

The door opening onto the unknowable and onto glory was Jesus; he said it himself. In the course of the eleventh century an idea slowly made its way to the surface: the terrifying God whose throne, above the door at Moissac, towered over a throng of judges, the God who vented his wrath by visiting plagues and famine on mankind, along with war and the unknown looters who had poured out of the remoteness of Asia, the God whose return was eagerly awaited, was none other than the Son, that is, man himself. Gradually, dimly, the notion of incarnation gained ground.

What do we know about it? Was it stronger among the laymen than in the cloister? We can sense that certain groups among the faithful were shaken by ill-defined tendencies that made them oppose the Church, rendered them more receptive to the words of wandering evangelists and hermits (there had always been many hermits in Italy, but at this time they were also to be found throughout Gaul). These inspired men spoke of a poor God, a God who did not delight in the gold heaped about him by his priests, an exacting God who found the prayers of a sensual clergy repugnant. The people believed that the sacraments opened the door to salvation, and as the movement to reform the Church developed, it stimulated their desire to see those propitiatory gestures made by purer hands. The throngs in Milan that clamored for priests without concubines and rebelled against their simoniacal archbishop were demanding precisely that. They suffered to see the sacerdotal mission sullied, whereas the magical communication between the human and the divine depended on it. But what were the spiritual pressures that drove one man in Champagne, whom Raoul Glaber described as a peasant gone mad with iconoclastic fury, to knock over crucifixes and smash images of the Savior? As for the thirteen canons of Orléans "who seemed purer than the others" and whom King Robert had burned as heretics in 1023, what particular attribute of divinity did they especially revere? And what about the people in Aquitaine "who rejected holy baptism, the virtue of the cross, and everything that constitutes holy doctrine, who abstained from eating certain foods, appeared to be like monks, and feigned chastity"? If they were considered more Manichaean than others, was it not because they made a principle out of the incompatibility that everyone felt between the God of the Bible and the forces of darkness and were more radical about relegating all fleshly concerns to the overall climate of dread surrounding the end of time? If they reacted against excessive ritualism, was it not precisely because the presence of evil in this world and the mystery of God's incarnation tormented them, because they yearned for a clearer definition of Christ and an explanation of how that divine essence had lowered itself to the point of becoming flesh, living among men and saving them?

The two movements that began to take shape within the Church after 1050 seemed to respond to such anxieties. On the one hand, the scholars began to argue, advance reasons, and, by means of dialectics, tackle the problems that the poor people's faith stumbled over: the Trinity, the eucharist and, specifically, the intrusion of God in man. Already in the reformed monasteries of Normandy, John (the nephew of William of Volpiano who, in 1028, became the abbot of Fécamp) had meditated on the text of the Synoptic Gospels. In them he still sought the mediations that could deliver man from his condition, as a captive in a world of evil. Jesus appeared to him as the way leading to the radiance of God the Father:

> He was circumcised so as to cut us off from the vices of the flesh and the spirit; presented to the temple so as to let us move forward, pure and sanctified, toward God; baptized so as to wash us of our crimes; tempted so as to protect us from the devil's attacks; captured so as to free us from the Enemy's power, mocked so as to shield us from the demons' sarcasms; crowned with thorns so as to wrest us from the clutches of the original curse; raised on the cross so as to draw us to him; given gall and vinegar to drink so as to lead us into the lands of boundless joy; sacrificed like an immaculate lamb at the altar of the cross so as to bear the burden of the world's sins.

John of Fécamp's theology followed the sinuous paths of the anagogic meditations, in which words and images correspond to one another and, as in the liturgy, everything is directed toward the dazzling revelation of a theophany. Magically, it transmuted lowly matter into the nobler qualities of the unknowable. But it also led the way for the queries raised by the Italian, Saint Anselm. He, too, was the abbot of a Norman monastery, then archbishop of Cantebury between 1094 and 1098. In an effort to answer his own question, *Cur Deus homo?,* Why God [made] man?, he outlined the scholastic method and inaugurated the theology of the incarnation. Its visual equivalent was to be contributed by the Gothic style of architecture.

The second movement was still more internal to monasticism. Some religious found the text of Revelation less exalting then that of the New Testament. In a movement that went counter to the ceremonial and sumptuous display of the Cluniac liturgy, they began to preach a way of life that would not attempt to imitate the glory of the seraphim; instead, on earth, in Christ's footsteps and in his poverty, it would turn God's servants into true apostles. By 1088, just when Abbot Hugh inaugurated work on the new basilica, the great days of Cluny were coming to an end and another period was beginning. The new monasteries strove for austerity. While colleges of clerics agreed to live the communal life of monks, spreading the word of God to the people at the same time, and gradually brought the entire body of canons back into the fold of a regular existence, while the Gregorian reformers' efforts gradually restored the Church's dignity, which in turn soon made it possible for cathedrals to spring up, the steady progress that gradually refined religious sensitivity tended to restrict the overriding influence of liturgical practices. The pivotal point of the new religion was no longer the effulgence of the celestial Jerusalem but instead the humanity of the Son of God.

This turnabout was aided by the movements of piety that culminated in the Crusades. When pilgrims chose to proceed toward Christ's tomb rather than visit the reliquaries of the tutelary saints, and when the penitential rites proposed to knights anxious for their salvation deflected their aggressiveness in the direction of the Holy Sepulcher, the cross began to take on a new meaning. Until then it had been one of the symbols that helped to create awareness of God's power over the world. As a cosmic sign, the intersection of space and time, or a tree of life, it stood for all of creation, and God had chosen it as the place on which to suffer precisely because of its esoteric values. When men depicted Christ's body on the cross, they did not show it as tortured, but instead as a crowned and triumphant living body, raised on the cross and exalted by it rather than dead on it. The kings became the ministers of this victorious cross; Robert the Pious, for one, played the role of Jesus in the symbolic Holy Week ceremonies. Nevertheless, the symbol slowly took on greater presence, at the same time as its meaning imperceptibly altered.

Toward the end of the tenth century, the bishops of Germania—princes whom the emperor had endowed with all temporal powers over their city and its approaches, and who combined the pastoral mission and the powers of royalty in their own persons—dared to break with the tradition that had held men back from showing the cross as an instrument of torture. The great wooden crucifixes erected in the very center of the Ottonian basilicas were the first to hold up a victim for all to see, and not a crowned and living figure. The appearance of the first crucified Christs in the West, one thousand years after Christ's death, marked a turning point in the history of religious sensibility.

The change gradually grew clearer. In 1010, when a monk from Saint-Martial of Limoges saw "a great crucifix erect high up in the sky and on it the image of the Lord hanging on the cross and weeping an abundant shower of tears," this marvel made him think of Christ's suffering. With the same thought in mind, certain knights strove to respect the truce of God on the Thursday and Friday of each week, "in memory of the Last Supper and the Passion of our Lord." It had long been the privilege of emperors and kings to order gold crosses from their court goldsmiths and distribute them to the churches. This was a gesture of prestige, largely what we would call a political gesture. But now they lost their monopoly on this privilege, and in fact on all of their regal powers, which melted away into the feudal system. Throughout the eleventh century the wearing of the cross was progressively vulgarized. In 1095 all who were preparing to leave for the Holy Land wore the sign of the cross. It was emblematic of the peace that God had promised to mankind, of his victory over the torments of the times. The same sign was placed by the roadside to mark off the areas where one would be safe from attack, pillage, and extortion, the places of asylum that the peace-promoting institutions had recently established all about the churches. Sewn on the crusaders' garments, the cross announced to the world that they were on route to Golgotha. It had a further meaning, imprinting on their bodies the mark of the paschal sacrifice, of an alliance with the powers of the Eternal. It designated them as chosen people, placing them already within the pacified realm of the Last Day. Abbot Odilo of Cluny had shown the cross to his monks as a promise of universal salvation, as the purifying sign which was to prepare mankind to follow Christ amid the celestial glories, and as symbolizing the two principal virtues of the monastic life, humility and poverty. As bearers of that insignia, the crusader-adventurers—all of them—became Christs in turn, just as in earlier days the sovereigns—and only they—had become Christs through their anointment during the coronation rites. What the crusaders were about to relive in Palestine was the adventure of the Savior's life on earth.

When the most sagacious churchmen were asked, in about the year 1000, what "such a great convergence of people on Jerusalem" could mean, they answered that they believed it was a portent: "the coming of the wretched

Antichrist" and the end of the world were imminent. "All of the peoples smoothed the way from the Orient along which he was to come, and the nations prepared to march straight to meet him." In fact, at least some of the pilgrims of the cross seemed to come home changed men. Perhaps it was because he had recently visited the Holy Sepulcher that the count of Angoulême wished to die "while worshiping and kissing the wood of which the Cross was made." One thing is undeniable. When the ecstatic travelers who had swarmed like bees toward the Promised Land, stimulated by eschatological expectations and fascinated by the splendors of the invisible Jerusalem, later reappeared (except those who had died on the way) in their native cathedrals, castles, or villages, they were all less ignorant of who and what Jesus had been.

Were they already beginning to identify the Son of Man, whose burial place they had venerated, with the admirable image of justice and sovereignty that the sculptors of 1120 placed over the portals of the monastic churches? Doubtless there was still an incommensurable distance between the Christ shown in the Cluny Ascension and the men who came upon that image when, at journey's end, they reached the threshold of the abbey church; or between the portrayal of the Eternal at Moissac and the ingenuous sculptor who placed that despotic figure in the center of the tetramorph amid the twenty-four elders playing musical instruments. But in the narthex at Autun that distance had already shrunk considerably; there Jesus was seated in the midst of his apostles, and their faces were marked by love more than by sacred terror. What Autun showed was not the invisible but, for the first time, the human universe, with its temporal dimensions measured by the twelve months of the year and its spatial dimension extending to the strange tribes that peopled the edges of the world. As the twelfth century approached, the Romanesque dream was vanishing, and the evangelical message seemed at last about to reach every corner of the earth, freeing man from fear and spurring him on to conquests. At this instant of maturity, and at the doorway of the monastery where, before the king of France, Saint Bernard was soon to preach another crusade, there appeared the most majestic figure of the living God that Christianity has ever conceived.

Both Gislebertus, who signed his work at Autun, and the master of Vézelay probably derived their skill and certainly their inspiration from the art created at Cluny. What counts, from the standpoint of a historian of culture and of aesthetic sensibility, is that all of these works of sculpture, carved immediately after the First Crusade and on the impetus that extended its mood of exaltation, mark a crucial stage in the progress of Western Christianity. Until then the images of Christ had never resided within the realm of creation. Either they were pure abstractions—the esotericism of the cross, of the alpha and the omega, or the labarum—or else, like the painted pages of the liturgical manuscripts, they were situated outside of time and space, in the nonreality of mystical visions. They had no more weight or tangibility than the souls in Purgatory described by Raoul Glaber. They all belonged to that indiscernible empire, the secret principles of whose architecture the Romanesque churches were intended to reflect.

Until about 1120 this was the case—for then, in the cathedral schools of the Frankish lands, the dialecticians began to debate over the nature of the three divine beings and to wonder how God had made himself man. And the great sculptors freed the images of God from the realm of the supernatural and established them in an earthly context. Sculpture, creating images in the densest and most stable matter of all, made matter of them in turn, rooted them in the world. It incarnated them.

After 1130, Suger, abbot of Saint-Denis, was possibly the most active instigator of such incarnation. In any event, he was the creator of the art we term Gothic. He belonged to the Benedictine order. His thought pattern, like that of the eleventh-century monks, was shaped by analogies; their digressions and associations were intended to uplift the meditations of cloistered men immeasurably high, to the lofty spheres of God. He embraced all the symbolism of Romanesque art, and we may safely say that it came to full fruition in his work. For the porch as Saint-Denis, Suger wrote an inscription that can be interpreted in several ways. Here is one possible translation of it: "The golden door foretells to you" (art, it must be said again and again, prefigures the essential realities that shall be revealed to the human mind once it has passed over into death, into resurrection and the opening up of the heavens on Judgment Day) "what shines here within" (this means inside the edifice but also inside the heart of the world itself, the heart of time, the heart of man—the heart of God); "through palpable, visible beauty, the soul is elevated to that which is truly beautiful, and rising from the earth, where it was submerged, an inert thing, it is resuscitated in heaven by the radiance of its glory." It is fair to say that eleventh-century art helped to reveal God's face. It shed light. It claimed to offer man the sure means of coming back to life bathed in light.

PART TWO

THE CATHEDRALS 1130–1280

By definition, a cathedral was the bishop's church, hence the city's church; and what the art of cathedrals meant first of all, in Europe, was the rebirth of the cities. Throughout the twelfth and thirteenth centuries they grew both larger and more animated, while their outlying districts stretched alongside the roads. They were lodestones drawing wealth. After a long period of obscurity they became the principal centers, north of the Alps, of the most advanced culture. But for the time being virtually all of their vitality still came from the surrounding fields. Most of the manor lords decided at this time to shift their places of residence to the city. Henceforth the products of their estates converged in the cities. In those cities, the most active traders were the wheat, wine, and wool merchants. Thus, although cathedral art was urban art, it relied on the nearby countryside for the major factor in its growth, and it was the efforts of countless pioneers, clearers of land, planters of vinestocks, diggers of ditches, and builders of dikes, all flushed with the successes of a flourishing agriculture, that brought cathedral art to its fulfillment. The towers of Laon rose against a backdrop of new harvests and young vineyards; the image of the oxen used in plowing, carved in stone, crowned those towers; vineshoots appeared on the capitals of all the cathedrals. The façades of the cathedrals in Amiens and Paris showed the turning of the seasons by depicting different types of peasant labor. It was only right to honor them in this way, for it was the work of the harvester sharpening his scythe, of the vine-grower pruning or layering his vines or spading about them, that had made the edifice rise little by little. The cathedral was the fruit of the system of manor lords—in other words, of the peasants' labor.

Nowhere was the impetus of rural prosperity stronger at this time than in northwestern Gaul. The world's lushest farmland was developed in the heart of that region in the plains surrounding Paris. And accordingly the new art was acknowledged by all of its contemporaries as being specifically the "art of France." It blossomed in the province where Clovis had died, between Chartres and Soissons. Paris became the central point from which it radiated out.

Paris was the king's city, the first city in medieval Europe to become what Rome had long since ceased to be: a genuine capital. Paris became the capital not of an empire, not of a certain Christendom, but of a kingdom, of *the* kingdom. The urban art which culminated in Paris in what we term the Gothic style was perceived as a royal form of art. Its major themes celebrated the sovereignty of Christ and the Virgin. In cathedral-building Europe, the power of the kings shook off the feudal yoke, asserted itself, and gained recognition. Before Suger devised the formulas of a new aesthetics for Saint-Denis, he had, for the benefit of the Capetian ruler, forged the image of a sovereign king; the king was at the summit of a pyramid-shaped hierarchy and his hands had a firm grasp on all of the powers which, under the feudal system, had been dispersed for over a century. Of all the states that became whole again after 1200, there was one that was more extensive and had a sturdier framework than all the others. This was the realm whose master resided in the city of Paris. In all of Latin Christendom, no monarch was haloed with greater prestige than Louis IX, Saint Louis. None possessed greater wealth. And that wealth came to him from the flourishing fields and vineyards by way of seigneurial fees and vassals' obligations.

Yet this king of France who in his lifetime was unanimously considered a saint, did not take the view that his power was chiefly temporal and lay power. Instead he wished to be—and felt that he was—a man of the Church. From reading Joinville we can see how when Saint Louis, who had been a fun-loving youth, reached maturity, and when his failure in the Orient convinced him that he was a sinner and that his sin was reflected on his entire kingdom, he eventually came to renounce worldly joys, "to love God with his whole heart and to imitate his works," and to live the way his friends, the Franciscans, told him that Jesus had lived. He was sacred. In the middle of the thirteenth century the king of France was always aware that he was bound to live an austere life. His most lavish spending had to do with God and the liturgical rites. He built churches, not palaces. It is of course true that like the bishops, Saint Louis was fond of dressing in fine fabrics, but he did not adorn his residences, and it is equally true that when dispensing justice he used to sit quite simply under an oak tree at Vincennes or at the top of a flight of steps. Better than the German emperors had, he received and understood the heritage and the glory of Charlemagne who was immortalized in the *chansons de geste* and, like Charlemagne, he drew on his treasures for funds with which to build a chapel. His ancestors before him, in their generosity toward the bishops, had been the true builders of the new cathedrals in the province of France.

Built by the donations of kings recovering their power, the art of France —like the art of Cluny—is essentially a liturgical art. Whatever secular works it may have given rise to were minor and ephemeral; nothing remains of them. Its most influential forms were designed within the small circle of prelates who surrounded the throne, a restricted and very wealthy milieu in the vanguard of intellectual research. These bishops, situated at the loftiest level of the feudal hierarchy, along with the body of canons who shared with them the revenue of the mother church, owned the best land, and their enormous granaries were filled to the rafters with the tithes payable on every harvest. They also controlled the cities, exploiting their markets and their fairs. Hence they profited directly from both the land and trade. The rest of their resources came from rich laymen who always made large donations because they were concerned about their souls. Because society was more diligent than ever before about confining the poor to a state of need, because the wealth produced by agricultural growth went to keep a fortunate few in luxury, and because the pyramidal structures of the state now culminated in the king who knew he was a priest and sat on his throne surrounded by bishops, the cathedrals were the product—the royal product—of rural prosperity. The influence of success on two fronts—monarchical and clerical—infused the art of France with serenity. It became a smiling expression of joy. Since in the king's own person the sacred and the secular were closely intertwined, and the temporal and the nontemporal miraculously came together, that joy was not only of this world. The art of the cathedrals culminated in the celebration of a God incarnate and attempted to depict the peaceful oneness of the Creator and his creatures. In so doing it transformed the glad-to-be-aliveness of the young knight heedlessly trampling flowery meadows and harvests as he galloped through them, shifting it to the realm of the supernatural, making it truly sacred.

Yet it would be a mistake to assume that the thirteenth century wore the beaming face of the crowned Virgins or the smiling angels. The times were hard, tense, and very wild, and it is important that we recognize all that was tumultuous and rending about them. The bishop of Laon who designed the new cathedral could not forget that his predecessor had perished in a riot, massacred by the rebellious burghers. In 1233 the burghers of Reims rose up against the excessive taxes levied by another church-building prelate; they forced him to halt the work for a time and to lay off the masons and the image-carvers. These were fortuitous occurrences, eddies and swirls of violence that reveal the contradictions latent in feudal society. Three groups confronted one another: the clergy, the knighthood, and the crushed, exploited, dominated mass of the poor. But the knighthood bristled at the Church, at its moralizing, at everything that tried to rein in the unhampered joy of fighting and loving. And artistic creativity was affected by this climate of antagonism.

But nonetheless this society remained firmly on its foundations. Between 1130 and 1280, the deeper movements that wrought imperceptible change in its structures had little influence on the narrow circle of clerics who gave orders to the artists and supervised the worksites. Consequently they had only scant repercussions on works of art as such, whose evolution depended largely on the evolution of religious thinking. As a result we must be more versed in theology than in sociology or economics in order to understand the art of this age.

Throughout this period of European history, accelerated by the continuous growth of production and the flourishing state of trade, men's souls were more and more torn between their passion for wealth, their eagerness to obtain it, their yearning to enjoy it, and that profound aspiration toward poverty that was held up to all Christians as the surest way toward salvation. These were times of kingdom-building, and the question was ever more anxiously asked: Who should wield sovereign power and govern the world, the spiritual forces or the temporal? The pope or the emperor? The Church or the king? And all of these opposing pairs were intermingled within one final—and fundamental—conflict: that between orthodox beliefs and heretical deviations. At this time the outstanding concern of every bishop in his cathedral, and soon of the princes as well, was to combat the false prophets, overcome their arguments, and find out the members of their sects. Moreover, they were anxious to place the Christian faith safely out of reach of the uncertainties and mists of prelogical thinking, to build a broad, diverse, and firmly ordered doctrinal edifice, to display its convincing attractions to the people. By so doing they would reveal the weaknesses of the heretics' teachings, and thus bring all stray believers back into the straight and narrow path. The heretics' effervescence was symptomatic of the impulse toward growth enlivening all of Western culture at the time; this accounts for their strength. Throughout the twelfth and thirteenth centuries, the presence of heresy and the threat it represented determined all of the developments that took place within a type of art whose first role was as a sermon on truth.

Yet the Gothic style that the leaders of the theological vanguard devised by no means summed up all of European art. Several factors—the diversities of a world that was still tightly partitioned, the prestigious novelty of Romanesque aesthetics, and thought patterns that were reluctant to change—offered stubborn resistance to the success of the Gothic style, initially a French and a royal innovation. It struggled to gain acceptance in certain provinces. In marginal areas, very broad outlying fringes, it failed.

Anyone wishing to grasp the real links between the birth of works of art, the structure of social relationships, and trends of thought must constantly examine the complex geography of culture at its most elaborate. Above all, we must bear in mind that the horizons of European civilization underwent profound change between 1130 and 1280. The change did not come about through a slow process of germination or peaceful blossoming, but abruptly, by fits and starts. Chronology is of the essence here. The aim of this essay is to indicate the different stages in, and the permanence of, the various forces which were continually opposed to one another throughout this period.

5

GOD IS LIGHT 1130–1190

In 1130 the most royal of churches was not a cathedral but a monastery, Saint-Denis-en-France. Since the time of Dagobert, Clovis's successors had chosen Saint-Denis as their burial place, and there the three dynasties which governed the kingdom of France in succession had continually buried their dead. Charles Martel, Pepin the Short, and Charles the Bald lay in the royal tomb near Dagobert and his sons, near Hugh Capet, near his ancestors, the dukes of France, and his descendants, the kings. Compared with this lineage of sepulchers, Aachen was like a mere interlude, an offshoot, an adventitious bud. The roots of the trunk of sovereignty—the kingdom which Clovis (helped, through his baptism, by God himself) had built on the remains of Roman might—reached far into the crypt at Saint-Denis. It was here that the kings of France came, after their anointments, to deposit the crown and the emblems of their power. It was here that they came to collect the oriflamme when they set out on military expeditions, here that prayers were said that they might be victorious, here that the chronicle of their deeds was written. It was around this *maître abbaye* that the legends grew, and they in turn nourished the epic verse chronicles recited at the assemblies of knights, lionizing Charlemagne, *"douce France"*, its sovereigns and their brilliant conquests. Heaped with royal donations, the monastery of Saint-Denis overflowed with opulence. It reigned over the great Parisian vineyard, over the Lendit fair where the Seine boatmen came to load the barrels of new wine onto the barges that would carry them to England or Flanders. On the threshold of the twelfth century it grew steadily wealthier as crops and commerce flourished, and its prestige grew along with that of the kings of Paris. The process of transference which gradually retrieved the major forces of Christianity from the Empire that the Ottonians had earlier renovated in Germania and restored them to the kingdom of the fleur de lys quite naturally directed itself toward Saint-Denis. The old Francia got its revenge over the Teutonic hegemony. Here the Carolingian tradition, annexed by Capetian power, returned to its source—in the plain of France, and not in Franconia. More than anything else, the new art that was born at Saint-Denis embodied this swing of the pendulum.

It was born out of the determination of a single man, a monk named Suger. Though not of the high nobility, he was the king's childhood friend, and that friendship was to propel him up to the apex of political authority. As abbot he saw more clearly than anyone else the symbolic values of the monastery for which he was responsible. He looked on his responsibility as an honor—in fact the highest honor, requiring great ostentation. Although a Benedictine, his concept of the monastic vocation had nothing to do with poverty or total renunciation of the world. Suger thought instead along Cluniac lines and, like Hugh of Cluny, believed that an abbey, being situated at the very summit of all earthly hierarchies, should gleam far and wide with magnificence for the greater glory of God:

> Let every man think as he may. Personally I declare that what appears most just to me is this: everything that is most precious should be used above all to celebrate the Holy Mass. If, according to the word of God and the Prophet's command, the gold vessels, the gold phials, and the small gold mortars were used to collect the blood of the goats, the calves, and a red heifer, then how much more zealously shall we hold out gold vases, precious stones, and all that we value most highly in creation, in order to collect the blood of Jesus Christ. Those who criticize us object that a saintly soul, a pure spirit, and faithful intentions should suffice to celebrate Mass, and indeed we agree, that is truly more important than all else. But at the same time we maintain that the sacred vessels should be enhanced by outward adornment, and nowhere more than in serving the Holy Sacrifice, where inwardly all should be pure and outwardly all should be noble.

Anxious to provide that outward nobility, Suger devoted the wealth of his monastery to creating a splendid setting for the liturgy. Between 1134 and 1144, despite opposition from the partisans of total poverty, he undertook to rebuild and adorn the abbey church. He was working for the honor of God, and for that of Saint Denis, but also for the honor of the kings of France—the dead kings who slept in his church and the living king, his friend and benefactor.

He was proud of his achievement and described it in two treatises, *On His Administration* and *On Consecration*. They enable us to understand his intentions clearly. He meant this monument in honor of kings to be a summing up of all of the aesthetic innovations he had admired earlier when traveling through southern Gaul and visiting its new monasteries. Because his monastery was a royal monastery, he also wanted it to stand above all others, just as the sovereign should surpass all the lords of his realm. And lastly, Suger innovated. As guardian of the sepulcher of Charles the Bald, and anxious to establish that the power of the Capetians was a logical sequence to the power of the emperors, he chose to use the Carolingian tradition, which was genuinely Frankish, in association with the styles of Aquitaine and Burgundy. Accordingly, he imported the principles of Austrasian aesthetics, which underlay the artistic achievements of Aachen and of the Meuse valley, to France in order to combine them with the Romanesque art that had been developed in opposition to them. Above all, Suger designed Saint-Denis as a monument of applied theology.

Naturally enough, that theology was based on the writings of the abbey's patron saint, Denis—that is, Dionysius the Areopagite, or so it was believed. For the remains of the kings of France lay near the original tomb at this site, that of Dionysius, the Christian martyr of the region called France. Not only Suger but also all his monks and all the abbots who preceded him identified this hero of the conversion to Christianity with Saint Paul's disciple, Dionysius the Areopagite, traditionally held to be the author of the most imposing mystical construct in the history of Christian thought. The text of that work, written in Greek during the very early Middle Ages by an unknown thinker, was preserved in the monastery of France, that is, Saint-Denis. In 785 the pope had given a manuscript of the work to Pepin the Short, king of the Franks, who had been a pupil at Saint-Denis. In 807 another copy was sent to Louis the Pious, emperor of the West, by Michael, emperor of Constantinople. The first Latin translation of it, a poor one, was done by Hilduin, an abbot of Saint-Denis. Then, during the reign of Charles the Bald, Johannes Scotus Erigena, who had a better command of Greek, produced a far better translation with a commentary. So it was that the *Theologia mystica* was held in awe at Saint-Denis. On it Suger's thinking and his art were based. Dante placed Dionysius at the very summit of his *Paradiso:*

> And Dionysius with such great desire
> set himself to contemplate these orders
> that he named and distinguished them, as I.
> [*Paradiso* 28:130–32]

The treatise attributed to Dionysius in fact depicted the visible and invisible universe in hierarchical terms: *Of the Celestial Hierarchy—Of the Ecclesiastical Hierarchy;* and Suger doubtless drew on that image directly when he conceived of the power of the king within a feudal system in similar terms. At the core of the treatise was one idea: God is light. Every creature stems from that initial, uncreated, creative light. Every creature receives and transmits the divine illumination according to its capacity, that is, according to its rank in the scale of beings, according to the level at which God's intentions situated it hierarchically. The universe, born of an irradiance, was a downward-spilling burst of luminosity, and the light emanating from the primal Being established every created being in its immutable place. But it united all beings, linking them with love, irrigating the entire world, establishing order and coherence within it. And because every object reflected light to a greater or lesser degree, the initial irradiance brought forth from the depths of the shadow, by means of a continuous chain of reflections, a contrary movement, a movement of reflection back toward the source of its effulgence. In this way the luminous act of creation brought about of itself a gradual ascension leading backward, step by step, to the invisible and ineffable Being from which all proceeds. Everything returned to that Being by means of visible things which, at the ascending levels of the hierarchy, reflected its light more and more brightly. Thus, through a scale of analogies and concordances, the created led to the noncreated. It followed that by elucidating those analogies and those concordances one after the other, one furthered one's knowledge of God. God was absolute light, existing more or less veiled within each creature, depending on how refractory that creature was to his illumination; but every creature in its own way unveiled it, for before anyone willing to observe it lovingly, each creature released the share of light contained within it. This concept held the key to the new art—an art of light, clarity, and dazzling radiance. This was to be the art of France, and Suger's abbey church was its prototype.

The work began with the porch, an earlier form of church harking back to the Carolingian tradition. It was still massive, compact, and dark, for it was really only the initial stage, the first step in the procession toward the light. Moreover, as it was intended to set a tone of sovereign authority at the entrance to the royal monastery, it had a military look, for all power at this time was based on armed strength, and the king, by definition, was primarily a military leader. This is what the two crenelated towers set in the façade were meant to convey. Yet the towers carried a series of blind arcades. Three entrances allowed the light of the setting sun to reach inside the edifice. Above them was a rose window, the first ever to be pierced in the west side of a church; it lighted the three high chapels, dedicated to the celestial hierarchies, the Virgin, Saint Michael and the angels. Thus what was to constitute the façade of all future cathedrals was born here at Saint-Denis, a direct result of Suger's theology.

It was in the choir of the new church, however, that the mutation in aesthetics took place. Suger naturally placed the glowing center, the point where the approach to God became most dazzling, at the other end of the basilica, at the culmination of the liturgical procession turned toward the rising sun. At this point he therefore decided to take away the walls and urged the master builders to make fullest use of the architectonic resources of what until then had been merely a mason's expedient, the ribbed vault. And so the years between 1140 and 1144 saw the construction of a "semicircular sequence of chapels, which caused the entire church to glow with marvelous uninterrupted light, shining through the most radiant of windows." It was necessary, in the early twelfth century, for an abbey church to include a number of chapels, for now virtually all monks acceded to the priesthood, and altars had to be provided at which they could say Mass daily. From Romanesque models came the basic plan of an ambulatory from which recesses radiated out. Suger was determined to make them penetrable by the natural light of day. By altering the structure of the vaults, he was able to open up bays, replace separating walls by pillars, and so realize his dream: that the coherence of light be used to extract the essential oneness of liturgical celebration; that all of the officiants be gathered in unison by the semicircle itself and, still more, by one unifying source of light; that within that radiance their simultaneous gestures harmonize like voices raised as one voice in the plenitude of choral singing; that the parallel rites of the liturgy, all bathed by the same light, come together to form one unanimous celebration. Suger's dream was symphonic. On the day of the choir's solemn consecration, mass was said "amid such joy and intimacy that the concordance and harmonious oneness of their exquisite singing composed a sort of symphony that was more angelic than human."

Since the principal theme of Dionysius the Areopagite was the oneness of the universe, still another necessity appeared: from the choir to the door, outpouring light must spread throughout all the inner volume of the church with not one obstacle in its way, so as to make the entire edifice a symbol of the mystical creation. "So that the beauty and magnificence of the church would not be dimmed," Suger took away the rood screen, "which was as dark as a wall and cut the vessel in two." Every partition, everything that interrupted the flow of the divine effulgence and then its reflection was removed. "Once the new rear portion was joined to the forward portion of the church, its middle portion, now luminous as well, made it a splendid sight, for that which is brilliantly coupled with brilliance is likewise brilliant, and the noble edifice is resplendent with the new light that floods it."

Suger had made additions to the two extremities of the abbey church. He did not have time to build the nave that would have linked the porch and the choir together, but he did at least indicate how it was to take shape in the future. Taking the new techniques for building vaults and applying them to the traditions of Neustrian architecture, he would doubtless have conceived it as a single space without discontinuity, prefiguring the internal unity which was to be achieved one hundred years later in the cathedral at Bourges.

Architecture was not the only field to sum up both the poetics of light that embraced Suger's theology and the aesthetics that derived from it. Twelfth-century religious believed that the divine radiance seemed to be condensed in certain specific objects; these were like the architectural features of an edifice in that they appealed to the soul to make the transference from the created to the noncreated world, from the tangible to the ineffable. Precious stones in particular had such mediating power. Religious thinkers assigned them a singular moral value, making each of them symbolic of one of the Christian virtues. They imagined that the splendid and radiantly perfect celestial Jerusalem would be built of just such stones. When King Louis VII came to lay the foundation stone for the choir of Saint-Denis, he was handed a number of gems so that he might place them near the stone while the clergy chanted from the Book of Revelation, "Thy walls are precious stones." Inside the church itself the presence of more jewels was deemed fitting; their sparkling would correspond to the light which streamed through the windows and converged on the chancel, focal point of the divine service. Here that love of stones, enamel, crystal, and all translucent materials which had always fascinated the barbarian leaders found its justification, in both liturgical and mystical terms. As Suger explained,

> when the enchanting beauty of the house of God has overwhelmed me, when the charm of the multicolored gems has led me to transpose material things to immaterial things and reflect on the diversity of the sacred virtues, then it seems to me that I can see myself, as if in reality, residing in some strange region of the universe which had no previous existence either in the clay of this earth or in the purity of the heavens, and that, by the grace of God, I can be transported mystically from life on this earth to the higher realm.

In praising to the skies the mediating values of lavish adornment in the church, Suger was following the tradition of the monastic movement's great leaders. But in his church the Dionysian concept of light endowed precious objects with a different role, another function. The saints' reliquaries, embellished with gold and precious stones, were now displayed to visitors in the transept, the middle portion of the abbey church, which was "now luminous as well." As a result, the basilica ceased to be what the Romanesque monastic churches had been until then: the mere superstructure of a hypogeum, a *martyrium,* of some dark, enclosed, underground place where terrified pilgrims descended in single file and groped in the darkness until at last, in the light of tapers, they perceived the martyrs' sanctified remains. At Saint-Denis the relics chamber emerged from the penumbra of sacred grottoes, the dim half-world of magic where a groveling religion had confined it, and merged into the radiant openness of the church itself, its reliquaries visible in broad daylight. The remains of Saint Denis himself, swathed in gems, triumphantly occupied the center of the church and shone with an uninterrupted light. It was the light of his own theology—a reflection of God, a mirror of divinity, helping the faithful to find enlightenment.

The gold frontal of the high altar was a gift from the emperor Charles the Bald. Suger added three other panels, so that "every side of the altar would be as of gold." Around the altar he arranged all of the valuables making up his treasure:

> For use at the altar we have adapted a porphyry vase, an admirable piece of polished sculpture, originally in the shape of an amphora, now transformed into an eagle adorned with gold and silver. We have acquired a priceless chalice carved out of a single block of carnelian, and another vase of the same stone but of different shape resembling an amphora, and still another vase that appears to be of beryl or crystal.

Suger had a passion for rare substances, for the way light glanced off of them, for the way it was caught and then sent back by them. A team of artists devoted their efforts to conferring functional value on these collectors' items. With the aid of "a noteworthy miracle that the Lord sent us in this connection," Suger placed the crowning touch on his church by standing a great cross, seven meters high, in the middle of the edifice, where it could be seen from all sides:

> The lack of precious stones had forced me to halt work on it, and I was unable to buy enough with which to continue, for, being rare, they were very costly. Then religious from three abbeys, that is, Cîteaux and another Cistercian abbey, and Fontevrault [the interpretation of the Benedictine rule in those three monasteries was ascetic, inclining more to poverty, and their monks did not embellish their churches] entered our little chamber adjoining the church and offered to sell us such an abundance of gemstones, amethysts, sapphires, rubies, emeralds, and topazes as I had never hoped to acquire even in ten years. They had received them as a donation from Count Thibaud. I gave thanks to God for having delivered me from the anxiety of having to search for such precious stones. We gave them four hundred pounds for the stones, yet they were worth a great deal more, and not only these stones but many other gems and pearls enabled us to make this very holy ornament a sumptuous one as well. I recall having used, in its manufacture, some eighty marks of pure fine gold. We were able to have several goldsmiths—at times five, at times seven—from the Lorraine complete the pedestal adorned with the four Evangelists, as well as the column which bears the holy image, done in very delicate enamel work, and the story of the Savior with all of the allegorical figures from the Ancient Law depicted, and the Lord's death shown on the upper capital.

The great cross was placed near the altar frontal, which was Carolingian. But since Suger's taste spurred him to avoid any disparity of style between older works and their more recent complements, he had artists come to Saint-Denis from the Meuse valley, the Carolingian province where the old imperial art was still alive. In so doing he attracted the whole aesthetic heritage of Austrasia to the Ile-de-France. At the very moment when Saint-Denis was preserving the legend of Charlemagne so as to glorify the Capetians, Suger was adding the Austrasian contribution to his creation. This amplified to a remarkable extent the mutation of which he was the instigator, for the art of the goldsmiths from the Lorraine—an imperial, renascent, humanistic art, infused with references to antiquity—remained profoundly different from Romanesque aesthetics, notwithstanding their considerable influence on each other. Their art had no room for a dream world of monsters and delirious fantasy. It exalted the plastic values. It created a setting and, in its very center, placed a truthful image of man.

Thus when Suger—who had just revolutionized accepted notions of architecture by transforming an edifice into the tangible demonstration of a theology of light—chose to reinstate the Carolingian forms of the glorification of monarchy close by the tombs of Pepin the Short and Charles Martel, he was associating himself with the second "rebirth" centered in the regions along the Loire and the Seine. At that very time the prominent figures in Latin letters—Hildebert of Lavardin, John of Salisbury, and all of the admirers of Ovid, Statius, and Virgil—were urging precisely such a return to the classical models. In annexing Charlemagne to his eulogy of the Capetian dynasty, Suger was also endorsing the Ada Gospels, the doors of Hildesheim, and the Reims ivories. On the art of the region called France, he imposed its other characteristic traits, its anti-Romanesque features.

This is most visible in the stained glass that Suger commissioned for the "most radiant of windows." The fruit of Lotharingian or Rhenish experiments, their colored panes transposed the art of enameling, found in the Meuse valley, into transparence. They were intended as devices by which to ennoble the divine light, infuse it with ruby- or amethyst-hued iridescence, the colors of the celestial virtues, and thereby lead the viewer's unseeing spirit "along the paths of anagogical meditation." Just as the Ottonian lectionaries and the enameled altars of the Meuse region had done earlier—and the mosaic floorings of antiquity long before them—these windows show the human figure isolated in the middle of their colored medallions by lead separations. In so doing they freed the human figure altogether from the architectural setting in which the Romanesque image-carvers had striven to keep it imprisoned. The solutions adopted in stained glass windows were borrowed from the ninth-century goldsmiths and limners, and Suger decided to apply them to monumental statuary as well. In Burgundy and in

Poitou he had seen abbey churches whose portals were adorned with sculptures. These he imitated. The large stone figures Suger had set in place were the first such north of the Loire. But in the porch of Saint-Denis they stood on either side of bronze doors, like those of the Ottonian basilicas. This meant that the surface relief of the stone uprights had to blend into that of the metal. As a result, the carved figures at Saint-Denis do not emerge from the wall like outcroppings of masonry. Instead they are objects separated from the architecture by a niche, a canopy like that found in Carolingian ivory carvings: objets d'art, like the finely wrought ornaments, the precious pieces put on display. The wise virgins of Saint-Denis were the first framed statues in medieval art.

And ultimately all of these images—in the narthex, in the stained glass windows, those that adorned the gold cross and the treasure displayed at the foot of it—were so many examples of what lay at the basis of Suger's theology, namely, the principle of incarnation:

> Whoever you may be, if you wish to pay homage to these doors, admire not their gold nor their cost, but instead the work they represent and the art. Like gold, a noble achievement gleams, but it gleams nobly; may it enlighten men's minds and may its true lights lead them to the true light of which Christ is the true gateway.

At Saint-Denis all the riches the world had to offer were gathered together to honor the Eucharist, and it was through Christ that man could gain entrance to the light-filled sancturary. The new art of which Suger was the creator was a celebration of the Son of Man.

The artists who decorated Cluny and Moissac had not overlooked Jesus, but they had seen in him the Eternal, and the glow of the burning bush or of apocalyptic visions continued to dazzle them. The Christ of Saint-Denis was the Christ of the Synoptic Gospels; he had a human face. Saint-Denis was built amid the climate of exaltation that followed the conquest of the Holy Land. All of the heroic literature whose themes were delineated all around the abbey church eulogized Charlemagne as crusader en route for Jerusalem, and King Louis VII himself left for the Crusades shortly after the choir of Saint-Denis was completed, making Suger regent in his absence. In the half-century after the tomb of Christ was delivered from Moslem hands, during which period flocks of pilgrims set out almost every year on the holy migration, all the types of religious attitude—among men of the Church, noblemen, even peasants—were attracted, as by a magnet, by the appeal of a redeeming Orient where Jesus had lived and suffered, by the great mirage that drew the entire knighthood of France irresistibly toward the unknown, by the crowned Christ who was king of that Orient. And what were the Crusades, after all, but the tangible, concrete discovery—in Bethlehem, on the Mount of Olives, or at Jacob's well—of God's humanness? Crusaders who came to watch progress on the building of Saint-Denis conversed about the Holy Sepulcher.

In this climate of evangelical fervor, the relics of the Passion—the nail from the cross, the fragment of the crown of thorns—that Charles the Bald had entrusted earlier to the monastery's keeping took on a more essential value. Thus Suger's theology culminated in an effort to link the new image of God—the living Christ of the Gospels—with the old image—God the Eternal—which monastic meditation had dwelled on until then.

This theology stemmed from the intellectual sequences which for generations had characterized the thought patterns of the Western world's monks. It was a gloss of the Holy Writ. In the ninth century Walafrid Strabo had worked out a basic commentary of the Scriptures, and all churchmen with even a smattering of learning had either heard it read aloud or had copied it over themselves. Starting from the idea that man is composed of three principles—body, soul, and spirit—Walafrid determined to look for three types of meaning—literal, moral, and mystical—in the verses of the Bible. The entire effort at comprehension made by cloistered monks in subsequent generations was based on such exercises in elucidation. They also read in Saind Augustine that "the Old Testament is simply the New Testament covered with a veil, and the New is simply the Old, unveiled." The Augustinian concept of historic growth considered that men's destiny was divided into two phases, separated by the birth of Christ. It maintained that Jewish history had been a living prophecy, that in it Christian history had first been symbolically acted out before actually taking place. Hence the text of the Bible constituted a sequence of premonitory events with spiritual significance and, as Saint Augustine said, the key to the "mystery surrounding them was to be sought in reality itself and not only in words." The New Testament was the model for that history; the Old Testament prefigured it. The Old Testament was the effect, and not the cause, of the truth, even though it took place prior to that truth; Christ was the realization of the Old Testament figures and, as such, canceled them out. It was against this background that Suger's theology developed. It was expressed, however, not by a text but in images, in the decor he invented for his edifice that was made of light and intended to shed light, by means of analogical equivalences, on the concordance between the Old Testament and the Gospel stories which had become so meaningful for his contemporaries, the crusaders. The iconography used at Saint-Denis incorporated all of Romanesque symbolism but deliberately aimed to deflect it toward producing an image of Christ.

The teaching of concordances, which began at the very entrance to the church with the ornaments of the porch, immediately appeared as a vindication of orthodoxy, a profession of unswerving faith, opposed to heretical deviations. The portal was triple; three priests, carrying out the same rites at the same time, had consecrated it together. And because it was triple it stood for the Trinity, explicitly depicted at the top of the archivolt on the central portion of the door. For the theology of Dionysius the Areopagite was organized around the theme of the Trinity, which in turn was a symbol of the Creation. In the early twelfth century, the mystery of the Trinity was the focal point of the most impassioned debates among theologians; the Council of Soissons, in 1121, had just condemned Abelard's *De Trinitate* as suspect. However, the images on the portal singled out for special emphasis the one of the three persons who, since the Crusades, had come to be considered the main figure: Jesus, "the true gateway." For that reason, and for the first time, the columns holding up the transverse arches at Saint-Denis were in the form of statues. Statues of the Old Testament kings and queens. Assembled in a triumphal escort at the beginning of the new era inaugurated by the incarnation, these historical figures constituted the royal lineage of Christ, son of David; they were his prototypes but also his flesh-and-blood ancestors, the beings through whom he was incarnated and took root in the created world. And in addition, placed as they were on this Capetian monument, they were the visible symbols of royal authority.

The theme was reiterated in the center of the church by the great gold cross. As the glowing symbol of victorious redemption, the insignia that the Holy Land adventurers displayed on their clothing, the cross loftily refuted all the half-formed doubts and defied the clandestine preachers in their shadowy sects who denied that man could be redeemed by the death of a man made of flesh and blood. It mutely condemned the heresiarch, Peter of Bruys, who had recently lighted a bonfire of crucifixes in Saint-Gilles on the southern border of Gaul. The cross was also a demonstration of the concordances between Old and New Testaments, thanks to the sixty-eight scenes that adorned it; they juxtaposed episodes in the story of the Savior and personages from the Ancient Law. The three eastern chapels reiterated the same lesson: to the south, Moses, *novum testamentum in vetere;* to the north, the Passion, *vetus testamentum in novo;* and in the center, the Tree of Jesse. By tracing Mary's genealogy, the Tree enveloped the Christ—the embodied God—in a human family and placed him at the very heart of history, made him exist in terms of duration and the flesh. The inscription included in one of the windows, showing Jesus crowning the New Law and tearing the veils off the Ancient Law, was like a manifesto of Suger's theology: "That which Moses hath veiled, the doctrine of Christ unveils." All of the analogies worked together to refute the appeal of dualism and glorify, not God's transcendence, but his incarnation.

As Suger's attention fastened on the Psalms, the Books of Kings, the Book of Revelation, and then on the Synoptic Gospels, he quite naturally showed God joined as one with human nature, situated the Virgin Mother at the heart of the iconography displayed in stained glass, depicted the Annunciation, the Visitation, and the Nativity on the high altar, and in one of the stained glass compositions, among the elements of the tetramorph, installed a crucified Jesus, different from the image of the Eternal at Moissac. At Saint-Denis, just as at Conques, the Last Judgment was the theme of the central tympanum above the door, but at Saint-Denis it merged the text of the Book of Revelation with that of the Gospel according to Saint Matthew. Relegating the music-playing elders to the archivolts, it made room instead for the Foolish Virgins and the Wise Virgins, representing mankind divided between heedlessness and the anticipation of God's coming. Furthermore, in the Last Judgment as depicted at Saint-Denis, Christ's arms were outstretched in the gesture of crucifixion, and the instruments of his torture were placed near him. Beside him were the apostles—Saint John, possibly, on his left, and the Virgin Mediatrix on his right. In this way the true identity of the glorious apparition on the Judgment day and of the scene on Calvary was expressed. There could have been no clearer way of conveying the hopes of the first crusaders marching toward Golgotha, where they aspired to find the dazzling celestial Jerusalem of the end of time. And Suger was so bold as to have himself depicted as the reverent donor at the bottom of the scene. This was doubtless the proud gesture of a creator satisfied with what he had wrought, but still more a wish to affirm man's presence in the very midst of the Second Coming. After all, in the hierarchies established by Dionysius the Areopagite, even the most humble of human beings shared in the light and the glory of God. The Christianity embodied in the basilica of Saint-Denis was no longer a matter of music and liturgy alone; it became theology as well, a theology of the Almighty but, still more, of the incarnation. In this respect Suger's work created a new dimension, that of man graced with illumination.

The new church was wide open to the light. On the horizon of the plain in the region called France, above the peasants' hovels and the vinegrowers' storehouses, it stood at the crossroads in a province which the process of land reclamation had made the very nucleus of economic and political growth. The example it set was earth-shaking. All the new art emanated from Saint-Denis. Over against this example we can now look at the first cathedrals that attempted to make its message more rational, the Cistercian cloisters that stripped away its ornamentation and, lastly, the heresy that rejected it.

As the (spiritual) son of Saint Benedict, Suger had built what was possibly the most urban of monastery churches. But it was the bishops, presiding over cities that were coming back to life, who carried on his work. In the middle of the century the stained glass windows of Saint-Denis inspired those of Chartres, Bourges, and Angers, all of them cathedrals; its statues-cum-columns inspired those of Chartres, Le Mans, and Bourges, again all of them cathedrals. Between 1155 and 1180 the architectural innovations found at Saint-Denis were copied or adapted in Noyon, Laon, Paris, Soissons and Senlis, all descendants of the cathedrals of France. This direct-line relationship was only natural; in Suger's view, the power of the consecrated king was based not so much on the feudal hierarchy, of which it had laid down the principles, as on the Church. Suger looked upon the bishops as the true pillars of monarchy, as in the days of Louis the Pious and Charles the Bald. Furthermore, the fact that artistic initiative shifted from the abbey toward the cathedrals reflected the far-reaching change in social structures brought about by the great urban impetus in northern Gaul.

In Carolingian times, the cities, hidden away in the forest, had virtually disappeared. Determined efforts to clear the land had resuscitated them. Being a lord of the Church or a temporal lord meant living in luxury and so standing out from the common herd. When the masters of the great rural estates appeared, they were bedecked in the finest raiment. They desired good wines and novel foods to do honor to their banquets. Agricultural expansion, by making them wealthy, had put them in a position to satisfy their tastes. And so they in turn brought prosperity to the boatmen, all of the floating merchants who navigated the Seine, the Oise, the Aisne and the Marne and converged on Paris. The dealers in good wines, spices, and many-colored cloths did a flourishing business. By the end of the eleventh century Italian traders had come to join them on the roads of France, and sixty years later Champagne witnessed the first of the fairs that soon became the main focal points of European merchant activity. The merchants of these times were itinerant adventurers, but they did establish their warehouses in the towns and ultimately were responsible for repopulating them. The few cities that the Romans had founded in the northernmost portion of Gaul had sunk out of sight amid profoundly barbarian surroundings, and were not able to come back to life. Instead, inhabited areas without any past sprang up at the busiest points along the roads near a monastery or a castle. But in the center of Francia the old Roman cities were denser and more robust. The merchants set up their stalls just below their walls. A new district grew up along the bank where the boats were pulled up and around the market place, and it expanded throughout the twelfth century as business swelled. In these dingy wood and mud shacks the largely clandestine stocks of goods that created wealth were heaped up. The new wealth was not in landed estates—the traditional, and visible, fortune of the nobility—but a matter of moveables: coins, ingots, and cargoes of spices that were concealed from the tax collectors and fructified through trade, exchange deals, and moneylending. The bishop and his council, lords of the city and all that surrounded it, drew on this hidden treasure in order to rebuild the cathedral.

The cathedral in fact looked out of fashion. Hardly any building activity had gone on in these regions during either the tenth century, for then piratical Norsemen overran the land and sacked everything they could lay their hands on, or the eleventh, while reconstruction gradually went ahead in the rural areas. But now money was pouring in. The canons took an active part in trade, selling the wheat and wine from their estates and their tithes at high prices and managing, despite fraud, to levy profitable taxes on the port and the market. The townspeople were their "men," in other words, their subjects, bound to pay them tailles and capitation. No matter how adroit the merchants were at concealing their profits, they were known to be rich, and the lords of the Church put pressure on them, confiscating their barrels and their bales. In this way they extorted part of the savings put aside by the traders, who grew more numerous and wealthy with every passing day. Sometimes these merchants balked, and in the ensuing violence and riots the commune—a combat association—sprang up. Sometimes a few canons or even a bishop would get killed, but in the long run agreement was reached on a treaty that granted the town certain franchises and promised that taxation would be less arbitrary. Every time, however, it ultimately tightened the cathedral clergy's grip on the wealth of the bourgeoisie.

Another way in which that wealth found its way into the bishop's purse, although in smaller quantities perhaps, was in the form of alms. The fact was that the new traders had bad consciences. Again and again they were warned that "no merchant can be acceptable to God" since a merchant grew rich at his brothers' expense. In twelfth-century France, it was still considered a mortal sin to make a profit through trading. An aging businessman, worried over the fate of his soul, would try to redeem himself by donating large sums of money. He was perfectly free to do so, for his savings belonged entirely to him. They were not like the land which made up the fortune of the nobility: that land was the collective property of a whole family whose members presented a common front so as to prevent their heritage from being dispersed and fought long and hard with the churchmen if their ancestors had made overgenerous bequests. In earlier times the rural aristocracies had given open-handedly; indeed, the power of the monasteries was based on those offerings. But now they were becoming niggardly, and under Kings Louis VII and Philip Augustus it was from the townsmen who had grown rich that donations streamed into the churches. Usually these were no longer in the form of land but of money, and so it was that coins earned in the traders' stalls or at the moneylenders' benches came into the hands of the bishop and the canons. And when the prelate inaugurated the worksite of a new cathedral, he could expect great things of the king, who gave more lavishly than anyone else. The bishop was sometimes the king's brother or cousin, and certainly his friend. He did all he could to have the sons of his vassals and the clergy of his chapel appointed to the best canonical prebends. He never refused any favor. And this is how it was possible to build the French cathedrals, almost all at the same time.

The first aim of the incredibly costly episcopal initiatives, sustained by all of these sources, was to assert and celebrate the prelate's power, magnify his glory. The bishop was a great lord, a prince, and as such, demanded that people take notice of him. For him, a new cathedral was a feat, a victory, a battle won by a military leader. When we read Suger's descriptions of his construction projects and achievements, we can feel him quivering with vanity. It was this urge to acquire personal prestige that accounts for the wave of emulation which, in the space of a quarter century, swept over each and every bishop of the royal domain. Later, too, it stirred the archbishop of Reims to have his own image included in the cathedral's stained glass windows, surrounded by his court of suffragan bishops, and to have the porch redesigned so that it would be still more magnificent than the one just built by his rival, the bishop of Amiens.

A rebuilt episcopal church signified something else as well: the alliance between Melchizedek and Saul, between pastoral and royal power. At least as much as Saint-Denis, if not more, it was a royal monument, with the same towers comprised in the façade, the same ambivalent statues-cum-columns in which the average unschooled onlooker recognized King Philip of France and Queen Agnes rather than Solomon and Sheba. Lastly, the new cathedral was a eulogy to the entire urban settlement, the amorphous collection of merchants' stalls and workshops which had all helped to build it and which it overlooked and exalted. It also embodied the townspeople's pride, as its plenitude of spires, gables, and pinnacles thrust up toward the heavens a dream city, an idealization of the city of God which magnified the urban landscape. When the communes began to adopt the custom of having each its own seal, they could find no better image of their power than the silhouette of the church that reared above the city. Its towers were a supervisory presence, guaranteeing the security of commerce within the city walls, and its nave was the only covered vessel in the center of town, for outside its house of worship each city was nothing but a tangle of narrow lanes, open sewers, and pigsties.

Prayer was not the only reason that brought the townspeople into the cathedral; the guilds assembled there, and so did the entire citizenry for their lay meetings. Moreover, a merchant who was the church's "liege man" could count on appreciable privileges and exemptions from customs duties. Accordingly, businessmen looked upon the cathedral as theirs to cherish and embellish. This led to another form of rivalry or emulation. The merchants of Amiens who sold the colors used for dying draperies realized that their power was expressed in the beauties of their cathedral. In Chartres, every one of the city's guilds wished to have its own stained glass window in the cathedral. In this way, enormous sums of money were invested in the cathedrals and, far from draining away the town's prosperity, consecrated it to God, redeemed and glorified it. But at the worksite it was not the wine merchants' or drapers' orders that the masons, the glassmakers, and image-carvers carried out. Instead they had professors to guide them.

In the twelfth century the cathedrals of the Capetian realm were schools, in fact the only living schools. During the Carolingian period the kings of the Franks had done all in their power, amid the prevailing cultural wasteland, to revive the luster of teaching based on models from antiquity and from Rome. They had re-created schools, great libraries, and scriptoriums. As was only natural in the midst of an entirely rural world, where only God's servants had access to books and to scholastic knowledge and the abbeys were the cornerstone of the entire ecclesiastical edifice, the instruments of knowledge were all to be found inside the monasteries. For centuries the monks had been the best teachers. They educated the novices and welcomed the scions of the nobility; the king himself sent his sons to Saint-Denis. After the period of imperial decadence and consequent upheavals, during which the secular Church sank into the general state of knightly and rustic simplicity, the monastery schools were the most brilliant centers of study in northern Gaul. After 1100, however, their luster dimmed very quickly. They retreated within themselves and reserved their educational efforts only for members of the monastic community, rather than disseminating knowledge outside it. In the name of asceticism the cloisters cut themselves off from the world. The monks' only duty was to pray and seek God amid total seclusion; teaching became the monopoly of the clergy, specifically the bishop's task. But the bishop was too much of a great lord; he was in evidence at the courts of kings, or acting as judge, or, clad in armor, leading military expeditions. Most of the time he delegated his intellectual functions to the clerics and canons of his church, and would put one of them in charge of the school.

The part of town surrounding the cathedral—still called the cloister even though it was open—began to swarm with pupils. And because scholastic activity shifted from the monasteries to the cathedrals, the principal centers of artistic creativity moved to the heart of the city. These twin movements stemmed from the same changes in society, from the rebirth of trade, and the fact that it was becoming easier, and more common, for men and goods to move about. These gave impetus to the innovations that took place in liturgical art.

For the teaching dispensed in the bishop's school was of a new kind. It relaxed and began to open onto the world about it. The abbeys, on the contrary, had turned their backs on the world; they were separated and protected from it by the wall beyond which no monk was allowed to go. Education in the monasteries was not a matter of teams but of pairs; each young monk was attached to an older one who guided his reading and his meditations, initiated him and led him step by step along the path of contemplation. A cathedral school was quite the opposite; a group of disciples sat at the master's feet, and for all of them at once he read and commented on a book. These students did not live secluded from the world. They were part of the times they lived in, could be seen going about in the streets. True enough, all, or nearly all, of them belonged to the Church; they were tonsured clerics, they were subject to the bishop's jurisdiction. Learning was a religious act. But the mission for which their education was preparing them was an active one, and a secular, pastoral one. It was a verbal mission. They were to spread the Word—the knowledge of God—among the laymen.

Progress was shaping a new world, less crude than the old, and it called for more and more men capable of grasping the changes and expressing themselves. The youths, who had laid down their arms and abandoned the life of knighthood in order to serve God, realized that the more mental discipline they acquired, the better would be their chances of holding important positions within the Church. So they were attracted in ever greater numbers to every episcopal see. But the ranks of students were very mobile, and either swelled or melted away depending on the quality of the master. For word got about that in such and such cathedral chapter there was a bigger or better selection of books, or the master was more learned or clever, and that in future it would be useful to be able to say that one had benefited from his teaching. For these reasons, some schools outshone others, and soon intellectual activity was concentrated in a few major centers where students could hear lessons given by several professors at different times where the curriculum began to be arranged in various cycles. In the early twelfth century Laon and Chartres offered the most abundant opportunities for schooling. But by the time work on Saint-Denis was completed, Paris had definitely supplanted them both. Its victory owed much to the glory that haloed Abelard, the most brilliant teacher of his day. By 1150 hundreds of students were pouring into the royal city, not only from the nearby Ile-de-France region but also from Normandy, Picardy, the Germanic countries and, above all, from England. Teaching was still dispensed in the cloister of Notre-Dame but now study centers were also to be found on the Montagne Sainte-Geneviève on the left bank of the Seine. Bolder, more independent-minded masters—whose audacity attracted greater numbers of students—rented stalls on the rue du Fouarre and on the Petit Pont. In 1180 one former student, an Englishman, founded the first college for poor students. South of the Seine a whole new district, devoted entirely to study, was growing up opposite the Ile de la Cité—the district of the king's court—and the Grève and the Pont-au-Change—the business district. Little by little Paris, from which the art of France was to radiate outward, acquired a threefold vocation, as the royal city, the merchant city, and the university city. In the narrow lanes where the schools were situated a new spirit was born.

Inside the monasteries, and even at Saint-Denis, studying was no open-ended exercise. It rested entirely on contemplation, on solitary meditation over a sacred text and on the mind's slow advance over a path marked out with symbols and analogies. In other words, it differed little from prayer and choral singing. But in Chartres, Laon, and Paris, on the contrary, the same dynamic spirit that led businessmen into commercial ventures lured young clergymen into mental conquests. They not only read and meditated, they debated. Masters and students faced each other in verbal jousts—and it was not always the masters who came out victorious. The cathedral schools were lists, the scene of intellectual exploits that were as thrilling as military exploits and, like them, prepared the combatants to take over the world. As a young man, Abelard had distinguished himself in such tournaments. His victories had brought him—as to a heroic knight—glory, money, and womanly love.

Although the line of study grew more diversified in the bishops' schools, it was still imprisoned within the framework of the "liberal arts," the same framework that the scholars who surrounded Charlemagne had long before, for the benefit of the monasteries of their day, unearthed from certain didactic treatises that had come down from declining antiquity. The novelty was that after the middle of the twelfth century the exercises making up the trivium came little by little to be confined to a preparatory role, leading up to what had now become the cleric's principal function: to read the *divina pagina,* make critical interpretations of the sacred writings, and bring doctrine into sharp focus in order to disseminate the truth. Students were initiated into grammar and rhetoric. Since their aim was to comment on the Bible, they first had to learn to scrutinize the meaning of words—Latin words—and clearly perceive their arrangement. Accordingly, the masters would read to their beginning pupils the classic texts of Latin civilization on which the Cluniac cloisters looked with mistrust: Cicero, Ovid, and Virgil. The best pupils were able to perceive their beauty and to make others share their enthusiasm. All their lives long, Abelard, Saint Bernard himself, and many others were fascinated by these models. In this way teaching leaned to classicism, and the vigor of the urban schools was instrumental in giving those who were to plan the aesthetics of the new cathedrals a renewed taste for antiquity and the sense of human fulfillment. Their eyes were opened. They looked with detachment at the traditional Roman art and found that they preferred the Carolingian ivories and the fullness of the bronze and enamel work of the Meuse valley. The source of the revival movement which would ultimately lead to the Visitation of Reims, with its classic harmonies, was in the schools of Chartres and in those along the Loire, for they were more devoted than the others to belles lettres.

But this was only a matter of preliminary training. In Laon and especially in Paris, logic became the major branch of the trivium. As the art of reasoning and critical analysis, logic made the power to reason the most important of a clergyman's capabilities. A century earlier the pedgogue Berenger of Tours had proclaimed that reason was what "did honor to mankind." Not only man's source of pride and honor but also his specific light, the way his existence reflected and projected divinity. All of the teahcers and all of their disciples held intelligence to be the best weapon, the one that would lead on to the real victories and make it possible gradually to penetrate God's mysteries. Since it was believed that the principle of all ideas sprang from God the Creator and that in the Scriptures ideas were imperfectly expressed, veiled and concealed under terms that were obscure and sometimes even contradictory, it was incumbent on logical reasoning to dispel the clouds of confusion and clarify the contradictions. Students must take words as their basis and discover their deepest meaning, but not by letting themselves be carried along in dreamy meditation, as in the cloisters of Cluny. No, now they must apply the rigorous dialectical methods. They must begin by doubting. "We seek through doubt, and by seeking we perceive the truth." So said Abelard who, in his *Sic et Non,* compared contradictory passages from the Scriptures in the hope of lessening the discordance between them. The method with which he experimented—and triumphed—was to tackle isolated passages and let the intelligence turn them inside out and interpret them one way or another, then to call them in question, discuss them, and, finally, come to a conclusion. This free approach was abundantly criticized as presumptuous, pernicious, and even demoniacal. Abelard defended it:

> My students clamored for human and philosophical reasons. They did not need affirmation but rather intelligible explanations. They maintained that there was no point in talking if one did not indicate the reasons for his opinions and that no one could believe something which he had not first understood.

Methods of reasoning were soon perfected, as the West gradually assimilated intellectual processes that it derived from the science of the Moslem world and through it, that of ancient Greece—cultural areas situated outside Latin Christendom and far richer in that respect than it had ever been. Hardly was Christianity victorious over Islam than it began to pillage Islam's intellectual riches. In the reconquered city of Toledo teams of Latin clerics and Jews had immediately begun to translate the Arab books and the versions they contained of Greek texts. Since the armies that forced the infidels to retreat little by little were made up chiefly of French knights, it was

French priests who were the first to turn the military victories to intellectual use. So the schools of France—in Chartres first, then in Paris—benefited from the work of those Spanish translators, and their libraries welcomed the new books. These soon included Aristotle's treatises on logic, which provided the masters with a dialectical tool of which until then the monks of the West had seen only a deformed and paltry reflection through Boethius. After 1150 John of Salisbury, who had studied in Paris, looked on Aristotle as *the* philosopher, and on logic as the supreme member of the *trivium*. Logic was the basis for all the progress which the mind could make; and it was the mind which, by means of the *ratio*, went beyond the experience of the senses and made it intelligible, then, by means of the *intellectus*, related things to their divine cause and comprehended the order of creation, and ultimately arrived at true knowledge, *sapentia*. At the same time as Peter Lombard in Paris was outlining in his *Book of Sentences* the first logical analysis of the biblical texts, Peter of Poitiers was boldly stating, "Although certainty exists, nonetheless it is our duty to doubt the articles of faith, and to seek, and discuss."

From such doubting and seeking and discussing the new theology drew its strength; it became more austere but firmer, vigorous, exacting. Abelard had won the lasting hatred of the monks at Saint-Denis because he was the first to question whether the "Denis" whose relics they venerated was actually Dionysius the Areopagite, and had the courage to propose another *Theologia*, in opposition to the Areopagite. In fact it too was based on the idea of illumination.

> The light of the physical sun is not the result within ourselves of our efforts to apprehend it, but instead, and of itself, it bathes us in radiance that we may enjoy it. In like manner we draw nearer to God exactly to the extent that he draws nearer to us by giving us the light and warmth of his love.

Thus for the teachers of the day God continued to equate with light, and that is why the cathedrals they erected were still more luminous than Saint-Denis—the first in that tradition. But they also became more evangelical, for the theology taught in the schools continued to emphasize the transfer from Old Testament to New. It became more keenly aware of the incarnation. It drew more heavily on the preamble in the Gospel according to Saint John and all of the texts that showed that God's Word was the true light by which all things had been made, which was life, and which "lighteth every man that cometh into the world." Because the masters of the urban (i.e., nonmonastery) schools wanted to have rigorous demonstrations and to understand what they were talking about, God no longer appeared to them so often as the glowing heart of light whose nontemporal splendors dazzled the contemplatives in the monasteries. Instead they attributed to him a human form. Like themselves, Christ was a doctor who dispensed the benefits of his intelligence. Like them, he came bearing a book; like them he taught. He was their brother.

This line of thought was meant to be lucid. It freed man from formalism. It distinguished between the will and the action. (For Heloise's benefit, Abelard proclaimed, "The crime lies in the intending, not in the doing.") Its method was analytical, progressively dissociating the elements of a complex whole. It maintained that "nothing exists if not the individual." It proposed an articulated image of reality whose oneness—like the oneness of the new style of cathedral—brought together in one sum the variety of its distinct parts. When it looked at the universe it saw nature—and explored it, for, as Abelard (once again) put it, "in the grasses, in seeds, in the nature of the trees and the stones, there are many forces capable of stirring and soothing your souls." Which is what Saint Bernard said as well in almost identical terms. The new theology—and the sculpture on the cathedrals—described nature as the eye saw it. Thierry of Chartres was the first to give an interpretation of the text of Genesis based on physics rather than, as before, on symbolism. He reduced God's creation to the interplay of the four elements of the cosmos and of the concentric spheres. Fire, being lighter, slipped away toward the edges of space; evaporating water gave birth to the stars, while warmth led to life and all of the animate creatures in the world. The universe ceased to be a code that the imagination strove to decipher. It became a matter of logic, and the cathedrals were to restore the pattern of it by situating all visible creatures in their respective places. Henceforth it was up to the geometers, using the deductive science of mathematics, to embody in stone the fantastic airiness of the celestial Jerusalem which Saint-Denis aspired to achieve solely through the effulgent radiance of its stained glass.

Mathematics was a revelation made possible by the conquest over Islam. In Spain and northern Italy clerics poring over Arab books gradually discovered not only the philosophy of the ancient Greeks but also their science. Euclid, Ptolemy, and treatises on algebra were translated for the schools in Chartres. Geometry and arithmetic took a prominent place in the new classification of the branches of knowledge which little by little replaced the old *trivium*. The Parisian pedagogue, Hugh of Saint-Victor, ranked the mechanical arts alongside the liberal arts in his *Didascalicon*. At Saint-Denis, for the first time in the history of any edifice, the plan had been drawn "with the help of geometrical and arithmetical instruments," and there is every indication that the plan of the crypt, which had to respect the ninth-century substructure, was the result of working drawings and the use of a compass. This method freed the new architecture from the empiricism that had guided the building of Romanesque structures. Its framework of logic freed it from the constraints inherent in the material used, and so made it possible to design edifices that would be less narrow and thickset, and more translucent. And the mathematician's calculations made it possible to turn these products of a reasoning mind into reality. Flying buttresses, invented in Paris in 1180 for the purpose of raising the nave of Notre-Dame higher, were the offspring of the science of numbers. The art of France, itself the offspring of the cathedral schools, often depicted the seven liberal arts on the subfoundations of its churches. By the end of the twelfth century it had become a logician's art. It was to become an engineer's art.

The new cathedrals were born into a society that continued, for some time to come, to hold the monastic life as the ideal of holiness. In the days of Abelard and the flying buttresses of Notre-Dame, the broad spiritual movement which ever since the triumph of Christianity and the collapse of Rome had sought salvation by renouncing the world, had not yet run its course. Under the reign of Philip Augustus, escaping the dreaded peril and saving one's soul still meant, above all, being "converted," donning the habit of Saint Benedict's followers and withdrawing into a cloister. Not the open cloister of the canons and their pupils but the closed world of the monks.

The monasticism which this century had in mind was actually a reformed and renovated form of monasticism. The old Cluniac interpretation of the Benedictine rule, which had adapted itself so perfectly to the seigniorial structures of the first stage of feudalism, was now outdated. The Cluniacs were criticized for living like noblemen and not being impervious enough to the outside world. They were accused of refusing to work, of cherishing the creature comforts, of flaunting a taste for ostentation which still supported Suger's ambitious undertaking. Now people were growing prosperous, attuned to money and pleasure, enjoying luxurious adornment and, by way of contrast, they took as their models of perfection poverty, solitude, work, and the total renunciation of worldly goods and comfort. In order to assure their own salvation, they placed their faith in ascetics, and venerated hermits who went to dwell in the heart of the forest and subsisted on herbs and roots. Henceforth if a knight was touched by divine grace and decided to turn his back on warfare, glory, and the world in general, he no longer entered a priory of the Cluniac order, for there he would not be able to make a sufficiently clean break with the atmosphere of power, nobility, and luxury from which he wished to flee. Instead he adopted the trade of the charcoal burner.

Thus in the years shortly before and after 1100 new religious orders sprang up. La Grande Chartreuse proposed the radically new virtues of oriental, desert-style monasticism—a remote existence among the rocks, a diet of bread and water, the silence of the cell. However, the most successful patterns of monastic life were those that contrasted less harshly with Cluny and even tried to reconcile the Benedictine ideal of communal living with the ideal of asceticism. In the same year that the choir at Saint-Denis was consecrated and work began on the royal doorway at Chartres, France witnessed a second triumph of monasticism. For by 1145 the Cistercian order, founded at Cîteaux, counted over 350 monasteries throughout the Western world; a Cistercian sat on the papal throne, and Saint Bernard of Clairvaux was the most influential figure in all the West. Of course one can dislike this violent, emaciated man; seething with the fury of God, he relentlessly crushed Abelard and lashed out at the Roman Curia with its propensity for temporal glories. But there is no denying that it was Saint Bernard of Clairvaux who launched the Crusades, who counseled and lectured the kings, and who went to Albi to preach against the Albigensian heretics. He was everywhere at once. Elected archbishop of Reims, he refused that dignity; monk he was and monk he would remain. He led the white-robed monks to conquest over their Church and their era.

The Cistercian triumph, ascribable to Saint Bernard, continued after 1200. For a long time Cîteaux was the nursery, as it were, of good bishops, and the spearhead in the struggle against heresy. Its offshoots were omnipresent; in fact some two hundred more Cistercian abbeys were founded in the course of the thirteenth century. The court of the king of France was thick with Cistercians, and they surrounded Blanche of Castille. The monastery dearest to Saint Louis' heart was Royaumont—a Cistercian establishment. There the king strove to live according to the same rule as the monks, doing manual tasks in silence. He wanted his entire household to follow his example:

> At the time a wall was being built at the abbey of Royaumont, the saintly king often came to this abbey to hear Mass or some other service, or simply to inspect the work in progress. And since the monks set to work after terce, as was customary under the Cistercian rules, carrying stones and mortar to the place where the wall was being erected, the saintly king took the handbarrow loaded with stones and carried it. He held the front end of it and a monk behind carried the other. At the same time the saintly king had his brothers and other knights in his retinue also carry handbarrows in like manner, and because his brothers sometimes wished to talk and cry and amuse themselves, would say to them, "The monks observe silence at this time and we should do the same." As his brothers loaded their barrows very heavily and wished to rest when they had carried them but half the way to the wall, he would say to them, "The monks do not rest, and therefore nor should we." In this way the saintly king compelled the members of his household to do right.

By the time Saint Louis came to the throne, Cîteaux had actually begun to outlive itself. Its monasteries had benefited so much from the progress made in agriculture that they had become far too rich. Now it was their turn to be criticized. But it is nonetheless true that the Cistercian mystique left a strong imprint on the age of the first cathedrals.

The spirit of Cîteaux was diametrically opposed to that of the bishops' schools. Its monks, having fled the cities, rose up against them, just as they also rose up against the clergymen, whom they placed on a very inferior rung of the spiritual hierarchies, and against the scholastic type of teaching, which they considered useless, and against Paris. Paris was the new Babylon, a den of iniquity where young souls were led astray. In 1140 Saint Bernard had come to Paris himself solely in order to "convert" the scholars by enticing them away from their studies. The sermon he preached to this end, *On Conversion,* was successful in some cases. It urged that Babylon be replaced by the only way to salvation: by a refuge, a retreat into the (spiritual) desert. The masters' lessons, he warned, "placed a separation between the soul and Christ, to no good end." Therefore what was the point of attending them? "In the forests you will find more than in books. The trees and the rocks will teach you things that no master will tell you." Saint Bernard considered it a sin to argue over any part of the Scriptures. There could be nothing more pernicious than dialectic; the science of reasoning was merely a vain effort to make the faith intelligible. So fierce was his opposition to the professors that he summarily convened a synod in Sens to condemn Abelard's logic and another in Reims, to condemn that of Gilbert de la Porée. Like the abbot of Saint-Rémi in Reims, Peter de la Celle, Bernard held that "the true school, the one where you do not pay your master and you do not argue" was Christ's school. While Cîteaux and the religious circles that came under his influence did not refuse to study the Scriptures and reflect on their meaning, they oriented their study differently and were convinced that the most accurate reflection of God in man was constituted not by reason but by love. "Intelligence is love itself."

So it was that in reaction against the rationalistic artifices of the modern philosophers, whose minds they considered warped, Saint Bernard and the Cistercians shaped a counter current of thought. Because it sprang from the main source of Latin mysticism—that is, Saint Augustine—it was able to win over the educators at some of the chapter schools—particularly the masters in Chartres—which had not gone so deeply into dialectic as the Parisian schools had. As early as the year 1100 the teachers in Chartres had constructed their lessons around the few writings of Plato that were accessible to them, a few fragments of the *Timaeus.* Suger's theology owed much to their teachings. These Platonic concepts, which had more to do with the outpourings of the heart than with the use of logic, radiated outward from Chartres and somewhat later took root in another urban school in Paris itself. This was not the cloister of Notre-Dame but the abbey of Saint-Victor, a hermitage founded at one of the city gates by a teaching canon, himself a recent "convert." There his disciples lived an ascetic existence; yet they were clerics and continued to accomplish their unique mission, which was to teach. But what they showed their pupils was the Augustinian approach to contemplation. Not that the Victorine monks explicitly condemned the use of dialectics to discover the Scriptures; Richard of Saint-Victor in fact defended the humanists and philosophers of Notre-Dame and the Montagne Sainte-Geneviève, saying that the soul must use every one of its capacities, particularly reason, that God was reason, and that man could approach God by that means. But that was merely an approach. Only through love, the great impulse, was it possible to reach the highest level of knowledge, the plentitude of illumination.

Hugh of Saint-Victor, like both Saint Augustine and Suger, maintained that every image perceptible to the senses was a sign, or "sacrament," of the invisible things that the soul would discover once it was freed of its corporeal envelope. In order to lead his disciples to this vision, Hugh urged them to embark on a gradual spiritual ascension, according to Saint Augustine. They should start with the *cogitatio,* an exploration of matter and the perceptible world, on which abstract thought was necessarily based. The inner man, however, must rise higher until he reached *meditatio,* the point at which the soul gazed introspectively into itself, and ultimately *contemplatio,* which was the intuition of truth.

This was the doctrine that the Cistercians borrowed and expanded. And it was in their monasteries, where total abstinence was the rule, that such exercises in illumination through contemplation were developed. William of Saint-Thierry, who in 1145 engaged in dialogue with the Carthusians, eulogized the mediating powers of love. As a humanist, he found that his philosophy was sustained and enriched by reading the Ciceronian treatise, *De amicitia,* and Ovid's *Ars amatoria*—the very same texts that were in use at the time by the clerics in the schools along the Loire and the troubadours they encountered at princely courts. Such reading helped him to develop and refine his theory of another (this time, nonreligious) choice in matters of love. This was chivalrous love. Just as a chivalrous knight was expected to gain his lady's love little by little by carrying off a series of exploits and sublimating his desire, so William of Saint-Thierry exhorted his disciples in mysticism to progress gradually from the body, or center of animal life, to the soul, the center of reason, and finally to the spirit which, as the center of loving ecstasy, crowned them both. Thanks to the ardors of love—the true intelligence of God—"the soul moves from a world of shadowy figures to the brilliance of high noon, the full light of day shed by grace and truth."

And Saint Bernard, the man of the century, made himself the ardent champion of this concept. He carried it to its utmost culmination in his great work, the series of sermons on the Song of Solomon. Bernard was overwhelmed by the sense of God's greatness, the greatness of the One God. He could not bear the dialecticians—the Abelards and the Gilberts who questioned his oneness and shattered the Trinity—their rational analysis was powerless to elevate man to the level on which the mystery lay and could only belittle God and tear him apart. How could man grasp the ineffable in all its fullness? Through perfect renunciation. Not until a man had achieved purity by vanquishing his own body and climbing one by one up the twelve steps toward humility could he then hope at least to know himself as the image of God. A faithful image which differed from divine perfection only by the sin that tarnished it. And man must let that sin be taken away by love. "What causes us to love God is God himself." *Quia amare dei est deus.* These Latin words sum up the two-way movement which, among the hierarchies established by Dionysius the Areopagite, gave rise to the circulation of light. Saint Bernard used Dionysius's luminous metaphors in addition to nuptial metaphors borrowed from the Song of Solomon. The ecstatic joining of the soul with God was a wedding, a union of love, "the bride's embrace." A harmonious meeting of wills, without commingling of substances, which verily deified the soul. "What the soul experiences then is altogether divine; to be affected in such a way is to be deified." In this joining, the soul dissolved as air flooded with the sun's light dissolved into that very light; but the soul could achieve this only if divested of all extraneous traces. "How could God be all in all if there remained in man anything that was human? The substance shall remain but it shall assume a different form and have a different type of power and glory." Dante, ascending to the empyrean in his *Paradiso,* took Saint Bernard as his guide.

Bernard's philosophy, so close to Dionysius's theology, was to give rise to an art that harmonized with Suger's—except in one respect, of prime importance. It could not tolerate Suger's ostentation. The art of Cistercian cloisters and the churches that flanked them was stark. It refused all adornment, and was like a permanent accusation leveled at Saint-Denis. Bernard himself inveighed against Saint-Denis in these terms:

> I shall not mention the astonishing height of your oratories, their exaggerated length and excessive width, the sumptuous manner in which they are decorated and painted, so that the onlooker is curious to gaze on them, and the attention of the faithful is distracted and they are less disposed to self-communion—no, I shall not mention any of these things, which remind us somewhat of the rites practiced by the Jews, for I am perfectly willing to believe that all this is only intended to glorify God. I will merely use the same terms, in speaking to other religious, like myself, as a certain pagan used in speaking to other pagans like himself. O pontiff, said he, what is the good of displaying all this gold in the church? And I, changing only the verse but not one whit of the poet's thoughts, I will say to you, what is the good, among poor people like yourselves—if, that is, you are truly poor—of all the gold that

> glitters in your churches? You display the statue of a saint, male or female, and you think that the more overloaded with colors it is, the holier it is. And people throng to kiss it—and are urged to leave an offering; they pay homage to the beauty of the object more than to its holiness. Likewise in the churches, it is not crowns that are hung from the ceiling but wheels covered with pearls, surrounded by lamps, encrusted with precious stones which gleam more brightly than the lamps. And the candelabra are like veritable trees of bronze, most admirably worked, and the gems that adorn them are no less dazzling than the tapers that they bear. Oh vanity! vanity! and folly even greater than the vanity! The church sparkles and gleams on all sides, while its poor huddle in need; its stones are gilded, while its children go unclad; in it the artlovers find enough to satisfy their curiosity, while the poor find nothing there to relieve their misery.

All ornament was banished from the church; there were to be no more images; renunciation was the order of the day. As soon as Saint Bernard became influential in the Cistercian order, the white-clad monks hesitated to illustrate their books, and as long as he lived the admirable painting workshop of the early days never fully recovered its vitality. The Cluniac notion of demonstrating truth on a monumental scale, of placing a sculptured framework around and above the entrance to each monastery, met with the same disapproval. Cistercian abbeys had no façade, not even a doorway; each one was inward-turned, bare, and simple. "Let those whose concern with internal things causes them to despise and neglect all that is external raise up edifices for their use which have the shape of poverty, inspired by saintly simplicity and faithful to their father's sobriety," declared William of Saint-Thierry. As the cornerstone of faith and the image of Christ, each church, by virtue of its very structure, of the rhythms embodied in its construction, and of its symbolic arrangement, was to elevate the spirit to the realms of mystery. Within its motionless setting, the light of day described circles that echoed the way to contemplation. Saint Bernard put it this way: "It is not by changing from one place to another that you must seek to approach God, but instead by successive illuminations, and not of the body but of the spirit. The soul shall seek the light by following the light." The proportions of each church humbly complied with the discretion prescribed by the Benedictine rule: no vertical tension, no vainglory; instead an equilibrium in harmony with the vastness of the universe. In both its intellectual patterns and its conception of architectural volumes and the ratios that linked them, Cîteaux was an extension of the Benedictine tradition. Its churches were thickset, like all of the Romanesque churches of southern Gaul.

Yet in two ways Cistercian art was similar to Saint-Denis and the first cathedrals. The first way had to do with the significance attached to light. It flooded in through broad bays; their panes were nonfigurative grisaille but they let in abundant light. In order to hollow the bays out of the wall, Cistercian churches used the ribbed vault. As a result, the Cistercian order, whose first establishments were in Burgundy and Champagne but whose "daughter" abbeys soon spread from one end of Latin Christendom to the other, helped to disseminate the art of France, the *opus francigenum,* throughout the Christian world—as far as the restive Midi, Poblet in Catalonia, and Fossanova in central Italy.

Secondly, Saint Bernard sang the Virgin's praises. He saw in her the bride of the Song of Solomon, the nuptial mediatrix. He made Cistercian art a Marian art, like that of the cathedrals. Suger had introduced Mary into his system of iconographical concordances, for, as the mother of God, she was instrumental in the incarnation. Yet she had been given only a minor role at Saint-Denis, whereas all of the cathedrals of France were dedicated to Our Lady, and depictions of the divine motherhood, which galvanized the devotion of the masses, were now central to their decoration. These carved figures, in the lofty hieratic positon of the gilded idols in the Romanesque churches of Auvergne, were not yet eloquent of tenderness; instead they conveyed an impression of sovereignty and victory. The Virgin Mother wiped out woman's sinfulness; she drove back demons, and routed unspeakable desires and unpure reveries. She redeemed all women. The mystical effusions of the Cistercian monks, of the canons who had to live a life of celibacy, in fact of all the men who strove to remain chaste, focused on the Virgin.

Majestically, the Virgin took her place in the context of twelfth-century piety, escorted on all sides by female saints. Mary Magdalen, the woman who had sinned, the prostitutes' hope of redemption, triumphed at Vézelay and in Provence. And just as Christianity began to veer toward an appreciation of the feminine values, the notion of womanhood began to be exalted at the courts of knights and noblemen throughout the Loire valley and the Poitou region. The charms of the local lord's wife, the lady, were celebrated in song, and all the young noblemen vied with one another, in the jousts that were part of chivalry, to win her favors. Worship of the Virgin and worship of one's lady stemmed from different movements; their impetus welled up from the profoundest mental patterns, whose potency and rhythm history has barely begun to glimpse. Yet each of the developments corresponded to the other. One fact stands out as clearly as can be. The Latin poems that Abbot Baudry of Bourgueil dedicated to the princesses of Anjou, and the songs composed by Cercamont and Marcabru to be sung in the chambers of the ladies of Aquitaine, and all the romances built around themes from antiquity—the story of Aeneas, the story of Troy—the early recitals of adventures that were both amorous and military—all of these coincided with William of Saint-Thierry and all of the Ovid he worked into his *De natura amoris*. They sprang from the same humanistic sources, employed the same vocabulary, recounted the same series of ordeals designed to test the protagonists' steadfastness, and conveyed the same desires and the same hope of being united with their object. An entirely new type of literature, both sacred and profane, flourished at the same time as the statuary of Chartres and corresponded to Saint Bernard's lyrical Mariolatry. The France of this period discovered—love. Both chivalrous love and the love of Mary. Hence a certain ambiguity, and the prelates, particularly the monks, were faced with the task of sublimating the eroticism of the flesh, collecting the various currents of sensitivity and draining those energies into liturgical rites. In honor of the Virgin in majesty, the Venerable Peter, who was abbot of Cluny, and Bernard of Clairvaux, and countless others composed hymns and sequences which blended into the intoned message of the liturgy amid the manifold sources of light and the wafting smoke from incense. The incantations were the prelude to the ceremonies marking the consecration of the Mother of God.

For the sake of the Virgin, his queen, Saint Bernard challenged not only the learned professors but also the knights who filled the princely courts. He would have wished to convert them all and bring them back into the straight and narrow path of truth. His preachings had provided the basis for the rule governing a new religious order: the Knights Templars. They were "converted" warriors who had become monks and yet continued to be knights, a *nova militia* whose valiant champions aimed their weapons at the enemies of Christ and their love at Our Lady. Saint Bernard had enjoined all the knights of France to follow their king on a new crusade, so that their turbulence would be safely channeled into service under God's banner.

Similarly, he strove to channel into the realm of mysticism the feelings exalted in the newly-coined love songs and romances. He was not altogether unsuccessful. Under his influence, part of the lyricism of chivalry was devoted to a conversion that culminated, after 1200, in the sylvan spells of the Quest for the Holy Grail. Already, more than a decade earlier, Chrétien de Troyes had shown the first signs of this change when he narrated the exploits of Perceval. Whereas his first heroes still practiced a ritualistic religion, Perceval on the contrary embodied a type of Christianity composed of prayers and adoration and love of God the Savior. This was a Christianity of repentance, and its outstanding virtue was purity. Thanks to Saint Bernard, the young noblemen of France now looked upon the dubbing ceremony—the old rites of initiation into warriorhood—as a veritable consecration. They arrived for the ceremony amid an entourage of priests; they prepared for it by spending the night in prayer in the chapel; they bathed, and this bath, like a new baptism, cleansed them of their sins. They were about to be inducted into an order whose members practiced—or were at least supposed to practice—Christ's own virtues. But in fact the Cistercian zeal was only partially, only superficially, successful. Knighthood's instinct for nonreligious joy, its hopes of conquest, and its taste for luxury and earthly pleasures were not easily overcome.

At any event, by 1190 the Cistercian order was becoming an indistinguishable part of the times it lived in. It was whispered on all sides that its abbeys, deep in their respective forests, were overflowing with opulence—and it was true. The white-habited monks now had their tithes, their tenant farmers, and their serfs. Like the manor lords, these monks lived on other people's labor. In ever greater numbers they were emerging from their hermit existence; they were becoming too visible. Saint Bernard had been indignant at an attempt to elect him archbishop—but Pope Eugene III left the cloister in order to ascend the papal throne. And as the thirteenth century drew near, many of the brothers had followed his example, becoming bishops. They in turn became cathedral-builders. They had been students themselves, and soon the order founded an offshoot in Paris that led directly to study in the schools. The clergy in Toulouse chose as their bishop Folquet of Marseilles, abbot of the Cistercian monastery of Le Thoronet. He was a former troubadour, and the churches of the Ile-de-France were to serve as models for the rebuilding of the bishop's church in Toulouse. But just at this time Christianity was faced with a glaring fact. Cîteaux had failed utterly in its final campaign: to wipe out heresy in southern France.

By 1190 the new aesthetics—based on light, logic, lucidity, and the yearning for a God in human form—had taken possession of the entire northern portion of the kingdom, from Tours up to Reims along the axis of the Carolingian renascence, within the purview of the great bishops' schools, throughout the revived rural regions criss-crossed by busy waterways, and in the areas under the Capetians' direct dominion. Thanks to Cîteaux, the influence of the new aesthetics was felt far more widely. It reached into the county of Champagne and into Burgundy, where the choir at Vézelay was rebuilt along the new lines. As the power of the king's throne expanded, so did the art of Saint-Denis. The limit of the king's possessions had just encompassed Mâcon and reached into Auvergne, and the king in person had traveled beyond the borders of his kingdom, as far as La Chartreuse, and Santiago de Compostela, and Jerusalem. In both Germany and England, whose bishops had received their education from the teachers in Paris, new cathedrals—Canterbury and Bamberg—imitated the cathedrals of France, and reflections of those models were discernible in the far-away narthexes of Compostela, Saint-Gilles, and Saint-Trophime in Arles. For Klosterneuburg, the goldsmith Nicholas of Verdun devised an enameled ambo whose iconography of concordances was a direct descendant of Suger. The old Romanesque imagery retreated before the victorious new art, taking refuge, in the Ile-de-France, in the shadowy nooks and crannies of various portals, among the demons of Judgment Day and all the creatures that writhed and slithered over certain capitals and the consoles of certain statues, depicting evil trampled underfoot, sin, and death. But this does not mean that the old familiar imagery was defeated everywhere. In the provinces farther removed from Paris and Chartres, its monsters still disported themselves in broad daylight.

In every direction, in fact, the Gothic invasion encountered resistance in the form of traditions, beliefs, and thought patterns that differed from those in France proper. In England and Ireland it was checked by the wellsprings of imagination that produced intricate, dreamlike, coiling, spiraling motifs—and Scottish monks brought them as far as Regensburg (Ratisbon) in southwestern Germany. In the Empire, opposition came from the vigorous Ottonian heritage; the art of the bronze-makers conquered Italy and flourished, devoid of any French influence, on the cathedral doors in Pisa, Benevento, and Monreale, as well as in Poland, at Gniezno. And all along the southern flank the taste for Romanesque art continued undiminished. Both at Ripoll and in Notre-Dame-du-Port in Clermont, the Romanesque decor dates from the last years of the twelfth century. In those regions, everything that came from the Middle East, with each successive Christian conquest, strengthened resistance to the appeal of the Gothic style. From Spain came other influences; the Mozarabic vision provided inspiration, in approximately 1190, for the final series of illustrations for the *Commentary of Beatus*. Above all, there was the influence of Byzantium, which spread from the Bavarian marches throughout the eastern portion of Latin Christendom and from the court of the kings of Palermo through all the south. During this same period Rome continued to blend the classicism of antiquity with Romanesque techniques and the influences of the Middle East.

The specific history of each of these reluctant provinces can shed light on the types of resistance they offered to the spread of the French aesthetic. In some regions tardy development was what kept the old artistic traditions so vigorous. For in fact not all parts of rural Europe had benefited at the same time from the agricultural renascence that had begun in the area between Chartres and Soissons much earlier than elsewhere and had there surrounded the local bishops with the opulence needed in order to encourage innovation. In mountainous Auvergne, ageless churches sprang from a peasant context that was perennially outside of history and continued to distribute the small change, so to speak, of eleventh-century creativity in the form of an unchanged rustic art. Provence had been cut off from the rest of the world; now the enlivening movements of trade began to bring it nearer to the mainstream. Ireland, Scotland, and Scandinavia, on the remote misty edges of the world, were still barbarian lands. Neither England nor forest-clad Germany had any real cities. The countries of the Empire, where Charlemagne was canonized, were still slowly assimilating Carolingian culture. All of these regions were lacking in schools, or else the schools they had were not aware of the new spirit. They knew nothing of the new liturgies based on light and the idea of incarnation. Their masters had not been gripped by the adventurous, questing spirit, had not yet felt the need for clear-sighted wisdom with which to sustain their faith. Choral singing still constituted the basis for their teaching. Moreover the faithful who attended the cathedral chapters were products of the feudal system. The archbishop and the canons of Lyons and likewise of Arles were great lords, quick to do battle, more inclined to practice their combat skills than to hone their reasoning powers. In these provinces the monasteries were still the foremost centers of religious life, but they confined themselves to liturgies in the style of Cluny. Whenever a new line of thought developed, it followed a roundabout route. Abbess Hildegard of Bingen, in writing her treatise *De divinis operibus,* drew on an allegorical poem only recently written by one of the teachers in Chartres, but the substance that she took from it was transmuted, in her mind, into a sequence of diffuse visions bathed in the phantasmagorical atmosphere of the several *Beatuses.* And when Joachim of Fiore, a Calabrian abbot, borrowed Suger's theology in order to meditate on the concordances, he treated it in such a way that it evolved into a sort of messianic utopia. Examples of how a universe of lagging mental activity resisted novelty.

Elsewhere, the stimuli that radiated out from the Ile-de-France encountered new forces released by an impulse toward growth as keen as any in the countryside around Paris but oriented differently.

South of the Loire the chivalrous spirit rose up with all its might against the bishops' art. Aquitaine had never bowed to Carolingian authority. Obstinately it had fought against Pepin, Charlemagne, and Charles the Bald, rejecting their schools, their concept of a church infused with learning, and that blending of spiritual and temporal that the Frankish kings embodied. Instead, the people of Aquitaine continued to keep religion—the perfection attainable through a cloistered existence—distinct from life with its earthly joys. In the eleventh century Aquitaine had been the outstanding scene of ecclesiastical reform. Here the synods had extricated the religious communities from the grasp of the great secular powers and separated monks from laymen more clearly; chastity was reserved for monks, arms and love for laymen. The princes of Aquitaine did not maintain that their power sprang from any sacred source and did not concern themselves overmuch with liturgy; their courtiers relied on prayers said in monasteries to achieve the salvation of their souls, assuming that by giving alms generously they would be safely in the Almighty's good graces and could go on enjoying life unhampered.

Not only did they love war and the hunt as much as did the knights of France but in addition they were able to taste of civilian, peacetime pleasures, for they lived in towns and cities where the old Roman traditions of refined courtesy had not been so weakened as in the north. In about 1100 one man, count of Poitiers and duke of Aquitaine, composed the first love songs that we know of, by fitting "lyrics" in praise of his lady to the melodies of Gregorian chant. All the youths at his court imitated him, and invented the amorous game in which the lover covets his lord's wife and she becomes the focus of all the devotion, respect, and services that a vassal owes to his superior. The refinements and ritual of courtesy were developed within an aristocracy whose impulses went relatively uncurbed by the Church (whose attention was riveted by its cloisters and its litanies of redemption) compared with the aristocracy north of the Loire. They spread throughout Provence and the region of Toulouse and then into Italy, and the nobility of the provinces of France as such ultimately adopted them, somewhat hesitantly, in the second half of the twelfth century. Louis VII, king of France, had married Eleanor, heiress of the dukes of Aquitaine, but could not reconcile himself to what he considered her frivolous ways. The monks about him—Suger chief among them—convinced him that they were the work of the devil and persuaded the king to repudiate her.

Eleanor quickly found another husband in the person of Henry Plantagenet; king of England, he also held Normandy and had inherited Anjou from his ancestors. After his wedding, Henry extended his control over a whole string of possessions that covered roughly half the kingdom of France. His dream was to outshine the Capetian monarch, and he commanded the intellectuals at his court to construct a type of aesthetics that would rival the aesthetics of Paris. What his ecclesiastics came up with was rooted, not in faith and intelligence, but in pleasure and dreams. It was the fruit of a marriage between the refinements of courtesy, or "matière d'Aquitaine," and the "matière de Bretagne"—that is, of Britain. At the edge of Wales the abbey of Malmesbury—the equivalent, for the sovereigns on that side of the Channel, of Saint-Denis in France—harbored a nucleus of legends about King Arthur, entangled in the intricacies of the Celtic imagination. From these legends the men of letters in Henry II's service derived their themes, and they began to recount marvelous adventures of knights errant pursuing dragons in order to reach their mistresses. The somber tale of impossible love between Tristan and Isolde offset the epic recitals that exalted the feats of valiant champions and helmeted bishops escorting Charlemagne, and the mystic quest of Percival for the Holy Grail.

In the western regions, resistance to the art of France developed in like manner. Although the cathedral at Angers, for example, used the Gothic ribbed vault, it was faithful to the volume of the Romanesque churches in Poitou. The fact is that the Plantagenet house did not succeed in creating its own architectural style; its new aesthetics was almost entirely a matter of poetry and was virtually never transposed into the arts except in the English miniatures—whose linear effects were a denial of the statuary at Chartres—and in the only nonsacred art objects that France has preserved from this period: the Limousin bowls, studded with coats of arms, in which water with which to wash themselves was brought to the lords and their ladies as they arrived to partake of court festivities. Only in certain Italian cathedrals do we find a translation into stone of the poems written for the princes of western France: the characters from the *roman de Troie* appear in the mosaic floor at Bitonto, and the knights of the Round Table decorate one of the tympanums at Modena. There is nothing surprising about such a long-distance transference. As I have said, the elite in various parts of Italy welcomed the style of *la vie courtoise* and, in the Italian cities, the cathedrals—descendants of the ancient basilicas—were still at least as much civilian as religious edifices. Far more than its counterparts in France, each Italian cathedral belonged to the inhabitants of the city and was really their house.

In the southeastern part of Latin Christendom there were other forces at work, possibly more deeply-rooted, certainly more vigorous. Little by little, revived by the vitality of the great Mediterranean trading currents, they repulsed the cultural models proposed by the Ile-de-France. The cities in these regions had never really been snuffed out even when the barbarity of the Dark Ages had smothered Western civilization, and they came back to life earlier here than elsewhere. The Germans who rode down from the Alps for the imperial coronation were astonished—and scandalized—to see how powerful the southern cities were. The *communes* had forced the feudal barons to retreat into the meager castles of the *contado,* and had made the bishop and his priests give in. They defeated Frederick Barbarossa and brought the imperial eagles triumphantly back to Milan. The type of culture that developed inside their walls freed itself, as in Aquitaine, from the Church's grasp, yet was based on the schools, for the Italian schools were not intended for clerics. They did not provide theological training, and the Italian clerics who wished to study theology went away to Paris to do it. Instead, and in accordance with pure Roman tradition, the schools in the Italian cities—Pavia, for instance, and especially Bologna—taught chiefly law. Toward the end of the eleventh century they had rediscovered Justinian's *Digest,* and it occupied the same key position in the lessons their masters taught as the Scriptures did in the *studia* of the Ile-de-France. The commentary on it was subject to the same methods of dialectical analysis as was the commentary on decrees of canon law. Gratian, in drawing up his *Concordia discordantium canonum* in about 1140, used Abelard's own weapons. Yet the new science was meant for nonecclesiastics; its purpose was to train men of law who would then serve the emperor and be leaders in civic life.

Farther south in the Italian peninsula, close to the provinces that had been under Byzantine and Islamic rule, still other forms of education were developing. They too were temporal, but they had to do with the body rather than the soul. Students were initiated into the secrets of medicine, or of algebra and astronomy, which were useful for drawing up more accurate horoscopes. Translations of Hippocrates, Galen, and Aristotle were read and commented upon. It was not Aristotle's works on logic that the pedagogues read but instead his *Book of Meteors,* and they strove to find in his writings what links the four elements of the cosmos to the humors of the human body. In this Italy of victorious communes, what was taught in the schools had to do with practical day-to-day matters, with life on this earth. Their stock of learning was meant to be of immediate use to each citizen, and not to instil new life in sacred art. Religious life was contaminated by heresy; for in Italy just as in Aquitaine it sprung up among the laity, who were abandoned by God's best servants: the hermits living their recluse existence in remote grottoes, and all the Cluniac or Cistercian monks withdrawn into their cloisters.

Indeed, in the cities of southern Europe the Church had not yet thought of basing its docrine on reasoning. It did not preach so much as it sang. Yet civilizing forces were making headway, and they sharpened the awareness of the elite among city-dwellers—the knights, and the jurisconsults, and the merchants—until there came a time when liturgical rites ceased to satisfy them. They all knew that they were more or less condemned by God, and wanted to save their souls. Since they could no longer find any spiritual nourishment in the cathedrals, they went to listen to the itinerant preachers who stood at the crossroads and talked to them in their own language. They were turncoats, these tormented clerics: they had either felt out of place among the canons or else had not been able to gain entry to the cathedral chapters, which were like closed circles, accessible only to the sons of wealthy families. Neither the monk's cloistered life nor the hermit's existence appealed to them. They were spokesmen for the divine—but violent spokesmen, for the bishops hounded them.

Most of them preached repentance. The mainstream of heresy was a striving for reform of the Church. This was actually nothing new, but instead a continuation of the eleventh-century reform movement, and its themes were simple. The clergy of the cathedrals were unworthy because they lived impurely and amid riches. Distributed by such sin-stained hands, how could the sacraments be of any value? How could the songs that issued from such corrupt mouths be acceptable? What the lay population needed was rites, and prayers that were answered. Well then, the people must get rid of the bad priests and steer the Church back to its spiritual mission. Words such as these, sounding amid a context of communal struggles, intensified them; for if the bishop's temporal power were wrested from him, did not that act at the same time liberate the entire city? Apostolic poverty was an imperative, justifying urban insurrections. In Italy it was Arno of Brescia, an ecclesiastic who had studied under Parisian masters, who led the movement toward purification and opened the way for the establishment of a commune in Rome, in 1146, that invoked the poverty of Christ. Nine years later he was burned at the stake as a heretic because he had called upon prelates to live the same ascetic life as Jesus.

As it spread through bourgeois circles, however, the mystique of renunciation gradually became less entangled with political intentions. Peter Valdo, a merchant in Lyons, was no rabble rouser. He had had the Gospel translated and upon reading it discovered that because of his wealth, the entrance to the kingdom of God was closed to him forever. He therefore sold all his worldly goods and distributed the product of that sale to the poor. Then, deciding that he would help the people of his city to free themselves from evil, he began to preach. But because Valdo was a layman, the archbishop did not want him to talk about religion; he condemned Valdo in 1180, and then had the pope confirm the condemnation. From then on Peter Valdo's disciples, the "*pauvres de Lyon,*" or "*Vaudois,*" went into hiding—which did not prevent this clandestine sect, cut off from the Church and violently opposed to it, from acquiring a huge following among the cloth merchants, horse traders, and weavers in all of the market towns, hamlets, and villages of the Alps, Provence, and Italy.

Meanwhile, in the county of Toulouse, crowds were following other agitators and listening to a doctrine that differed fundamentally from Christianity, even though it used the name of Jesus. In opposition to the established Church, a different church—the church of the Albigensians—was taking shape. The groundwork had been laid early in the twelfth century by certain unorthodox preachers: Peter of Bruys, and a monk named Henry of Lausanne. At the beginning, they also berated the unworthy ecclesiastics. The bishops called them Manichaean, for in their sturggle to achieve and protect the spirit of poverty and purity they were inclined to separate the two principles—the spirit and the flesh—more sharply and posit their mutual incompatibility. And since in the society that heard them laymen were more isolated from the servants of God than were laymen elsewhere, that society was receptive to the doctrine of a world torn between two antagonistic powers.

Half a century later this spontaneous dualism had taken on greater weight. It already had numerous followers; in some places they must have outnumbered the Catholic faithful. They proliferated to such an extent that

Saint Bernard hastened to the scene and used all his eloquence against them, but in vain. The party that came off victorious from this confrontation was not Bernard, the Cistercian abbot, but the patient, obstinate organizers of the movement. Some of them came from the Middle East. In the Languedoc and in northern Italy they installed heretical bishops and in fact an entire parallel hierarchy which was enthroned in the empty cathedrals. At this point the chapter general of Cîteaux received an appeal for help from Count Raymond of Toulouse: all of his aristocratic vassals were contaminated, down to the last man, and in the region around Albi a whole section of Christendom had broken away from the Church of Rome and gone over to the competing religion.

It did more than just deviate from established Roman doctrine; it was actually another dogma. We will never have a very accurate picture of Albigensian dogma, for in the century that followed the inquisitors wiped it out, harried whatever seemed to be an expression of it, and destroyed all of the books it had spawned. The manuals that served to guide this repressive campaign give us a glimpse of the heretical doctrine, based on the opposition between a God of good and a God of evil, a God of light and spirit struggling with a God of darkness and the flesh in an equal combat which would decide the fate of the world. Man's very destiny was at stake. If he wished to attain unto the light after his death, instead of being reincarnated in a body of flesh, then he must take part in the victory of the principle of light by fleeing everything that was tinged with Satan, refusing money, eating only the least impure foods, and refraining from all sexual intercourse. The act of procreating increased the hordes of evil and encouraged material resistance to the powers of light. Only a tiny number of men so pure they were called the "perfect" were actually capable of such total asceticism. At least these pure men had the power to lead their weaker brethren to salvation; all they needed to do, in order to impregnate them with the coveted Spirit, was to stretch out their hands over them before they died. The people of Aquitaine were used to such intercessions, accustomed to delegating the vocations of poverty and chastity to others on their behalf, relying on the ritual gestures of the specialists in salvation, while they themselves, laymen and nonspecialists, went on serenely enjoying what life had to offer. But the perfect of the Albigensian heresy had an advantage over the monks of Moissac, Conques, or Saint-Gilles, in that they set the example of genuine destitution; they were less hypocritical and demanded less of an effort from the laity. Therefore their mediation appeared to be more effective. The troubadour knights and all of the wealthy merchants who followed them were "consoled" by them *in extremis*. Under their guidance, the wives of the lords of Aquitaine came together in communities of perfect life to spend the remainder of their earthly existence.

We can suppose that all of these men and women had only a blurred perception of the radical antinomy between what the perfect taught and what the Church of Rome taught. The Albigensian dualism had borrowed the vocabulary and some of the symbols that the Catholic clergy used and as a result there were imperceptible transitions from the preachers' diatribes against the bishops to the rigors of the heretical dogma. But the doctrine rejected the hierarchical orders established by Dionysius the Areopagite, with their processional comings and goings, and the very notion of creation. Matter was evil; it could not possibly stem from the God of good. Albigensian doctrine also rejected the principle of the incarnation, apparently considering Jesus just an angel sent by the God of light—and pointed to the beginning of the Gospel according to Saint John to justify its rejection. For how could the divine glory ever have sunk into the darkness of the flesh and taken shape inside a woman's womb? How was it possible to venerate Mary? The Albigensians also rejected the idea of redemption. How could the God of light ever have experienced bodily suffering? What value could be placed on the pain felt by any mortal body? The perfect looked upon the cross as no more than a paltry emblem and a mystification. They stood resolutely apart from Saint-Denis, from theological speculation on the Trinity, from the entire iconography depicted in the cathedrals.

By the end of the twelfth century, heresy in its many forms—the throngs of Albigensians, the secret meetings of Vaudois who carried out purity rites without the benefit of priests, the countless hesitant sects that swarmed in the outlying districts of the southern cities, and the flourishing civilization of *courtoisie* that surrounded those centers on all sides—constituted the most serious obstacle to the influence of the schools and religious edifices of Paris. And heresy did still more. It endangered the very unity of Christendom. It crystallized within it all the dread and anguish of the world at this time. This was the chief cause for concern among the heads of the Church; they might not be able to devote as much attention to Jerusalem and Christ's tomb, for now the West itself had been poisoned, and they had to focus on that world. The Cistercians, who were the best of all monks, had just failed to carry out their mission; their crestfallen abbot had come back from it amid an overly visible escort of horsemen. In this crisis the Church of Rome had to bring all of its weapons into action, including the weapons supplied by art.

In Italy, art was already an instrument of orthodox propaganda. In 1138 William of Lucca had countered the miscreants who doubted the virtues of Christ's sacrifice by placing before them the image of Christ on the cross. And in the choir of Santa Maria in Transtevere artists had created, in mosaic, the triumphant image of the Mother of God. The truth of the incarnation was proclaimed in both of these works. In 1178, when it came time to decorate the ambo of the cathedral in Parma, the pulpit from which the Gospel was read aloud to the people, the clerics had asked Benedetto Antelami to borrow an image found in Byzantine art: the Deposition from the Cross. How could anyone, seeing Christ dead on Calvary, amid the soldiers and the saintly women and Mary kissing his right hand, refuse to believe that God was not only spirit and light? That he had taken bodily form in order to suffer and undergo death, so as to bring mankind to redemption?

A few years earlier, between 1160 and 1170, the portal of Saint-Gilles—in the very hotbed of dissidence—had constituted an exhortation against heretics that was raised up for all to see, above an enormous theater. On this portal, the apostles, witnesses of the Word made human, appear between the columns of an ancient temple, trampling underfoot the forces of evil and the ferments of misguided beliefs. These apostles are the athletes of the true faith; they embody its strength. The Gospel story unfolds on the frieze which they are holding up and, on the pier of the main door, focuses on the Last Supper, which proclaims the truth of the Eucharist.

So it was that by the end of the twelfth century the Romanesque art of southern Europe had become a convincing form of visual propaganda. But it was the art of the Gothic cathedrals throughout Christendom which, at that point, became the instrument—possibly the most effective one of all—of repression by the Catholic Church.

6

THE AGE OF REASON 1190–1250

As the year 1200 drew near, the Church of Rome was like a city under siege. Of all the hostile forces that surrounded it, that had already made its bastions capitulate and were undermining its last defenses, the most zealous and most visible were the forces of heresy. At the same time, however, progress in various branches of learning gave rise to other, more insidious threats. They in turn encouraged the schools in Paris to take bold new tacks, launch into disturbing deviations. Long practice in reasoning about Dionysius, about the mysteries of the Trinity, and about the Creation eventually made Amaury of Bène, for instance, decide—and teach—that "everything is one, for whatever is, is God," and that consequently every man was a member of God and was therefore untainted by sin. Was it not enough for a man to know that God was within him, in order to live joyously and freely? This type of doctrine harmonized with the optimism and lyric flights of chivalry—and therein lay its strength—but it also implied that the priesthood was useless—and this made it seem pernicious in the eyes of the Church's leaders.

At about the same time the teachers of the Paris schools were gradually discovering the full breadth of Aristotle's pagan philosophy. In 1205 the pope had sent some of them to Constantinople, to the source of Greek philosophy, while in Toledo teams of translators, who had at last made the entire logical system of the *Organon* accessible, now revealed the contents of Aristotle's *Physics,* then of his *Metaphysics.* These texts revealed to the theologians a corpus of demonstrations which provided a rational and coherent explanation of the entire universe—but starting from premises that were thoroughly incompatible with the teachings of the Scriptures. The theologians' mission was to strengthen the framework of dogma so as to drive back heresy. Was it possible that they in turn would let these books entice them away from the true religion? The soul-searching and first twinges of bewilderment occurred amid a vigorous context of prosperity, an overall urge to get rich that was imperceptibly beginning to rock the foundations of society. The structural principles of the Chuch, based on a monastic ideal of withdrawal, dated from an earlier, stagnant peasant-and-warrior society. But by now it was clear that they were no longer relevant to a changed world and to the movements that were leading it into a new phase. There was an urgent need to rejuvenate those principles and reinstate unity. The Church's reaction was to stiffen and take on a rigidly monarchical, totalitarian form, centering on the throne of Saint Peter and on one pope in particular, Innocent III.

For nearly two centuries the pontiffs of Rome patiently expanded their web of power. They had successfully braved the various emperors. The theocratic doctrine, tailor-made for the popes by the legal experts of the Curia Romana, assigned to them an *auctoritas* in this world that was greater than any temporal power. Each pope claimed to have moral jurisdiction over the entire earth, sent his legates everywhere, and dreamed of making the bishops obey his law. Innocent III, elected pope in 1198 at the age of thirty-eight, carried this protracted effort to its culmination. A member of the Roman nobility and an intellectual, he had first studied law in Bologna, in the style of Italy, and then theology in Paris, in the style of France. He was the first pope to state clearly that he was not only Saint Peter's successor but also Christ's lieutenant; hence the king of kings, *rex regum,* who stood above the princes of this world and passed judgment on them. On his coronation day he proclaimed,

> I am he to whom Jesus said, "I will give to you the keys to the kingdom of heaven, and everything that you shall bind up on earth shall be bound up in heaven. See then this servant who rules over the entire family; he is the vicar of Jesus Christ and the successor of Saint Peter. He stands halfway between God and man, smaller than God, greater than man."

And the pope attempted—and nearly managed—to include all of the sovereigns of Europe in an intricate web of feudal homage with himself at the summit. Toward the end of his reign, emboldened by this success, he held a council at the Lateran Palace which played the same role in medieval Christendom as the Council of Trent was to play in modern Christendom, and with regard to problems that were comparable. Its agenda included these items: "Eliminating heresy and reinforcing the faith, but also the reformation of morals by uprooting vice, sowing virtue, and warding off all excess. Furthermore, the resolution of quarrels, the establishment of peace, the repudiation of tyranny, and ensuring that truth prevails everywhere."

This was reactionary. The Church was girding its loins, entrenching itself, getting rid of foreign bodies. An earlier council, in 1179, had ordered that all unpure creatures, carriers of purulent diseases, and all madmen, possessed by the devil, be shut up in leper colonies far from God's people, whom they contaminated. Acting along the same lines, the council held by Innocent III decreed that Jews must wear the *rouelle,* a distinctive round cloth badge, a sign of their exclusion from Christian society.

Then the Church attacked. For the sake of Catholic unity, the Crusades were deflected from their original purpose and turned against the schismatics—in 1204 the crusading army took Constantinople—but also and especially against the outstanding danger, namely, the heretics. In 1209, the pope summoned the knights of the Ile-de-France to pillage the Languedoc region and exterminate the Albigensians; in exchange he promised them indulgences from the Holy Land. We should note that the Church of Rome had long since given up counting on the monks to assist it in this particular struggle and in its fierce effort to establish its supremacy on every front.

The old monastic orders were discredited, objects of ridicule among banqueting knights. In the last years of the twelfth century, the didactic poems composed for the nobles of France in their language were filled with criticisms of the Benedictines and the Carthusians. They were reproached for living in isolation—and living too richly. "They are regular money-grabbers." What they were actually blamed for was their religion based on rejection and complacent egoism. The Knights Templars and Knights of Saint John of Jerusalem, who were both knights and monks at the same time, were looked on more favorably. They at least fought in the world itself rather than standing aloof from it; they exalted the ideal of valor and conquest rooted in *l'amour courtois* and projected the image of an activist Christianity. Yet the spiritualistic movements that were spurring the birth of new religious orders at this time urged mortal man to lead a religious life based on the love of God and men, not on jousting and the clash of swords. Emulating Jesus in his devotion to the poor, the Order of the Holy Ghost bent its efforts to caring for the sick, and the Order of the Trinitarians, to ransoming prisoners. They provided an answer to the evangelicalism that was spreading among the lay public, and they alone could hope to overcome the heretical sects. Pope Innocent III realized this; he himself succeeded in bringing part of the Vaudois movement and of the heterodox poverty sects back into the fold of the established Church, by accepting such sects as the Catholic Poor and the Humiliated, and encouraging lay repentance.

But the real leadership of the new movements that were signs of the times fell to two apostles: Providence, in order to bring the Church nearer to Christ, her spouse,

> ordained on her behalf two princes,
> who on this side and that might be her guides.
> [Dante, *Paradiso* 11:35–36]

These two were Saint Francis and Saint Dominic.

In 1205, when the knights of Paris had not yet begun to gallop through the Languedoc region to massacre its heretics—and others—in the name of Christ, one of Pope Innocent III's visitors was the bishop of Osma, in Spain, who was accompanied by Dominic, the subprior of his chapter. On their way to Rome they had traveled through the regions where the Albigensian movement was triumphant, and in Montpellier they had met the discouraged Cistercian legates. They had clearly perceived the reasons why Catholicism was being bested; its clergy had grown amoral and overrich. And they told the pope that "in order to shut the mouths of the wicked, the clergy must follow the Divine Master's example in the way they acted and the way they taught, stand humbly in the sight of God, go on foot, spurn gold and silver; in short, they must imitate the Apostles' way of life in everything they did." This bishop and his canon offered to suit action to word by giving up the lordly ostentation, the mounted expeditions, the ornaments and the insignia of temporal power that all the prelates of the Western world since Charlemagne's day had enjoyed. Their wish was to return to the dissident regions they had traversed, but this time as Christ's witnesses, true evangelizers living in total poverty. The pope gave them his blessing and his encouragement.

So Dominic and the bishop of Osma reappeared in the region around Narbonnes—at Pamiers, Lavaur, Fanjeaux—and there they publicly challenged the "perfect." This time it was plain for all to see that the upholders of the Church of Rome were as penniless, womanless, and weaponless as their adversaries. They clashed in jousts of eloquence. Heresy had won over the monks, but now the schoolmen were entering the lists, for Dominic and his companions were clerics and intellectuals. They prepared their arguments ahead of time, in writing. They had come to fight the Albigensians on grounds of dogma and demonstrate that it was wrong for theological reasons. They could speak Occitan, and it was in that tongue that they outlined those reasons. An audience of noblemen and bourgeois designated the victors of such tournaments; in the end, only Dominic remained.

Then he founded a monastery at Prouille—a convent, rather, for women, to rival the conventicles to which the ladies of the country had withdrawn to live according to the Albigensian ascetic ideal of perfection. Dominic decided that this convent would be governed by the rule of Saint Augustine, entirely devoted to poverty. Although it may be just as well not to look too closely at his role in the bloody tumult of the crusade, at least he later resumed his preaching. The new bishop of Toulouse included him in his group of disciples, in the heart of a region that had been ravaged by Simon of Montfort's raiders, a region where Catholicism took over by force, like a tyranny rising out of the debris amid the mute resistance of an oppressed, decimated, hostile people. The handful of preachers struggled, determined to win over men's minds this time, and undertook a campaign of spiritual reconstruction. Dominic appeared at the Lateran Council, at the very place where the assembled Church leaders were striving to halt the proliferation of sects. They looked mistrustfully at the new orders, but Dominic overcame their reluctance. They did however succeed in making him abstain from inventing his own rule for his new order, and choose instead an already established rule. He took the rule of the Augustinian canons—the one he had given to the nuns at Prouille—but by adding decisive touches to it here and there, he managed to innovate nonetheless. So it was that he founded the Dominican order, the order of Preachers.

The very core of the Dominican vocation was absolute poverty. Not the artificial poverty of the Cistercians; the true poverty of Christ. Wealth was corrupting the modern world, and the battle would have to be waged essentially against wealth. Chapter 26 of the Rule, entitled "Of the Rejection of Property," included this fundamental precept: "We shall receive no property nor income of any kind." Landholding was no longer the only form of wealth in the society of the early thirteenth century. Now in the midst of that society there appeared for the first time a religious order which did not take root in a given piece of land and decided not to derive its livelihood from its own fields; instead it was determined to go begging from door to door. A Dominican friar owned nothing—except his books. His books were his tools. His mission was to spread the true doctrine, to wrestle unflinchingly with the demons of unbelief—subtle enemies that only the illumination which sprang from the Holy Spirit could slay. To this end he had to practice, hone his intelligence, read, study, learn to wield reason as a weapon. The masters of the cathedral schools had already shown that the only way to study effectively was to study as a team. Therefore the Dominicans lived together in religious communities—like the canons of the cathedrals, like the Benedictine monks—but not for the purpose of singing the Lord's praises in unison at every hour of the day, as the Benedictines did. The liturgical framework in the life of a Dominican friar became simpler, more flexible; whenever he felt it imperative he could free himself from the obligation to attend ritual prayers, disregard prescribed hours to some extent. The Dominicans were not slaves to the cosmic rhythms that had timed the chanting of psalms throughout stabler centuries gone by. Each preaching brother felt a vocation that committed him to embrace the hazards that action involved. The struggle could not be put off. It was not in the solitude of the desert, or even the fields, that the enemy was lurking. No, he was posted wherever men were to be found. And in this novel world, where the rural life was not the only life that counted, that meant it was in the towns that the enemy had to be sought out and faced. Accordingly, the Dominican monasteries were set up in the very heart of the urban masses they were supposed to enlighten.

But those monasteries did not mean a cloistered existence encompassing the friars' entire life. A Dominican monastery merely offered physical shelter; once the friars had accomplished their given tasks, they came back to sleep and to share the food for which they had gone begging in the outlying districts. At the same time the Dominican houses became known—like the cathedral cloisters with their schools—as centers of intellectual effort and training. In fact, this was their major function. Each one of them had a reader whose duty it was to read passages from the Scriptures and comment on them. The rules required each religious to possess three books, all copied over in his own hand: a Bible, the *Book of Sentences* by Peter Lombard, which was a condensation of theological science, and Peter le Mangeur's *History,* in which they could find specific themes for their sermons. These were not the heavy, elaborately decorated volumes that were borrowed from monastery libraries for purposes of celebrating Mass or patiently meditating. Instead they were real textbooks, and each preaching friar carried them about in the bag slung over his shoulder, ready to be referred to if necessary, for he had already committed most of their substance to memory:

> They must not base their studies on the works of the pagan writers or the philosophers; at most they may use them for casual reference. Nor shall they learn the secular sciences or even the so-called liberal arts, unless, on occasion, the master of the order of the chapter general deems it wise to decide differently with regard to certain individuals. The father superior can grant students a dispensation such that their studies will not be interrupted nor hampered because of divine service or for any other reason.

What counted most in this passage from the rules governing the order, what constituted the significant innovation or key intention with clear implications for the future were not the prohibitions, which were formal, traditional matters, but in fact all the dispensations, like so many doors opening onto intellectual research; cautious though that research was, it was also vigorous and bold. The reasoning was this: since the friars were called upon to be doctrinal militants, they should enter the fray well armed, as experts in dialectics—a "secular science"—and be familiar with the rational demonstrations of that pagan philosopher, Aristotle. The new order in fact carved out its niche in the very midst of the scholastic system of the period. In all of the large cities that had become study centers (Montpellier, Bologna, Oxford) and, to begin with, on the rue Saint-Jacques in Paris, the Dominican houses blended into the existing teams of theological researchers and soon formed the vanguard.

The Dominican order, the order of preaching friars that had developed out of a cathedral chapter, eventually moved away from it so as to adapt the cathedral's teaching missions more closely to the modern context, and to place those missions at the service and under the control of the monarchy in

Rome. The Franciscan order, on the other hand, stemmed directly from the urban laity and its spiritual frustrations. Francis of Assisi, born in a commune which chose an Albigensian *podestà,* was the son of a wealthy businessman. In his youth, Francis gave himself over to the joys of *courtoisie,* composing lovesongs, plunging into a chivalrous existence. Then the anxieties that were gnawing away at the bourgeoisie of southern Europe began to affect him too, but not through the Albigensian movement; no, it was the crucified Christ who spoke to him. Like Peter Valdo, he decided to cast off all worldly things. And when he appeared naked before his father, throwing his adornments and his fortune at his feet, it was the local bishop who covered him with his cloak. Francis remained faithful to the Church. He too was a mendicant. He did not stop singing the Lord's praises, and at the same time he became God's juggler. Troubadour-fashion, he continued to serve one mistress—Dame Poverty. He preached not only repentance but also the beauty of the world, Brother Sun and all the stars. Young people, his friends, began to follow him. Just as Jesus had sent forth his disciples, empty-handed and wearing sackcloth, so did Francis send his out to live among the poor, to hire themselves as farm laborers and craftsmen's assistants, and, when evening came, to sing to their companions of the perfect joy achieved through humility. And should it happen that they could find no way to earn a wage, then let them go begging for their bread. God would not let them die.

In 1209 Pope Innocent III, who was anxious to bring the poverty sects back into the fold, authorized Francis to preach and approved his very simple rule, a blend of various fragments of the Gospel. Immediately, the Minorite brothers began to spread to all the cities of Europe; in 1219 the first Franciscans came to Paris—and were eyed mistrustfully. Impassioned mendicants, they were taken for heretics, and were obliged to show their letters of credit from the pope. But by 1233 there were Franciscans established in every city of northern France. Among the aristocracy of the day the condition of the wives and daughters was beginning to improve. The spiritual aspirations of women as a whole—wealthy women at least—deserved the clergy's attention. Clara, a noblewoman of Assisi, founded a community of nuns analogous to her friend Francis's Minorites. Soon a sort of halfway-house had been organized which offered, to people who did not want to break with the life of their day, patterns of apostolic life that were suited to their condition. Francis himself went further in his vocation of brotherhood with Jesus; so ardent was his love and so completely did he identify himself with Jesus that he received the stigmata on his own body. In the Tuscan towns the masses venerated him like a saint and looked on him as the model of a new type of perfection. He corresponded to the young urban society's yearning for humility, for a life of total simplicity, charity in action, lyrical joy, and sentimental effusions. Francis's way of fighting heresy was not with the sword, not with reasoned arguments, but with whole-hearted enthusiasm and the living example of his own style of existence. Better than anyone else he made the simplicity of the Gospel a tangible presence in this life. Francis was actually the great hero of Christian history, along with Christ himself, and it is no exaggeration to say that whatever still remains of living Christianity today comes directly from Saint Francis.

Although neither he nor his first disciples were priests, nor had any desire to be, he did not try to undermine the priests' authority in any way. By talking directly to the people, he merely aimed to help the men who consecrated the communion wafer over and over again every day. For at this time the Church of Rome, in contrast to the Albigensians, the Vaudois, and all others who rejected the priesthood, exalted the Eucharist. The Lateran Council laid down the dogma of the Transubstantiation. The Last Supper was carved on the entrances to the churches in Beaucaire, Saint-Gilles, and Modena, towns that were contaminated by heresy; these scenes showed Jesus holding out bread to Judas himself. Saint Francis was the clergy's faithful servant; he argued in defense of the priests:

> If the blessed Virgin Mary is so highly honored—as is only fitting—because she carried the Christ child in her holy bosom, if the blessed John the Baptist trembled most violently and dared not touch the sacred head of his God, if the sepulcher in which Christ's body was laid for a time is so highly venerated, then how saintly, just, and worthy must he be who with his hands touches the body of Jesus Christ, takes it into his heart and his mouth, and gives it to others to eat.

And in his spiritual will Saint Francis went on to say,

> Even were I as wise as Solomon, if I came upon some poor priests living worldly lives, I would not go preaching in the parishes in which they dwelled if it was against their wishes. My intention is to love those priests, to fear them and honor them as my masters. And I do not pay any heed to their sins, because in them I discern the Son of God and because they are my masters. And why have I so much respect for them? Because I cannot see, here in this world, any tangible witness of that Son of God Almighty except his most holy body and his most holy blood, and these the priests themselves consecrate, and they alone administer them to others. And my wish is to honor and venerate those most holy mysteries above all things and place them in settings that are magnificently adorned.

In the beginning the Franciscans' preaching, as a humble and reverent adjunct of the sacerdotal function, was naive. All it offered was an example rather than arguments based on logic. For that reason it was remarkably effective. But the cardinals wanted to reinforce it, give it a disciplined structure, in the belief that what was most urgently needed at that time was not so much to proclaim the love of God and of his creatures as to wipe out the doctrinal deviations, rectify the faith of the believing masses—in other words, construct dogma in a rational way. The pope considered the inspired enthusiasts and devotees of Christ less useful than logicians and learned men. Despite protests from Saint Francis and a whole segment of his disciples, the Holy See compelled the Minorites to become a militia of priests and intellectuals modeled on the Dominican preaching order. The Franciscans were pinned down in their convents, prevented from expressing the lyrical vagabond penchant that had initially led them to wander over the gentle Umbrian countryside. They were given books and teachers. For their benefit *studia* were established in Paris and other scholarly centers. By 1225 they constituted a second army of knowledge and were under the pope's orders. Inside the cities marked out for conquest they had taken up their positions within the clerical scheme of Catholic repression.

Indeed, Innocent III had decided that henceforth the repression must be based on the network of parishes where the local priests, assisted by itinerant "squadrons" of mendicant friars, would be able to keep a close watch on the faithful. A dense grid of antiheretical surveillance was superimposed on all of Christianity. It was in the thirteenth century that the notion of local communities came into being throughout rural France, within a structure of parishes. Each peasant was designated "parishioner" of a given place; he was forbidden to go and receive the sacraments in any church other than the church of that place, and attempts were made to compel him to practice his religion regularly. The Lateran Council advised all laymen to take communion and to confess once a year. The local priest was supposed to be able to spot any laymen who tried to avoid complying and thus to track down clandestine heretics and launch more effective witch hunts. The village priest, a prosperous figure and secure in the knowledge that his flock were under his power, became the petty tyrant mocked in the *Roman de Renart,* in droll stories and collections of *fabliaux*. Similar cells were created in the newer districts of the cities. And the bishop presided over the entire supervisory operation throughout his diocese.

The bishop was given two specific missions. The first was to police the heretics. His "ordinary court," called the *officialité,* received and acted on complaints concerning run-of-the-mill breaches in ecclesiastical discipline. Alongside this court an exceptional procedure was instituted. This was the inquisition. Its action was based on investigations conducted without waiting for accusations to be made, and in this the bishop took the initiative. The rules for this emergency jurisdiction were laid down by the Lateran Council and soon applied in the Midi. Suspects were those whom rumor denounced. They were pursued, arrested, and interrogated in front of witnesses. Confessions were forced from them. If they persisted in their misguided ways, they were turned over to the secular arm to be burned by the purifying flames. If not, the inquisitor sentenced them to do penance either by going on a pilgrimage or—more often—going to prison ("the wall") for life.

This, then, was one of every bishop's functions: repression. The shepherd must smite the black sheep; he must purge the body of Christianity—already shielded from contact with the lepers and the Jews—of the harmful germs that infested it. The bishop caused noxious elements to be burned at the stake. His other mission was to enlighten men, to shed the right light onto their souls. This was a traditional matter—disseminating dogma, spreading the truth. The priest himself should teach, or at least do all he could to foster the scholarly life in his town.

Because the Church of Rome had a structure like a centralized monarchy, the greatest centers of study were answerable directly to the pope. These theological workshops, which gave dogma its backbone, were an essential part of the defense mechanism of a religion which sought to shield itself in intellectualism. The leading research centers organized themselves into more coherent bodies called "universities"; they lay outside the bishop's control, but Rome tried to keep a grip on them. Teachers and students had long since begun to form guilds, analogous to the various professional guilds in the towns, with the aim of becoming autonomous, and together they fought to free themselves from harassment by the local lord and control by the local chapter. In Paris, this guild had wrung significant freedoms from both the king and Notre-Dame. Pope Innocent III officially recognized it, and his legate gave the *universitas magistrum et scolarium parisiensium* its statutes—in order to run it more effectively from on high and link it more closely to the pope's overall efforts. Immediately it was placed under strict surveillance. The doctrine developed by Amaury of Bène was condemned, and ten university professors who stubbornly insisted on teaching it were burned at the stake. Texts considered pernicious were removed from the curriculum; the teachers of Paris were forbidden to introduce their students to Aristotle's new philosophy, his metaphysics, or Avicenna's commentary. And since it was felt that the mendicant orders could supply more reliable teachers, room was made for them in the university. There, with the pope's support, they filled the principal chairs in theology.

This development focused intellectual activity on logical thinking. The days of vain preoccupation with aesthetics, of nonfunctional curiosity, were over. In the early thirteenth century Paris became one enormous mechanism designed to produce reasoning that was straight and true. In the preparatory arts college where the future theologians were trained, dialectics pervaded everything. The "lesson," or direct contact with various authors, gave way to "disputation" or formal exercise in debating, intended to equip students for mind-to-mind doctrinal combat. The old exercise of commenting on texts was gradually replaced by purely syllogistic jousting. Grammar ceased to be a prelude to belles lettres and began to resemble a type of structural linguistics, to speculate on verbal logic and analyze modes of expression in terms of the several mechanisms to which reasoning subjected language. What was the use of reading Ovid or Virgil? What was the point of seeking delectable pleasure in literature when words were now no more than the precision tools that were essential to demonstrate reasoning? This new trend made humanistic impulses wither rapidly and dampened the fervor which had made teachers and pupils alike, and the Cistercian monks themselves, revere the classical poets and take them as their models during the entire twelfth century. Scholasticism cast out all ornamentation and gradually slid into a dessicated formalism; but at least in Paris and other university cities, including Oxford and Toulouse, a certain body of theological doctrine appeared. Deliberately designed as a reaction against heresy, it very soon became a more rigorous affair.

The preaching of truth was based on that theological edifice. In the towns it was a matter of the spoken word, and the preachers were chiefly Dominican and Franciscan friars. They were specialists, better at preaching than the bishop or his priests, who were obliged to give way to them. They became familiar figures everywhere. Because they were more attentive to the currents and crosscurrents of the new state of consciousness, they knew how to make the broadest spectrums of men listen. They appealed to what men were most sensitive to, spoke in everyday language, avoided abstract notions, and made use of striking images. Into their sermons they worked different kinds of anecdotes, depending on the social status of their public. Already they had begun to use the appeal of theatrics in conjunction with their propaganda by showing the first miracle plays (*Miracles de Notre-Dame*) to the Parisian populace. And whereas art, until then, had been a form of prayer and homage, in praise of the divine glory, the new urge to persuade and convert now made it a means of systematically edifying the laity.

In the first half of the thirteenth century the mendicant orders had not yet begun to contribute directly to creative art. They had hardly settled anywhere; their conventual buildings were more like inns, and their chapels like hangars. The preaching friars (Dominicans) and Minorites (Franciscans) left it up to the clergy to decorate the churches, and in fact the new iconographic themes developed in their preaching encouraged the clergy to do so. Although Saint Bernard of Clairvaux had banished all images from the Cistercian abbeys, he had already accepted the idea that figurative art could decorate churches in the towns so as "to enable their bishops, who have a duty to all men, both wise and ignorant, to stimulate the people's physical devotion by means of tangible images when they could not achieve this with spiritual images alone." And Saint Francis, considering that the churches harbored the body of Christ, wanted them "magnificently adorned." Accordingly, in the days of the first Dominican and Franciscan missions, a new generation of cathedrals appeared, rising above the city skylines like three-dimensional sermons. The wave of cathedral-building now speeded up (Notre-Dame in Paris was completed in 1250, but work on it had been under way for nearly a century) because of a combination of factors: the bourgeoisie was growing more and more prosperous, donations to the Church were more effectively channeled to where they were needed, and it was felt urgent to win over men's minds. Each building site became the scene of intense activity, as if it were a crucial battlefront in the struggle for truth. In Chartres, work on a new cathedral began in 1191, and twenty-six years later the cathedral was completed. In Amiens the work went even faster, and in Reims, where construction began in 1212, the major portion of it was finished by 1233.

These building sites were enormous affairs, the focal points of the biggest investments and the most gigantic artistic undertakings of the entire medieval period. The chapters now entrusted the task of overseeing them to technicians who went from one site to another, one commission to the next. One of them, Villard of Honnecourt, kept notebooks which have come down to us. They reveal his concern with mechanical improvements, and his interest in hoisting apparatus that might save labor and make the work go faster. Furthermore, they show that he was capable of applying theoretical formulas and of conceiving an entire edifice in the abstract. These technicians, "doctors of the science of building," had assimilated the science of numbers that was taught in the schools. They called themselves "masters," stressing their kinship with the universities. In point of fact, each of the buildings they were responsible for erecting was a demonstration of Catholic theology, a transcription into inert matter of the professors' philosophy and dialectical thought processes.

More than ever before, Catholic theology at this time was a statement about light. In order to combat the temptations offered by the Albigensian heresy, the best of the theologians harked back to the system of hierarchies described by Dionysius the Areopagite, and sought to shore up that monument with sturdier reasoning and enrich it with the progress that had been made in physics. Robert Grosseteste, who founded the first schools in Oxford, the nucleus of the future university, read Greek fluently; he was familiar with Ptolemy and the new astronomy and with the Arabs' scientific commentaries on Aristotle's *Treatise on the Heavens.* In Grosseteste's philosophy, God was still light, and the universe was a luminous sphere that radiated outward from a central source into the three dimensions of space. All of human knowledge stemmed from a spiritual irradiance of uncreated light. Were it not that sin makes the body opaque, the soul would be able to perceive the blaze of divine love directly. It was in the body of Christ, both God and man, that the corporeal universe and the spiritual universe reverted to their original oneness. Hence Jesus was designated—and, along with him, each of the cathedrals, as so many symbols of Jesus—as the center from which all things proceeded and received their light: the Trinity, the Word incarnate, the Church, mankind in general, and all of creation.

These concepts in turn shaped an overall aesthetic concept:

> Physical light is the best, the most delectable, the most beautiful of all the bodies that exist. Light is what constitutes the perfection and the beauty of bodily forms.

Here Robert Grossteste was stating in philosophical terms what the Franciscans had dimly expressed in their praise of Saint Claire:

> Her angelic face was *clearer* and more beautiful after each prayer, so *radiant* it was with joy. Truly the gracious Lord, in his generosity, so filled his humble spouse with his *rays* that she gave off the divine *light* all about her.

And the Dominican, Albertus Magnus, defined beauty as a "splendidness of forms."

So it was that the second-generation cathedrals were illumined, to an even greater extent than the churches from which they derived, by the splendors of the divinity. The upper portions of the Sainte Chapelle in Paris were nothing other than an airy snare intended to catch every passing ray of light. The walls had disappeared, and from all sides daylight streamed into a perfectly homogeneous inner space that would have delighted Suger. For the cathedral of Reims, John of Orbais imagined windows made entirely of fretwork; Villard of Honnecourt hastened to design them, and this new style of window began to appear everywhere. Then came Gaucher, a master builder who did away with all of the tympana over the main doors and replaced them by stained glass. Rose windows blossomed everywhere, opening so wide that they touched the framework of the buttresses. As perfect circles enclosing perfection, symbols of the cosmic rotating force, they represented the gushing burst of creative energy, the outward voyage of light and its return, the whole universe of radiant emanations and reflections described by the theology of Dionysius the Areopagite.

Robert Grosseteste's meditations culminated in a *Treatise on Lines, Angles, Figures, Reflections and Refractions of Rays*—in other words, in the practical geometry of working diagrams. It was to such geometry that thirteenth-century architecture owed its character, both rigorous and radiant at the same time. The learning dispensed in the arts colleges of the universities acquired new emphases, and these were reflected in the geometry of the cathedrals, making them less rhetorical, less concerned with mere ornamentation, and more of a showcase for the dialectical analysis of structures. The ambition embodied in each cathedral was to achieve clear scholastic demonstrations. The forms used in a cathedral were the mental offspring of the ecclesiastics who sharpened the weapons of argumentation all year long in preparation for the great Easter tournaments, the *disputationes quodlibet,* fencing matches between razor-sharp wits. Like these intellectual masters, the construction foreman proceeded by dissociation, isolating parts from one another, then doing the same with the parts of those parts, and finally placing them in the groups where they logically belonged. Each cathedral was a fabric of geometry interwoven with light, the vertical development of an exercise in persuasive intelligence.

The ornaments placed in and outside these new cathedrals were not selected for their ability to charm the beholder. They were meant, instead, to display a certain Church theology to the people, and were boldly offered to them, thrust into the midst of city lanes like a conquering army's proclamations of power. In both Reims and Amiens the statues were no longer tucked away in embrasures; they stepped out to meet the faithful and mutely preach the values of the priesthood. These carved figures exalted the mission of all the members of the clergy—the masters who taught, the priests who consecrated the wafer and the wine, the bishop, and the inquisitor as well. Melchizedek was shown holding out a wafer to a knightlike Saul. Since each cathedral's purpose was to combat the erring ways of the Vaudois sect, the sculptors who adorned it took care not to depict Christ in a context of physical poverty, solitude, and betrayal; instead they showed him as the founder of a church, enthroned, like a bishop, with his clergy on all sides of him. And since each cathedral was also meant to contradict the Albigensians in their negation of creation, of incarnation and redemption, its decor conveyed essentially the omnipotence of a God who was three and one at the same time: God the creator, God made man, God the savior.

Early in the thirteenth century the pantheism preached by Amaury of Bène was vigorously rooted out; it was vitally important, in the Church's view, to avoid all confusion between God and God's creatures, and between the specific values of body, soul, and spirit. Yet the Church neither condemned the tangible world nor set it aside as some hostile principle separate from or opposed to God, for it continued to look on the dualism taught by Manichaean doctrine as the greatest danger. If the theology of Dionysius the Areopagite was given a prudent interpretation, it could provide a fulcrum, since it showed that nature stemmed from God, returned to God, and supplemented God. In this vision, this two-way current of love, the creatures were seen as substances distinct from the divine being who existed separately from them, but their manner of being conformed to the example contained in God's presence. Although God's creatures were illuminated by

God and filled entirely full with God, yet they were only a reflection of him. In the Dionysian system, and in the orthodox theology based on it, the material world was part of God's splendor. It glorified God and led to knowledge of him.

This is certainly how the jubilant optimism of Saint Francis of Assisi conceived of the tangible world:

> Words cannot express how moved he felt upon finding in God's creatures the sign, the power, and the beauty of the Creator. Just as the three children in the fiery furnace had urged all the elements to praise and glorify the Creator of the universe, just so Saint Francis, being filled with the spirit of God, found reason in all of the elements and all of the creatures to glorify the Creator and Master of the world, to offer him praise and benedictions. . . . If he but saw a flower-studded field he immediately began to preach to the flowers as if they had been rational beings and urged them to praise the Lord. With the utmost simplicity he exhorted everything—harvests and vineyards, running brooks, green gardens, earth and fire, air and wind—to love and obey God wholeheartedly. He called all creatures brother, and his heart, enjoying a prerogative denied to all others, divined all of their secrets, as if he had been delivered of his body and was already experiencing the glorious freedom of God's children.

As brother to Jesus, Saint Francis also felt the ties of brotherhood with the birds in the sky, and with the sun and the wind, and with death. As he wandered through the Umbrian countryside, all of the forms of beauty made him a glad escort. Young people were imbued with the tradition of *l'amour courtois,* and such a degree of oneness with the joy to be found in the world harmonized with their desire for conquest. It was strong enough to entice the flocks of youths and maidens, intent on celebrating the Maytime, back to God. It was by welcoming nature—the wild animals, the freshness of dawn, and the ripening grapes on the vine—that the cathedral-building Church could hope to attract the hunter-knights, the troubadours, and believers in the formidable and pagan powers of rustic nature. Saint Bernard of Clairvaux had said it earlier, with great determination: "You will see for yourselves that it is possible to draw honey from stones and oil from the hardest rocks."

By rehabilitating matter—the tangible, created world—Catholic theology smashed the very foundations of the Albigensian movement, and it may have been the Franciscan rapture over the earthly creatures that was decisive in defeating heresy. By choosing to revere God as creator, God in the act of creating, the theologians made reconciliation with the visible universe central to cathedral art. Both the rose window in the north transept at Reims and the transverse arches at Chartres show God causing the light and the stars to burst forth, separating day from night and earth from water, and shaping the plants, the animals, and, finally man. They in fact spread out an inventory of creation for the faithful to gaze upon. At the same time they treated the story of Genesis without symbolic overtones. It was possible to do what Thierry of Chartres had already attempted: bring the text of Genesis into harmony with the laws of physics as they were taught at that time. Henceforth the successive stages in the creation of the world became a clear and lucid vision, a sight for all to contemplate. Since all the creatures in nature could be perceived by the senses with which God had endowed man, man should look at and observe them rather than continuing to fantasize about them as before. Saint Thomas Aquinas urged that the soul derive all its knowledge from the perceptible world. If man wished to see what God had shaped, he must open his eyes. This new outlook made the fables, the fantastic bestiaries, all the figments of the imagination, retreat into the background. At a time when crusaders, merchants, and missionaries were setting out to explore unknown regions, the new outlook scattered the mists and the phantasmagoria; real live beasts replaced the monsters that the heroes of tales of chivalry used to encounter in the course of their adventures, and leaves such as anyone could see in the nearby forest became more relevant than the visionary flora of Romanesque illuminations.

In the provinces which gave birth to the art of France this new attentiveness developed at the beginning of the thirteenth century. The romances of Jean Renart described certain aspects of life as it really was, with its greedy bourgeois and blustering braggarts. Thomas of Quintampré's *Book of Nature* was still intended to guide the reader through the complex allegorical interpretation of visible things, but it did not merely describe the relationships between the virtues and each of the creatures; it also tried to define wherein lay their practical value. And all the theological constructions of the day followed Aristotle's example by pairing off their metaphysics with a concept of physics that was based on the experience provided by the senses instead of, as before, on analogies. These compendiums of knowledge claimed to be scientific and went out of their way to assimilate facts and figures borrowed from Arab and Greek scientists. The leading field of research at this time was optics, along with the geometry implicit in it. This was Europe's age of astronomers and of the first accurate measurements of the stellar universe.

It was also the age of naturalists. Saint Albertus Magnus arrived in Paris in 1240 and immediately introduced his pupils to Aristotle's *Natural Philosophy,* although it was forbidden to do so:

> If, on questions of faith and morality, Saint Augustine does not agree with the philosophers, then it is Saint Augustine whom we

> must heed. But if it is medicine we are talking about, then I rely on Galen and Hippocrates, and if we are concerned with the nature of things, I turn to Aristotle or some other expert on the question.

Albertus himself wrote a *Compendium of Living Creatures,* in which he methodically described the features that characterized the fauna in the various regions of his native Germany. For the Dominicans enjoyed relaxing in a natural forest setting, just as other men did. The cities were not so enormous or so self-contained as to shut out the scent of spring. Within their new defensive walls there were gardens, vineyards, and even wheatfields. Material civilization had not cut off thirteenth-century man from contact with the cosmos. He was still an animal leading an outdoor existence, and the rhythm and savor of time as he experienced it varied with the seasons. The intellectuals generally lived amid a setting of orchards and meadows rather than in the isolation of bedchambers and studies, and every cloister was enlivened by a garden filled with birds and flowers.

Because of this familiarity with the bounties of nature and this feeling that they bore God's own mark, rather than a burden of guilt, and revealed the divine visage, the sap gradually rose, so to speak, in the shafts of the columns in Notre-Dame in Paris until its effects became visible in the style of the plants that decorated their capitals. In the choir, completed in about 1170, their botanical decoration was still a purely mental projection expressed with geometrical regularity. Ten years later, when the first spans of the nave were built, the flora that adorned them was already closer to its living models; deliberate symmetry had vanished and the diversity of actual nature was visible, so that it is possible to identify a given leaf or distinguish a given species. Yet even so these plants were still chiefly symbolic, and it was not until other parts of the edifice were decorated, after 1220, that they became true to life.

Nonetheless the trend toward realism stopped short of certain limits. The purpose of man's exploring the universe was to define certain types or categories found in it in the hope of discerning the order in which God had arranged them. Scholastic doctrine taught that each individual being, in its uniqueness, belonged to a species the ideal of which existed in the mind of the Divine Being. When an artist decorated a cathedral, his mission was to depict that ideal and specific form, rather than any of the real-life variations which might deform it. In order to achieve this, the artist had to let his visual experiences decant and then take a rational approach to them; for God's thought processes, like man's, worked logically, and the forms that they engendered projected themselves in the same way as light did, that is, in accordance with geometrical laws. When Villard of Honnecourt sketched animate creatures—animals, or men fighting or playing dice—in his notebooks, he built them, so to speak, around corners or along straight lines or curves, like the architecture of the cathedral as a whole. This adherence to a rational framework revealed the hidden structures—the true reality, for a theologian—that underlay the accidental surface. Hence Gothic imagery was governed, possibly to a greater extent than Romanesque imagery, by geometry. The novelty was that the geometry in Gothic art, instead of applying, as before, to the realm of the imaginary now applied to the way the real world was perceived, and it respected the proportions found in nature. Geometry's role was to equip each figure with the flawless framework that, according to the divine plan, underlay the model established for every visible creature.

All of these images would be meaningless, however, if they remained just so many isolated efforts. It was up to the master planner at each work site to coordinate them so that together, arranged in a suitable order, they would represent the whole of the created universe. For nature was one, just as the God from which it came was one, and each cathedral aimed to depict nature in its entirety. The ornamentation of a cathedral was not just a choice of samples. It was supposed to constitute, in itself, a "compendium of living creatures," a full and detailed inventory, the faithful reflection of a sublime coherence. Nature, in the view of Alan of Lille, was the "lieutenant of Almighty God," giving off a multiple reflection of the divine simplicity. This concept implied that all parts of the divine creation were interrelated, that a network of harmonies existed among them. The realism which the art of France took as its goal was all-encompassing, concerned with distilling the essential rather than with pointing out singularities. This art embodied lucidity and respected the hierarchies decreed by Dionysius, establishing each and every element of the cosmos, each star, each genus, each order, each species in its rightful place. This was an art that ordained an indivisible whole, for, as Saint Thomas Aquinas put it,

> divine nature arranges all things as best suits them and without confusion, in such a way that all are coordinated within a concrete and coherent system wherein each thing maintains its specific purity at the very point where it becomes involved in a series of reciprocal coordinations.

Every word in this definition counts, every word helps to furnish the key to the aesthetics that shaped Gothic art. Dante soon borrowed these words and carried their implications further:

> All things
> have order among themselves, and this is the form
> that makes the universe like God.
> Herein the high creatures behold the imprint
> of the Eternal Worth, which is the end
> wherefor the aforesaid ordinance is made.
> In the order whereof I speak all natures
> are inclined by different lots,

nearer and less near unto their principle;
wherefore they move to different ports
over the great sea of being.
[*Paradiso* 1:103–13]

An artist's ultimate goal should be to create an image of each creature that was at the same time an image of fulfillment. "Whatever we take away from the perfection of the creatures we are actually taking away from the perfection of God himself," said Saint Thomas Aquinas.

Although the laws of nature strove for that perfection, they would have trouble achieving it were it not for man's intervention, forcing them to make progress in that direction and removing whatever hindered the development of nature's own rhythms. This was man's role; God had endowed him with reason that he might play that role. Like Romanesque man, Gothic man lived in the center of the cosmos. The interplay of "reciprocal coordinations" enabled him to adhere to it, and every bit of flesh in his body underwent their influences. His humors or moods were in correspondence with the elements that composed matter. The course of his life was oriented by the course of the heavenly bodies. At least he was neither crushed by the weight of the universe, as Romanesque man had been, nor passive, for the Supreme Artist who had placed man above all other tangible, visible creatures, on the very highest level of the hierarchies contained in the visible world, called upon man to work with him. In creating man, God's intention was that man himself should be an agent of creation. The theology embodied in each cathedral accompanied and translated, as it were, the great forward impulse that made new meadows, fields, and vineyards gain ground as farmers brought fallow land under cultivation, that made the cities spread out, attracted and impelled traders to the fairs, knights to combat, and Franciscan friars to the conquest of men's souls. The new age was astir with joyous activity, for the creation was not yet complete, and man, through his works, took part in the act of creation. So it was that not only the material world as such but also manual labor were rehabilitated. The teachings of the Paris and Oxford masters reproved the disdain for manual labor that had been professed by the aristocratic classes during the preceding periods of stagnation and that Cluny and even the Cistercians themselves still professed. The Albigensian perfect had refused to make any physical effort that would serve the cause of mere matter; but the Lombardian sect of the "humiliated" and the Minorites of Saint Francis of Assisi all performed manual labor. They transformed the world and contributed as best they could to the continuous creation of the universe, just like the obscure and pioneering clearers of land who, during this same period, were correcting the courses of myriad waterways and replacing thorn thickets by neat ploughed fields. Under the new rules applied to confessions, any profession that was founded on labor was justified, and moralists began to seek reasons to consider profit legitimate. The various types of manual labor that corresponded to each of the seasons were depicted on the doors of city churches, and these images took on their full meaning amid the economic growth of the thirteenth century. And when the guild masters offered a stained glass window, they wanted it to show the techniques of their trade in minutest detail. Each workman was a conqueror, and the cathedral itself meted out praise to him.

Hence the human figure was situated in the very midst of creation and of the iconography used in the cathedrals. Gothic man had a recognizable physical type. He was never shown with the emaciated features of an ascetic or the puffy features of a prelate who suffered from gravel and died of apoplexy. He was spared the deformations that come with age or a life of work—or of pleasure. Fruit of the divine mind, he was born adult, at the point of culmination to which his growth would bring him and from which the aging process would bring him down. He was twin to the potterlike God who shaped him out of clay on the transverse arches at Chartres. It would be sacrilege—an attack on God's perfectness—to deform man's body for the sake of excessive realism or instead to bend it unduly to make it fit inside a framework, as the Romanesque artists did. The rational harmonies that united man to creation as a whole must be visible in his image since they were what determined the specific forms of his face and body. On Bamberg cathedral the shapes and visages of both Adam and Eve are produced by the harmonies of geometrical perfection. They have experienced salvation; they are cleansed of all sin and are to be resurrected in a cloud of glory. Already the rays of God's light illumine them and draw them toward eternal joy. The smiles on their luminous faces are almost angelic.

At the same time, however, Gothic man was a human being. On Reims cathedral, a humble Servant of the Presentation makes her appearance, amid the saints and apostles, near the Virgin, and not far from Jesus, who resembles her. She is a free person, responsible for her actions, fully conscious. Thirteenth-century Christians, who were learning to go to confession regularly every year, to examine their consciences and discern the motivations behind their sins, were practicing the introspection that Abelard had already advocated. As a result, the statues that the learned doctors chose to adorn the façades of the churches were no longer mere symbols of men and women but instead poised and adult human beings, delivered from the grip of blind forces. They were imbued with love; and love, along with reason, was what made it possible to attain unto the ultimate source of all light. This is why their lips quivered and why they gazed wide-eyed on the splendors of the world. It was this gaze which beamed all the messages that human beings exchanged, all the communication latent in the universe. Through the eyes, the divine light reached into each human being's heart and there fanned the flames of charity. The human gaze was a living thing, central to the light-filled metaphors employed by the theologians, and it was what endowed Gothic man with a destiny. Man the creature was born, he would die; he had sinned; his life was part of the timespan punctuated by the course of the heavenly bodies. Yet the learned doctors' philosophy wrenched him away from this crushing sequence, delivered him from the occasional fluctuations that occurred in the sublunar world, rescued him from the forces of corruption, and, with the motionless motion of celestial time as a backcloth, leaped ahead to envision him in harmony with his everlasting model. Just like Jesus, who had taken bodily historical form, yet had existed before Abraham, and who lived and reigned for all eternity.

In the theological system established by Dionysius the Areopagite, time ceased to exist within the mystical concept of circulation that governed the pulsating, two-way movement of creation: God's condescension and the love that his creatures bore him in return. Saint Thoms Aquinas commented that

> God's wisdom and goodness transpire in his creatures, but this movement can also be envisaged as a reason for a reverse current flowing toward the supreme fulfilment; and this is accomplished by the gifts of sanctifying grace and glory which alone make us one with God, who is the supreme purpose. In the efflux of the creatures proceeding from their primary principle, there is a sort of circulatory or respiratory movement, as all created beings revert ultimately to that from which they proceed, as from their principle. Therefore we must observe the laws that enter into their returning and their proceeding.

Saint Thomas Aquinas looked for reasons and based his argument on Aristotle, but it was to the Dionysian system that he applied his efforts. In the mid-thirteenth century the Dominican and Franciscan masters teaching in the schools of Paris managed, in their striving for lucidity, to reconcile the rational methods of scholasticism with the impulsiveness of Saint Bernard of Clairvaux. Their aim was to use the methodology of logic in order to discern the laws regulating that creative respiration and to observe the visible features of life on earth in order to discover the God of nature, who was the same as the God of the celestial realms. But they let themselves be swept along by love.

> Even as fire moves upwards
> by reason of its form, being born to ascend
> thither where it lasts longest in its matter,
> so the captive mind enters into desire,
> which is a spiritual movement, and never
> rests until the thing loved makes it rejoice.
>
> [Dante, *Purgatorio* 18:28–33]

At the junction between love and reason, at the point where the outward-streaming procession of love met the returning procession, where the created and the uncreated, the natural and the supernatural, the eternal and the historical came together, is where Christ was situated, as God made man. He was "light born of light," yet was made of solid flesh. Ever since the building of Saint-Denis Gothic art had strained to express the incarnation; gradually, and more and more skillfully as time went by, it outlined the specific images that ultimately reached perfection in the thirteenth-century cathedrals. Rooted in the Gospels, these images emerged from all the obscure movements which had begun, as early as the eleventh century, to shake Western Christendom. They had already existed in embryo in the first efforts of the faithful to devise an image of God that would resemble them and provide a remedy with which to ease their fears and dreads. For instance, in about 1050, the Patarine sect in Milan had centered their hopes on the cross; to them it symbolized victory over death and the forces of darkness. Likewise, the groups of pilgrims who had set out for Jerusalem—empty-handed at first—soon after the year 1000 and whose travels led the way for the crusaders' expeditions, did much to prepare for the blossoming, in Gothic art, of depictions of the Word incarnate. By 1100 the reformers' models were not the patriarchs of Old Testament law but instead the apostles. They found substance for their arguments in the Acts of the Apostles, in Saint Matthew who spoke to them of poverty:

> The friars have described diverse itineraries—called the rule of Saint Basil, or of Saint Augustine, or Saint Benedict—but these are not the foundation itself of religious life, not the roots but only the buds and the leaves. There is but one rule leading to faith and salvation, one prime and essential rule whence all others flow, like so many streams from a single fountain, and that is the holy Gospel that the apostles received from the Savior. Cling to Christ, for he is the true vine of which you are the shoots.
>
> Insofar as he himself will allow you to do so, strive to follow the precepts of his Gospel. In this way, should any man inquire as to your condition, your rule, or your order, you will reply that you are following the prime and essential rule of Christian life, which is the Gospel, the source and the principle of all other rules.

The man of faith who, in 1150, wrote this prologue to the rule of Grandmont was expressing what the most enlightened of the era's knights and burghers were still confusedly feeling. Peter Valdo discovered his vocation in the Gospel. Christ himself induced Saint Francis of Assisi to spurn wealth and speak to the poor. And as Pope Innocent III convinced himself that Jesus in person had conferred his power on him, he found justification for his actions in the will of the Divine Master. All of this feeling that welled up from deep inside the people, as their sensitivity gained in refinement and culture progressed, made the living God central to the art deployed in the cathedrals. We can even postulate that the Albigensian movement itself owed most of its success to its ambiguous vocabulary, for it disguised its total rejection of the concept of incarnation under a cloak of evangelicalism, and it was this cloak that the Church of Rome tore off the heretical sect so that the populace would be disenchanted with it. The people then began to follow Saint Francis of Assisi, who erected the first nativity scenes. Devotion to the Christmas story—the birth of an infant human God—enabled Catholicism to triumph.

Actually, however, the theologians who created Gothic art pictured Christ not as an infant but a king, the sovereign of the world. The edifices which the kings of France helped to build had shown Christ first as a doctor, his head circled by a crown, and then seated on a throne and in the act of crowning the Virgin. The Virgin was his mother but at the same time his spouse; she was woman, but also the Church. For in the role that Mary had played in the incarnation, the authors of Catholic dogma had finally found justification for the fact that in the course of the twelfth century the people had taken the Mother of God to their hearts. Marveling, they acknowledged that Mary's image now stood alongside Jesus' at the center of their theology and the center of cathedral art. The artists of the first half of the thirteenth century did not look to the ladies of chivalrous society for their inspiration; and since they heeded the lords of the Church, who were the king, his bishops, and his theologians, the Our Lady whom they depicted was not an embodiment of tenderness or suffering. Instead they showed her surrounded by glory. Incarnation was not a matter of rejoicing; it was swathed in mystery. The sculptors and stained glass makers made Mary's image all the more majestic because the scholars considered her the symbol of the New Testament and the fulfillment of the Old. In her person mankind was united with God, the soul was mystically wed to its Creator. Mary was the concrete image of the assembled body of the Church, for surely the spouse in whom God had become flesh was the Church itself, strong in its opposition to heresy? In other words, Mary's coronation in each cathedral was actually the formal affirmation of the sovereignty of the Church of Rome.

As the Church grew stronger, Marian iconography developed apace. In 1145 the royal doorway at Chartres had still exalted the power of the Romanesque God by placing his image in the center, haloed by the glory of Judgment Day and victorious over darkness. Yet because the Albigensian movement was so influential, that same door also carried the message that God had been incarnated; one of its lateral tympanums bore evangelical scenes of the Christmas story. It was in Chartres, center of the Beauce, that the first stone statue of the Mother of God appeared, because in this region the cult of the Virgin grafted itself onto old traditions that went back to Carolingian times, the fertile seeds of spirituality that the Frankish kings and the monks had sown throughout Neustria. Charles the Bald had given to the cathedral in Chartres handsome pieces of cloth that had been brought back to him from the Middle East; since then it was assumed that they constituted the gown that Mary was wearing when the angel Gabriel came to hail her, and throngs of dazzled ruffians and peasants prostrated themselves before them. The people were led down into the crypt—and there they beheld the effigy of the Virgin majestically seated on a throne. After Suger's time, reliquaries were no longer hidden away in the darkness of underground sanctuaries; instead they were displayed for all to see, dazzling in the God-given light, and the prelate who designed the royal doorway had that reliquary-statue reproduced in the stone of the tympanum above the west door, amid the story of Christ's infancy, a discreet accompaniment to the Virgin's presence. The Ile-de-France shepherds, in their humble role, seem to be blinded by another dazzling supernatural vision: the timeless, mystery-shrouded figure of the Mother of God. This Virgin, hieratic like the Virgin of Torcello, but seated, is the "throne of Solomon," the "seat of divinity" that even the Venerable Peter, Abbot of Cluny, was lauding at this time. The artists who decorated the cathedral of Laon a few years later still used symbols from the theology of concordances to pay tribute to Mary, expressing her virginity by such biblical prefigurations as the burning bush, Gideon's fleece, and the Hebrews in the fiery furnace.

The decisive change came about in Senlis in 1190, just as the Church, under stern papal influence, had begun to take a tougher line. It went into battle proclaiming the doctrine of God's incarnation and glorifying the Virgin, who had been the instrument of that mystery. The Church became accustomed to seeing its own image in the image of the Virgin. The cathedral at Senlis was the first whose porch was devoted entirely to the Mother of God. It showed the funeral of the Virgin Mary or rather, her passage from an earthly existence to glory, for according to eastern Mediterranean beliefs recently adopted by Latin Christendom, the Virgin was not dead. She was asleep. Her body would be spared the fate that awaited all flesh and blood creatures, for soon the angels would come to take it and carry it up to heaven. The ecclesiastics of Senlis decided to depict Mary and Jesus together side by side on the same royal seat at the very top of the tympanum; Christ has placed his mother at his right, associating her with his kingship. This simple sculpture illustrated the rites of the feast of the Assumption, at which two sequences from the psalter were sung: "The queen was seated at his right side in a garment of gold." "On her head he placed a crown of precious stones." And this theme, devised just at the time when Pope Innocent III was claiming universal sovereignty for the assembled Church of which he was the leader, spread very quickly. By about 1220, at Notre-Dame in Paris, the theme had found its perfect form of expression.

And yet even there it was still confined to only one side of the portal, whereas thirty years later, when the cathedral of Reims was completed, figures of Mary were visible in every part of it. John of Orbais, the first master builder at Reims, left behind him plans for a narthex whose central portion was to be reserved for the patron saints of the episcopal church, as minor intercessors. The plans were altered in such a way that the Virgin, as mediatrix sovereign above all others, replaced the saints. They were relegated to the north door, and she is in their midst, reinforcing their efforts to redeem man. The Virgin appears again on the south door, which depicts the end of time, and her presence intensifies the mystical meaning of the apocalyptic vision. The entire façade of the cathedral of Reims was intended as a demonstration of truth visible by all, and now, just as at Senlis, it was arranged around the Virgin. Mary is placed on the pier of the central door, flanked by monumental statues of the Annunciation, the Visitation, the Presentation in the Temple, and King David, Mary's ancestor. The carvings on the transverse arches tell Mary's human story, while the other images symbolize her virginity. Solomon and the Queen of Sheba prefigure the Virgin's wedding with Christ the King. The rose window recounting the Creation is balanced by another to the west, dedicated to her Assumption. And lastly, at the very top of the gable, Jesus bestows the insignia of sovereign power upon his mother with his own hands. As the new Adam, he crowns the new Eve, his wife. Surely his incarnation assured the triumph of the Church in this world?

The thirteenth-century theologians' concept of the creation and the incarnation relieved man of his feelings of guilt and abolished his terrors. At least a portion of Western Christendom—the part that was emerging from its earlier uncouthness—no longer believed that sin could be redeemed by ritual or by haggling based on predetermined prices, or that it was the magical intervention of divine power that made it possible to distinguish the criminals from their victims when both were subjected to the judgment by ordeal. Now men knew that they must earn their salvation through their actions and, better still, their intentions, through love and through the reasoning powers that proved to each man his identity with God and stimulated him to come back to God and imitate him more faithfully. Yet the state of sin subsisted, it made matter more impenetrable, made the flesh a burden on man, and prevented the uncreated light from shining through. In all this world only Jesus had overcome that obstacle. Only Jesus could save man. Wherefore each man must follow in his path and, like him, bear his cross.

All of the mendicant Franciscans, champions of the renewed faith, spread this message everywhere. Saint Francis of Assisi enjoined, "Speak to me not of any other way of life than that which the Lord himself has mercifully shown me and given me. The Minorite brothers' entire lives consist of following one rule, which is to observe the Sacred Gospel of Our Lord Jesus Christ." The Gospel in its simplest version, that is, without any superadded commentary—*sine glossa.* Saint Dominic's highest ambition was to be "a man of the Gospel." Although the preachers of truth now considered joy as one ingredient in it, the emphasis was still on repentance and, ultimately, on experiencing the suffering of the Passion. Saint Francis of Assisi achieved this on the Alverna. "Some time before his death we saw that our brother and father Francis resembled our Lord when he was crucified; on his body were wounds that were the genuine stigmata of Christ." At the first light of dawn, Francis kneeled and, with outstretched arms and his eyes turned to the east, beseeched his Savior:

> O Lord Jesus, two blessings do I ask you to grant me before I die. The first is that if it be possible I should suffer the same cruel pain as you, gentle Jesus, felt throughout the Passion. And the second is that if it be possible, I should feel in my heart the same boundless love that enflames you, Son of God, and causes you to suffer so greatly and so willingly for our sakes, miserable sinners that we are.

And fifty years later, when King Louis IX—Saint Louis—felt a similar vocation, that was because, Joinville said,

> he loved God with all his heart and imitated his works. This can be seen from the fact that, just as God died out of love for his people, so our sainted king several times placed his person in mortal danger out of love for his people.

For those who had a share in the new wealth, the thirteenth century was a time of joyful conquests. Each successful stage in its progress engendered euphoria—but simultaneously sermon after sermon exhorted the people to repent, so that the triumphal current would flow in the right direction, sweeping God's people along to the Promised Land. Like the crusaders' guides, the sculpture adorning the cathedrals bore the sign of the cross. They displayed scenes from the Passion, and we must remember that they were meant as symbols of victory for all to see, affirmations that the God who had been made man had gone through death himself and that, in the triumph of resurrection, Christ carried all of mankind along in his wake, toward the veritable joys that are not of this world.

When Latin Christendom began to meditate on the sufferings of Christ, it followed a penchant for spirituality that had already caught up eastern Christendom long before. Ever since the eleventh century, the Byzantine clergy had urged the faithful to look upon the rites of Mass as a reenactment of Christ's death, burial, and resurrection. This liturgy dramatized all the episodes in the life of the Savior; the Eucharist became a summing up of all the incidents of the entire Gospel story, and the iconography used in the Macedonian frescoes soon provided a visible transcription of them. We can get an idea of those images at Cefalu. The crusaders gazed at these figures at the same time as they discovered in the Holy Land a Jerusalem that was truer than the fascinating eschatological symbols that had released the great crusading impulse of 1095.

Then in 1204 bands of Frankish warriors captured Constantinople. This was a crucial event. It was thought that it would put an end to the schism, that at last Christ's body, which had been rent in two, would be brought back together. The conquest proved to be an opportunity for the West, at any rate, to take possession of all the marvelous relics of the Passion that the churches of Byzantium had been protecting. Robert of Clari was struck dumb by such wonders as two pieces of the true cross, the lancehead, the two nails, the tunic, and the crown of thorns. All of the apparatus connected with the crucifixion ceased to belong to a world of dreams and became real. The knight-plunderers bought it or stole it, piece by piece, and carried it away with them. Count Baudoin of Flanders was able to bring a few drops of Christ's blood back to the vicinity of his castle at Ghent. For centuries the Western world's unrefined faith had been sustained by the dubious remnants incased in the reliquaries that were, in turn, housed in the crypts of the abbey churches. Now the adventurous crusaders were bringing back relics that appeared far more authentic, and they had to be placed in a setting worthy of them. Existing chapels were renovated and embellished, new chapels were built:

> King Louis IX [Saint Louis] had the crown of thorns of Our Lord Jesus Christ, and a large piece of the holy cross on which he was placed, and the lance with which his side was pierced, and a great many precious relics which he acquired. He had the Sainte Chapelle in Paris built for them and spent on it a good forty thousand *livres tournois* and more. He had the chapel and the reliquaries in which the holy relics rested adorned with gold and silver and precious stones and other jewels, and it is believed that these ornaments were worth one hundred thousand pounds and more.

A figurative ornament was placed on each reliquary to explain the origin, meaning, and virtues of the miraculous remains enshrined inside. The feverish urge to decorate which gripped the early thirteenth century stemmed directly from the sack of Constantinople.

The artists who were asked to glorify the new relics had to innovate. They found their iconographical models in Byzantium, so recently pillaged by the crusaders. The aim of the militant preaching Church, the Church of the Catholic repression, was now to convince the masses, and this required touching what lay deepest within them. God's suffering had to be depicted in less abstract, more soul-stirring ways, conducive to repentance. So the men responsible for mapping out the program that artistic endeavor was to follow delved into the living tales found in the Synoptic Gospels; and, just as Eastern artists had done some generations earlier, so these thirteenth-century leaders chose to have the episodes of Christ's Passion illustrated in sculpture and stained glass. Villard of Honnecourt's notebook includes a scene in which Nicodemus unnails Christ's feet from the cross; and we know that the original plan for the narthex of Reims cathedral was altered and that, as a result, the crucifixion appeared for the first time on a cathedral door. In the same spirit, the modifications that Suger had already made in the Romanesque theme of the Last Judgment were accentuated until its meaning was totally altered. At Chartres, the sculptures done after 1204 showed Christ no longer as a resurrected and glorious sovereign but as a humble, despoiled man who displays his wounds, while the instruments of the Passion—the lance, the crown of thorns, and the wood of which the cross was made—are visible all about him. These were the signs of the Son of Man, said the Gospel according to Saint Matthew. Yet it was neither Christ himself nor his torturers who bore them but rather angels, and they held them out as if they were relics. Creatures of light though they were, they dared not touch them with their hands; a sacred shroud protected them. Indeed the theologian who planned this scene did not intend to convey the savior's physical suffering or the sagging of his tortured body; the cross, far from being a mere place of execution, was ever a sign of glory. Similarly, Jesus' wounds did not merely bear witness to his torments. Instead, said Saint Thomas Aquinas, they proclaimed his strength. "He triumphed over death."

At this particular period the doctors of the Church militant did not dwell on the events of Good Friday. They focused on the victorious Easter Sunday. On the back of the door of the cathedral at Reims, in which window openings were cut so that the portal, too, could let the divine rays flow through, the exuberance of thicket and vineyard surrounds the figures of the redemption. This time they are real people rather than symbols. Still, they are not yet true-life participants in a dramatic event. All of these statues have a specific mission: to represent the spiritual values of which the crucifixion was the sign, and to provide the eucharistic equivalents of them. Because thirteenth-century Christianity was more ecclesiastical then ever, exalting the functions of the priesthood in determined contradiction of the heretics, and furthermore, because Gothic art was created by priests, the statues of Reims cathedral distributed communion, that is, the major sacrament that elevated the ministers of the Catholic religion high above the Albigensian perfect and the Vaudois preachers. They took Jesus' death and transmuted that event into the everlastingness of the rites of the Church, into peace itself. On the level of the rose window—where iconographical innovation culminated in about 1260—above these serenely assembled statues, the original plan called for a gallery of kings. At the last minute it was decided to replace them by a different cohort: the multitude of witnesses who saw Christ reappear after the Resurrection. At the very peak of the ascensional movement with which the entire edifice soars toward heaven, those witnesses proclaim that death has been overcome and every mortal man shall joyously attest to this miracle of immortality. They bespeak the hope that mankind will be redeemed. The Church of Rome, knowing full well that the lay masses were still tormented by their dread of the after-life, was eager to convince them that deliverance was at hand, and offered a more effective type of "consolation" than the Albigensian perfect had. To all who were willing to place themselves under its protection, the Church promised that they need not fear the straight and narrow passages that would lead to the haven of divine light. Saint Francis of Assisi had praised the Lord, in his *Canticle,* for

> our sister, the death of the body, which no living man can escape; doomed are they only who die in a state of mortal sin, while blessed are they who have done God's holy will, for no harm shall be done them by the second death.

Death no longer mattered. The resurrection had stripped it of all its powers.

Rome allowed the mightiest men of the day to have their burial place inside the churches and have images of themselves carved on their tombs. This was the period when artists began to decorate sepulchers as well, and the starting point for the long procession of Europe's recumbent tombstone effigies was the oratory of the Knights Templar in London. Saint Louis decided to make the basilica that Suger had designed at Saint-Denis into a mausoleum where the tombs of his ancestors would be on display. Peter of Montreuil was ordered to arrange the church accordingly and install the tombs in the central portion of the transept, like so many ceremonial beds. But rather than depicting corpses lying in a horizontal position, he erected column-type statues whose anonymous faces exuded the serenity of the kings of Judah. These kings and queens were of the fleshly lineage of Jesus himself, reaching beyond death, beyond mortal notions of duration; for in the eyes of the Eternal, did the passion and resurrection of Christ signify anything more than a mere stage in an overall process? They were not only historical events but also signs of more to come, foreshadowings. In truth, the resurrection of all mankind, and of each individual man, already existed for all eternity in Christ's resurrection—and in each man's death. For what was an individual death but the return of the light encompassed in the soul to the principle in which it originated, the movement by which created life flowed back to its divine model? And this is why the reclining figures atop thirteenth-century tombs are of no specific age and have no identifiable physiognomy. Since they need no longer partake of the accidental nature of life—and death—they have reverted to their initial type, which is God incarnate. The ecstasy that Saint Bernard was seeking was realized at last in these recumbent statues. The illumined faces of the resurrected humans carved on the cathedral of Reims, still atremble as they emerge from the shadows of death, bear the same traits as the Son of Man himself, the Christ resplendent with glory, who exposes the wounds in his hands and side. The same traits as God the Creator. Man's destiny culminates in redemption. But both redemption and creation are epitomized in the incarnation.

7

HAPPINESS

1250–1280

It was in Paris, in the university, that the best weapons for fighting heresy were forged. All the prelates of the Christian world, the bishops of Scandinavia, of Hungary, of Morea, of Saint John of Acre, of Nicosia, flocked there to learn, and the popes, its former pupils, protected it. The students and all the people of the town had escorted the triumphal procession bringing back the caged prisoners whom their victorious king had taken at Bouvines. He had defeated the emperor; he had assumed the name Augustus, he had supplanted all his rivals. And now the virtues of Louis IX added the halo of saintliness to Capetian success. Saint Louis adjudicated the quarrels of the princes; he was the master of Languedoc, where the inquisitors labored in his name to root out the last vestiges of heresy; his brother commanded Provence, Naples, and Sicily. Europe ordered itself around his throne. To noblemen throughout the world he offered the model of a new type of chivalry, a *prud'homme,* valiant in arms, gallant to ladies, but fearing God. The marveling knight of Bamberg wears his countenance. All the lords of Christendom strove to speak his tongue. The unreal atmosphere of Breton romance and the sensuality of the troubadours gradually faded away before the springlike allegories and lucid visions of the first *Roman de la rose.* Through school and royalty, Paris carried all before it in the mid-thirteenth century, as did the art of France.

That art had won new territory when some provinces—Normandy, Artois, Anjou—had brought their allegiance to the royal domain, or others—Champagne, Burgundy, and Flanders—had bowed before the preeminence of the sovereign. At Trondheim and in Castile and Franconia, the bishops had introduced architectural schemes they had accepted as adhering profoundly to theological constructions at the time of their studies in Paris. The Dominicans and the Franciscans had just begun to alternate with Cîteaux in making those patterns better known: the basilica of Assisi and the Minerva in Rome were both Gothic churches. The struggle against heresy had destroyed most of the barriers hindering the progress of the French cathedral style. Now it implanted it by force in the vanquished South, at Toulouse, at Clermont—soon at Limoges, Narbonne, Bayonne, Carcassonne, in all the citadels of Albigensianism. French sculptors had appropriated the best of rival arts and proceeded to adorn their achievements with their spoils. Mingling with the statuary at Reims were forms borrowed from the fonts of the Meuse and from the antique cameos of which replicas were being made in Paris. Art historians ponder over what may even have been borrowed from Greece.

Since the middle of the century, however, Paris, the focus of the triumphant style, had sensed the stirrings of a deeper movement which had begun to change the face of the world. The major work on the Sainte Chapelle had been completed in 1248; at Notre-Dame in 1250; at Amiens in 1269; the monumental sculpture of Reims was finished in 1260. It was precisely the latter date which Joachim of Fiore, in his messianic view of human destiny, had singled out as the appointed time for a reversal of history. He had predicted 1260 as the advent of the third era of mankind; after the reign of the Father and the reign of the Son would come the reign of the Holy Spirit; the eternal gospel heralded in Revelation, a golden age when the people of God would accede to total poverty in joy; there would be no more need of the Church: humanity, composed wholly of monks and saints, would form a new purified church of the spirit. These writings had circulated everywhere and many men began to look upon Saint Francis as the precursor of such days of light. In the university, the Franciscan theologian, Gerard of Borgo San Donnino, commented on the works of Joachim. Opposing him, another professor, William of Saint-Amour, drew up a treatise shortly after 1250 entitled *The Perils of the New Age,* condemning the mendicants, the rivals of lay scholars, as pseudo prophets. And thereby aiming at the pope, their protector.

What William of Saint-Amour actually expressed was the reaction of a modern world chafing at the bit. Those reactions were twofold. In the first place there was general resentment at the tyranny of the Roman monarchy and all who were in its service. The papacy wished to rule the world and keep it beneath its rod. It had already added a second coronet to its tiara, that of the kings of the earth, "as a mark of empire," and laid claims to supremacy over the whole of the West as the heir of Constantine the Great. Byzantium had been conquered and was occupied by Latin knights. The emperor, Frederick II, had been defeated by the pope. On his death in 1250, the Roman Curia appointed no successor, leaving a yawning interregnum. Its intention was to remain alone at the head of the world. The unlimited power it assumed over the whole of Christendom was required, it said, by the danger of heresy: and it was against heresy that Pope Innocent IV authorized the inquisitors to use torture in 1252. But it was plain that repression had done its work. Montségur had fallen. No avowed Albigensian was to be found. So what was the purpose of such a concentration of authority round the Holy See? It was solely concerned with temporal interests and with satisfying the avidity of the cardinals. Rome had succumbed to the earthly temptations condemned by Saint Bernard. It had become the handmaid of Mammon. Rome, clearly, was the great whore of Revelation.

> Ah, Constantine, of how much ill was mother,
> not your conversion, but that dowry
> which the first rich Father took from you!
> [Dante, *Inferno* 19:115–17]

The indictment of papal tyranny, expressed in the dream of a Holy Spirit which would invade the world and render the priesthood meaningless, lay at the heart of the prophesies of Joachim of Fiore. In 1252 the reading of the *Evangelium eternum* [Eternal Gospel] was banned in Paris by the Holy See. Yet opposing Rome in the south of Christendom, in the areas wrested from Albigensianism, but where the seeds of the spirit of poverty had not altogether died out, an insurgent section of the Franciscan order preached the utter destitution of the Poverello and the freedom of the spirit. At Hyères, on his return from the crusades, Saint Louis had heard a mendicant friar vituperate against all the ecclesiastics who basked in the lap of luxury at the royal court; Joinville, also in the audience, could not brook the papists either—though for other reasons, because they reproached him with his fine array, because they were hypocrites, and because the bishop's agents extended their right to administer justice on his own estate, and at his expense. The main resistance to the Roman Church, in fact, was asserted within the kingdoms, within the states which had grown stronger and were in the process of splitting up Europe. Like the Italian communes, like thirteenth-century Rome, the city of God found itself parceled out among closed hostile abodes, in fortresses whence each power kept watch on its rivals and made ready for attack. The time of the great wars was at hand. The unity of the seamless tunicle, which the symbolism of the cathedral had celebrated in the crowned Virgin, seemed a myth, and heavenly Jerusalem merely a hope, a regret, a yearning—no longer a part of experience. The reality of 1250 was the secular state and its young army of officials, eager to defend the prerogatives of a master whose authority made the mark of their own prestige. The audacity of William of Colonna, who soon slapped a pope in the face in the name of the king of France, could be felt brewing among the servants of the princes. By the mid-thirteenth century all sovereigns claimed to be masters in their own houses and scoffed at the temporal pretentions of the Roman See. Even Saint Louis, prepared to serve Christ but not the bishop of Rome, protected Frederick II and sided with his own vassals against the trespassings of the Church.

The resistance the modern world put up to ecclesiastical constraints was due to the steady growth which sustained the West and to the wave of prosperity which was still gathering momentum. The contradictions of feudal society became keener. For the poor there was no way out of despair, while the happy few rebelled against the morality of the priests, designed to rob them of their pleasures on this earth. Messianic images, the obscure hope of a golden age which would restore the children of God in the equality of the first days of creation, fired the imagination of the exploited masses, of the workers on the outskirts of the towns—where heresy, persecuted, found a final refuge—the drapers, the fullers, the dyers, the "blue nails" in the Flemish cities who organized the first strikes in history in 1280, and roused a famished proletariat in the wilds of the country, causing sudden gatherings here and there around a rebel monk or a seer in the guise of an archangel. Groups of men set out blindly in quest of the Savior, looting the granaries of the Church as they passed. Such were the *Pastoureaux* in 1251; streaming over the fields of the Ile-de-France behind a preacher called the Master of Hungary, wishing to wrest good King Saint Louis from the grip of the infidel who held him captive. In the eyes of those errant cohorts, spurred on by poverty, both the pope and the bishops who blessed their persecutors, who stimulated knighthood to drown their rising in blood and to thwart their impulsive hopes, bore the features of the Antichrist. Whereas for the nobles, pope, bishops, and mendicant friars were downright nuisances: people who claimed to deprive them of the riches God had bestowed on well-born men, promising the uncertain joys of the afterlife in return. In the most delightful of the romances written at that time, young Aucassin is afraid of being bored in paradise where there may be no pleasures other than the litanies of the priests; if fair ladies must betake themselves to hell, he would prefer to go there too. Such were the restive forces developing in the new age.

Another dream collapsed: that of the imminent conquest of the universe, at last wholly united in the Christian faith. It was a dream which had enticed Europe since its first successes against Islam: but now came the rude awakening. That disillusionment may have been responsible for an insidious uneasiness which made the serene precepts of the cathedral images of creation appear derisory. Jerusalem, on which the entire West had riveted its hopes, had slipped from the grasp of the knights of Christ. The crusaders of 1190 had made a vain attempt to reconquer the Holy Sepulcher. Throughout the long siege of Saint John of Acre, they had grown accustomed to meeting paladins worthy of respect among the Saracens as well. They had subsequently returned a sorry sight, sick, empty-handed, and had then set out once more, but this time to plunder Christian provinces, the region of Narbonne, or else, guided by the merchants of Italy, Byzantium. Even Saint

Louis had been taken prisoner and had had to pay a ransom. He had been unable to lead his pilgrimage to Christ's tomb. In 1261 the partisans of the schism expelled the Franks from Constantinople. And in 1270, when Saint Louis wished to lead his vassals into the Holy Land again, "in my opinion," said Joinville, who refused to follow him, "all those who counseled the king to undertake the journey committed a deadly sin." The king, the model of chivalry, was in fact to meet his death in the failure of that fruitless venture. Many Latins, colonists, bishops, and monks, remained in the Levant and generations of knights were still to dream of crusades. But the blithe ardor was past. The hope of one day seeing all the nations of the world assembled in common expectation round the Holy Sepulcher was dead. Western armies could no longer advance. They were checked by superior forces, hounded from their outposts. Europe itself was threatened. It felt the entire weight of Asia and was beginning to realize its vastness. It perceived the vigorous impulses surging forth again, not unlike those which had proved a match for the Roman Empire. The Mongol hordes poured out from the heart of the steppes. In 1241 and 1243, Christians in Poland and Hungary had had to fight against those assaillants with their strange-looking faces. In their terror they had identified them as the peoples of Gog and Magog, the horsemen of Revelation, the harbingers of the end of time.

Churchmen, consequently, also became aware that the region won over to Christianity was but a small section of the universe and that it was no longer legitimate to believe in a near triumph of Christendom capable at last of absorbing the whole world in continuous advance. The dissemination of knowledge and the strides made in the cultural sphere had opened their eyes and compelled them to face facts: the world was infinitely larger, more various, and less docile than it had seemed to their forefathers; it was full of men who had not received the word of God, who refused to hear it, and who would not be easily conquered by arms. In Europe, the days of the holy war were over. The days of explorers, traders, and missionaries had begun. After all, why persist in struggling against all those infidels, those expert warriors, when it was more advantageous to negotiate and attempt to insinuate oneself in those invincible kingdoms by business transactions and peaceful preaching? In 1271 Marco Polo set out along the silk route after having studied its various stages from the accounts of the Venetian merchants, his compatriots, and the tales of the mendicant friars. The new vitality of the Italian traders superseded the old vitality of the knights of France. Moreover, reading of the Gospel brought out more plainly every day all that was barbarous and, ultimately anti-Christian, in the wish to exterminate misbelievers, or even to force them into baptism by the sword as in the days of Charlemagne. They needed to be talked to, to be set living examples of Jesus. The prelates laid down Turpin's helmet. Many wore Franciscan homespun. And at Damiette, Saint Francis himself had been able to see that the crusading army was no nobler than that of its adversaries and just as in want of conversion. With a handful of the Minorite brothers he had flung himself between the two camps and the sultan had authorized him to preach the Gospel in his land, to no immediate avail. But a new hope had been born. It appeared that Nestorian communities were still to be found in the little-known regions of Asia ruled by the Tartar khans. The Tartars had left these peoples in peace and would therefore presumably be easier to win over to the true faith than the Muslims, the common enemy. From then on the Mongols seemed like good savages. No longer the scourge presaging the fire of God, but possible allies who would enable Islam to be taken from the rear. The Minorites ventured forth in the attempt. Saint Louis dispatched to the Asiatic court "a chapel of scarlet cloth, and to attract them to our belief, had images carved which portrayed the Annunciation of the Angel, the Nativity, the Baptism received by God, the whole of the Passion, the Ascension and the advent of the Holy Spirit. He added chalices, books, all that was required to perform mass, and two preachers to sing it to them." To engage unbelief, Europe no longer sent out men in arms, but its best preachers, the ceremonial they had learned to give to their sermons, all the new imagery of the cathedrals. Yet it had to be admitted that these spiritual weapons were hardly more successful than the others: Christendom would remain only one part of the world.

After 1250, when the Christian West was being made aware of its relativity in space, it also discovered the relativity of Christian history. Up to then, time had offered a homogeneous whole in which by divine example past and future were inseparable from the present and entertained mystic relations with it. The creation and the end of the world merged, in relation to eternity, mingling with actual experience. This conception of duration had been expressed by Saint Augustine and Dionysius the Areopagite. On it rested Suger's concordances, the biblical examples of Peter le Mangeur, and the entire symbolical structure in which cathedral art reduced time to the cosmic whirling of the rose windows. Past events did not explain the present, they prefigured it while completing it. By the second half of the thirteenth century, however, fissures had appeared to undermine that idea. Humbert of Romans, the master-general of the Dominicans, was ordered by the pope to reflect on the history of the Greek schism. A concilium, which would try to unify the two separate Churches, was being prepared. The discussions would be based on historical fact. The attempt was new. In the short *Treatise in Three Parts* he wrote in 1273, Humbert endeavored to find reasons for the events of his day, but reasons which were no longer solely supernal. He therefore refrained from applying his study to the mystic relations which could make historical evidence agree with the texts in Revelation: he did his utmost to discern the true relations among the actual facts and to see where they were connected with the changes perceptible in their material and psychological environment. Humbert's attitude toward history contrasted radically with that of someone like Joachim of Fiore: the age of the Holy Spirit was not to come, it had passed, and the present age was of the Church. This outlook was an even plainer indictment of the idea of duration fixed by exemplarity: history was infused with a constructive force, that very impulse which had spurred on cultural progress in the Ile-de-France and raised the cathedrals when Humbert was young. His book overflows with the optimism and the spirit of enterprise of the constructors and the mendicant Friars who left for the fight to face concrete realities, rejecting the dreamworld, learning Arabic to try at last to convert Islam. Yet its author was familiar with present experience, with failure and imperious venturing. He had lived among the counselors of Saint Louis for a long time. He had witnessed the return of the defeated king, his new ill-starred departure and his martyrdom, the fall of the emperor Frederick, then that of the Latin Empire of Constantinople. He dared to say that the Greeks were not heretics but estranged brothers and not the only ones responsible for the estrangement. He no longer believed in the unity of Christian history, nor in its necessity. He perceived it as contingent, relative, human.

Like all his learned contemporaries, Humbert was well aware that the oriental schism, Islam, and the immense pagan population of Asia, were not the only coherent groups outside Western Christendom. Arab and Greek thought compelled European intellectuals to convince themselves of the relativity of their theology. The discovery was overwhelming; and it too, doubtless in a more far-reaching manner, brought into question the world of the cathedrals. The papal prohibitions which had sought to ban from the universities all Aristotle's treatises on subjects other than logic, had been defied. Albertus Magnus freely commented on the *Natural Philosophy*. In 1252, the English community in the university of Paris widened its arts syllabus to include the reading of *De anima*. Even the Dominicans, who were established in the Byzantine bishoprics still obedient to Western Christendom, set about translating the whole of the *Metaphysics* directly from the Greek. Finally, after 1240, the even more corrosive interpretation of his commentator, Averroës, reached Paris. Of all the dangers inherent in the new age the greatest was perhaps the spell this system of thought exerted, in the small world of professional thinkers, on the men who furnished the intellectual models for works of art. It was a solid cogent entity which had to be accepted as such. It provided the key to the universe and its diversities, a clear and total explanation. Aristotle had first of all been regarded as a necessary instrument, the most effective of the weapons used in rational progress. He had served as a guide for exploring the mysteries of nature, he had helped to classify species and types, to order them, in short, to draw nearer to God. But, on closer acquaintance, his philosophy had to be recognized for what it really was, which is to say, anti-Christian. And

Averroës set forth in broad daylight the basic antinomy of dogma and the Aristotelian system, together with all the attractions the latter offered.

In Aristotle's thought there was no creation. From time immemorial minds had been activated by God, the prime mover of the celestial spheres. Neither matter nor the cosmos ever began. In Aristotle's thought, there was no such thing as free will. Neither individuals nor individual destiny existed, only a human species. Each body decayed, like all things, and died; reason survived—but a form of reason common to all, which once separated from the flesh, was lost in impersonality. Neither incarnation nor redemption had any meaning within that bleak abstract universe. But the fact remained—hence the concern—that it was a philosophy which commanded respect and possessed singular power. How could one hope to dissociate its elements, dismantle it, refute it? The logic with which the university had equipped Catholic dogma had admittedly overcome Albigensianism, but it could be no match for the philosophy of Aristotle, which rested on the very mechanisms that had governed the dialectics of the Christian masters from the first. They had borrowed its framework for their theology. How could it be confronted now? And it was doubtful whether they were capable of annexing it, of reconciling the Bible, Saint Augustine, and the movements of procession and return of Dionysius the Areopagite with such a closely coordinated and seemingly indestructible whole. Certainly the influence of Aristotle and Averroës affected an extremely narrow circle. But it shook the very point which was the pivot for all the promoters of cultural life. Young people, students at the faculty of arts, who threw themselves enthusiastically into studying it, were not to be restrained. After 1250 the enemy was no longer the perfect, but the Philosopher. The fight had to be steered in his direction. Once again the papacy took the lead and marshaled its militia, the mendicant orders. It had just condemned Joachim of Fiore. At the university it protected the Dominicans and the Franciscans against the attacks of William of Saint-Amour. In 1255 Alexander IV commissioned a refutation of Averroës from Albertus Magnus. Three years later, he gave the two main chairs of Parisian theology to Thomas Aquinas and Bonaventure, a preaching friar and a Minorite: two Italians.

Between 1250 and 1280, economic growth continued in Europe, but its course slowly shifted. Expansion had sprung from the country. The provinces best fitted for agricultural activities had consequently moved ahead. Leading the vanguard was the Ile-de-France. Then a deeper current had carried prosperity to the towns, rousing the slumbering cities in the same provinces. Urban centers continued to thrive in those areas throughout the second half of the century, but in northern France peasant conquests had reached their limit. The land was cleared no longer. Fields had stretched over all the fertile ground. They had even progressed too far, here and there, at the expense of the thin soils which were rapidly exhausted. Disappointed farmers forsook them, leaving them to revert to scrub. A recession set in. Technical improvements came to a halt. On the lands which had been tilled for too long already, production sometimes began to drop. Yet the demographic rise showed no signs of abating. In the villages it swelled the numbers of the landless peasantry who did not know where to look for employment and accepted the lowest wages, whereas the great landlords benefited, recruiting hands at the least cost, selling their corn without difficulty and amassing wealth. On the other hand, many workers were wretched and hungry. The overpopulation was responsible for all the anxieties, the flares of revolt, the abortive marches, and the children's crusades which periodically reiterated the hopeless venture of the *Pastoureaux*. In the regions where Gothic art had originated, there was an increasingly marked contrast between the country, once again a prey to famine, epidemics, and terror, and the town, locked within its walls, ever active, perhaps even more so than before, where men ate their fill and drank wine, and where money flowed in. Late thirteenth-century fortunes were middle-class. They were the fortunes of the moneylenders, of the patricians who had bought the estates of spendthrift nobles, who had the farmers, their debtors, in a stranglehold and who attracted the sons of the peasantry into the city workshops so as to obtain cheaper labor. In Paris, at the fairs in Champagne, in the draper towns of Flanders, all businessmen grew rich. The most successful strove to emerge from their cultural ignorance. Some married young ladies of high birth with no dowries. They endeavored to copy the manners of the knights and many encouraged the poets in their turn. It was to entertain the bankers of Arras that the songsters and theatrical producers invented comedy. In France, however, at the end of the thirteenth century, the middle classes were still basically country bumpkins. This was not so in Italy, the true land of the towns.

For a long time the great traders of the north had been purchasing their most alluring merchandise, which brought the best profits, from across the Alps: spices, pepper, and indigo, and precious cloths which they offered to illustrious princesses and to archbishops, silks from Lucca, figured linen from Florence. But Italy above all brought them money. The economic strength of French towns was based on a region where gold remained scarce, secured in church treasures to a very great extent, in altar ornamentation, in countless reliquaries, and in the gleaming decorations the great lords chose for their personal attire. Trade lacked means of payment: the Italians provided it. Dealers from Asti and Piacenza set up at the fairs and erected their stands in the marketplace, exchanging money and agreeing to lend at interest. These foreigners aroused suspicion and envy. They were hated as much as the Jews. But the prince protected them because they were his creditors. In Paris, the Lombards had their street near the Grève, whence they controlled the royal finances and the entire movement of capital within the city.

And once pieces of gold began to be minted in Europe again, toward the middle of the century, most of them came from the workships of Genoa and Florence.

The monetary preeminence of Italian towns may be regarded as the distant fruit of the Crusades. Few knights had set out from that part of the world, but the expeditions had excited the spirit of enterprise of all seafaring adventurers, luring their vessels to the shores of the eastern Mediterranean, to the flourishing ports and the bazaars filled with tempting wares. In the eleventh century, as soon as the piety of the Christians of the West had turned toward Jerusalem, the maritime cities of Italy had begun building ships to carry the first parties of pilgrims to the tomb of Christ. The passengers paid for their fare. They had sold their estates to the monasteries or had left them in pawn and thus amassed a little money. Part of it went to the boatmen and was thus put into the first business transactions. Then came the crusade. Its large armies reached the Holy Land by road, but the fleets of Pisa and Genoa aided in conquering Palestine, staunchly supporting the efforts of the knights of Christ. In the thirteenth century most knights embarked in Pisa, Venice, Genoa, on ships ever improved and found in ever increasing number thanks to prosperous trading. This meant fresh profits for shipowners and seamen. The princes who led the Christian expeditions placed fortunes in their hands, granting trading counters and customs exemption in the merchant centers won over to Christianity. If they were unable to acquit themselves otherwise, they did services during the voyage. The finest stroke was that of the Venetians who, wishing to protect their commercial privileges, succeeded in diverting a whole crusade which, in 1204, took Byzantium for them, the treasure house of the world.

All the local townspeople entrusted their capital to the sailors to be traded in the Levantine ports, for speculation on exchange rates, to bring back goods which could be sold at very high prices at the fairs in France. The pope forbade commerce with the infidel. The merchants paid no heed. Many perished at sea, or from fever, but the others collected pieces of silver and sent their partners to place them in banks across the mountains. By the mid-thirteenth century Genoa had strengthened its fleet and its ships sailed into new waters; in 1251 one of them carried 200 passenges and 250 tons of goods to Tunis; in 1277 another sailed around Spain for the first time and reached the ports of Flanders. This inaugurated the new itinerary later to ruin the fairs of Champagne and divert certain trading routes that still guaranteed the prosperity of a few regions in France. That trend, which had been gaining ground for two centuries, carried Italian businessmen to the head of world economy in 1250, imperceptibly placing the levers of cultural creativeness in their hands. Although the tradition which had brought intellectual and artistic inspiration from Greece to Rome and then from Rome to Paris was still acclaimed on all sides, a new transference was taking place, confusedly and as yet not advancing very far. The university of Paris was to hold sway for many years more and there was no contemporary Italian monument that could compare with Notre-Dame of Reims. Yet the great saint of the thirteenth century was no longer Louis, king of France. He was the son of a merchant of Assisi.

In the cities of Italy, the strides made in business had allowed a new society to emerge. The townspeople had long since succeeded in reducing the urban clergy to purely liturgical duties and had freed themselves from the power of the barons. Whereas municipal authority in France was represented solely by ordinary citizens, in Italy it remained aristocratic. In the early stages the nobles had been predominant, but by the thirteenth century the active sector of the population in the most prosperous cities had begun to compete for power and to supplant them. At all events, the barriers between knighthood and commonalty were far lower there than anywhere else. And they dropped still further. Many nobles, whether compelled or not, joined commercial companies and took part in trading and banking, while middle-class patricians adopted their way of life, built towers, bore arms, and solicited acceptance through courtly jousts. It was as a knight that Francis of Assisi had spent his youth. In Italy in 1200, at the summit of city society, businessmen found adornment in aristocratic values.

Such an association engendered a cultural life which began to show its singularity in 1250. It had first found expression in the yearning for poverty, which initially deviated into heresy then enthusiastically followed the footsteps of Saint Francis. In the Italian communes the clergy were still held in suspicion. Most of the episcopal schools vegetated. Both nobility and commoners turned naturally toward the enlightened hermits who praised God in the grottoes of the *contado* or toward the mendicant friars. The worship professed in the cities was ardent but lyrical, filled with affectionate outpourings. Intellectual activities developed outside the Church, taking the form of practical studies, such as law, which provided training as a judge, or arithmetic, useful in conducting business. In the Mediterranean ports, merchants' sons learned Arabic. Some knew it well enough to read a few treatises on arithmetic. In 1202, the Pisan, Leonardo Fibonacci, revealed the entire corpus of Islamic algebra in his *Liber abaci*. But it was the accountants rather than the builders of churches who put these mathematical processes to use. The new outlook was slow in acquiring artistic forms of its own.

Money worked in business. When loaned to the king of France and his bishops, it helped to construct the cathedrals beyond the mountains. Within the city itself little was invested in works of art. The accession of the merchants to municipal authority together with the power of evangelical trends restrained inclinations for luxury. Dante was soon to denounce the profligate elegance of the Florentines. But in actual fact, in Florence, as everywhere else in Europe, the externals of profane life were extremely sober. And there was scant imagination even in the ornamentation of the churches: Byzantine models guided the mosaicists and the painters; Romanesque models supplied the architects and the sculptors. The only vibrations which gradually relieved the general tone came from Franciscan saintliness. Not, as yet, from ancient Rome. Jurists had begun to discover Roman maxims but its poets were scarcely read and its artistic achievements lay buried beneath cultural deposits which had progressively masked them since the end of the Empire and were being thickened by the renewed contacts with the East. The pope had studied at the school of Paris. He regarded the patterns of French art as the most apt for celebrating his power and the power of the Church. These were the forms he propagated, since classical art possessed the drawback of enhancing the secular power of the emperors, his rivals. Consequently, the first resurgence of Roman forms did not occur in the cities of Lombardy or Tuscany or even in Rome, but in that part of Italy where imperial rule had become well established, before eventually foundering beneath papal blows, in the kingdom of Sicily.

A strange world. Could it still be called Italy? Even Latin? It lay beyond the boundary that had separated the Greek and the Latin sectors in antiquity and had not been noticeably dislodged despite all the upheavals of the Dark Ages. In 1250, Sicily, Calabria, Puglia, and Campania, at the crossroads of the new sea routes, were still open to the three cultural traditions of the Mediterranean, Hellenic, and Arab as much as that of Western Christendom. Byzantium had long dominated that part of the world. Islam had partly colonized it. Then, in the mid-eleventh century, mercenaries from Normandy had succeeded in making themselves its masters. They founded their rule on the institutions of vassalage and feudalism they were familiar with and on royal magistracy. They safeguarded the tax system and all the prerogatives and regulations at the basis of the despotisms they replaced, and so doing built up the most powerful monarchy in Europe. They welcomed Latin priests and monks to their court and became the faithful allies of the pope. Yet, under their harsh taskmasters, the populations of that land went on living in their own way, preserving their language and their traditions. Their kings favored the troubadours. But Greek and Arabic were spoken and written at their court. The precepts of Islamic physicians and astrologers were readily adopted. Palermo far more than Ratisbon, but also far more than Antioch, whose princes were Sicilian, far more than the outposts set up by Genoa on the farther banks of the Pontus, more than Venice so closely bound to Byzantium, even more than Toledo, was a meeting place where Western curiosity could drink its fill. It no longer consisted in a few colonies here and there, established by the sword, girt with hostility, a few dens for youthful adventurers, or even in privileged townships where victorious barons sought a brief spell of repose from plunder. Palermo, the capital of a state formed in antiquity, with solid foundations and extremely vast, gazed peacefully on the horizons bounded by the sea. The alms donated by its sovereigns had enriched Cluny. The kings of Europe stayed there on their way back from the Holy Land, at home among men of their own faith whose conversation they understood. Yet it was the East. Its princesses, new Theodoras, with their silks and perfumes, walked in the gardens beneath the orange trees. This East was truly vanquished, possessed, but in no way robbed of its ornamental prestige. The court officials translated Hippocrates and Ptolemy into Latin and when Romanesque cloisters were built for the Benedictines in the twelfth century, their arches were at once clad in luxuriant rare vegetation, vanishing beneath chiselled medersas and the sparkle of mosaics.

At the beginning of the thirteenth century, it came about that by a chance alliance, Frederick Barbarossa was made the grandfather of the very young king of Sicily, and that the pope set him on Caesar's throne. Frederick II of Hohenstaufen was not German. It was he who embodied the return of the Roman Empire to the Mediterranean. Opposite Saint Louis, his contemporary, his cousin, his ally, he showed a totally different visage, as strange as his kingdom. Nervous, sickly—"one wouldn't have given two cents for him as a slave"—eyes bright with intelligence: an upsetting man. A mortal enemy of the Holy See, excommunicated on several occasions—but what did excommunication mean in those days?—he alone of all the Christian kings succeeded in reopening the pilgrim road to Nazareth and Jerusalem. *Stupor mundi,* amazement of the world, but also *immutator admirabilis,* the admirable master who kept the universe under divine order. A thousand startling tales were told about him in his lifetime. For the Guelphs he was the Antichrist, the beast rising up "out of the sea . . . and upon his heads the name of blasphemy . . . like unto a leopard, and his feet were as the feet of a bear, and his mouth as the mouth of a lion." Whereas the Ghibellines saw him as the emperor of the end of time: one senses Dante's sorrow at being obliged after all to include him in his *Inferno.* His figure soon merged with that of Frederick Barbarossa, whose body had been borne away forever on the waters of an Eastern river. He died defeated like Siegfried, and was to become the old man of the Kyffhäuser who would one day be roused from his sleep and whose return would herald the awakening of the Empire. Even historians find it hard to rid themselves of these myths. The Florentine Villani, writing a hundred years after the emperor's death, was already a prey to an ambiguous legend:

> A man of utmost worth and valor, of universal learning and wisdom, he knew Latin, our common tongue, German, French, Greek, and Saracen; he was noble, generous, skilled in arms, and infinitely feared; he was dissolute at all events, keeping many concubines and

> mamelukes as the Saracens do; he wished to taste all the pleasures of the flesh and led an Epicurean life, behaving as if there were none other. He and his sons reigned in great worldly glory, but for their sins at last they came to a bad end and his line was extinguished.

Frederick II admittedly was fond of women, and made free with them—but so did all the princes of his time, except Saint Louis. Admittedly he put out the eyes of his chancellor: but it was not cruelty, just mere application, customary in those parts, of a torture borrowed from Byzantium. A Moorish guard kept garrison in his fortress at Lucera; he counted the sultan of Egypt among his friends, exchanging presents and knighting the infidel ambassadors. Does that entitle one to speak of unbelief, or even skepticism? His faith in Christ was unquestionable. There was no smile on his face when he led the crusade. But he had an enquiring mind and liked to be told who was the God the Jews and of the Muslims. Just as one day he asked to meet Francis of Assisi. Even so, he persecuted the heretics, upheld the inquisition more energetically than any other and when dying donned the Cistercian frock. Contrasts, generosity of spirit accepting the world in all its diversity, anything but easy to understand for singleminded thirteenth-century ecclesiastics: a Sicilian.

What is important first of all is that he loved science. But a different type of science from that of the theologians of Paris. A science which came from Aristotle, but also from other books, translated from Greek and Arabic at the emperor's expense. And from experience. Frederick himself wrote a *Treatise on Hunting* in an endeavor to explain what he had observed about animals. While a popular rumor relates that he once put a man to death in a hermetically sealed jar for no other reason than to find out what might become of the human soul. Southern Italy made up a very special province of scientific activity. By virtue of its prelates and its inquisitors, it belonged to the Catholic world: its jurists, who had studied at the university of Bologna, taught it the methods of scholastic reasoning. Yet Euclid, Averroës, all the knowledge of Islam and Greece, were not on alien soil; their sources were native. The king presided at debates conducted, as in Oxford or Paris, according to the strict rules of dialectical argumentation, with challenge and answer, but the subjects discussed were algebra, medicine, and astrology. Restless, concerned with destiny, Frederick II, like the sultans, questioned soothsayers, alchemists, casters of horoscopes, necromancers, delving into oriental night in the hope that the secrets of occultism might allay his fears. Like the emirs, he was passionately interested in the properties of things and beings. Peter of Eboli composed a poem for him on the waters of Pozzuoli and their virtues; his shoeing smith wrote a treatise of farriery; his astrologer brought back the *Astronomy* of al-Bitruji and the *Zoology* of Aristotle from Toledo.

The emperor and the scholars at his court applied the same deliberate lucidity to the observation of natural phenomena as the Parisian masters. But they were less bound by the desire to arrive at God as a conclusion to their analysis of the created world; and their physics was not intended to merge with theology. It remained autonomous and profane. That these men believed in the divinity of Christ and the power of the sacraments of the Church was beyond doubt. They regarded Aristotle, Averroës, and all the Saracen and Jewish masters who taught them, cared for their bodies, scrutinized their stars, as miscreants. But their religion, like that of the Tuscan cities, preserved its lyrical note. It did not wholly command their intellectual exercise or their curiosity about the mysteries of the visible world. Throughout the period when Chartres and Reims were being built, the south of Italy kept aloof from the dogmatic syntheses of the cathedral of France. Alive to what was real, it strove to discern the hidden forces governing plant life, the habits of animals, and the movement of the stars—but freely, as in the schools of Islam, possibly because its Christianity was less sensitive to the values of incarnation, because it attributed to its God the transcendence of Allah, an omnipotence which raised him incommensurably above nature. At all events it was in the circles of Frederick II that a natural science distinct from divine science developed for the first time in the Christian world. And there that the feeling for the concrete, reflected in the art of Italian cities a century and a half later, was shaped. That realism, totally different from the realism of the Gothic cathedrals, was not, as has been repeated all too often, the product of a middle-class mind but of the favors of a prince renowned throughout the courts of Europe for having lived like a sultan.

No monarch except Saint Louis commissioned so many works of art at that time. After becoming sole king of Germany in 1218, then emperor two years later, Frederick II ordered the artists in his service to break away from the Byzantine traditions of his Palermitan ancestors. He was a Swabian by his father's line and could rely for support on the order of the Teutonic Knights. He dreamed of an imperial art and consequently refrained from ordering adaptations of the art of France, which celebrated the glory of the Capetian kings and had been taken up by the papal Church. The forms proposed to him had just made their appearance on imperial territory, at Lucca and Modena. Their remote roots thrust deep into the forests of Ottonian Germany. In the early days of his reign, the Lombard style completed its conquest of southern Italy: zoomorphic capitals related to those of Parma were carved for the palatine basilica of Altamura; in Bitonto, the emperor himself was portrayed as a donor, with the features of a Romanesque idol. But the young ruler gradually formed a clearer idea of the values conferred on him by his coronation in 1220. All about him, men lauded the power of "Caesar, the admirable light of the world." He moved among jurists who professed the maxims of Justinian. His troops crushed the militia of the Lombard cities in league against him: he had the trophies of his victory borne triumphantly to the capitol. From then on he was expected to live up to his emblems. The art of the bishops of Tuscany and Emilia could not adequately render the meaning of his sovereignty for long. He had expelled the papacy from Rome; his rule stood out against the liturgy, asserting itself as a military and civil force. After 1233 he built castles, symbols of his majesty, not churches. Constructed on an octagonal plan like the Carolingian chapel of Aachen, Castel del Monte represents the imperial crown, or rather the heavenly Jerusalem. But its eight walls, the perfect image of eternity according to the mystics of numbers, were not arranged as an environment for psalms chanted by the chapter, or to house relics. They were designed to display on all sides the earthly might of the Christian Caesar, the true lieutenant of God in this world. And, decorating the fortress, the careful elegance of Champagne was everywhere substituted for Romanesque reverie. Lastly, at the very moment when King Saint Louis was about to raise the Sainte Chapelle to the glory of the Christ of Gothic coronations, Frederick II had a statue of himself erected in Capua. The statue of Augustus. This time it was ancient Rome that emerged victorious from the depths of the ages.

In 1250 the great emperor died and the reality of the Empire with him. To his contemporaries his fall looked like one of the most conclusive signs of the advent of a new world. The descendants of Frederick II died too. Yet Charles of Anjou, the brother of Saint Louis, hoisted to victory by the papacy and established in the kingdom of Sicily in their stead, did not sweep away the cultural flowering, of which the seeds had been planted by the Hohenstaufens and had fructified because of the dynamic progress of Italy. The royal prince embraced all the ambitions of his predecessors, the Norman kings of Palermo, and their dreams of conquest on the three fronts of the Mediterranean. He did not dismiss the astrologers, physicians, and translators from his court. Peter of Maricourt, the "master of experiments," made astrolabes for him and his stone statue was soon to be seen imparting the ponderous majesty of its Roman models. He wished to appear as a sage, a profane sage, like the king of Castile, Alfonso the Wise, across the sea, already writing *On the Knowledge of Astronomy*. Under the reign of Charles of Anjou, the sculptors of Campania continued to steal their images of civil awe from classical sarcophagi, readily admired and copied. In the communes of central Italy such models began to be regarded as better attuned to the new awareness than Romanesque or Byzantine symbols and the patterns offered by the art of France. The decoration of Ameins was barely completed when Nicola Pisano began work on the pulpit of Pisa. Amid the rising dangers, the art of the new age took shape at the southern tip of Europe on the ground prepared by Frederick II.

After the middle of the century, the artists who built the French cathedrals slowly lost their genius for invention. They applied schemes which were the acme of perfection, more and more logical, better and better distributed, flooding the sanctuary with light, but imperceptibly emptied of their spiritual content. The reasons for the exhaustion are manifold. It was partly the result of the new direction taken by research in the centers of learning. The university sacrificed everything to improving the mechanisms of dialectics, allowing genuine cultural life to run dry. Its graduates were rarely more than skilled technicians in the science of reasoning. The cold syllogism had invaded theology and had its consequent repercussions on religious art. Furthermore, although the exclusive purpose of great art was still to celebrate the glory of God, the prelates themselves were no longer so closely associated in its creation. Their numbers were increasing and they were chosen from the mendicant orders. Many were of humble stock. "Fils de vilain et de vilaine" [son of villeins]: Joinville thus upbraided the Franciscan, Robert of Sorbon, who had picked a quarrel with him, and proceeded to reproach him with having betrayed the simplicity of his forefathers. Some of these ecclesiastics who attained the status of great lords through the episcopate found it hard to resist the attractions of luxury in fact. They let themselves be dazzled: what they most appreciated in a church building was polished rendering, effect, and skilled construction. The best of them, those who sincerely lived in a spirit of poverty, were more concerned with preaching than with building, and the new paths they discovered through meditation were those of humility, of worship from the heart. This led to a general indifference towards monumental forms. Saint Bonaventure did not undertake the construction of cathedrals. He left that to the king of France, who was nevertheless regarded as a model of saintliness at that time, although not himself a theologian. Powers over creative activities were gradually transferred to specialists, to the masters of works, whose fortunes were about to begin.

These men now raised themselves far above the simple craftsmen they had to direct. They no longer carted the stones. They even ceased hewing them with their own hands. They wielded the compass. They presented to the canons minute parchment drawings of the elevation of the future building. "Some work with words," said a preacher at that time. "In these great constructions there is usually a principal master who fashions by words alone and never or rarely puts his hand to them. Standing by with rule and compass, they order the stonemasons: 'Just cut here.' They do no work, yet they receive the highest wages." These men had a remarkable knowledge of their craft. They were on familiar terms with the doctors of theology, their peers, sharing their knowledge of numbers and dialectical prescriptions. But they were not priests. They did not consecrate the body of Christ. They had not spent hours meditating on the word of God, scrutinizing its darker passages. They accomplished, but were not, like Suger or Maurice of Sully, directly inspired by the contemplation of divine hierarchies. Problems of dynamics and statics preoccupied them more. While they were still imaginative, they proceeded like virtuosos, not mystics. Their victories consisted in mastering the resistance of the material, not in elucidating mysteries. Those whose minds had a logical bent committed their success to geometrical rigor. The most sensitive among them strove for grace, instead of truth.

At Saint-Denis, toward 1250, the work of the great Peter of Montreuil consisted in refinement rather than innovation. He was in possession of a technique which allowed him to reduce the building to its stone frame, distributing the light for the pleasure of the eye. The two rose windows in the transept, one converging toward the center, the other contrasting its radiant clarity, employ all the resources of perfect mathematics to demonstrate the dual movement of procession and return which the theology of Saint Thomas Aquinas had borrowed from Dionysius the Areopagite. But the equilibrium between the structural elements and the ornamental decor is gone. The architect has masked the separate functions of the masses by emphasizing their elegance. Similarly, although the sculptures in the Sainte Chapelle have harmonious proportions, they lack a soul, as if all the spirituality had evaporated from the statues of Reims. And even at Reims, Gaucher, the last of the great masters of works, neglected the strict application of doctrinal teaching initially planned in his arrangement of the great carvings in the portal. He upset the intelligible order of the theologians, no longer feeling its necessity, giving priority to the position which best enhanced the visual values of the statues rather than conveyed their meaning. There are no signs that the canons made any protest at this choice. They, too, were becoming sensitive to the charms of gracefulness. Artists henceforth sought to please. The body of the Synagogue already rested its whole weight on one leg and the hip stance which gradually led the virgins and the saints into courtly dance was introduced. The same inflections appeared in the stained glass windows and on the pages of illuminated manuscripts, in the modulations of a line traced for the sheer joy of the eye. The congregation and the clergy who guided it toward salvation began to be aware that the living God and his Mother were beautiful.

The shift toward aestheticism reflected the crisis of theological thought in Paris and all the underlying forces responsible for it. Obeying the pope, Saint Thomas Aquinas and Saint Bonaventure led the fight against the new deviations. Aquinas based his arguments on reasoning. In disputation with Aristotle, he engaged the Philosopher and the Commentator in a dialectical tournament designed to unsaddle them. But his colleague from the Franciscan order assigned no more than a preliminary purpose to the instruments of logic: "Philosophical science is a way toward other sciences. Whoever wishes to halt there remains in darkness." Returning to Saint Augustine, he urged the distinction between the knowledge gained through science which only grasped appearances and that deeper knowledge, which could apprehend the glories of the world to come. His *Itinerary of the Mind toward God*—or rather *in God*—progressed from rung to rung, driven by the impulse of love. What was the point of reasoning against Aristotle? It was more salutary to advance in the contemplation of light. A last precept marked the limitations of intellectual striving: "In that contemplation, beware of thinking that you understand the incomprehensible." His approach was more attuned to the trends of the new age than that of Saint Thomas. It embraced the spontaneous upsurging of naïve souls who trusted in the illumination of the Holy Spirit to find God. It consequently triumphed over Thomism, and Bonaventure set about formally rejecting its premises in his *Lectures on the Gifts of the Holy Spirit.* In 1270, terrified at the daring of dialectics, heedful of the turmoil stirring the popular mind, Catholic theology deliberately set its course toward mysticism.

The Ile-de-France, however, the opulent Paris of Philip the Hardy, of university dialecticians and of the fine ladies of chivalry was not the land of choice for mysticism. Doubtless, that was why the forces which had thrust the towers of Laon, Chartres, and Reims up to the sky forsook the area and, in the second half of the thirteenth century, traveled eastwards, toward the Rhine valley, toward the region where small mystic communities of Beguins, men and women, were beginning to flourish. By then commercial progress had reached Germany, streaking it with brisk trading routes. Towns sprang up on all sides; forests were razed in order to build them. Before 1250, Albertus Magnus had left Paris to teach in Cologne, the new center of learning he was to carry to fame, where he commented on Dionysius. In his wake, the Dominican friar, Ulrich of Strasbourg, developed the aspects which subordinated rational method to illumination, pushing a stage further along the way Meister Eckhart was soon to enter. Cathedral art was bequeathed to the Germania of the brothers of the Free Spirit and the Minnesängers. The last of the great Gothic constructions was begun in Strasbourg. The sculpture of Reims cast as far as Naumbourg to penetrate a world still shrouded in mists.

But the manner it inspired there tended to be expressionistic. Statues of princesses in the full bloom of their beauty were allowed to stand not very far from the scenes of the Passion of Jesus. On those forest lands, near the convents of visionary nuns, French art lost its limpidity. The monsters of the Romanesque bestiaries belonging to the old world of phantasms and uncontrollable powers enriched it, mingling with the convulsive or mannered forms Byzantine models had evoked in response to the German soul. In the churches of Thuringia and Franconia, Suger's aesthetics, stripped of its logician's framework, dissolved into a play of opacity and Marian tenderness. It adapted to the taste of pious men seeking spiritual tranquility in the outpourings of the heart.

It was precisely then that Paris proposed a new way, ever rational, but one which led to happiness on this earth. Its intellectuals eagerly claimed the right to philosophize and were encouraged to do so by the new mystic leanings of theology: since Christ, by his sacrifice, had come to save all men and since it was enough to surrender oneself to his love to accede to heavenly joys, why deny oneself the freedom of reflecting on profane matters in this life and why reject worldly pleasures? The lay professors at the faculty of arts took no part in theological discussions. Their task was to expound Aristotle. They commented on his work to very young pupils, many of whom aimed to pursue lay careers. They proclaimed that thinking was the token of human dignity. Thinking in utter freedom. The philosopher's condition was the noblest of all, it led to supreme good. After all, what was his assignment but to discover the laws of nature, in other words, true order? If nature was acknowledged as the instrument of God, the mirror of his mind, the work of his hands, how could it be bad? To glimpse its secret workings was to uncover the rules of a perfect life, in agreement with divine purpose. "Sin is inside man," wrote Boethius of Dacia, "but honest ways spring from natural order." If man endeavored to follow that order, he could be sure of pleasing God. What was more, he would live on this earth in harmony and joy. What the younger generation had just proposed was happiness.

Happiness made by man alone, happiness which could be won by intelligence. Dame Nature, his mistress, promised that those who served her would attain perfect beatitude here below. That was the moral of the second *Roman de la rose* written by Jean de Meung toward 1275 not far from the schools of Paris. He condemned the corruption threatening divine precepts from all quarters: the will for power, but also the sophistication of courtliness and the hypocritical preaching of the mendicant friars. He recalled the perfect order of the first ages of the world. "Formerly in the times of our first fathers and mothers, as testified in the writings of the ancients, men loved one another with fine loyal feelings, not through covetousness, or the desire for rapine, and happiness reigned throughout the world. The land was uncultivated, and was as God had arrayed it, and yet it gave sustenance to each." All was spoiled by deceit, pride, and falsehood.

These ideas had originated in Averroism. But they also proceeded very directly from the antiheretical propaganda proclaiming the rehabilitation of the created world in opposition to the Albigensians. They were rooted in the theology of creation developed in cathedral art. They also agreed with the naïve optimism of the early days of Franciscanism, which the Minorites abandoned in obedience to the pope. Lastly, they concorded with the simple beliefs in millenarianism, the expectations of the poor who had been led to understand that God had created all his children as equals. Parisian philosophy in 1270 bore every appearance of being a new stage in the progressive discovery of the incarnation, a major turning point at which clerical thought became desacralized and offered itself to profane society.

The proposition of material happiness, once rid of clerical constraints, was principally addressed (Jean de Meung had written his book in courtly language) to all knights in love with life, to their ladies to those who had refused to accompany Saint Louis on his last crusade There was no pilgrimage in those days and no one left his country to explore savage lands." It was the joy of courtly poetry to a different tune. It was an invitation to gaze upon the beauty of all creatures and to rejoice in a simple life. It had already found expression in the childlike laughter of the Chosen of Bamberg, in the irony of Rutebeuf, and in the fresh melodies composed by Adam de la Halle, less elaborate, more natural and direct than the scholastic polyphony of Pérotin the Great. Saint Louis had not been insensitive to it in the carefree days of his youth. The smiling anticlericalism of the nobles of the court of France was swept along on its impetus together with a whole body of young people, sane and free, for whom the false prophets, the harbingers of the end of time, were not the dialecticians of the universities or the troubadours, but the sanctimonious papists and the friars whose objurgations to penitence hindered the return to an untrammeled golden age. It was echoed by the graces of the new sculpture. It brought forth the generous sap swelling the decorative plants of the last capitals and allowing them to blossom in the sun. In response to its exhortations to happiness, the Resurrected Souls of Bourges displayed the gentleness of an adolescent body in the light of God. In Paris, it bore the hope of carnal beauty suffusing sacred cathedral art toward ultimate fulfillment.

Three centuries of continuous progress in the Ile-de-France had provided the mold for the philosophy of happiness. Businesslike Italy was ready to accept it. But in a land where ecclesiastical structures were less robust, there seemed a danger than Christendom might disintegrate altogether and open the way for ungodliness—the ungodliness already ascribed to Frederick II. Are we to believe Benvenuto Imola, who said "there were soon more than a hundred thousand nobles, men of high condition, who thought that paradise was only to be sought in this world, like Farinata degli Uberti and Epicurus"? In his *Inferno* Dante admittedly traversed the circle where he found:

> Epicurus with all his followers,
> who made the soul die with the body
> [*Inferno* 10:14–15]

and where Farinata disclosed:

> Here I lie with more than a thousand.
> Here within is the second Frederick.
> [10:118–19]

Yet it was in paradise that Dante Alighieri placed the "eternal light" of Siger of Brabant, the greatest of the Parisian philosophers, the distinguished leader of the new school. In his theory of universal orders, Dante arranged Church and state, grace and nature, theology and philosophy in two parallel yet distinct sequences, showing,

> how Nature takes her course
> from divine Intellect and from Its art;
> and if you note well your *Physics*,
> you will find, after not many pages,
> that your art, as far as it can,
> follows her, as the pupil does his master;
> so that your art is as it were grandchild of God.
> [*Inferno* 11:99–105]

The *Divine Comedy* may be regarded as a cathedral, the last. Dante based his work on what he had learned of scholastic theology from the Dominican preachers of Florence who had studied at the university of Paris. Like the great cathedrals of France, this poem leads in successive stages, according to the enlightened hierarchies of Dionysius the Areopagite and through the intercession of Saint Bernard, Saint Francis, and the Virgin, to the love which moves the stars. As a poetics of the incarnation, the art of the great cathedrals had wonderfully celebrated the body of Christ, in other words, the Church triumphant, the world itself. But at the dawn of the trecento, the processes which imperceptibly released European thought from the influence of the priests turned the men of the West away from immaterial things, guiding them along other routes toward other conquests. "Nature, the art of God." An art bound for happiness. Dante himself, and his first admirers, sped toward the new shores.

PART THREE

THE PALACE

1280–1420

During the fourteenth century, the signs of a retraction in the corpus of Western Christendom grew more acute. The crusading spirit was as vivid as ever, even obsessive. It lay at the center of Church policy and governed the conduct of all the knights. But slowly it drifted toward myth and nostalgia. Between the fall of Saint John of Acre, the last Frankish possession in the Holy Land, in 1291, and the rout of the crusaders at Nicopolis by the Turkish army invading the Balkans, in 1396, real events marked a gradual relinquishing of the eastern Mediterranean. By 1400, Byzantium was no more than a nervous, beleaguered fort, a kind of condemned outpost against the pressures of the infidel and Asia. If Europe retreated rather than spread after 1300 it was because the number of its inhabitants, which had been expanding continuously for at least three centuries, had begun to dwindle. The great plague of 1348–50 and the ensuing epidemics converted the regression into disaster. In the early fifteenth century the population in many European countries had shrunk to half the size of a hundred years before; countless fields lay fallow, thousands of villages stood deserted, and many urban districts, within enclosures grown too large, fell into decline. Added to that were the upheavals of war. The aggressive energy formerly expended abroad in victorious campaigning began to be felt at home. It caused uninterrupted conflict between states great and small, as they consolidated their influence and parceled out Christendom, vying for power. Everywhere, in the fields, around beseiged cities, was the sound of battle. Everywhere troops of mercenaries, *routes, condotte,* looting and laying waste. Everywhere brigands and fleecers, the professionals of war. It was during the fifty years framing the turn of the thirteenth century that the material history of civilization in Europe met with one of its great reversals. There have been two broad sweeps of development in European history, separated by a very long depression. The fourteenth century ushered in a stagnant phase which was to last until the approach of 1750.

Withdrawal, depopulation, and distress are inescapable facts but do not warrant the pessimism oversensitive authorities have extended to the history of ideas, beliefs, and artistic activities in Latin Christendom. At the cultural level the fourteenth century was anything but a period of contraction. The very degradation and disorder of practical life seem to have stimulated the onward march of creativity, in three main ways. First of all, by noticeably modifying the geography of prosperity, therefore by transplanting the seeds of intellectual and artisitic activity to the new areas.

Epidemics, chaotic production, and military turbulence had severely harmed several German regions, the kingdom of England, and, more cruelly than anywhere else, France, the former privileged focus of expansion. In Rhenish Germany, in Bohemia, in a few Iberian regions, in Lombardy above all, towns were growing, business thriving, and new interests and concerns beginning to take shape. As the navigators of Genoa, Cadiz, and Lisbon ventured farther and farther along the Atlantic routes, the direction of European trade was reversed toward the ocean, soon very largely to compensate for all the losses in the Mediterranean. And in some respects the mishaps of the fourteenth century and the dramatic demographic situation in particular were not debilitating factors at all. They favored the concentration of individual wealth and a general rise in living standards, and in that way provided the practical conditions for more active patronage and the diffusion of great works of art. In those times, troubled by a sequence of calamities, with the population dropping by fits and starts, rich men no longer seemed so few and far between. Wealth certainly had increased during the serene prosperity of the thirteenth century, but not as quickly as the number of men. Many customs and tastes, once reserved for the highest aristocracy, therefore gradually filtered through to the ever-widening lower social strata, whether it was a matter of drinking wine, of wearing underclothes, or even of using books, of adorning one's home or one's tomb, of comprehending the meaning of an image or a sermon, of commissioning an artist. Thus, despite the decline in production and the standstill in trade, the propensity toward luxury, instead of slackening, became exacerbated. Last but not least, the failing material structures caused the crumble and collapse of a number of values which had so far been the cultural mainstay of the West. This made way for a confused state of affairs which at the same time had a rejuvenating effect and to some extent brought a feeling of release. In those days, men were certainly more tormented than their ancestors, but by the strain and stress inseparable from innovation and freedom. All who were capable of reflection, at any rate, were aware, sometimes dizzily aware, of the modernity of their epoch. They knew that they were blazing a trail. They felt that they were new men.

The great literary productions that appeared about 1300, the second part of the *Roman de la rose* or the incomparably more beautiful *Divine Comedy,* bore a clear testimony to the new awareness. These works were addressed to all. Composed in the vernacular and therefore intended for audiences not of the Church, they were the sum of all the intellectual conquests and all the knowledge of the previous age. Their primary aim was to make the higher cultural experience of the schoolmen and the clerks at last available to the leading lay sectors so desperately anxious to improve themselves. Their success was immense, quickly arousing commentary, public lectures, and discussions. They were immediately regarded as classics. Subsequent generations gradually found their bearings with respect to the compendium of learning they supplied and the system of the world they imparted, introducing literary criticism, or rather aesthetic appreciation combined with a sense of the past, a sense of history as it had been lived, a sense of what was modern. Renewal was the keynote of all intellectual and spiritual activities at that time and it naturally spread to religious attitudes as well. What began to be called *devotio moderna* toward 1380 was the new way of approaching God. But the freedom such modernism involved, even in the field of prayer, remained basically operative at the level of the ecclesiastical officials, of the priests. As cultural life became more popular in the fourteenth century it entailed an emancipation from the clergy. And art—which is how it became modern—ceased, at that major turning point in material and spiritual history, primarily being a vehicle for what was sacred. Henceforth it looked toward men, toward more and more men, like the call or the reminiscence of pleasure.

Ars nova was an expression used in the fourteenth century to define certain forms of musical composition characterized by profuse ornamentation, a spirit of gratuitousness, a search for pure aesthetic delectation, and a striving, whether conscious or not, to introduce worldly joys into sacred music. In short, it marked the entry of the instrumental arabesque into liturgical chant, of all that had germinated in the springtime stage music of Adam de la Halle and well before in the melodies of the troubadours: it was an outburst of profane values in religious art. Parallel trends could be traced at the same time in all areas of creative activity: for architects, sculptors, goldsmiths, painters, and those who recruited them, the fundamental purpose of a work of art no longer lay in the liturgy of the incarnation which had radiated throughout Europe from the center of France in the thirteenth century, portraying man, reason, and nature, the perfect forms in which God was made manifest, in their rightful place among the harmonies of creation. Artists and patrons alike, the men who claimed to be modern, no longer regarded art as a means of dispelling the mysteries of the world and revealing its inner order, as the contemporaries of Saint Louis had continued to do and as friends of Lorenzo de' Medici were to do again later. Art in their eyes became an illustration, a narrative, a tale. It was intended to provide an immediately intelligible relation of a story—or of stories—of God, but also of the knights of the Round Table, and the conquest of Jerusalem. There lay the really profound change. Artists were no longer the companions of the priests in the celebration of the liturgy, no longer the auxiliaries of a ministry. They placed themselves at the service of men. Of men eager to see the materialization of their dreams—art invited escapism more than ever—not a portrayal of everyday reality. In the fourteenth century, creativity turned into the pursuit of fancy. As a result, its major objective was not to provide a space conducive to prayer and suitable for processions or psalmody as before, but one designed for display. Thus painting, the most appropriate medium for suggesting visions, raised itself at that very moment in Europe to the highest rank of the arts.

The mainsprings of such a far-reaching transformation must be sought in the interplay of three simultaneous forces. The evolution of society, which had its repercussions on the circumstances and intentions of the creative act, the evolution of beliefs and intellectual outlooks, which modified both the content and the destination of works of art, and lastly the evolution of forms of expression. Like the philosopher and the writer, the artist employs an idiom rooted in the past, fixed, numbed by routine, and only succeeds in overcoming its resistance slowly and painstakingly and always imperfectly. The implications of these three factors are well worth a few preliminary considerations.

8

NEW MEN

It seems valid to take a sociological approach to art as a point of departure: the spirit of renovation and freedom characterizing the fourteenth century sprang very largely from the new human relationships being established at that period. Great art, the substantial art handed down by time, the vestiges of which we still see around us, had owed its achievements ever since the conversion of Europe to Christianity to a homogeneous social circle whose members all shared the same outlook and all had the same cultural background, the small group composed of the high dignitaries of the Church. That handful of men, educated at the same schools, had been the creators of liturgical art and the guardians of its unity. But after 1280 the social nucleus on which great art depended widened considerably, becoming more mobile and as a result more complex. It splintered into different cultural zones, engendering a situation which warrants close attention.

In actual fact the condition of the artist altered little during that period. In the fourteenth century all artists, or almost all, were laymen—but most of their predecessors in the thirteenth and twelfth centuries had almost always been laymen, too. Their work was organized through the medium of highly specialized craft associations. These bodies provided a substitute for the family unit, offering shelter, facilitating movement from town to town and from site to site, and consequently furthering acquaintance, apprenticeship, and the dissemination of techniques. Like all closed societies, they had their conventions, and were dominated by elderly members suspicious of personal initiative, although there had also been stonemasons' and goldsmiths' guilds in the thirteenth century. After 1300 corporative organization merely spread to the other crafts, especially to painting. Sometimes well-matched teams of traveling artists, the *condotte* of aesthetic conquest, were set up, led by a contractor, such as Giotto, who accepted the commissions, signed the agreements, and distributed the work to his assistants—but on the cathedral sites, similarly structured companies had been active well before. Finally, like the commanders-in-chief in the wars, the great directors of enterprises emerged more and more from anonymity in the fourteenth century. They were respected, known, mentioned by name, all of which marked a step forward in recognizing a creative personality—yet cathedral architects had also insisted on signing their works. The only significant change lay in the growing trend toward secularization which applied to most of the arts simultaneously, or in the steady promotion of painting—one of the chief aesthetic innovations at that time.

What must be remembered is that up to the end of the century, up to the generation which attained its creative majority about 1420, the artist continued to occupy a subordinate position where his relations with his customers were concerned. The artist plied a manual trade, was of humble stock, generally from the urban poor. The value of his work was always regarded as minor in comparison with that of the material he was required to transform. Famous artists admittedly began to appear in Christian Europe in the fourteenth century, successful artists whose services were coveted and who sometimes managed to choose their customers. Giotto, the first of the great painters, was one. But neither Giotto, nor even Ghiberti a hundred years later, were free. They remained executants—using the manifold resources of their craft in their own way—but always faithfully, in utter obedience.

A few modifications in the artist's relations with those who paid him could be discerned nevertheless. Trade in works of art was making its tentative beginning. It concerned pieces finished in advance and subsequently proposed to eventual buyers, displayed in shops or entrusted to Italian businessmen who acted as brokers all over Europe. The first transactions must almost certainly have included books, small ivory ornaments, prayer accessories such as traveling dyptiches, or toilet accessories, such as mirror cases or perfume boxes. And tomb stones. Paris seems to have been the great marketplace for such wares and the principal place of manufacture (though imported works of art, like the painted panels from Italy, had been sold in Paris in 1328). Trading went from strength to strength, flourishing on account of the reduced dimensions of the pieces, which made them more portable. And more significantly—since the smaller size was merely a consequence—as a result of the evolution of personal fortunes, the emergence of an ever-growing body of citizens who could acquire decorative art, who were no longer content with enjoying collective masterpieces, who wished to possess works of their own and amass, for their private pleasure and prestige, a lesser equivalent of the treasures formerly kept only by churches and kings. It was the combination of this extensive popularizing movement and the increasing secularization of cultural activities that sustained the growth of the commerce of art.

The fact that the extremely wide influence exerted by the dealers helped to determine the actual conditions of artwork cannot be emphasized too often. It accelerated the dissemination of technical processes and styles, it encouraged comparisons, it precipitated aesthetic merging: without the importation of the ivory statuettes manufactured in Paris, the sculptors, painters, and goldsmiths of central Italy would certainly have been far less well acquainted with Gothic forms. But above all it liberated the artist. By reversing the relationship between customer and executant, it gave the initiative to the latter, although the area of freedom admittedly lay at the lowest level of creative activity. It was the less well-endowed of art lovers who bought in the shops and what they found there was but the small change of the great works. No imagination was spent on the articles brought out in series. They were never more than swift reproductions of major pieces, repetitions in a more ordinary key. In order to supply as large a public as possible, the merchants strove to reduce the cost of manufacture by speeding up the processes and by employing second-rate materials. Wood-engraving, for instance, was used for producing pious images on paper at the lowest price. But to be sure of appealing to that wider clientele recruited from the less cultivated levels of society and of keeping up demand, they also sought to simplify the subjects, make them more readable, place them more on the plane of sensibility and less on that of the intellect, give space to narrative portrayal. Popularization became the specific purpose of the art of that day whenever it was a matter of trade. But the motive force of the genuine works lay elsewhere, in the action of the patrons.

Nowadays, when a very great artist has more money than any possible patron and can consequently sponsor himself, composing and creating in utter freedom for his private delectation and his private use, it requires something of an effort to assess the magnitude of the duties that fettered the artist to the buyer in the days of Cimabue, Master Theodoric, or Sluter. All important works of art were commissioned and all artists closely bound by the wishes of his customer, one would be tempted to say his master. The ties were formed in two ways. By a contract in due form, authenticated by a notary, concerning a specific undertaking, a reciprocal agreement which not only set the price and the delivery dates but also the quality of the material, the details of the rendering and lastly, and above all, the general theme of the work, the ordering of the composition, the choice of the colors, the arrangement of the figures, their movement and their bearing. Or else, and in that case the alienation was carried even further, or at any rate lasted longer, the artist was incorporated in his patron's household for a time, placing himself at his orders, living on his premises, receiving full maintenance and at best filling a specific post in return for a wage. Dependent situations like this were sought by the best artists because they freed them from the constraints of the corporations, the workshop, and the team. They held out the promise of the highest profits. Finally, they offered an introduction into the most brilliant and most open-minded circles—a place at the crossroads of fashion, research, and discovery. An opportunity for true social promotion. It was in the homes of the great nobility that a certain respect for the artist's standing and his professional freedom began to dawn at the threshold of the fifteenth century. In reality, however, painters, sculptors, image cutters, resident goldsmiths, and, at the greatest courts, the master of works who directed them all, coordinating the processes of decoration, bowed before the will of a lord. No doubt it was too early to suppose even the beginnings of an exchange between artist and patron: Giotto discussing an aspect of the compositions for the chapel of the Arena with Enrico Scrovegni; the Limburg brothers submitting their project for the calendar of the *Très riches heures* to John of Berry. Throughout the whole of the fourteenth century the ties of domesticity, like the clauses in the contract, made the significance of a work of art entirely subject to the wishes, tastes, and whims of a patron.

The patron of course only dictated the framework, the subject, and, more tactfully, the substance of what was to be expressed. The true master of the piece was always the artist. His gifts had a life of their own which developed independently of outside recommendations. It is important to underline this fundamental fact. This was the mark of the freedom of artistic activities within the social structure and explains why, at all time, painting, sculpture, and building, just as literary composition, scientific research, and philosophical thought—and sometimes even more so—have been operations of discovery and exploration, aiding in impressing a new image of the world on the art-loving public. Surely it is needless to add that vast scope lay open for personal inventiveness. And among all those captive artists geniuses were not lacking. Within the limits of their commisions they made very wide use of their talent—wider perhaps than modern artists who choose their own subjects but find it hard to vary their manner. But genius resists analysis. The aspects which reflected the history of society and taste—it is not my purpose to discuss anything else—still depended to a very large extent on the customer. So it is advisable to try to find out what it was the customer wanted.

In the previous period, art had flowered within a settled society with stable hierarchies. The extra wealth produced by peasant labor converged on two small aristocracies, the one military and destructive, squandering its resources in festival, the other religious and liturgical, consecrating its possessions, in the strongest sense of the word, by using them to celebrate the glory of God. Uniting the two groups was the figure of the king, a war leader, but anointed. And it was the largess of one king, Saint Louis, that had carried very high art to fulfillment in the thirteenth century. After 1280 that order disintegrated. Certainly the spirit of generosity, which was the main value attributed to an offering, to a donation of precious things, as the symbol of a dual assertion of power and humility, continued to dominate the outlook of the rich and to urge them to maintain artists. What changed was the status of the patrons. Two separate currents were instrumental in bringing this about.

The first shook the hierarchy of fortunes, leaving the ruling class, which possessed the financial means of supporting the major artistic undertakings, in disarray—and precipitated a renewal. The forces were twofold, but were chiefly the general outcome of the demographic evolution and the recurrent ravages of death almost everywhere in Europe in the second half of the century. In certain places the epidemics, first of all the Black Death of 1348–50, decimated entire teams of artists. If English miniature painting, which had been that country's great and certainly most original art form up until then, declined sharply in the middle of the century and later stagnated at the lowest level, it was probably because the workshops, emptied by the plague, could not be set up again afterwards. Consequently, collective death sometimes directly affected creative activities by striking the actual craftsmen. But in the main such immediate action seems to have been limited. In fact, in England again, but in other artistic fields where the teams of executants were probably larger and more resistant, no real break can be discerned: the amazing architectural feat of Gloucester Abbey was carried forward at the height of the demographic disaster. Death seems actually to have affected the customers in a far more serious way, provoking a rebound on the models required of the artists and even on the way they expressed themselves.

In the fresco work and the painted panels in central Italy, for example, an impressive cleavage occurred about 1350. Suddenly the dignified restraint and elegance which had marked the narratives of Giotto or Simone Martini were there no more: more commonplace overtones followed, in Andrea of Florence or Gaddi. No one will deny that the sudden disappearance of certain masters caused havoc in the workshops, that the rupture was also the outcome of the crashing bankruptcies which stirred the world of the great businessmen in Florence, ruining some and elevating others. Yet the drop in intensity demonstrated by the invasion into painting of the picturesque, of the anecdote, of the touching effect, arose quite plainly and decisively from a vigorous renewal of the city corpus. The plague of 1348, then the periodic epidemics which followed, left large hollows in the upper layers of urban society, already penetrated by humanism. The gaps were filled by the rapid rise of uncultivated parvenus, or rather of men whose learning, based on the popular preaching of the mendicant friars, lay several degrees below. In order to adjust to their taste, artistic expression had to curb its ambitions. Swift social ascension in trecento Tuscany, just as everywhere else in Europe in the fourteenth century, was responsible for a marked regression in aesthetic acuity.

Such speedy promotion was not solely the result of the plague. It was also furthered by the hazards of war—almost permanent in the Europe of those days. Not that military encounters killed many rich men. The constant improvement in armor guaranteed effective protection, and in any case their opponents did not usually wish to slay them in combat. They preferred to take them alive. Warfare in the fourteenth century was a chase. Everything hinged on money; everything ended in ransom. A self-respecting knight consequently scorned wealth and dreamed only of his fame, at heart hoping that when he was taken prisoner his conqueror would set the highest price on his release since it would be a concrete demonstration of what he was worth. Thereafter he blithely accepted his ruin. Ample transfers of fortune followed all battles and all tournaments. And it sometimes turned out that the lucky contestants, enriched by their prizes, chose to devote a portion of the windfall to commissioning artists. Lord Beaverley undertook the construction of Beverston castle after returning victorious, laden with gold, from one of the great battles of the Hundred Years War. Though he was rich in any case. However, if the war, like the plague, brought men from the middle sections of society, of less refined cultural traditions, into the upper aristocracy, it was because fighting by then had become a professional matter for mercenaries, *condottieri,* and soldiers of fortune. These men made haste to adopt the customs of the nobility, particularly its aesthetic leanings, but did so as upstarts, clumsily, and always over ostentatiously. During the fourteenth century the dual movement thus merged into one by stimulating the rise of new men who were bound to alter taste, and played its part in the growing fondness for the genteel.

The other current affected not only individual destinies but the social corpus as a whole. It tended to modify the circulation of property, consequently to upset the order of inheritance and to shift the wealth necessary for patronage to fresh areas. Fortune had formerly been based on the land, on rural estates which generated a stable revenue; as we know, the entities best endowed with profits from the peasantry were the great religious communities, the monasteries, the cathedral chapters, all the ecclesiastical organs which had previously produced the most outstanding artistic achievements. Disorder was introduced in three ways after 1280. In the first place a mutation of the agrarian economy perturbed the estate system, depriving the landed gentry and particularly former religious establishments of a good part of their revenues. On the other hand, the princely states continued to grow stronger and in particular succeeded in setting up a very efficient fiscal system which worked to their advantage. At that time Europe as a whole had begun to adopt state taxation. Or rather a mechanism which channeled a considerable portion of the money in circulation into the coffers of the prince, so that he could indulge in luxury and in the display he felt beholden of his dignity and through the idea, also new, that each formed of his own majesty, last of all in the enrichment of those who served him. In that way, a few lavish centers—the princely courts—could let shine an ever brighter beacon despite an ebbing failing Christendom. But that very readiness to do so—the third force—furthered the activities of a number of great businessmen, able financiers, who acted as the auxiliaries of the sovereigns in collecting taxes or in issuing coin, benefiting by it while at the same time furnishing the courts with sumptuous objects. In the majority of towns, business and banking had begun to decline because of the depopulation but continued to thrive in the capitals, at the principal meeting places of the great trading routes for gold and luxury cloths. There, a few citizens who had grown rich through services rendered near and far to the great Western princes acquired the same liking for splendor, for the gratuitous gift, as they acceded to the level of fortune and cultural maturity at which a wealthy man could think of giving artists ambitious commissions.

These economic changes largely explain why the influence of Church institutions in artistic activities steadily dwindled throughout the fourteenth century. Ruined, exploited, crippled with taxes by the pope and by the kings, disorganized by the new methods of recruitment and of granting prebends, monastic or canonical communities almost generally ceased to count as promoters of great works of art from then on. In ecclesiastical society only a few institutions and a few men were still active: first certain religious orders, the Carthusians, the Celestines, and above all, the mendicant friars. Paradoxically, these orders were the strictest. Their aim was to be the symbol and example of destitution and the contempt of all things earthbound. Presumably they should have condemned all forms of ornamentation and taken a stand as the direst enemies of the creation of works of art. Some did. If Giotto was obliged to cut down his decorative program for the chapel of the Arena in Padua it was at the insistence of the Augustinian hermits who supervised the execution of the work, and reproached him with producing many things "far more for the sake of pomp and empty pride than the glory and honor of God." Yet most of the convents of the poor orders were active focuses of trecento art. There were two reasons for this. First, as they were established in the towns or at their gates, they collected plentiful alms from the princes and the notables, because the virtues of extreme poverty and asceticism embodied by their corporations attracted the worship of all who were rich, or too rich, whose consciences labored under the opulence and luxury in which they lived. Then, the poor communities also discharged the major social duties of funerary celebration and preaching, neither of which could be imagined at that time without ceremonial and some recourse to imagery.

Other patrons emerged from the fourteenth-century Church nevertheless, abbots, canons, bishops, cardinals above all, and popes. But when these prelates gave their support to artists, they no longer behaved as ministers of a cult or leaders of a community, but as individuals, prompted by the desire for personal aggrandizement. More obviously still as princes. Apart from the poor orders, the only sections of the Church to participate in the creation of works of art were the ones closest to the temporal world, the least liturgical, those which were virtually secular. The bishops of England or France who pursued the decoration of the cathedrals, while not princes in their own right, were at any rate the servants of princes. Royal fiscality provided their wealth just as papal fiscality provided that of the cardinals. They acquired princely tastes and princely purposes, and especially an eagerness for displaying their own magnificence by endowing the church in their care with an ornament bearing their personal stamp. When Pope Boniface VIII in Rome and Pope Clement VI in Avignon in their day exercised widespread stimulating patronage, when they encouraged the research of men like Giotto or Matteo da Viterbo, they were more concerned with using monumental prestige to convey the majesty of the state, temporal quite as much as spiritual, or which they held the reins, than with praising the glory of God.

In point of fact the princes themselves took turns with the Church in conducting largescale artistic programs and settled the avant-garde of creative work and research in their courts. The most brilliant and powerful of the courts were admittedly still those of the pope, the king of France, and the emperor, in other words, consecrated figures whose task it had been to assemble fine teams of craftsmen since the dawning of Christian art. But the fourteenth century was precisely the moment when profane values began to supersede religious values in the conception of papal, imperial, or royal rule, limiting the power of the priesthood and extending the role of the *imperium*, the civil idea of power which the intellectuals of the day defined more and more closely as they discovered ancient Rome. Secularization again. What was more, many of the wealthiest princes, like the French lords who found themselves drawn into renewing Parisian aesthetics after the lapse of royalty toward 1400, the duke of Anjou, the duke of Burgundy, the duke of Berry—or like all the "tyrants" who had taken charge of the *signoria* in the large communes of northern Italy—had not received divine unction and no longer felt any affinity with the priestly calling. Thus, in all the courts where men and finance were brought together, as exploring as ever and more and more receptive to the outside world, ideal centers for social promotion, the only ones where men of low birth might hoist themselves to the highest distinctions by arms, economic administration, or chapel duties, the liturgical interests of the household, of the great families and the courts, gradually gave way to political intent, the sacred yielded to the profane. The values now acknowledged were power and majesty, as represented in Roman law for the "legists" who had studied at the law faculties in the universities, and as in the Latin classics for other intellectual servants who had studied in the arts faculties at the universities—values of chivalry and courtesy, but all the more flamboyant, borne along and propagated in the general flow of social customs and rites handed down from the feudal Middle Ages.

It was precisely those academic and knightly values that were assumed by the few great businessmen here and there in urban society and above all in Italy who made up the only elite capable of truly creative patronage outside the Church and the world of the courts. The middle classes as a whole still played a very small part in conducting artistic activities. Their role almost always lay at the lowest level, in the area of popularized production. More often than not it also operated in a collective way, within the framework of the confraternities to which many citizens belonged and where cultural life was entirely subservient to the teaching of the mendicant friars. That is why it is rash to claim that there was a "bourgeois" art in the fourteenth century or even "bourgeois" values in art. The bankers and traders became patrons by leaving the middle classes behind, by moving in the princely circles they served or else, but very rarely, and only in a few large cities in Italy, by bestowing majesty, the *imperium* of a great lord, but also the attributes of courtly nobility on the commune, the collective principality they helped to govern. All the great businessmen, and on their heels of course the masses, fat or lean, were spellbound by the customs of the courts, by what they perceived of them, and by the twin ideal of clergy and chivalry they proposed. This was no middle-class frame of mind, it simply indicated the steady impregnation of courtesy, or knightly values, and humanism, or academic values, among small groups of men who had been born in the middle classes but had risen beyond. In other words, still scarcely more than faint popularization and strong secularization in society.

It is important to emphasize one of the ultimate effects of the changes wrought in the social fabric. In all the centers where very great art was being produced at that time, in the convents, at the courts, in the great urban communes, the new overtones of the fourteenth-century manner partly derived from the unmistakable importance of the individual decision taken at the outset. Whether it was a matter of purchasing an object in a shop, of instructing a household artist or drawing up a contract for a commission—though the patronage might appear to rest with a community, an urban brotherhood, the cathedral chapter of York, the Franciscans of Assisi, or the commune of Florence—at the crucial moment everything hinged on the intentions and the likings of one person. At the major turning points in his career, Giotto came face to face with Jacopo Gaetani dei Stefaneschi and the cardinal, Enrico Scrovegni, the heir of a moneylender. Man to man. And, as has been said, doubtless not for an exchange of views.

The artist was almost always at the service of an individual, of a man who asserted his personality more than ever before and felt far freer to state his tastes. That freedom, that liberation of self, insofar as the customer was concerned, showed yet another side of modernism.

The fact that the will of a single person and no longer that of a community had become the motive force explains some of the basic characteristics then leaving their mark on artistic productions. More plainly than ever, works of art were looked upon as articles for individual ownership. When private—or even when public, when offered to all, like a stained glass window or a statue in a church doorway—they always bore an imprint, or a sign of some sort, which showed that they had been created for so-and-so. The ubiquitous proliferation of heraldic symbols, the gradual invasion of the figure of the donor offering the pious image in order to save his soul and his family, and the striving for a likeness in these effigies were all evidence of the patron's annexation of the work he had caused to appear. And since he never lost sight of his own fame, least of all if he was of low birth, and since he felt that his commission was a means of displaying the extent of his achievements, it was usually he who suggested the materials, forms, and compositional arrangements. Depending henceforth on a personal decision, fourteenth-century works of art strove more readily for effect. They also tended to be smaller, consequently easier to own. Illuminated books, gold ornaments, treasure articles, jewels, made of extremely precious materials, condensing pomp and circumstance, which one could clasp in the hand, provided a more perfect answer to the taste of a society in the process of freeing its aesthetic pleasures from collective constraints than the vault of a nave or a monumental statue. Lastly, most of these objects bore the stamp of a temperament. Always that of the donor, who sought singularity, desirous of revealing the traits of his personality through specific details in the theme. Sometimes that of the artist, because not all patrons came from the Church, as before. Nor were they so frequently intellectuals. Less vigorous minds allowed more latitude in the execution of the themes they had conceived and more scope for one's own initiative and artistic sensibility. As a result, works of art gained in diversity, on the face of it at least, because deep down, from one end of Europe to the other, and at all levels of society, a few common cultural models continued to govern the personal wishes of the customer and the personal achievements of the artist.

The problem of the genuine relations between intellectual development, the evolution of beliefs, the transformation of the collective outlook, and the new accents expressed by means of art is difficult if not insoluble. And to raise it in connection with the fourteenth century immediately involves grappling with a whole network of uncertainties. By then contacts were far less direct than in the eleventh, twelfth, and thirteenth centuries when the sole creators of great art were learned men. Saint-Denis is obviously a straight translation of Suger's conception of the universe. The masters of works for the abbey buildings had been given strict instructions and no one will find it hard to see what Suger had in mind. He explained his intentions in any case and it is easy to corroborate that he constructed and adorned the basilica as he would have constructed and adorned a sermon, as he did in fact construct and adorn the *History of Louis VI the Great,* drawing on the same repertory of symbols, playing on the same arithmetical and rhetorical harmonies, very likely proceeding according to the stages of anagogical reasoning. Conversely, while it is undeniable that the *Jardin de paradis,* or any page from the *Très riches heures* also convey John of Berry's view of the world, the mechanisms are far less apparent. First of all because the intellectual attitudes of a royal duke in 1400 were far more elusive than those of a Benedictine abbot in the twelfth century. Next, and above all, because these translations depended on a host of subtle intermediaries.

Many fourteenth-century works of art were deliberately conceived as visual readings of a piece of doctrine. This was the case with the entire group of propaganda images, and notably of a large number of paintings influenced by the Dominican order. For spectators of average education, the *Triumph of Saint Thomas Aquinas* painted by Andrea of Florence in the Spanish chapel of Santa Maria Novella, and another *Triumph* by Traini for Saint Catherine's church in Pisa offered a simple, decipherable, therefore effective pattern, if not an actual portrayal, which settled Thomist philosophy securely in a system of knowledge in relation to the "authors," to Aristotle and Plato, to Saint Augustine and Averroës, and in relation to divine wisdom. Works so closely directed, however, were fairly rare. The new patrons took a less favorable view of the direct participation of professional thinkers. In most cases little can be discerned beyond a semblance of affinity between the artist's rendering and a certain view of the world at this or that intellectual level depending on the social status of the donor. Again, what was finally expressed was not so much a matter of thought, belief, or knowledge as of values linked with customs, rites, and social taboos. Because of the combined effects of secularization and popularization, fourteenth-century art paid less attention to instruction, to expounding dogmas or intellectual conceptions. It tended rather to reflect the cultural models proposed as a sign and justification of social superiority to a larger number of men of wide origin, who believed that they belonged to an elite and commissioned architects, sculptors, and painters as such.

Those cultural models, it must be insisted, were the same for everyone, for the prelates, the princes, and the great bankers. In the main, they could be related to two extremes, to two exemplary types of conduct and wisdom embodied in the knight and the clerk. Since the emergence of a knightly way of life, that is to say since the end of the eleventh century, these two figureheads of human accomplishment had not failed to vie with each other. Many fourteenth-century literary works, such as the *Songe du verger,* still consisted of a dialogue, in diatribes, between the representative of the clergy and the representative of chivalry, each defending divergent principles and ideals. One of the novelties of the period, however, lay precisely in attempting to associate the two cultures. Various forces urged a confrontation; first of all certain alterations in the social order. In the fourteenth century a growing number of men were members of both formations at the same time. On the one hand there were the clerks who had been thrust into profane activities and gradually contracted the worldly habits formerly codified solely for men of war, and on the other, the *milites literati,* or "lettered" knights, capable of acceding to book learning and eager to widen their knowledge. The courts, where the same tasks were assigned to knights and clerks indiscriminately, as they were expected to possess comparable abilities, offered the best meeting place. There a literature expressing the convergence of the two ways of life was allowed to flourish for the entertainment of the princes and more extensively and in a more far-reaching way "for the benefit of their subjects," an order of diffusion by then regarded as one of the major duties incumbent on a great lord. These books, written to be read, were intended for educated men, but not only for clerks. No longer in Latin but in the vernacular, they were the new vehicles of scholastic knowledge.

The books which most plainly demonstrated the growing receptiveness of courtly society to learning were the innumerable translations. In Paris, the attempts to place the Latin writings of school *auctores* within reach of men of knightly upbringing and calling had stemmed from the circles of the king of France at the very end of the thirteenth century. Three trends soon emerged with the adaptation of the military treatise of Vegetius of John of Brienne under the meaningful title of *The Art of Chivalry* and Philip the Fair's request for a translation of Boethius' *Consolation of Philosophy,* while his wife read a sum of amorous rhetoric composed in Latin two generations earlier and his daughter-in-law the *Metamorphoses* of Ovid. The king, who still felt himself a churchman, desired texts on sacred morality, the great lord, the flower and model of chivalry, technical treatises on the science of arms, the ladies, codes of courtly love and their best classical references. And when the movement gained shape along the same lines around King John the Good, around Charles V and his brothers after the mid-fourteenth century, something of the works of Livy, Petrarch, Saint Augustine, Boccaccio, Aristotle, and the university masters who had described the "properties of things" and scrutinized the mysteries of the physical world was introduced into the cultural system common to the knights and ladies of the court of France. Admittedly, only to a minor extent, on the surface, in rough snatches, in the fragments least ill attuned to the thought and interests of worldly society. Yet it was a victory, and a considerable one. It was progress that was to be matched by a new approach to knowledge.

At the court of the Valois, within the group of princely households gravitating round it, among the members of the intellectual staff leaving the universities and joining the clergy, a small nucleus of humanists began to form at the beginning of the early fifteenth century. They gathered around a few leading figures, around those who filled the post of secretary to the princes. In Paris such offices were new. Devised fifty years earlier at the court of the popes of Avignon, they spread through all the political capitals of Europe and the urban republics of Italy. Since the secretary was first and foremost a writer of princely documents, he needed to have a perfect knowledge of the purest Latin, therefore be an assiduous reader of the classics. And since his duties and his concerns had become strictly temporal, he was frequently led to consider profane Latin texts both from a critical and an aesthetic angle, no longer to treat them as preliminary exercises for liturgical practice or the interpretation of the word of God, to see them as models for political action, as testimonies of human history, the chronological depth of which was beginning to be perceived, to regard them above all as sources of joy and as examples of profane virtues. At that very high level, the change of attitude, and all the concomitant modifications in educational methods and intellectual training, half-opened the way for a radical desacralization of ecclesiastical learning. This occurred at the very moment when some of the texts which had been reserved for clerical teaching were disseminated in adapted form in worldly society. In the privileged circles of the princely courts, the cornerstones of the social edifice at that time, which provided such fascinating examples for all emulators from church and city, secularization and popularization accordingly combined to bring about a rapprochement between the intellectual outlooks of clerk and knight on the level of everyday human relationships. A more inward encounter, however, was obtained through the fundamental processes of change being wrought in each of the two cultural models.

For chivalry, in actual fact, it was less of a change than a confirmation. Ways became more stable, acquired a style and a consequent power of persuasion that imposed them, extended their influence, and made widespread the central values of joy and optimism. It was in the fourteenth century that the chivalrous spirit triumphed, although the various elements making up the ideal figure of the perfect knight offered in the romances and courtly love songs had taken shape and been put together far earlier. The first, the most deeply ingrained, had formed the keystone of aristocratic awareness at the turn of the tenth century when the type of society known as feudal was introduced into France. That primary nucleus consisted of strictly male and military virtues, strength, valor, and loyalty toward a freely chosen leader. Supporting it were prowess, display of courage, and technical ability, defining knightly perfection. The joy of fighting, vanquishing, dominating, asserting oneself through conquest still shone bright at the heart of profane society in the fourteenth century.

A second group of values was added when, at a very high social level, women began to emerge from their lowliness in the southwest of the kingdom of France at about 1100. The circles of men of war first of all had to admit the lord's wife, his lady. This involved the observance of new rules of courtly conduct, before which all knights alive to fame and honor henceforth had to bow. It also invented a new order of relationships between the sexes, in other words, Western love. War and love. Four words are enough to describe chivalrous culture: *Canti guerrieri et amorosi* (as the madrigals of Monteverdi were entitled, a sign that their glories had not faded in the baroque period). It had first found expression in song, in *chansons de geste* and *chansons d'amour* [epic poetry and love songs]. It also developed as a form of strategy, whether in order to rout an opponent or to win and retain the love of another's spouse. In either case, the plans were laid virtually at the outset, and took shape gradually, like a game. A game governed by rules, a game which entertained, but honorably. In other words, which strictly respected a code.

The code reached completion in the second half of the twelfth century. During the following generations, a superabundant literature diffused its stipulations among all men in Europe who were anxious to distinguish themselves. But the masterpieces of that literature had been produced before 1200, when the exemplary characters of the myths of chivalry, King Arthur or Percival, were brought to life, although their real success and the far-reaching effects they had on ordinary attitudes were not felt until the fourteenth century. At that period in the cultural history of Europe the knightly tale enraptured the aristocracy as a whole. It locked the parade characterizing that class in an increasingly rigid system of rites which bore less and less relation to natural behavior. Trecento realities were wild warfare, fire, rapine, death by the knife, a world entrenched behind fortresses bristling with lances in bleak deserted countryside, as Simone Martini staged so wonderfully in his back-cloth to the figure of the *condottiere*. Yet the *condottiere* was a would-be knight, one who swaggered in the middle of the fray in festive dress. At Crécy, Poitiers, Agincourt, the French lords, the flower of the aristocracy of the day, the most illustrious representatives of the knightly way of life, insisted to their utmost disadvantage on fighting like gentlemen; unheeding princes had themselves lashed to their steeds and led to the center of the battle to die in honor like the heroes of Lancelot—while blood-stained mercenaries vied for the love of princesses at court. When the evolution of the economy was in the process of ruining the old noble families, of lowering them beneath the newly rich who emerged from the war, from high finance, or from domestic service, of destroying the former hierarchies, those very hierarchies were transformed into vain symbols which proved extraordinarily effective in maintaining the values of play. Like the orders of chivalry founded in turn in the fourteenth century by the Castilian kings, the emperor, the dauphin in Vienna, the kings of France, the kings of England, and soon so many lesser princes, to surround themselves, like King Arthur, with more knights of the Round Table. The only way the new men could gain acceptance in worldly circles was to show proof of greater skill, more perfect respect for the rules in the strategy of love and war. It was around prowess and courtesy that the true liturgy of the day, the only one which still sprang from the heart, was performed at the festivals and parades on the field of battle as well as at the tournaments and midnight balls. This was precisely why the high arts failed to adjust to sacred liturgy in the fourteenth century and began to express profane ceremonial, and in so doing helped to establish its success. The greatest novelty of contemporary art perhaps lay in the lavish revelation of the chivalrous life.

Chivalry nevertheless soon found natural ties with clerical values. In feudal times, the Church had in fact concentrated on christianizing the knighthood, as one of the major components of society. Certain merits of men of war, strength and prudence, could easily be merged with theological virtues. But the Church pushed further. Eleventh-century Christendom even went so far as to condone aggressive violence: the crusade was the Christian justification of prowess. Yet, although the Church accepted warfare and swordplay and gave its blessing to massacre, it persisted in condemning the inclinations closest to the true spirit of chivalry and courtliness, the desire for earthly delights. The knight, like the best of monks, was expected to scorn gold and mercantile considerations, but while he sought to destroy them, he meant to secure pleasure in extravagance, luxury, and festival. Courtly love, adulterous as a matter of course, and carnal, appeared less easy to reconcile with the Gospel than military violence. The Church at any rate gave up its intentions of condoning that, too, after a few endeavors to channel emotions toward Marian worship. It reproved it. Thus, with veiled irony in *Aucassin et Nicolette,* violently in the songs of Rutebeuf, with naïve freedom in Joinville, thirteenth-century chivalrous literature confirmed the basic antagonism between those it condemned as papists or bigots, the upholders of a chill, austere, and penitent faith, and the genuine knights, those who wished to associate the more smiling principles of religious salvation with their love of life and the world.

Yet the joyful values of chivalry had already staked their claims within the precincts of the Church, initiating a major reversal in certain provinces of Christianity. As a rich merchant's son, Francis of Assisi had been nurtured in the courtly spirit. Before his conversion, he had dreamt of knightly adventures and composed carefree verse like all young men of his class. When he chose poverty as his lady, to serve love, he sincerely believed that he might thereby attain perfect joy, in accordance with the models of courtliness. Franciscan Christianity, more in agreement with the Gospel than any other, claimed to be fundamentally optimistic. Conquering and lyrical, it offered a reconciliation within creation, it proclaimed the goodness and beauty of God in the love of all creatures. By refusing none of the principles of the most demanding form of Christianity but by also accepting the world, embracing it in order to win it, Franciscanism followed the lighthearted ardor of chivalry. The message of Saint Francis was too new and too disturbing to be admitted as such by the Roman hierarchy. Part of it perished in the course of the thirteenth century. But at all events what survived subsequently pervaded the religious universe, spreading widely throughout the Church, beyond the Minorite order, reaching the rival militia of the preaching friars. In the fourteenth century, when sacred thinkers considered that all created things contained a particle of divinity and were consequently worthy of attention and love, when the Dominican monk, Heinrich Suso, in lyrical outpourings which echoed the *Canticle of the Creatures,* cried, addressing God:

> O admirable Lord, I am not worthy to praise thee, yet my soul desires that the sky may praise thee when, in its most ravishing beauty, it is illuminated in full clarity by the brilliance of the sun and the countless multitude of scintillating stars. That the fine countryside may praise thee when, amid summer delights, it sparkles in its natural dignity, in the manifold array of its flowers and their exquisite splendour,

they likewise placed themselves in the direct heritage of the Poverello. But through his teaching they also found themselves in agreement with the ethics of chivalry and courtesy. The latter forces not only prevailed among the educated laity as a whole, they also profoundly influenced the new forms of ecclesiastical culture.

The lay spirit infiltrated the academic world of professional sacred thinkers in another way—although, apart from the small civic schools set up by businessmen in the large commercial centers to enable their children to acquire the rudiments of writing and arithmetic which they needed to ply their trade, teaching and learning admittedly remained basically religious activities and the universities basically ecclesiastical institutions. The Church claimed all students, and all teachers, as its own. Yet not everyone wished to become a priest. Some faculties, occupying the least clerical rung of the university ladder, provided special training for profane careers. For at least two centuries, the schools where the texts of Roman law were read and commented on—the speciality of the schools of Bologna—had offered a place for reflection where the mechanisms of scholastic reasoning could be applied to strictly temporal problems, notably to those arising from the government of men. They forged the instruments of a political science emancipated from ecclesiastical tutelage, urging the supreme majesty of secular power, the emperor's power, and readily refuting the claims of the Roman Church to temporal hegemony. In those schools a whole aspect of ancient Rome, its laws, its emblems, some virtues, had been gradually coming to light since 1200. And the growing strength of the states, the need to recruit more and more better trained auxiliaries, constantly enlarged the role of the study of law and therefore of the university sector which naturally leaned toward secular thought.

However, the most substantial innovations were made at the faculties of theology in Paris and Oxford, the nurseries of prelates and preachers. The decisive crack which let in all liberated forms of scholarly thought appeared in 1277, when the papal ban against the teaching of the theses of Averroës at one stroke condemned certain propositions put forward by Saint Thomas Aquinas, casting suspicion on all the attempts of the Dominicans over the last fifty years to assimilate Aristotelian philosophy to Christianity and at last to achieve the reconciliation of faith and reason, the dream of all thinkers in Latin Christendom since the end of the eleventh century. The Dominican order reacted against the indictment. Its chapters general of 1309 and 1313 forbade all denial of Thomism within the brotherhood. In 1323 it obtained the canonization of Saint Thomas and used every means, particularly the painted image, to have its justification recognized by all. In Italy, where the universities remained faithful to the teaching of Aristotle and the traditional methods of scholasticism throughout the trecento, it succeeded. But in Paris and Oxford, the position of the preaching Friars proved so shaken that about 1300 advanced theological research transferred its allegiance to the rival order of the Franciscans.

Two Minorites, two English teachers who had studied at Oxford, where emphasis had long been laid on mathematics and the observation of things, forced Christian thought to accept a total reversal. Until then the general aim had been to use the rational methods of Aristotelian logic to elucidate the mysteries of Revelation. John Duns, called Scotus, showed that only a very limited number of dogmatic truths could be based on reason; therefore one should simply believe in the others instead of endeavoring to demonstrate them. It fell to William of Occam, following suit, truly to open the "modern way." His ideas were fundamentally anti-Aristotelian since he believed that concepts were symbols devoid of all reality, that knowledge could only be intuitive and individual, and that the processes of abstract reasoning were consequently perfectly useless—whether it was a matter of reaching God or of understanding the world. Man's only hope of achievement was to follow one of two separate paths, either by a profession of faith, by inner acceptance of undemonstrable truths, such as the existence of God or the immortality of the soul, or by logical deduction, but applied only to what the created world offered as matter for observation.

Since it espoused the natural trend of the day toward secularization, the Occamist doctrine stimulated the whole of Western thought after the first half of the fourteenth century. It was a twofold evasion of the constraints imposed by the Church. By asserting the irrationality of dogma, first of all, it prepared a way toward God which no longer lay through the intellect but through love. It gave free rein to the deep current of mysticism which had irrigated Latin Christendom since Saint Augustine but had been stemmed by the success of scholasticism and thrust back into the cloister, into Franciscan convents and the small communities of ascetic penitents. Fourteenth-century Christianity—which is why it became so widespread, opening its arms to the weak, the ignorant, the humble, and to women— claimed to be mystic. As it was far more personal and far less communal, it parted from the clergy. Now that the basic religious act lay in a loving search for God, in the hope of a fusion, a union, a "marriage" between divine substance and the inmost recesses of the individual soul, the "depths" of Meister Eckhart, now that it consisted in secret conversation in any case, what role could the priest play? His duties were no longer as closely linked with the liturgy because the faithful no longer needed another to pray for them; they were expected to attain inward illumination alone, in successive stages, by means of personal exercises and of direct contact with the word of God, by daily imitation of Jesus. The priest's assignment could no longer be to teach and to explain. It had to be restricted to meditation and example. The priest was the distributor of grace through the sacrament and the witness of Christ, which meant that men were more alive to all that might appear to contradict his calling, more demanding in his respect, more aware of his attitude toward power, riches, and covetousness. Occamism thus offered a guarantee for criticism of all that encouraged the Church to lean toward the temporal, for campaigns designed to curtail its ambitions, to condemn unworthy impure clerics, to entrust ecclesiastical discipline, and the task of confining it to strict spirituality, to a civil power.

But by urging the progressive penetration of the secrets of the sensory world through reflection on experience, William of Occam also asserted the full freedom of scientific knowledge. First and foremost, Occamism proclaimed the sharp separation of the sacred and the profane. The first realm, that of the heart, remained under the spiritual control of a purified Church, whereas the second, that of the intellect, had to elude all ecclesiastical interference. It was a doctrine which involved the secularization of science and simultaneously released it from all forms of metaphysics, notably the system of Aristotle. A Parisian teacher, Nicholas d'Autrecourt, was soon able to confirm that "there was some degree of certainty which men might attain if they applied their minds to the study of things and not to the Philosopher or the Commentator." The modern way proved gloriously stimulating when it insisted on direct critical observation of each singular phenomenon, untrammeled by preconceived systems. It was an invitation to imagine them as they were, in their diversity, therefore to replace the symbol of an abstract concept with the true picture of a particular creature. Occamism thus pointed directly toward what we call realism in art. However, the realistic element which gradually invaded painting and sculpture in the course of the fourteenth century bears no relation to the progress of an illusory "middle-class mind." The art of that day, it cannot be repeated too often, did not come from the bourgeoisie. Its outposts were established in noble households where great artists and great scholars rubbed shoulders. The realism it expressed went hand in hand with the front line of university thought.

And the academic mainstream flowed toward the deeper current springing from chivalry; the visible world was no longer to be neglected in the same degree, its appearances no longer to be scorned but regarded as good and worthy of notice. Where their views converged, both held out the optimistic rehabilitation of the created world, to a society which was more diverse, less stable, but in which it was daily easier to find men able to read, understand, follow an argument, analyze their own feelings, and achieve a personal religious experience, a society which some have claimed was a crumbling, declining civilization. The modernity of the fourteenth century resided to a very great extent in that optimism, that sensitive attention paid to things. But forms still needed to be invented to express it.

Latin Christendom had just forged a distinguished idiom to render the meaning of the invisible, of divine reason, and of a conceptual order of the universe, and it created a seemingly unsurmountable barrier. In Paris, in the middle of the thirteenth century, the commissions given by Saint Louis had carried to perfection the art of using stone and tinted glass to transcribe the liturgy of the incarnation. Having reached fulfillment, the forms of Parisian Gothic remained fixed, reduced to uncomplicated schemes, so pleasing that they disheartened further flights of the imagination. Their influence was paralyzing and weighed heavily. In the two generations following the completion of the Sainte Chapelle, Parisian artists seemed to be imprisoned in a manner, powerless to mold it to the changing outlook and the intellectual innovations reflecting the evolution of society. In the days when Boethius was being translated for Philip the Fair, when Duns Scotus was teaching in Paris, when William of Occam was working out his system, contractors, image cutters, glass designers, and illuminators continued to portray the patterns of a sacralized universe, that of Albertus Magnus, of Pérotin, of Robert of Sorbon. And the prestige of the university of Paris where all professional intellectuals trained, together with the thriving trade in painted books and ivory statuettes, disseminated those patterns throughout Europe, despite the fact that the conception of the world they conveyed was outdated.

By the turn of the fourteenth century, the forces of renewal had made themselves felt nevertheless. They came from two quarters. From within French Gothic, where a slow but strong inclination toward mannerism began to appear as patrons grew more alive to luxury and to earthly delights, urging greater refinement. To gratify them, artists introduced precious elements into the established Gothic idiom, choosing richer, more flattering materials, adding ornamentation to the uncluttered designs of rational architecture, and above all playing on line. It was through the curves of the arabesque, a product of the cloisonné of the stained glass window and the pure drawing of the great monumental figures, that the courtly spirit of play found a place within the precepts of liturgical art, only to transgress them almost at once. Graceful and slender, the arabesque translated the rites of worldly elegance, which gradually ousted those of the divine service, by the hip stance of the statues or more freely by the luxuriant vegetation adorning the margins of the illuminated books. Responding to the rhythms of the roundels and virolets, to the processes of amorous pursuit, to the thousand vicissitudes waylaying the knight errant in his quest, its modulations betrayed a concern for elegance, a lighthearted search for pleasure and adventure, the first erotic perversions of courtly society. It was expected to illustrate that society's dreams. But if those dreams were to be linked with the reality they transposed into poetic fiction, a few scrupulously observed fragments of that reality needed to be easily recognizable in between the fractures and projections of the line just as in between the fractures and projections of the harmonies of *ars nova.* French drawing accordingly turned to the experience of the sculptors who had bedecked the cathedral capitals with the real foliage of the gardens and the copses of the Ile-de-France and the more recent experience of the tomb manufacturers whose customers wished funerary effigies to bear a likeness to the deceased. In order to express courtly fancies, French artists needed to be thoroughly versed in symbolism, poetic allegory, and realistic illusion. Through its unexpected sinuous meanderings, the nervous, mannered style they succeeded in wresting from Gothic classicism toward 1320, like the dream idiom, linked up obvious fragments of truth on an unreal and unfamiliar ground.

It was then that the echo of more overwhelming innovations arrived from central Italy. Because of the introduction of papal fiscality and the general changes in Western economy, that region, where merchants and bankers handled the most fruitful affairs from one end of Europe to the other, had just become the focus of the greatest financial powers. This accumulation of wealth permitted a flowering of artistic activities that flaunted original modes of expression rivaling Paris. The hegemony of Parisian forms fostered by increasing importation of French pieces had also been felt in those areas, but submission remained on the surface. The basic aesthetic outlook of central Italy derived from two solid traditions. The one consisted in the vast contribution of the East, the splendid stole of mosiacs and icons deposited by Byzantium in successive layers throughout the Dark Ages up to the twelfth century, which remained a living entity maintaining ties with its sources through the trading routes which linked it with Constantinople, the Black Sea, Cyprus, and Morea. The other, more deeply rooted, was local, a genuine matrix regarded as the national heritage, handed down from ancient Rome, present in countless ruins and the large number of monuments still in full use, and from an even remoter past, the depths of the Etruscan era. The artistic impulse, endorsed by the growing wealth of the Holy See and the cardinals who protected the order of Saint Francis, which Sienese and Florentine businessmen supplied with gold, was to cast off Parisian influence. By also rejecting Byzantium, by ridding itself of the reputedly colonial yoke of foreign tastes, and deliberately opting for Romanism, it revived antique forms out of fidelity to Italian soil. It was a genuine movement of national liberation. Giotto was its hero. At the very moment when Dante decided to write *The Divine Comedy* in Tuscan dialect, Giotto—according to the first critic who reflected on his art, Cennino Cennini, a fourteenth-century Florentine painter—"changed the art of painting from Greek to Latin." From Greek, a foreign tongue, to Latin, a native dialect. In actual fact some sculptors had employed its terms before Giotto. Those who had re-created the setting of the Caesars for Frederick II in Campania in the second third of the thirteenth century, then the sculptors of Pisa. Pisa, still rich from fortunes won on the eastern seas, Pisa, a major stage on the road taken by the kings of Germania when they went to Rome and received their diadem, a city more imperial than Rome itself, where the power of the emperors conflicted with the power of the popes. In Pisa, in the cathedral apse, the effigy of the city, kneeling before the Virgin like a queen mother, was placed beside that of the emperor. And below the pulpit carved by Giovanni Pisano after 1310, the statue of the city was shown supported by four Virtues opposite that of Christ, supported by the Evangelists. There civic pride allied with devotion to the empire to bring about the revival of Roman visual art.

The artistic overtones perceptible on the threshold of the fourteenth century were twofold. In France, it was the touch of laughing grace, of rippling litheness or nonchalance as in the Eros of Auxerre or the Tempter of Strasbourg. In Tuscany, in Umbria, even in Rome, the note was graver, more stable in its majesty, more secular in its strength. Both first appeared in sculpted stone. But as here and there the purpose of art became more and more narrative and visually demonstrative, it was not long before both found their full resonance in painting, before both expressed the outburst of profane values. Yet while the new inflections in the Gothic style merely signified a slow substitution of rites, the insidious penetration of knightly and courtly manners in the ceremonies of Church and royalty, and the infiltration of Franciscan joy in worship alongside a gradual reinstating of the natural world, the Roman key marked a sharp break. The triumphant Italy of the princes of the Church, of the imperial representatives, of the *podestà,* of the *condottiere,* of florin lenders, of merchant companies, of cities bristling with towers, and of hills where an immense amphitheater of terraces, olive groves, and vineyards was being erected, had not just adapted the language, it had upset the order, with a jolt. And what its businessmen distributed to the great European courts they supplied with ornament, what it proposed to the pilgrims of Rome, to the princes of France or Germany in search of lucky adventure contained the mainsprings of a keen will for secularization. The models of antiquity revealed recipes for an illusionism in trompe l'oeil which brought out the vanity of symbols. Conceived for civic pomp, to conduct the dead to a feared but apprehensible beyond, the sculptures of Rome and its Etruscan hinterland spoke of the divinity of man, justified his worldly conquests, his power, and his fortune. They were an invitation to rise from prostration before the priests. Not yet to deny God, certainly, but to look him in the face.

The idiom of the Pisans, of Cavallini, of Arnolfo, of Giotto, of Tino di Camaino expressed the hopes of the Ghibellines and the striving for independence in the great communes. It enabled Pope Boniface VIII to proclaim the majesty of the papal see and its calling to rule the world as if it were an empire. It enabled the cardinals who directed the great site of Assisi to conduct the worship of Saint Francis, to disarm it, to transform the Poverello into a hero of the primateship of Rome. But it was too aloof and too different. It was not fully intelligible to all the new men who had been granted access to very high art precisely as a result of the thriving Tuscan economy. To those from beyond the Alps it seemed totally alien. And since Gothic prestige remained so powerful, since the Roman tone seemed unsuited to courtly manners and since secularization was inseparable from a popularization which required the use of a more familiar, less disconcerting means of expression, it was not the idiom the fourteenth century West adopted in order to convey the new spirit. The artistic forms introduced into Tuscany and Rome about 1300 merely acted as stimulants to hasten the evolution of the French manner, to hurry it to discard its liturgical wrappings. It should be added that this invigorating influence bypassed central Italy, because the transfer of the papal see to Avignon, the slow ruin of Pisa, the failures of imperial policy, the upheavals in upper Florentine society caused by a series of banking disasters, and lastly the ravages of the plague, quickly reduced the cultural radius of that province. Nor did it affect Paris where Gothic traditions had sturdy roots. But it reached a few great princely courts which upheld knightly values and were more receptive to trends from the heart of Italy. Successive encounters turned those courts into a series of relays along the road to renewal in artistic expression.

The court of the French princes of Naples was the first to play such a role. Both Cavallini and Tino worked there. It may also have been there that Simone Martini succeeded in enriching his style with all the linear modulations of courtly design. Some time later in Avignon, Pope Clement VI opened the vastest building site of the century, which became a meeting place for artists from the north of France and for Italian decorators. Simone Martini, the most famous of living painters at the time, was asked to direct the undertaking. He died in 1344 and almost nothing remains of the frescoes except the admirable sketches in Sinopia red deposited on the preparatory coat. By 1368 the essentials of the program had been completed by the team of another Italian artist, Matteo Giovanetti of Viterbo. In a very free manner, this painter achieved the first true fusion of Gothic lyricism and the spatial conquests of Tuscan painting. Moreover his work was exhibited at the greatest crossroads of the world, visited by all princes and prelates and their train, whence they departed laden with gifts offered by the pope and the cardinals. At the heart of the trecento and at the heart of Christendom, Matteo's synthesis in Avignon was a major stepping-stone in the artistic itinerary. It was then that the emperor, Charles IV, a descendant of Charlemagne, an heir of the Caesars, a thorough admirer of Parisian taste, in love with precious stones and glittering things, called the architect, Matthew of Arras and the painters, Thomas of Modena and Nicholas Wurmser of Strasbourg, to his court at Prague. For Czech painters it was an opportunity to be made the most of. Bohemia had ceased being a land of ploughmen and swineherds. It had grown rich. It had thrown open its doors. Prague became the central knot in a vast network of trading connections and the princes, religious and lay, who reaped the benefits of the estates, asked local painters to ornament the settings in which they spent their lives. Shortly after 1350, the anonymous author of the Vysebrod cycle treated the linearity of French stained glass window design in a majestic key and Master Theodoric lent the faces of the saints an expressive fulfillment rejecting the evanescence of Gothic aesthetics. Finally, in the last third of the century, the courts of the northern Italian "tyrants" fostered a similar striving for synthesis. The princes who had assumed the government of the urban centers and maintained close ties with the Parisian court, wished to be models of chivalry and elegance. Like the lords north of the Alps, they were passionately fond of horses, dogs, and the sport of amorous intrigue. The heroic poetry, romantic tales, and lyrical themes from France found a dying bloom in their society. But they were more alive to the glories of ancient Rome than their Parisian contemporaries. Giotto had painted on their territory and the Italy of the sacrophagi was next door. At the hand of the painters who decorated the libraries of the lords of Milan and the patricians of Verona, "Lombardy work" improved the illusionist techniques of classical art. More naturally than elsewhere, realistic renderings won a place amid courtly arabesques.

In 1400 Paris was thus the most promising place for the conclusion of the stylistic synthesis which had been in preparation throughout the trecento in the entourage of the great European princes. Paris was able to impose the outcome on all Western aristocrats united in one body, speaking the same language, sharing the same customs, the same dreams, and the same tastes, meeting at festivals, tournaments, on summer crusades into Prussia, and during unceasing military roving from one province to another. The long English wars had just been brought to an end in the favor of the king of France, who emerged more powerful and, above all, richer and henceforth able to devote the gold which had flowed into his coffers, thanks to the fiscal machinery forged during the fighting, to his personal pleasure. After the death of Charles IV, the empire had lapsed back into anonymity. A schism opposed the two popes. There was nothing to challenge the absolute primacy of the court of the king of France and the attendant courts of his uncles, the dukes of Anjou, Berry, and Burgundy.

The splendid commissions from the king and the dukes attracted artists from all quarters to Bourges, Angers, Mehun-sur-Yèvre, the Carthusian monastery of Dijon, and to Paris above all. The Lombards brought the modernism of illusion, concrete vision, the precise accurate portrayal of the singularity of the world offered in the Veronese illustrations of the *Tacuinum sanitatis*. They taught the precepts of trompe l'oeil to all the image makers who arrived from the Netherlands in the wake of the sculptors of funerary effigies, and adopted them, applying them less delicately, but with more vigor and a sharp sense of rustic, slightly primitive comment. Contributions from north and south fused with the daintiness of Gothic tradition, engendering forms which trading in in objects of art, princely presents, and the influence of the royal court quickly bore to the far corners of Latin Christendom.

Throughout the itinerary, and more than ever in the synthesis which brought it to an end, French modes of expression had undoubtedly carried the day, which after all was scarcely surprising. The secular powers that triumphed in the fourteenth century were those of chivalry, not of Rome. And chivalry came from France and was conducted in the French manner, whether in Cyprus, Pamplona, or Windsor. Or Florence. The idiom accepted all over Europe and even in Tuscany in 1400 was Gothic to the core. Linear, precious, insensitive to values of weight, sturdiness, the quality of empty spaces, it had ignored almost everything in the newly discovered Roman forms beyond a few techniques which allowed a better rendering of the appearances of things, because patrons expected their artists to provide images of the pleasure of living, not monuments of stoic authority. In other words, a transposition of reality into dream and play, identical with the social transfer toward the rites of prowess and courtesy which had been taking place for some time. Those demands were filled by an ever closer alliance between the arabesque and trompe l'oeil.

Through their use of the arabesque and trompe l'oeil, the artists of the fourteenth century achieved courtly expression in the true sense of the word, yet at the same time released creativity from the sacred, gradually establishing it within reach of man. There lay the essential: the new art was no longer addressed to the priests, but to men in general, even to a man holding a religious office. When Giotto undertook to relate the life of Christ, he chose to display it as a theatrical performance surrounded by a symbolical set. His art was no more realistic than that of the cathedrals. Yet the universe he proposed had ceased to belong to the supernal world and to liturgy. It had become the universe of mankind. A true story took place, a human story, the drama of Jesus the man and Mary the woman. On the same plane, the other actors were real men, raised to the level of the living God solely by the majesty of their attitudes. In his Roman heroic manner Giotto consequently portrayed a particular and perhaps the essential aspect of Franciscanism: man's striving to live like Jesus, like God, like a god. A hundred years later, in a Gothic rendering of the collapse of the tortured Christ, the moving art of the Master of the Hours of Rohan also carried the humanization of divine figures to an extreme, but in the opposite direction.

According to the mysticism of an author like Tauler, humility allows man to draw so close to God that he becomes "divine." Such proximity of a God embodied in the attitudes and sufferings of his creatures obviously implied a victory over a number of taboos, over ecclesiastical indictments of human virtues and pleasures. Delivered from the priests, the new man found that he was solicited both to further his conversations with Christ and to enjoy the world. In everyday life, the answer to the dual way, mystic and natural—the one opened by William of Occam—was found in dual behavior. Prince Louis of Orléans and Queen Isabel of Bavaria lived enthralled by worldly festival. Yet he withdrew from time to time to a cell in the Celestine convent, the most ascetic of the religious orders, to hear five masses a day; and she had a meditation on the Passion of Jesus composed for her daily exercises. The castle of Karlstein, built by the Emperor Charles IV as the crystallization of a dream, opened on to the forests of Bohemia. It was reached through courtyards laid out for jousting and for gathering the pack. But, by degrees, by stages which faithfully translated the progress of mystic illumination, the path mounted to the shrine prepared for the emperor alone and for his communion with the relics of Golgotha. An ascension to a world beyond, yet a world obsessively present—in reality a parting. Freed from liturgy, trecento man remained a prisoner of himself. The pleasure of living meant the *Angst* of living. Man fled toward festival, or toward the love of a God he strove to believe was compassionate. In art as in life, human desires were torn between the imitation of Christ and the possession of the world.

9

THE IMITATION OF CHRIST

To a very great extent, the modernity of the fourteenth century lay in the new attitudes adopted toward religion and the "modern" devotional forms which were the outcome of the great conversion of medieval Christianity. In the course of a long march punctuated in its preliminary stages by the first signs of heretical unrest in the eleventh century, then suddenly hastening to an end after 1200 with the preaching of Francis of Assisi, the Christian religion had at last ceased being a matter of rites and priests. In the fourteenth century it slowly enlisted the masses. That period, as already said, became declericalized. Which did not mean that it was less Christian. If anything, it was more Christian, in a more private and certainly far deeper way, owing to the dissemination of the Gospel and its impact on the popular mind. Up to then Europe had displayed the externals of Christendom; Christianity was truly experienced only by rare elites. After the total reversal nearing completion, it was to have every appearance of being a people's religion.

In the meantime, it had taken on a kind of naïveté. By annexing the simplest forms of worship, it had equipped itself against uncertainties. Undoubtedly, there was more credulousness among the crowds lately christianized than in the cloisters, the cathedral chapters, and amid the ranks of the university, less susceptibility to doubt, a blinder faith in the powers of another world. In fourteenth-century Christianity one feels a strength against the temptations of unbelief. Yet, precisely because it was closer to the people, it was more of a prey to inward fears. The religion of the great prelates of the thirteenth century had overcome such matters and developed peacefully in light and hope. The popular religion which the Church welcomed and endeavored to discipline left far more room for darkness and fright. It let out into broad daylight the demons which for a time had been relegated to the gloomy corners of the cathedrals by Gothic brilliance or which lurked clandestinely in the secrecy of heretical sects and in all the forests, near trees where fairies dwelt and beside healing springs. The laymen of the fourteenth century quaked before them just as before God the judge. And, since community ceremonies played a lesser role in their religious observances, they gave daily attention to the devout, prophylactic act which exorcized evil powers and earned the mercy of God. In the new Christianity laymen were no longer mute uncomprehending witnesses of the liturgy as their fathers had been. Everyone, the princes, Isabel of Bavaria, the rapacious knights of Thuringia, the poet Christine of Pisan, the bankers of Italy, her compatriots, the Hanseatic traders, the great farmers, and even the village jobbers practiced their faith as well as they were able. Helping to create art was precisely one of the ways open to them: by acts of praise and fervor—acts of sacrifice, the consecration of wealth—propitiatory acts, or acts designed to foster saving intercession. Works of art more than ever answered a religious purpose.

But the great change sprang from the fact that works of art were more than ever governed by the desires of the laity. Quite apart from the economic and social transformations succinctly analyzed above, the relations between the priests and their congregation had altered radically. For centuries, Western ecclesiastical institutions had operated as instruments of spiritual compensation. Clerks and monks prayed for all laymen who maintained them with their donations, and by those prayers earned graces, which were then distributed among the Christian people as a whole. Through alms, given according to set tariffs, each believer came into possession of graces for himself or his family. He expected that they would help to counterbalance his faults on the Day of Judgment. In the entrance to the great sanctuaries, the image of Saint Michael weighing the souls reminded every conscience of the redeeming virtues of such transference. It was for the salvation of all that clerks and monks erected the monuments of sacred art, which were truly public.

The favor the heretical doctrines found with the more advanced laity, anxious to emerge from a passive faith, had led the Church to revise its approach to worship in the course of the thirteenth century. In doing so, it had not been able to count on the support of the parish priests, poorly instructed, poorly recruited, and tending more and more frequently not to reside among their flock and to collect the receipts of their cure from afar. Nor had it been able to rely on the ministers of the district chapels, who were very poor. The mendicant orders provided the driving force, at least in the towns, where they rapidly improved their methods of winning and organizing the masses.

In order to group the laity into entities more active than the parish communities, the Minorites and the preaching friars enlisted into the Third Order all those who, while not embracing a religious life, nevertheless wished to be practicing Christians and no longer just uninformed observers who watched the liturgy from afar. Many of the tertiaries were men who had belonged to the heretical sects or who would otherwise have gravitated toward them. The less fervent were encouraged to form confraternities, the guilds and mutual aid associations with their periodic libations which for a long time had been condemned by the Church as hotbeds of pagan supersitition, but which in the fourteenth century it had taken it upon itself to stimulate, supervise, and direct. Meeting around a luminary whose permanent maintenance was guaranteed by a contribution from each member and around the image of a patron saint, the confraternities grew apace. There were trade societies, district and parish corporations, hospital and charity associations, penitentiary groups whose members obeyed a ritual self-discipline and performing groups like the companies of *laudesi* in Italy, committed to the fight for good dying, whose chief work consisted in staging for their own edification and sometimes extremely skillfully, the central scenes from the New Testament, the Nativity, or the Stations of the Cross, to *laudes* or community songs. The Third Orders and the innumerable confraternities offered to all their members, in other words, the majority of the laity in the towns and a fair section of the rural laity, a spirituality which emanated from the monasteries. Isolation in the closed garden of collective mediation, a heroic struggle for the arduous conquest of salvation, through renouncement and mortification, and lastly, through daily exercises, singing the Psalms, reciting the canonical hours. The new pastoral approach invited all men to pray individually, to repeat the words of the sacred texts themselves and, if they were able, to read and understand them when they were alone. It brought them the liturgy of the cloisters and the cathedral chapter houses but by transporting it into their daily life and the intimacy of their hearts.

To educate the people and so that the private exercises of the confraternities should be given their full meaning, the teams of organizers made plentiful use of mass methods of instruction, particularly the sermon and the theater, employing them in close association. When Saint Francis discovered that it was not enough to attain personal salvation alone and that the mission Christ had given him was to spread his message far and wide, he did so through words. He was not a clerk. So he sang of repentance, of the love of God, and of perfect joy, just as any minstrel, and everybody heard. Then he sent out his disciples on to the roads and the building sites in order to convince, in the same very simple way. Whereas Saint Dominic had founded his order specifically for preaching. The Dominican intellectuals who went into the field, attempting to defeat the heretical orators who lived with the people and spoke their language, succeeded in making a very efficient instrument of propaganda of the traditional homily given in the cathedrals and the monasteries, accessible only to those who belonged to the Church. They set about it by putting the learned rhetoric of the religious texts into the everyday dialect. They popularized the themes to bring them within reach of the humblest audience. Like the reading of the book of hours, in the thirteenth century the other clerical exercise, the sermon, left the cloisters and the closed communities to win the common ear, and popular preaching played an increasing role after 1300.

The great missions and the tours of the nomad orators began in the 1480s. Long preceded by tales of their mystical deeds, they were awaited at the gates of the towns by all the magistrates assembled in a body. Their presence soon filled the churches or the squares with enthralled ardent listeners. The throng expected miracles, the end of the plagues, and above all the regeneration of its life, ways toward salutary death. "He began his sermon at about five o'clock in the morning," said one report of the Franciscan friar, Richard, who preached in Paris in 1429, "it lasted until between ten or eleven and every day five to six thousand people attended. He preached from a platform almost a measure and a half high, his back to the charnel house, facing the Charonnerie, the place of the *danse macabre."*

These mass emotionalists readily played on trivialities. They wanted the people to weep at their words, they aimed at plucking the heartstrings which would set in motion the great collective conversions. Wycliffe condemned the baseness of the tricks they used, and Chaucer's Pardoner was a sinister charlatan. But their inexhaustible eloquence revealed to the popular soul a brotherly, moving image of Christ. This image was all the more convincing when the preaching formed part of a show or popular festivities and was surrounded by painted or carved symbols in good view, accompanied by sung processions and interspersed with theatrical performances.

Theater originated in the liturgy. As early as the tenth century it had been used as an adaptation for the people for religious purposes. But its development and decisive popularization dated from the fourteenth century; like preaching, it went from strength to strength. Linked with the two great feasts of Christianity, Christmas and Easter, and the feast day of the patron saint, countless *sacre rappresentazioni* were produced by the Italian confraternities in episodes which gradually took on more and more life, were included in the processions, ordered into scenes, enriched with dialogue, music, and a proper set. These performances were really personal exercises reserved for the members of the devout associations and intended for their private instruction, but they had a profound effect on inner awareness. Acting the sufferings of Christ aided in grasping the true meaning of his Passion, in becoming identified with him. Toward the end of the century, when the first great preaching missions were organized, the theater approached a wider public and confirmed its purpose of collective celebration. In Paris, in London, in other large towns, confraternities were specially founded to give an annual public performance of the Passion. This was when the fifty most fertile years in the history of European religious theater commenced.

The staging, the illusionist sets, the magical chants, the processions of flagellants, the speech, and the gesticulations of the preachers were not addressed to the mind. Their aim was to rouse the feelings, to strike each individual conscience and to call forth the pity and fear which would bring salvation. Within the confraternity, just as in the audience during the sermons or the performance of a mystery play, each man felt that he was the one concerned. His own soul, the preparation of his death, his personal salvation were at stake. It was he who was involved, his responsibility, his guilt. This less serene form of Christianity, rooted in the sources of emotional sensibility, stirred by holy dread, was also far more individual. It was organized in dialogue: the dialogue of the penitent and his confessor in the secrecy of contrition, in the whisperings of faults avowed and their absolution, in the dialogues of the soul with God. Through their sermons, through the theater, through every kind of direct action, the mendicant orders drew the faithful away from their rival, the traditional Church, embracing the anticlerical trends of all the heretical movements they had formerly been required to rally to orthodoxy and which their efforts now helped to restrain.

Those trends were swept up by fourteenth-century Christendom and continued to proliferate, sometimes dangerously. Along the southern flank of Europe, deeply undermined by residual Albigensianism and the heresy of the Waldenses, in Italy and in Provence, an entire branch of the Franciscan order slid into violent opposition against the Avignon popes. As Spirituals, the dissidents demonstrated their fidelity to the intentions of the founder of the order. But they also expressed their belief in the advent of a third age of the world, drawn from the writings of the Calabrian hermit Joachim of Fiore: after the age of the Father, after the age of the Son, the preaching of Saint Francis had brought the age of the Holy Spirit; its reign rendered ecclesiastical intermediaries meaningless, since the entire community of the faithful was directly infused with the Spirit—that very spirit betrayed by the Church of Rome. Such teaching was echoed in the Rhineland by the Bégard communities and the Brothers of the Free Spirit, whom the bishops persecuted and burned in 1326 because they too asserted the free sovereignty of the "perfect" and the identity of the soul and God in mystic union: "Because of the natural repose they feel and possess within, in their idleness they regard themselves as free, united with God without intermediaries, raised above all the practices of the holy Church, above the commandments of God, above the law." Their doctrine had curious repercussions in the convents of the Dominican nuns taught by Meister Eckhart. In one of his vulgate sermons Meister Eckhart said:

> The power of the Holy Spirit also truly takes what is purest, subtlest, highest, the spark of the soul, and bears it on high in fire and

> in love, just as with the tree: the power of the sun takes what is purest and subtlest in the root of the tree and causes it to mount to the branches where it becomes a flower. In absolutely the same way, the spark of the soul is raised into the light and into the Holy Spirit and borne thus to its first origin. It becomes wholly one with God, moves absolutely toward union, it is one with God more truly than food with my body.

Later, at the end of the century, the opposition to the hierarchy grew more brutal and more determined in England and Bohemia. For Wycliffe and the Lollard preachers, as well as the knights who listened to them, the corrupt clergy no longer had any role to play. The essentials of religious life lay in the direct worship of Christ the brother, nourished by the reading of the Bible. What was important was that the word of God should be translated into the vernacular so that the people would be able to understand it. And John Huss followed suit. He condoned the deeper movements of popular messianism which, for a very brief period, before the violence and butchery, on the symbolical mountain of Tabor, managed to achieve the fraternal and egalitarian community of the children of God, impregnated with the living Spirit in fervent expectation of the imminent end of time. Far more discreetly, however, without rebellion and without a break, the movement at last took on its full meaning in the Netherlands by bringing about what was very rightly called "modern devotion." Along the Rhine, small groups of "friends of God" had been flourishing for some time. These assemblies of laymen, priests, and Dominican fathers mutually encouraged one another to lead an orderly life in the fraternity of Christ, which would guide them toward illumination and would be progressively purified. In his *Spiritual Wedding* Ruysbroek pointed the way to total renouncement, so that each might attain union in Jesus. "A truly devout man relies on himself. He is free in respect of earthly things, his heart opens reverently toward eternal divine goodness. Then the hidden sky is uncovered. From the face of divine love, a sudden light flashes straight into that open heart. Within that light the spirit of God speaks to that loving heart: I am thine and thou art mine, I dwell in thee and thou in me." And before 1424, the Brotherhood of the Common Life, founded by Geert Grote after long vacillation between Ruysbroek's hermitism and the austerities of the Carthusians, produced the devotional book which had the most widespread success among the Christian laity: *The Imitation of Christ.*

Preparing oneself for a form of meditation no longer bent on piercing the mysteries of God but on joining Christ in his humanity and, by successive degrees, on fusing with him in ineffable union, did not exclude all recourse to the priest. Jesus was nowhere more accessible than in the Eucharist. Certain rites therefore remained necessary. Both Mass, conceived as a representation of the Passion, during which the blood might spurt from the host and the image of the Man of Sorrows rise from the chalice as once in Bolsena, and the extended showing of the Corpus Christi during the long solemn procession on that day, were of essential value and rendered the ministry of the priest indispensable. Yet the inward personal works were what counted most of all, prayer, the devotion of the heart, and the gradual exaltation of the depths of the soul. These were what gave full significance to the new forms of religious art.

For the performance of the collective rites of Christianity, the fourteenth century erected a number of very spacious buildings. In the regions where rural estates were still thriving, in England and in Spain, the abbeys and the cathedral chapters sometimes set about renovating their sanctuaries. Elsewhere communities were assisted by the generosity of a prelate, or a patron, or, as in southern France, a pope. Where the functions of the cloisters, capitulary halls, and naves were maintained, no attempts were made to alter the structures of the building. The innovations consisted in adding to the external decoration, to the adornments glorifying a donor, or to the refinements of the rood screen, the enclosure. In the Capilla Mayor in Toledo, the rood screen confined the community of the officiants behind a splendid but impenetrable barrier, isolating them in their secluded psalmody, cutting them off completely from the congregation, which was cast out. The last developments of the art of the high clergy consequently accentuated the division between the old liturgy and the people. However, large churches were constructed for the citizens in the towns.

The urban populations were anxious to celebrate the fame of their cities with parish buildings which, by relegating the small district chapels to an accessory local role, would be suitable for assembling the citizenry around the magistrates and the major corporations at municipal ceremonies, civil and religious. The central collegiate churches of the Flemish cities, Saint Mary Radcliffe in Bristol, or Tyn, the merchants' church in Prague, rivaled the cathedrals. They stood as prestige monuments, thrusting their naves and belfries to the highest as symbols of power. But not far away other churches rose up in answer to more strongly spiritual functions and better attuned to the new fervors: thus the mendicant churches of the mendicant orders. The communities of grey, black, or white friars, Franciscans, Dominicans, Augustinians, Carmelites, established on the outskirts of all centers of any size, built vast structures often with two naves, one for the brotherhood and the other amply welcoming the laity. It was there that the new schemes were applied.

The emphasis was on sobriety, as befitted the poor orders. The outside was strictly bare, no flying buttresses, just a single volume rigorously adjusted to its purpose and consequently very beautiful. Inside, the same simplicity, the same spatial unity. If there were several naves, they were always the same height, as both ecclesiastics and laity were equals before God, separated only by the occasional slender pillar. It was important for the crowds and the friars who inspired them to be able to gather in one body. Since the new architecture was devised to ensure the full participation of the laity, it developed as the very negation of the rood screen. It destroyed all forms of enclosure, it eliminated all partitions. Everyone everywhere had to be able to hear the sermon, to see the body of Christ being raised and even to read a book. To achieve these purposes the bays were enlarged and the stained glass windows, gradually invaded by yellows and greys, acquired greater transparency, dispelling the gloom created for lighting candles and for choral psalmody. Bare, sober, and vast, flooded with light, the mendicant churches—a design which soon influenced the municipal collegiate churches and even the new cathedrals—established themselves as meeting places perfectly adapted to what the externals of a devout life had become: a show. Along their lateral walls stood a row of chapels, erected for the private worship of confraternities and families.

The chapels were originally conceived for royalty, for a sovereign possessing *charisma* and the power to work miracles. Belonging to the house of the anointed king, who for a long time had been the only layman to pray like a priest, a body of domestic clerks waited upon the monarch with uninterrupted liturgical rites just as they waited upon the bishop in the chapter house. The central place of ceremony was the chapel. There the king had his throne, his chair, his *cathedra,* like a bishop. The members of his household stood about him. Opposite were displayed the relics belonging to his treasure. The sovereign was expected to assemble a considerable number of parts of the saintliest bodies in order to enhance his powers of intercession. Therefore, and perhaps above all, the chapel also served as a reliquary. It was arranged as a shrine on two levels, one for the care of the holy remains and the other for their display. The walls, inlaid with extremely precious materials, shed their glow on the relics and on the sovereign in his majesty, on his throne, invested with the emblems of his power. Such was the chapel raised by Charlemagne for his palace in Aachen on the plan of the oratories of the Roman Empire in the East. Such was the Sainte-Chapelle, built by Saint Louis, a crowned king, to house the crown of Christ, marking the culmination of the art of royal liturgies.

This perfect model was imitated by European rulers throughout the fourteenth century. Edward III of England, in order to assert his venturesome command opposite that of the king of France, whom he wished to equal, once he had snatched the power from his mother's hands, ordered the construction of a chapel dedicated to Saint Stephen in Westminster, near the tomb of Edward the Confessor, honored as the rival of Saint Louis. When Charles IV, king of Bohemia, set about restoring the influence of the imperial power bestowed upon him, he built Karlstein. A room for relics, set with gold and diamonds, tapestried with saintly faces, crowned the dream castle. That recipient of the holy cross was a kind of mystic fulfillment of the knightly and military virtues paraded in the courtyards below. Ending the ascension up to the sky, the chapel provided a secret, closed place, imbued with the awe of the holy remains, which a series of ramparts protected against all attack for private conversation between the emperor and the crucified God whose vicar he knew himself to be on earth.

But not only kings set up personal shrines in the fourteenth century. Princes who had not been anointed wished to possess one too. Duke John of Berry deposited the sacred pieces of his dazzling collection of jewelry in the wonderful chapel at Bourges. But the most significant innovation which illustrated both modern devotional trends and the general development entailing the popularization of culture was the vast proliferation of privately owned chapels designed for personal use. In actual fact, these chapels belonged to small groups, to brotherhoods maintained from generation to generation, to confraternities, or to families, not to an individual. The guilds, corporations, and all the devout associations needed a place where their members could gather for regular prayer meetings around the clerks who guided their spiritual exercises. Few of them had the means to undertake the construction of a separate building. They asked for shelter in a particular church and were conceded a special area near one of the altars beside the high altar, which was where the collective celebrations were held. But the rites no longer united the whole community of believers as solidly as before. Each family, each household, wished to have a sanctuary of its own. In the castles of the upper aristocracy for a very long time there had been private oratories patterned on the royal chapels and these began to increase. The rich strove to copy the customs of the noblest lords, to eat, drink, dress, and amuse themselves as they did. Every head of a household who could afford it accordingly appointed his own priest and had Mass said for himself and his family, in the manner of the princes—or at any rate attempted to obtain a special place against the choir stalls or along the aisles by means of a handsome payment in alms. He looked upon this as a way of earning social promotion, of enabling his line to rank beside those of the great. The mendicant friars did not refuse to allot portions of space in their churches to the most influential or the most generous members of the laity whose piety they administered: twenty-five private chapels surrounded the choir stalls of the Cordeliers in Paris.

The confraternity and family chapels answered two purposes. The first, which might be called external, concerned the altar, and developed a private liturgy with masses said regularly and especially intended by the members of the group—for the living members, but even more frequently for the dead members. The primary function of the chapel was funerary in character. The cult of the dead had always been central to the instinctive religious life of the people. Insofar as such feelings became christianized and more closely incorporated into the Church, Christian rites for the benefit of the dead increased. For everyone at that time, joining a confraternity first of all meant being certain of a properly conducted funeral and of the perpetual religious services future generations of members would hold for their deceased. Each line was conscious of similar duties toward its dead. The belief in the efficiency of the ritual gestures performed by the living to aid the dead in no way dwindled at that period. On the contrary, one feels that it strengthened. All was not lost with death. The pope in Avignon had proclaimed that immediately after the soul passed away, it appeared before the face of God and received its first beatific vision. But between that first appearance and the Last Judgment stretched a term during which the soul might still earn certain merits it lacked for admittance into paradise. Its friends who had remained behind on earth could also credit its account with the profits derived from the repeated performance of the divine sacrifice. Thus no will and testament ever neglected to apportion a fair share of its heritage to the organization of a majestic funeral service and above all to the foundation of countless perpetual Masses. Families were ruined in the process, but each regarded such legacies as the best safeguard against hell. Each also thought that the Masses had more effect when they were sung close to the mortal remains of the one they were designed to succor. The most practical arrangement consisted in assembling the tomb and the altar in one place, where the priests would consecrate the host to the end of time. A Christian concerned with his own salvation and that of his family accordingly founded a chapel in a church for his house as soon as he felt in a position to bear the expense, by no means negligible. He had to purchase the burial place, fit it out in a way that would demonstrate its particular purpose and, lastly, provide revenue for the personal maintenance of the "chantry," as it was called in England, the chaplain or chaplains attached to the foundation. A whole ecclesiastical proletariat competed for such duties, which offered a safe comfortable living and required very little care. In the *Canterbury Tales,* the Friar is an allegorical figure of harmless sloth. Yet, however great the number of clerks who aspired to such sinecures, they were loth to fill the demand in view of the exorbitant requirements of the rich once they reached the threshold of death. The will of one great lord of Gascony, the *captal* of Buch, ordered sixty-one perpetual anniversaries and eighteen chaplaincies in addition to fifty thousand Masses to be said in the year of his death, with the result that the spread of these practices deprived many parishes of their ministries and contributed to the disintegration of the communal institutions of the Church, replacing them with egotistical forms of liturgical ceremony.

Funerary liturgy was not the only purpose of the private chapel. The growing inwardness of worship gradually provided another. As religious life became more personal, chapels began to be regarded as places for meditation and retreat. The believer who entered the oratory to pray for the souls of his dead relatives or his fellows could also meet God, could slowly raise up the "spark" of his soul in the silence of his heart. The chapel was suitably embellished with ornaments conducive to such outpourings. In the manner of the royal chapels, it tended to become a shrine. Christianity, at the level of popular sensibility, fortified faith in the saving virtues of holy remains. In the twelfth and thirteenth centuries the refinement of ecclesiastical culture had gradually restrained and disciplined the worship of relics in the churches constructed and governed by the highest clergy. With the irruption of lay practicing it proliferated again. Relics were the most valuable presents that could be given or received in the fourteenth century, or at all events the ones which everyone wanted to have. Owning relics, like all things, became popularized and secularized. Furthermore, images which could comfort or enable the soul to accede to the illumination of the Holy Spirit began to be placed in the chapels. These figures filled the stained glass windows, mingling with the symbols of ownership, the heraldic emblems, the mottoes, or the portrait of the founder. Painted, or carved in wood or alabaster, they adorned the altar pieces standing behind the high altar. These collections of symbolical scenes were usually folded, closed to the public, and opened only for the special use of the owners, the founders of the chapel. The household character became even more pronounced, however, in the statues of the patron saints of the family or the confraternity. The members of the small privileged group sometimes brought these effigies out of the cupboard and set them up for their exclusive contemplation or exhibited them in processions as a statement of their authority.

Such objects, which were portable and not fixtures like an altar or a tomb, could in fact leave the chapel and extend their mystical functions abroad, in daily life. Why confine the exercise of the love of God to a particular building at particular hours? The new Christianity was intended to be an integral part of the life of the faithful. The progress of private devotions in the fourteenth century guaranteed the success of sacred belongings of a small size. These substitutes for the chapel, even more personal, could provide a setting conducive to the deepening of saving meditation at any moment and in any place. It was then that relics began to be mounted as jewels to be worn against the body in immediate permanent contact with the one they were designed to protect against evil and to impregnate with grace. Small diptyches or triptyches summing up the major scenes of the drama of the liturgy with a few figures were produced in precious materials. Like the altar pieces, they were opened for prayer, before battle, before a tournament, on a business journey, or in the secrecy of a bedroom. The psalter and the book of hours also became a kind of portable chapel for many laymen, and their miniatures, transposing the themes of the stained glass windows or the altar panels, offered fervent imagery on biblical topics, more persuasive than the Latin words in the prayers, and appealing more directly to the sensibility. Of all those objects, the ones surviving in modern collections were probably the most valuable. Their sumptuous forms were strangely similar to the accessories of worldly amusement, with which they were sometimes confused. Like the chapels, they belonged only to men and women of great fortune. Yet the inventories, wills, and records show that persons of average wealth, the lesser knights, the subaltern agents of power, the burghers of the small towns, owned similar pieces, not so costly. Toward the end of the century, for men less rich still and far more numerous, the woodcuts, the printed paper illustrations which could be pinned to the wall, sewn on one's clothing, or carried folded on one's person began to provide a very cheap equivalent.

Those prints, just like the ivory diptyches, the pages of illuminated books, or the reliquary jewels always showed the devout image framed by an architectural symbol, an abstract sign for a church. Constant recourse to a network of arches, pinnacles, and gables was more than a mere residue of the dominant functions formerly filled by the art of building. It bore witness to the fact that for the devout such objects, which were better adapted to modern forms of worship, not only effectively replaced the chapel where one withdrew from time to time but also the forlorn cathedral. Within the movement that handed Christianity over to the laity in that century, the shadow church rose up in remembrance of liturgies long past, but also as the symbol of an inner religion which had its sanctuary in men's hearts.

Modern worship had no other aim but to prepare the soul for its wedding with the Spirit, to guide it by successive degrees, to secure it at the decisive moment of death against the dangers of the passage. Accordingly, it invited the believer to draw nearer to the word of God, to make it the constant nourishment of meditation. How could one know the Father, the Son, and the Holy Spirit, but by acquaintance with the Bible? In the fourteenth century, for the faithful as a whole, immediate contact with the Scriptures became what it had been for the monks in the isolation of the Benedictine cloisters and the cells of the solitary orders ever since the beginnings of European Christendom: one of the essential moments of a devout life. The layman was no longer expected merely to listen from afar to the ritual words or the intoning of fragments from the Bible, but to understand them.

In actual fact, however, the ecclesiastical hierarchy, suspicious and haunted by the fear of heretical deviations, was not at all anxious for men to read the scriptures unguided. Thus in the large-scale efforts to place the Latin books used by the clergy within reach of a wide public, the translations of the Old and the New Testament held only a minor place. Toward 1340, a

Yorkshire hermit put the Psalter into Middle English, the language of the people. Fifty years later, teachers from Oxford produced two versions of the Gospel. But those translators were committed to the Lollards, who figured as agitators in opposition to the high Church. When John of Cy translated the Bible into French, with a commentary, he was working for the king of France, John the Good: his magnificent edition, a genuine treasure-piece, was in no way whatsoever intended to educate the people. At the beginning of the fifteenth century short extracts of the Sunday lessons or "moralized" simplified adaptations of the Bible were still the only books in the French dialect available to the lettered laity. It was through the sermons that they perceived the essentials of Holy Writ.

The preachers at least strove to give more impact to their words and to impress their meaning on their audiences. For the assembled throng they endeavored to translate the Gospel into gesture and mime, acting the parts themselves, organizing the performance of the central themes of their sermons in tableaux or parades. They invited their listeners to take roles in the divine drama in the general processions, at the meetings of the confraternities, and even in the intimacy of their own oratory. The sacred representation provided a visual means of reaching the humblest believer, those whose slower minds remained unmoved by the eloquence of the sermonizers, despite the deliberately popular note.

But its aims went further. By enjoining the physical participation of the faithful, through singing or better still through acting, it asked them genuinely to embody the scenes of the life of Christ, to identify themselves for a moment with their brother Jesus. Medieval piety had always sought to fortify the inclinations of the soul by the adhesion of the body. In the Benedictine monasteries, prayer was not silent, it was declaimed at the top of the voice in one breath, by the assembled community. Writing, copying the scriptures, because the parchment had to be "worked," were active tasks in which the wrist played as great a part as the mind. There was no reading in low tones, but muscular participation again in declaiming the text. To mime the word of God consequently appeared to be the most complete way of possessing it, of truly living one's faith. At night in the cloisters, bearing a cross, the Dominican monk Heinrich Suso went from one pillar to the next acting out the Passion of Christ. His Stations of the Cross ended in a conversation with the Virgin before the crucifix in the chapel. By such exercises he attained those moments of ravishment he has described: "It often seemed as if he were floating on air or sailing between time and eternity, on the deep tide of the unsoundable marvels of God." If the Christian people as a whole, banded together by the mendicant friars, did likewise, they would advance along the mystic way, toward the radiance that saves and ensures that death itself will be but the straits of release. Sometimes the entire townspeople would join in a vast collective operation. During the three days of Pentecost in 1400 the craftsmen of Avignon produced the Passion of Our Lord at their own expense: "Two hundred were required to perform the said play, with so many more costumed and armed that no one could tell their number. In the square in front of the convent of the preaching friars stood very many platforms holding men and women. Never was there so royal a festival, nor one which could command ten to twelve thousand spectators." The mystery plays were consequently not only acted by the specialized confraternities; they also tended to stimulate general theatricals in which every Christian had a role in daily secret performance.

The image intervened even here. It occupied a central position as the most efficient medium between the word of God and the fervent mimesis wrenching body and soul from all that fettered them, all that kept them from soaring "toward the nobleness of contemplation, the summits of a blessed life." The image was suited to the novice, it marked the threshold to the way. "My daughter," wrote Heinrich Suso, "it is now time for you to mount higher and to raise yourself out of the nest of the consolations brought by images to one who begins." The preachers were well aware that it was important to offer a show to the countless beginners who made up their audiences, and that it was advisable, to achieve a more lasting effect, to determine distinguishing features and colors which would leave their imprint on the mind and offer wavering souls a kind of springboard for new impulses long after the missionaries had completed their tour. At the invitation of Bernardino of Siena, the image of the name of Jesus, surrounded by a radiant sun, which he had made the focus rather than the illustration of his sermons, was inlaid in the façades of patrician palaces. Painted panels, polychrome sculpture, all the imagery widely disseminated by the woodcuts, were designed to prolong the impression of penitential preaching and the *sacre rappresentazioni*. Fourteenth-century religious art, intended to uplift a vast public easily moved but apt to lapse by the wayside, was fundamentally scenic.

Giotto owed his entire fame to the fact that on his church walls he had achieved more magnificent portrayals of the successive acts of a kind of mystery play than any of his predecessors. With his genius for staging, he perpetuated theatrical movement, he proposed model attitudes for all those who wished to imitate Saint Francis of Assisi, Joachim, the Virgin, or Jesus, and to enter into their characters so as to probe their spiritual substance. Lastly, the educators of the Christian community, the friars who were bent on spreading the knowledge of the New Testament even at the humblest levels of religious society, regarded the image as a far more persuasive vehicle than reading the Bible or even listening to it. The fourteenth-century Bible had become "storified" to be made more accessible to the laity, it developed in tales, relating a succession of episodes as lively and exciting as those of legend and romance. And for the faithful who did not know how to read, the Bible was presented in story fashion, the *Bible des pauvres,* the Bible of the poor, cut up into a series of simple expressive pictures which contained the essential.

All the organizers of the new manner in fact thought, like Eustace Mercadé, the author of a *Passion* acted toward 1430 in northern France, that:

Examples, stories, paintings,
done at monasteries and palaces,
were better for many people
who did not understand the Scriptures.
They were the laity's books.

As piety became more popular, it became more spontaneously imaginative. "Before a Calvary be aware of what your soul gazes upon and view carefully all the things that are against your Lord. *See* therefore, with the *eyes* of your soul, how some drive the cross into the earth, how the others prepare the nails and the hammer," say the *Meditationes vitae Christi,* attributed to Saint Bonaventure but probably composed in the late fourteenth century by a Franciscan of Tuscany. All the metaphors, even the deliberate purpose of these writings, bear witness to the major role assigned to sight in the progress of inner life.

Sight, as everyone at that time was convinced, watched over the birth of love and nourished it. For everyone, all affective relationships were formed by rays of light, and the eyes were the gates to the heart. In the thirteenth century, in opposition to Aristotle, Robert Grosseteste, the founder of the Oxford schools, had proposed a system of the world inspired by Dionysius the Areopagite based on the luminous principle. He claimed that the universe proceeded from an effluence of light which, on radiating, engendered the spheres and the elements and the forms and dimensions of matter. Once accepted and developed by the scholars belonging to the Franciscan group, such a doctrine signified more than an invitation to refresh physics with the study of optics. It joined the current that fostered mystical outpourings as a protection against the temptations of the intellect. Surely light, created, infusing the world, guaranteed the closest link between a creature and its God? It propagated grace. It was the means whereby the human soul attained beatific contemplation. Such ideas incited thirteenth-century intellectuals to glorify the poetics of light pursued in cathedral art. And when Christianity became more secular and more popular a little later, the learned doctrine of the Franciscans of Oxford was easy to match with old profane conceptions. The laity also believed that one had to see in order to love, and that the fire of love was transmitted by an exchange of glances. In the lyrics of the troubadours in the thirteenth century, the loving spark received by the eye descends to kindle the heart and the union of the two hearts is achieved by means of a bright liquid. "Flame," "heart," "ardor," "spark"; the sermons and letters of guidance of the mystics use the same vocabulary as the songs of chivalrous passion. Sacred eroticism met profane eroticism in the great encounter mingling ecclesiastical and chivalrous culture. The fervor of the courtly lover flared up at the sight of his chosen lady. Similarly, Heinrich Suso, imitating the Passion of Jesus, proceeded toward the contemplation of an image of the crucified Christ. The page of a manuscript of the second half of the fourteenth century illustrating Suso's spiritual itinerary with a series of figures, shows the soul in a wanton attitude at one of the main stations: rapt in the sight of the effigy of Jesus on the cross. In the sculptures above the tombs, on the panels of the altar pieces perpetuating their offerings, the donors are portrayed kneeling before the image of God the man and his Mother. Their ecstatic gaze allows the radiance of sacred love to stream into their inmost hearts.

That is why display held such an important place in fourteenth century rites. That is why the Mass paused so long at the elevation when the consecrated host was offered to the eyes of the people, imbuing them with love. That is why the reliquaries were designed as showcases, like transparent cages, permitting the gaze to fall on the holy bodies. Everyone wished to see the objects of his mystical desire and found the visual approach a remedy for anxiety and a source of trusting hope. At its lowest level, piety even went so far as to endow religious images with miraculous powers. Surely it was enough to behold the effigy of Saint Christopher to know that one would not die on the day of a bad death. The people wanted images of that goodly, barely christianized giant to be placed everywhere. They stood at all the crossroads and hung against the far wall at the back of the churches so that the believer might cast a last look for reassuring protection as he departed. The ecclesiastical hierarchy did not discourage the fondness for venerating images. On the contrary, it condoned the supernatural efficiency of certain of them: indulgences were promised to anyone who said a prayer before the figure of the Christ of Mercy at Saint Gregory's Mass, and to anyone who visited the Calvary in the Carthusian monastery of Champmol.

Yet voices were raised within the Church to condemn such practices and to proscribe the allegedly miraculous images. A treatise was composed "against those who worship images and statues." Later there were statements from Gerson and Cardinal Nicholas of Cues. A very sober English text set forth the sound doctrine: "Images are organized by the Church to serve as calendars for the laity and uneducated people, to introduce minds to the Passion of Christ, martyrdom, and the good life of the saints. But if man renders to lifeless images the worship due to God or places in them the hope he could place in God, he commits the greatest sin of idolatry." The most violent and intransigent attacks came from certain heretical circles. The adepts of a truly spiritual religion wished it purified of all the readjustments introduced by an affluent, corrupt, earthbound clergy, and their reprobation of the Roman Church included images. In 1387 two men, both Lollards, broke the statue of Saint Catherine in Leicester. A little later, in Bohemia, the puritans of Tabor rose against figurative church ornamentation. But the iconoclasts were never more than the extremist wing of heretical violence. In the fourteenth century, both monumental art and the small objects that sustained individual piety provided a vehicle for simple faith.

Devout art was naturally linked with religious writing, with extracts from the Bible or the lives of the saints, often transcribed on scrolls or forming part of a scene. The successions of pictures could be read almost as comic strips might be read today. They ensured wide and permanent dissemination of a text and at the same time endowed it with expressive impact. They were therefore expected to disclose the facts of belief to the eye; if they used symbols or allegories, more often than not, it was in order to insert the invisible in familiar appearances, to lend it all the singular overtones of life on earth. These images were no longer intended merely to represent, they portrayed. They had to embody a reality, which was why the artists of the day borrowed certain illusionist methods from classical models. Yet it was also important for religious likenesses to stay at one remove from the profane world. Their role was to urge the soul to lift itself up, to break away from earthly shackles. Consequently they had to appear aloof. Painters and sculptors could certainly arrange men and God face to face in the same pictorial area. But no one ever mistook the face of a donor for that of the Christ he was worshiping, nor even for that of the patron saint standing behind him as a protector. They belonged to different worlds. They were separated by a fundamental barrier which could be crossed only by death. To make that essential segregation manifest, Giotto used certain theatrical devices: the abstract blue of the back-cloth he hung behind his scenes set them outside ordinary time. Above all he employed the authoritative note brought to light by the newly discovered decoration of ancient Rome. The characters in his stately drama admittedly look human. Joachim sleeps as all shepherds sleep. But something prevents one from wishing to tap him on the shoulder, something undefinable, like the invisible wall separating the audience and the actor, the communicant and the priest bearing the host, Don Juan and the statue of the Comendador. The tritest altar piece executed for a craftsmen's confraternity in the humblest township took care never to lower the characters of the biblical story to the pedestrian life of everyday. An intact belief in another world raised an obstacle, called a halt at a certain point along the road to realism in the religious art of that time.

Beyond that limit, in that real but invisible realm which the image was intended to unveil, to offer to the eye before dreaded death, thus opening a way for the bright dart of love, dwelt a host of secondary characters, the population of the saints. They had been generously welcomed by simple Christianity, along with the demons and the malevolent powers they vanquished. These innumerable intercessors had very definite personalities and when they were shown in a group, the most skillful artists attempted to give each figure a special countenance. Each saint possessed his favorite places on earth, those he had known during his life, those where the remains of his body lay. It was there that they worked their miracles. Each possessed powers of his own which it was advisable to invoke in certain circumstances. Their personal histories were known through the *Golden Legend* of James of Voragine, a tale told to the whole of the West in a thousand episodes. They could be identified by their features, their dress, their symbolical attributes. There was no doubt whatsoever in the mind of Joan of Arc as to which saints had dictated her calling. Like the processions, religious imagery allotted considerable space to these powers that provided protection against dangerous death, to the accredited patrons of a particular social group or a particular confraternity, to these personal guardians entrusted with the care of each Christian's body and soul. The dissemination of the image advertised the renown of the newly canonized saints, Saint Thomas Aquinas or Saint Catherine of Siena. And it was through its control of visual decoration that the Church succeeded in governing the humble affections lavished on these supernumeraries of the sacred drama. The figurative program of Assisi aimed to present the image of Saint Francis as an integral part of the orderly structure of the papal Church.

Devout theater nevertheless gave the front of the stage to a central figure: God, God in three persons. A large number of confraternities placed themselves under the Trinity in the fourteenth century. Painters and sculptors were consequently required to portray the three divine images. In its most venturesome thrusts, the leading wing of Christianity laid emphasis on the third of them, the Holy Spirit. Like the *fraticelli,* many of the faithful were convinced that its reign was at hand. Its command of the relations between the soul and divine power was acknowledged by all. Yet the dove of the Holy Spirit was never more than an accessory item in the portrayals of the Trinity, a kind of lyrical symbol of union. The Father himself was never more than a backcloth, a kind of living throne. The entire composition was arranged around the image of the crucified Son. After a century of Franciscan influence, trecento figurative art was focused on a center radiant with love: Jesus. But which Jesus? The Benedictines of the Romanesque age had designed the tympanum of the abbey churches to show Christ on the Day of Judgment. The cathedral doorways built by thirteenth-century intellectuals contained figures of Jesus the teacher. The Christ demanded by a Christendom at last composed of the people was just a man, a man who stirred the heart, since modern worship had become "a certain tenderness of spirit causing one easily to break into tears." The Jesus of the preachers, as revealed in the *sacre rappresentazioni,* the Jesus of Christmas and the Jesus of Easter. A "storified" God, a character in a tale: Christ brought closer by the helplessness of early childhood, above all by his collapse in agony.

Christmas and Easter. The winter feast was joyous. It proclaimed hope in the gloom of night. But its joy emanated from the Mother rather than the Child. Appealing increasingly to women, popular Christianity plaited its sentimental arabesques around Marian worship. Marian themes were also very prevalent in clerical Christianity, becoming more and more widespred at a low level. In fourteenth-century art, the countless figures of the Virgin gradually lost their sacred character: Mary kneeling before her newborn Son, Mary overwhelmed in her meditation by the annunciation of the angel, Mary watching her child play among the sweet grasses and flowerlets of closed gardens, and Mary the protectress, the Virgin raising her mantle above the saintly host, assuming the tutelary role of all, sheltering the assembled Christian people beneath her blue cope as sole mediatrix. After the penitence and mortification of Lent, Easter burst forth, but was led in by the parade of divine sorrows. If Christ ultimately drew all men toward their salvation, it was by the accumulation of suffering; he was the victim, the Lamb bearing the sins of the world. At that time no performance was more popular than the Passion, and no image better known than the cross, the crucifix, the tragic axis of the religion of the poor. Attention gradually shifted from the humiliated Christ, the flagellated Christ, Christ nailed on the cross, to the dead Christ: in the lap of the Virgin of Mercy, no longer the happy mother of flowering orchards, coronations, and assumptions, but cooperating in redemption by the depth of her grief, by the sorrowful loving gaze cast on the despoiled son, lay a corpse. A corpse whose burial was staged for the first time in a theatrical performance of the Holy Sepulcher in 1419. Acting the part of Jesus, beholding the successive scenes of his sacrifice, seeing with the eyes of the soul "how some drive the cross into the earth, how the others prepare the nails and the hammer," sinking oneself in contemplation to the point of receiving the stigmata on one's own body, was to become so closely identified with him that one ultimately triumphed over death as he himself had triumphed. It was the dread of eternal night which led to the imitation of Christ.

More than an art of living, fourteenth-century Christianity was an art of good dying, and the chapel seemed more a place of funerary worship than of prayer and mystic vision. The combined forces of popularization and secularization established the awareness of death in that prominent position, centering religious rites and imagery around one primary question: what had become of the dead? Where were they?

High Church doctrine offered a reassuring answer. Death was a passage, the end of the earthly journey, the arrival at the port. One day, perhaps not far off, the world would witness the end of time, the glorious return of Christ, the resurrection of the flesh in its fullness. Then the righteous would be separated from the wicked and the vast host of those raised from the dead would be divided into two groups, one of which would proceed toward everlasting joy and the other toward everlasting pain. In expectation of that day, the dead reposed in a quiet, refreshing place, sleeping the sleep of peace. Such was the teaching of funerary liturgy. The conquering Church of the early Middle Ages had formerly persecuted the funerary practices of paganism in order to destroy them. It had threatened the direst penalties for those who persisted in giving food to the dead. It had emptied the tombs of their jewels, clothing, arms, the superabundant furnishings placed beside the body so that the deceased might live his mysterious existence in comfort and not return, dissatisfied, to disturb the living. Death had thus established itself unadorned, in tranquil sobriety. Startlingly bare: no ornaments or emblems accompanied the remains of the Carolingian princesses buried in the foundations of Saint Gertrude's basilica in Nivelles, and when the archaeologists opened the grave of Philip I at Saint-Benoît-sur-Loire, the only royal tomb still undefiled, they found nothing beside the body but the debris of a simple covering of leaves.

The priests had had to come to terms with overpowerful beliefs and had given more and more importance to funeral liturgy. They had accepted the myth of intermediate space and time between death and the Last Judgment, they had admitted that it might be entered by the souls of the dead awakening from their sleep: those whom Dante went to visit were not sleepers. Under the doubtful supervision of the Church, Purgatory stretched out like a province won back by pre-Christian conceptions of death. The scope of the reconquest was further enlarged in the second half of the thirteenth century when the clerks lost their influence on devout demonstrations and the mendicant friars worked to make Christianity a true people's religion. For a long time the Church had refused to admit tombs other than those of the saints, princes, or prelates inside the sanctuaries. But the desire of the living to lay their dead as close as possible to the altars, gradually overcame official reluctance. For the rich the funeral ceremony was yet another occasion for display. The deceased had to make his entry into the kingdom beyond the grave fully arrayed in accordance with his fame. Since a man's power was measured by the number of his "friends," of those who lived under his patronage in his obedience, the long procession of his household, followed by all the poor he had supplied with gifts, accompanied the bier. Lastly, his tomb was covered with many ornaments. Figurative ornaments. Anxious not to disappear altogether, the dead person wished his likeness at least to remain present on earth.

Contrasting with the Christian spirit of self-denial, the will to survive in one's sepulcher reflected the emergence of another possibly more basic trend in profane attitudes: the desire to defeat physical annihilation and human terror, not only of the dead, but of one's own death, of death itself.The Church had set out to domesticate that trend and mold it to its own purposes from the first. It had always invited meditation on the corruption of the body by representing it as a sign of the imperfection of the flesh, of its futility, as the condemnation of the transient pleasures here below, as the keenest inducement to embrace the true way, the way of God, by detaching oneself from the age. The image of the skeleton and the decomposition of the body offered one of the most persuasive illustrations of the merits of repentance. The *laudi* sung in Italian confraternities thus readily referred to the loneliness of the corpse, surrendered to the worms in the obscure grave. Matching this edifying undertaking was a figurative topic based on the poem of the Three Dead and the Three Living, which describes how three riders come across three open sepulchers and discover their own corpses in decay, suddenly revealing the vanity of the world to the living. The wriggling worms in the wasted flesh taught a double lesson. Putrefaction was first of all evidence of the intimate union of the carnal wrappings and sin. Only the bodies of the saints were believed to escape corruption, and when the preaching friars opened the tomb of Saint Dominic, they waited anxiously for that sweet "scent of holiness" which would prove to the whole world that the founder of their order effectively ranked among the blessed. But the sight of physical annihilation was also intended to spur on the believer to pursue a prudent life, to be ever ready, like the wise virgins, in a state of grace, since death was an archer who would let fly his dart when least expected, and catch man unawares. The view of the rotting corpse rose up amid the imagery of liturgical Christianity like a rampart against the pernicious charms of a tempting and condemned world.

By the turn of the thirteenth century, the progress of the lay spirit had brought about a total reversal of the theme. Beside the image of the Three Dead and the Three Living in the great fresco painted for the Camposanto of Pisa, the artist set another scene in radical contradiction, the Triumph of Death. Brandishing a scythe, the figure of death rushes like a whirlwind toward the delectable orchard where, amid the sweet joys of courtly life, a society of lords and ladies sing of love and earthly delights. It will mar their happiness at one stroke and, like the plague, like the Black Death, add that musical assembly to the pile of corpses already being heaped up. Here the image no longer has the effect of an example of the vanity of pleasure. It hurls out the anguish of mortal man at the powers of his destiny. The movement of the retreating horses, rearing up before the Three Dead and their open tombs, hints at renouncement, detachment. Whereas the lovers, carefree and careless of the whirling fury which will suddenly reap their bliss, on the contrary, cling to their happiness, to their lives. For them, as for the troubadours whose songs accompany their dances, this world is beautiful, full of enchantments. It is scandalous to be snatched away. If death, Petrarch's *donna involta in vesta negra,* borne along in the tumult of a hurricane as in Pisa about 1350, riding the skeleton of a mare in Palermo about 1450, appeared in the ineluctable power of a terrible triumph, it was because the thirst for carnal happiness in a society freeing itself from ecclesiastical morality had been the first to prevail in trecento culture. When man rose from prostration, it was to find himself face to face with a calamitous death, made to measure. His own.

The new symbols invaded the church walls. The preachers, the organizers of a devout life, proved powerless to restrain the love of the world, to stem the upsurge of secular optimism. But at any rate they sought to apply their teaching to the uneasiness inseparable from that optimism, to the horror of death, the destroyer of all worldly pleasures. The Pisa fresco resembles the illustration of a sermon which has reinforced the failing impact of an old theme with another, more disturbing, touching the mainsprings of a new sensibility in its tragic depth. Contemporary forms of the macabre took up their place at the center of religious iconography about the end of the fourteenth century. The first *Art of Dying* appeared in Germany about 1400. These collections of woodcuts described the drama of death in a succession of scenes, showing the dying person tormented with regret for what he was leaving, harassed by demons attempting a last offensive but finally routed by Christ the brother, the Virgin, and the saints. The *danse macabre* became organized at about the same period, perhaps in France. At the deepest strata of popular belief, the figure of victorious death was sometimes associated with that of the magician-piper. His artful tunes captivated men and women, old and young, rich and poor, the pope, the emperor, the king, the knight, the members of each worldly "estate," carrying them along irresistibly. The sermon-givers perhaps thought of having that terrifying triumphant sarabande acted, then the sacred representation became fixed with the use of imagery. In 1425, in Paris, the new symbol of human mortality stood in the graveyard of the Innocents, not far from the henceforth less convincing group of the Three Dead and the Three Living, erected there formerly by Duke John of Berry. From Coventry to Lübeck, from Nuremberg to Ferrara, the theme was taken up everywhere as an expression of the human predicament, attaining anxiety at its most sensitive spot, no longer transporting it into the distant confused beyond of Last Judgments, but confronting it with real present certainties, with an actual fact, the agony of death. "Whoever dies, dies in pain." Passing away no longer resembled the peaceful slumber of the traveler who had reached the haven of salvation, but a giddy opening onto a yawning abyss. Yet it was as a development of a long drawn-out movement which had been attuning Christianity to the religious desires of the laity for two centuries that the macabre prevailed, not as a consequence of the poverty of the day, the recurrent plagues, the wars, and the epidemics. Trembling in the face of death was not a sign of a depressed Christendom no longer as confident or as credulous: it betrayed a less discriminating Christendom widely accessible to simple men of unshakable but more limited faith, whose outlook was more concrete. The *danse macabre,* like the Italian theme of the Triumph of Death, like the image of the dead Christ in his mother's lap, suited a religious sensibility which came from the people and no longer from monks and university professors. It belonged to the rich and the poor who prayed in the Franciscan churches or in the chapels, surrounded by tombstones.

Once the idea of death had been accepted at the heart of a devout life in its simple forms, and authorized to command it, once the anxiety at leaving this world and the eagerness to live on had made the imitation of Jesus Christ above all the imitation of his agony, the tomb appeared in broad daylight as it actually had been for centuries behind the serene veil drawn by the High Church: a basic concern. In the fourteenth century, patronage seems to have turned its attentions mainly to funerary pomp. The majority of the commissions, and the ones which were most detailed, were for the tomb. The initial clause of all wills contained the selection of the sepulcher, the choice of the spot where the remains would be deposited, where they would be housed until Judgment Day. Anyone who thought of building a chapel, of devising its decoration, of amassing the revenue to ensure its maintenance, thought more about his tomb than about his prayers. It was the custom to prepare one's last abode well in advance, to supervise the construction and ornamentation personally, and to set down careful arrangements for the actual burial. The funeral ceremony was conceived as a festival, the greatest festival of a man's life. And at festivals one indulged in wasteful display. A funeral in those days was a last opportunity for ruinous show.

> This is how the king [poor King Charles VI of France, in 1422, amid the worst disasters of the Hundred Years War] was borne to Notre-Dame. Of the bishops and abbots, four wore a white mitre, including the new bishop of Paris, who awaited the body of the king at the entrance to Saint Paul to sprinkle him with holy water as he left. All the others went in except him, the mendicant orders, the university in one body, the colleges, the Parliament, the Châtelet, the people. Then the king was taken away from Saint Paul and the servants fell into deep mourning. He was carried to Notre-Dame as one carries the body of Our Lord on the feast of the Holy Savior; a gold dais was held above the royal remains by four or six near relations; thirty servants bore the body on their shoulders, possibly more, because it was very heavy. He reposed on a bed, his face

> uncovered, wearing a gold crown, in one hand the royal scepter and in the other the hand of justice giving the blessing with two gold fingers, so long that they touched the crown. Ahead marched the mendicant orders and the university, the churches of Paris, then Notre-Dame and lastly the palace. The latter were singing, but not the others. And all the people lining the streets or at their windows wept and wailed as if each were witnessing the death of the one he had cherished most in the world. There were seven bishops, the abbots of Saint-Denis and Saint-Germain des Près, Saint-Magloire, and Saints-Crépin-et-Crépinien. The priests and the clerks were in one row and the lords of the palace, like the provost, the chancellor, and the others, in another. In front of them were the poor servants dressed in black weeping heavily and bearing two hundred and fifty torches; further ahead still, eighteen chief mourners. . . . Behind the body, the duke of Bedford walked alone, with no prince of the blood royal of France beside him. It was thus that the dead king was taken on Monday to Notre-Dame where two hundred and fifty candles were lit. Vigils were said, and Mass early the following day. After Mass, the same procession formed again to take him to Saint-Denis where he was buried beside his father and mother after the service. More than eighteen thousand persons attended, small and great, and each received eight doubloons of two deniers tournoi. Dinner was given to all.

Of course that was the funeral of a great sovereign, but at the time everyone dreamed of being able to order the same sumptuous splendor. The account is interesting because, apart from the ceremony, it describes the figurative ornamentation which had become customary for royal tombs. The primary aim of fourteenth-century funerary art was to institute a show, to give permanence to the sacred representation performed around the corpse. Built onto the wall or standing in the center of the chapel, the sarcophagus lost its bareness. It took on the appearance of a bed for lying in state which had displayed the mortal remains to all during the ceremony. Surmounted by the processional dais which sheltered the monstrance during the rites of Corpus Christi, it supported the life-size effigy of the deceased. For the purposes of the funeral, the corpse had been embalmed and emptied of its entrails, which were often dispersed to be buried in various sacred places. Or had been replaced by a costumed leather doll, sometimes even by a live mannequin. The recumbent stone figure on the tomb consequently looked like a mummy. Arrayed in all the emblems of authority, it had a painted face. The procession itself was reproduced on the sides of the sarcophagus or on the surround at the back, with arches framing a symbolical church: the officiating clergy, the members of the family wearing mourning, and lastly the poor, bearing their lights as a sign of fervent prayer before receiving a last donation of money and food. The deceased was expected to show himself in all his glory to his people, whom he had assembled for a last banquet. He was also a subject for propitiatory rites, which funerary ornament again was designed to render more effective. Lastly, he was identified with Christ who, on his return, would bear him toward everlasting life. Tomb iconography culminated in the symbolism of salvation, sometimes by representing the Easter sepulcher, more often than not by illustrating the figures of the Resurrection.

The Christians who could prepare such monuments of hope for their mortal remains were very few. Most ended up in the public charnel house. Those who were not utterly poor ordered unpretentious gravestones from the tomb craftsmen whose industry was thriving; the designs reduced the mortuary likeness to a carved silhouette and the liturgical environment to a few inscriptions. But the royal tomb, like the royal burial, gave full expression to what was actually the desire of all. It demonstrated common conceptions of funerary ostentation, and at the same time gave them clearer shape. In arrangement and adornment, it rid the idea of death of its confusion as funerary art gradually espoused the new direction.

When funerary representation was reintroduced on the formerly bare tomb, developing first in England and Spain in the thirteenth century, it continued to reflect the influence of High Church art for a long time. The clergy had admitted reclining figures of the dead provided they were hieratic and serene. The faces of the kings of France sculpted for Saint Louis at Saint-Denis impart the peace bestowed upon them by funerary liturgy. With their eyes open, washed of all the accidents of earthly life, transfigured in the timeless beauty of a body prepared for resurrection, they sleep a cool and tranquil sleep excluding all duration. They crossed death to anchor gently on eternal shores. Lulled by the psalmody of the priests, they entered the conceptual universe of a way of thought which, by means of Aristotelian abstractions, was then discovering the rational order of a world beyond. By the late thirteenth century that tranquility was lost. Secular sensibility had undermined it and caused it to disintegrate. The dead were snatched from their repose. In their impassiveness, they had turned their backs on contemptible life but were now thrust into the concrete world and the concerns of the living. Admittedly, in the Gothic countries, the peace of the mortuary effigies remained deep and undisturbed for a long time. Although signs of a physical likeness could be traced on the face of King Philip III of France, whose tomb was erected between 1298 and 1307, the note of magnificence it conveyed and its liturgical overtones transported the body far out of time. But Italy, which up to then had disregarded recumbent figures, pointed to another way with the first of the overtly figurative funerary monuments produced by Arnolfo di Cambio after 1282 in the Dominican church of Orvieto for Cardinal William of Braye. It was a majestic way, as human and earthly as it was divine, and one eagerly followed by all Italian sculptors. The art of Rome and Etruria, which they gradually resuscitated, had in fact been largely devoted to the dead. But their dead did not repose in the sleep of grace and the expectation of an afterlife. They had wished to live on in this world in the splendor of their earthly fame. In Tuscany and Latium, in Naples, in Verona, in Milan, then in the countries beyond the mountains, the tombs of the princes of the Church and the world became complex mausoleums. The liturgical recumbent figures lying in state on the funeral bed signified the resurgence of Roman death and the anxiety of lay Christendom at death in general, but they were joined by other characters, praying figures, the decaying corpse, the heroic knight. The intrusion of the new images, as three different portrayals of the deceased, bore witness to the progress of the profane spirit in funerary art.

The rotting hairy corpse of Cardinal de Lagrange, the skeleton, as the strict residue of exact dissection, which Masaccio painted in Santa Maria Novella, merely portrayed the inside of the sarcophagus beneath the bedecked mummy stretched out on the lid. *Memento mori,* an image still in the direct line of ecclesiastical thought. Like the image of the Three Dead, it demonstrated the futility of a material world doomed to disease and dust. The patrons who commissioned such forms of representation wished to show their contempt for their carnal being at the gates of death, to detach themselves from it more completely, and to make their tomb an instructive act of humility, an exhortation to repentance. The appearance of pictures of decay on funerary monuments was largely the consequence of the old message of the Church to renounce worldly vanities. But in the beholders the sight could also awake the obsession with triumphant death. The figure of the corpse accordingly took up its position beside the Dance of Death and the Triumphs in the grimacing parade of the new macabre.

The donors who no longer wished to be shown sleeping in heavenly peace and the anonymity of the chosen were inspired by more profane feelings. They preferred more obviously lifelike guises, with personal features that were identifiable, therefore often not reclining on the bier but in the more active posture of prayer or even seated, like the emperor Henry VII on his tomb in Pisa, holding court, surrounded by the statues of his counsellors who were still alive. First and foremost, they wanted to be remembered for themselves. The sepulcher was not just anyone's, it was theirs. And it was important that everybody should know, because constructing a fine tomb in one's lifetime was a sign of social achievement and because the only justification for ostentatious art was that its author should be clearly designated. Above all, however, because the tomb was an appeal to the living. The deceased demanded prayers from passers-by. He demanded them for himself, for his personal salvation; the egoistic turn taken by piety was also expressed in the desire to leave a distinctive stamp on one's tomb. Heraldic symbols or the inscription of a name were enough to point to the identity of the dead person on most private sepulchers and on the gravestones purchased from the craftsmen who produced them in series. But the great patrons wished the portraits on their tombs to be true likenesses. The custom of taking a death mask, which was sometimes used for the funeral procession, eased the sculptor's task when the tomb had not been prepared during the owner's lifetime. Faces of reclining figures consequently became a privileged area in which fourteenth-century artists could practice their observation of the accidental.

The eagerness to leave one's mark on such an essential work of art as a funerary monument matched another desire, perhaps less overt but likewise belying the spirit of renouncement. To set one's features in stone was to shield them from the ravages of death, to overcome the powers of destruction, to endure. The unreal countenance of thirteenth-century reclining figures proclaimed the same victory but transferred it to the beyond. Men wished to survive in this world as well through a convincing semblance. During the funeral ceremony the deceased would sometimes be portrayed in activity by a series of live scenes. When Bertrand Du Guesclin was taken to burial at Saint-Denis "four knights armed to the teeth, riding four smart chargers in full array, represented the figure of the dead man when he was alive." At all events the funerary portraits of fourteenth-century Christians gradually assumed something of the arresting presence of the effigies of ancient Rome. The tombs with several tiers showing the figure of the sovereign either kneeling or ruling in all his power—Ferdinand of Castile in Seville toward the end of the thirteenth century or King Robert of Naples at Santa Chiara a little later, in lifelike attitudes and with recognizable facial features—signified a kind of revenge on the image of the decaying corpse which they rejected.

Such representations were found more and more frequently. Soon they left the tombs and accompanied the portrayals of saints and God on the altar panels, in more vivid and more carnal renderings, and slowly invaded the spaces which liturgical art had so far reserved for sacred figures. The emperor Charles IV wished to find his own features on the walls of the lower chapel at Karlstein. A faithful portrait of the count of Evreux filled one of the finest stained glass windows in the cathedral, in a position formerly held only by the aloof silhouettes of the prophets. The statues of real men stood against the church walls. In order to gratify his sovereign, Cardinal de Lagrange had ordered images of Charles V, his counsellor Bureau de la Rivière, the dauphin, his second son, and himself for the cathedral of Amiens. The façade of the cathedral of Bordeaux no longer displayed statues of Christ and the apostles but the pope surrounded by cardinals. Three centuries before, the monks of Cluny, braving the fear of sacrilege, had been bold enough to place the awesome figure of the everlasting God on the portals of their churches. That position was now occupied by the fatherly faces of the princes, and by comely princesses, by King Charles V, the duke of Burgundy, Philip the Hardy, and their wives, at the threshold of the Celestine sanctuaries, in the college of Navarre, and the Carthusian church of Champmol. Even inside the church, the human figure, an ordinary man, the individual figures of persons who had not wished to die altogether, won the area hitherto reserved for angels. The new men, who had discovered the tragedy of death, ushered in the era of the portrait.

In Verona, a heroic cavalryman, perched on the top of the funerary dais, completes the mausoleum of the "tyrant," Cangrade della Scala. The face is not a likeness. Yet it proclaims his victory and fame. That knightly figure was the product of two converging desires for profane survival. The one unquestionably came from Rome. The university professors who had discussed Roman law in Bologna and had been the first to allow a yearning for civic antiquity to creep into the medieval soul had set up their sarcophagi outside the churches, in public, like steles. They had wished their tombs to show them in power, dominating their disciples from their chair. The equestrian figure of Cangrande, continued by those of the other Scaligers, then the portrayal of Bernabò Viscounti after the dukes of Milan had conquered Verona, intoned imperial rule. In Capua, the emperor Frederick II, renewing ties with the classical manner, had laid the foundations for an art of political authority; that art on the public tomb of the lord, in the cities subjected to tyranny, led to the first monument of civic splendor. It endowed the dead princes with historical immortality. But those tall figures erect in the saddle, standing upright on their stirrups, conveyed yet another fame, likewise terrestrial: the glory of the heroes of courtly adventure. The current of chivalrous myth poured down the Alpine passes and across the Lombardy plain. The valley of the Adige led to Bamberg, to another empire, Christian and Germanic, knightly but feudal, possessed by the prowess of French epic, of Roland, Oliver, and Percival. Rather than other Caesars, Cangrande and Bernabò yearned to be paladins. The lasting victory their statues installed had been won in a tournament. They owed their survival to their chivalry, to the tales of their valor and "skill in arms" repeated in ladies' chambers. But they also represented Saint George. Their lances had slayed death like a dragon. Opposite the liturgy of the reclining figures and the moral teaching of the decaying corpse, the art of the new sepulchers set up the challenging figure of the knight.

10

POSSESSION OF THE WORLD

Girt in armor and in the pride of his victories, the knight of the Lombard sepulchers ranked among heroes. He was about to join the company of the nine paladins, chosen by worldly society as the symbols of his virtues and his love of life. Joshua, David, and Judas Maccabaeus, Hector, Alexander and Julius Caesar, Arthur, Charlemagne, and Godfrey of Bouillon, the nine exemplary figures whom Giotto had already depicted at the royal palace of Naples, who had appeared on so many tapestries woven for the princes and whose statues adorned the renovated knightly dwellings toward 1400, had all been immortalized by history. The first by the "holy tales" of the Old Testament. The next by classical legend brought to light with the growing success of the works translated from Latin literature. The last three by the accounts knit into a heavy fabric of episodes told in epic poetry and the romances concerning "the matter of France" and "the matter of Britain." The composition of the procession showed where chivalrous culture had found nourishment. The majority of its heroes had been drawn not from priestly literature but almost without exception from the profane tales. Rome in the center; on one side Jerusalem, on the other Aachen, *douce France,* and Windsor; in the background, dreams of empire, of the East and of crusades. No saints among them, no clerks. Men who lived by the sword, kings and warriors who had vanquished, in honor. Power and prowess. And, so that the model might also embrace the other side of knightly culture, nine ladies were soon added to the picture, nine female figures who also emerged, three by three, from the Bible, from classical story, and from the poetry of the courts, embodying the values of courtesy.

In the lives of the men and women whose desires fourteenth-century works of art were expected to illustrate, the imitation of the nine paladins and their ladies alternated with the imitation of Jesus Christ while completing it. It was as important to copy the acts of the heroes in life as to copy those of the Savior in the expectation of death. Literature offering a minute description of such exemplary behavior was copiously distributed on all sides. Festivals and ceremonies provided the symbolical transposition. Yet it was not the type of play which could be acted in the theater, although the *entremêts* which broke up the banquets with entertaining interludes often showed live tableaux. It mainly formed part of the ritual of the new orders of chivalry.

In 1344, carried away by the never-ending romance of Perceforest, Edward III, the victorious king of England, adopted the designs of his rival in chivalry, John, the future king of France, then duke of Normandy. Froissart relates that

> at that time it occurred to him to restore and reconstruct the great castle of Windsor, previously founded by King Arthur. There he formed and established the noble Round Table which produced so many fine valiant men, diligent in arms and prowess throughout the world. The king decided to create an order of chivalry which would comprise himself, his children, and the most gallant knights in the land. They would be forty. They would be called the Knights of the Blue Garter. A festival would be commemorated year after year at Windsor on Saint George's day. The king of England began by summoning earls, barons, and knights from the whole country and describing his intentions and his great desire to hold the festival. All joyously agreed, because it seemed an honorable thing which would nourish love. They then elected forty knights, deemed more gallant than all the others by opinion and report. They swore to the king in faith and by oath that they would keep and continue the festival and the order as they were planned and organized. The king founded Saint George's chapel at Windsor castle and provided an establishment for the canons, who would serve God. So that the said festival might be known in every province, the king of England had it published and announced by his heralds in France, Scotland, Burgundy, Hainaut, Flanders, Brabant, and also in the Empire of Germany. He granted fifteen days safe conduct after the celebrations to all the knights and squires who wished to attend. At the festival there was to be jousting in which forty knights would await the rest and forty squires, too. The queen of England would be there, accompanied by three hundred ladies in waiting and maids of honor, all of noble birth and similarly attired.

Thus a closed confraternity presided over by the sovereign, recruited by competition based on titles to prowess, assembled around a chapel like all brotherhoods at that time. A patron saint, Saint George, the hero of victorious jousts. A life commitment, a vow to accomplish certain virtues. A decoration, a symbol of valor, a device, lastly an annual feast on the day of the patron saint to celebrate the fame of the best among them before the ladies.

The new profane liturgy fell into place within a framework borrowed from the devout associations. Courtly romance was substituted for lauds, and exercises in worldly excellence for collective mortification. As exact replicas of the confraternities of the *laudesi,* the new orders of chivalry aimed to represent a code of ethics and to ensure its success by periodical adjustment of a collective game. Like them, they required figurative portrayal, a transposition into scenes and images. The rules of such a morality not only disciplined the closed companies surrounding the kings and princes, however. They governed a type of conduct which all those who dreamed of being introduced into the nobility and being considered as gentlemen accepted as the common ideal. Graciousness meant gentle birth. Those who were not born noble—captains honored by success in arms, citizens who had grown rich—were well advised to outdo everyone else at the game of chivalry and courtesy. The courtly myths and the rites allowed to materialize in daily life were consequently imposed on the rich at large, on the entire social group that indulged in patronage of the arts. For that reason courtly imagery stands as a symmetrical counterpart to devotional imagery in the fourteenth century.

Like the *Bible des pauvres,* the *Artes moriendi,* or the frescoes of the chapels, these illustrations were intended as examples for moral edification. They concerned three principal topics attuned to the three basic tonalities of chivalrous joy. In the series of tapestries executed for the king of France, Charles V, and his brothers, for instance, the majority showed religious scenes and were used to adorn the walls of the chapels. Of the others, the first included images of *guerrerie* or tournaments: Hector before Troy, the fight of Cocherel, or the jousts of Saint-Denis. "The knights of our day," says the *Songe du verger,* "order paintings of pitched battles on foot and on horseback for their halls so that by *means of sight* they may delight in *imaginative* combat." The primary function of the nobility, its essential duty, in fact, consisted in fighting for good causes. Through arms, a gentleman rid himself of his aggressive strength under the discipline of the rules of honor. Most of the profane tapestries were also spread with greenery. The decoration they displayed eliminated the walls and allowed the castle rooms to benefit from open nature. For the heroes of chivalry were outdoor men. They cantered through the spring forests, clasping the mayflower in their fist. Whenever a hare passed, they forsook the fray for the hunt. The forest provided the mysterious, magical setting expected of all adventure stories, and the lords made the orchard the favorite spot for their quieter sports. The last theme was love, governed by the code of courtesy. All the hangings of the *Triumph of Love,* of the *Goddess of Love,* which the princes ordered from the weavers of Paris, Arras, or Mantua around 1400, celebrated that ritualization of covetous desire in which knightly ethics found fulfillment.

Those three main values of conquest, the joy of fighting, the joy of hunting and frolicking in the freedom of natural life, and, finally, the joy of courtship, were joined by another, brought by the evolution of society, the promotion of businessmen, the gradual widening of the aristocracy to admit the newly rich, this time an accumulative factor: the joy of possessing. Certainly its progress was very slow, clandestine, unconfessed, because chivalry above all meant largess, in other words generosity, a spirit of magnificence and prodigality, prompt condemnation of anything mean. Yet a satisfied confidence in the well-being acquired by fortune gradually seeped into the morality of worldly society. It was a feeling which first took shape among the urban élite in central Italy, where it came face to face with the exhortations to poverty of the mendicant friars. Giotto is said to have written an extremely harsh song proposing another ideal, measure and equilibrium, instead of the total destitution of those who advocated abstinence. In the chapel at Padua, decorated for a rich banker, the queen of virtues, the only one to wear a crown, happens to be Justice, in other words, fair distribution of wealth. Certainly Petrarch praised the austerity of the Romans of the Republic and Boccaccio the detachment from the world taught by his Stoic models. Certainly the mendicant order of the Gesuati was founded in 1360 by a Sienese businessman, Giovanni Colombini, who had distributed all his goods to the poor, and Florentine worship was turned entirely toward Santa Croce and Santa Maria Novella, both mendicant churches—just as the royal princes of France paid their devotions to the absolute poverty of the Celestines or the Carthusians. But at the end of the century the Dominican father, Giovanni Dominici, also reinstated wealth, showing it as a condition which certain men might legitimately achieve by the grace of God. In that way he enlisted the preaching Church in the large prosperous cities in support of Leonardo Bruni, the secretary of the Florentine Republic, who proclaimed, basing his arguments on Cicero in the *Tusculan Disputations* and Xenophon in the *Economics,* that riches, provided they had been well earned, offered a safe way of attaining virtue.

The cheerfulness of profane ethics, the pride in being rich which it involved and which underlay the desire for happiness, accordingly enhanced the joys of living and were a reminder of all that men lost on dying. Its values stood in strong contrast to the spirit of devotion and their victory in the fourteenth century demonstrated the vanity of all the previous efforts made by the Church to christianize them. It was easy to represent affluence as the bounty of the Lord, to add a canons' chapter to a knightly confraternity and to bless its war horses, to discern the image of God in the beauties of nature and to dream of a transmutation of the lover's worship of his chosen lady into divine love—but this was to dress the virtues of society in borrowed robes which did nothing to disguise their attractions. It was to capitulate before the irresistible emergence of their power.

The outburst of terrestrial joy illustrated the profound conversion of that civilization: it became secular. It was a period which brought forth a bloom of outstanding goldwork in response to orders from the princes, no longer from the prelates. As in the Carolingian era, the creative peak seems to have been reached in the art of jewelry. Suger, who loved precious stones, regarded them as the crystallization of a divine light and the prefiguration of the splendors of a true universe still masked by the opacities of the sensible world and not to be unveiled until the Day of Judgment. But in the clenched fist of John of Berry, or his cousin, the duke of Milan, John Galeas, a jewel signified the joys of this world, wholly possessed at last.

For the knight and for the great citizen who strove to imitate him in order to be accepted as a gentleman, worldly wealth had to be squandered and consumed in festival. Feudal society could not conceive of the exercise of power and the practice of arms without a lavish environment. The good lord was the most magnificent, the one who drew from his coffers without stint, strewing happiness about him. In order to be loved and served he was obliged to live constantly in the grandest style, to organize occasions for rejoicing, to invite all his friends to participate in the collective satisfaction of their coveted desires, which had gradually become more refined and orderly.

Every action of a noble life was an excuse for a celebration. The liturgy which dictated the course of such a blaze of gladness was dual. In essence, festival was first and foremost a ritual of outward show: the lord was revealed in his power and his glory, wearing every gem in his treasure. He distributed new garments to all who replied to his invitation; he clad them in his own splendor. But festival was also and essentially a ritual of destruction, an offering made to the pleasures of living, a holocaust. It was a sacrifice whereby at one stroke the masters annihilated the goods slowly and painfully amassed by the toil of the poor. The wastefulness of the great disavowed the wretchedness of the serfs. Through festival a knight made himself uncommon. He dominated all those despicable beings who lived bowed by their labor and thought only of hoarding their gain. He dilapilated. Through festival he escaped the curse laid on the human race, condemned since the Fall of Man to earn its bread by the sweat of its brow. He displayed his distinction, his freedom. He triumphed over nature, plundered and ran away. And when he died, the funeral procession, the feast, the subsequent distribution of gifts, gave a last demonstration of his eagerness to conquer the squalor of life by extravagance.

In the fourteenth century, profane tastes consequently achieved their supreme expression in adornment and parade. The *Chronicles* of Jean Froissart, composed in order to glorify prowess—"a virtue so noble and commendable that one should not be too ready to discard it, for it is the very stuff and the light of a gentleman, and as no log can burn without fire, no gentleman can attain perfect honor and worldly fame without prowess"—

open with a description of the brutal festivities offered by the great battles of the Hundred Years War. They end with the more complicated and perverse festivities organized for King Charles VI of France, who was mad. In the Paris of 1400, the glittering focus of chivalrous pleasure, festival appeared to have reached the stage of a kind of inversion of nature, so as better to foster evasion from the real and complete the victory over daily constraints. It crossed the bounds between night and day, it thrust back darkness, it held its dances until point of dawn by flickering lamp-light amid the interplay of reflection and shadow. It culminated in travesty and masquerade. Lords and ladies felt released. Through sacred mime, they identified themselves with the penitent thief or the suffering Christ. At the ball, they became King Arthur or slayers of unicorns. And throughout the merrymaking, they played the game of love.

The ludic spirit of chivalry flourished in the wantonness of courtly sentiments. For two centuries, all the poems and romances composed for that purpose invited the knight to indulge in love. The priests resident at the princely courts had used the resources of scholastic analysis to draw up precise rules for the complex rites which were to govern the respective behavior of the gentleman and the well-born woman in noble society. The books which every lord had read to him in the evening, attended by his household, the pictures which illustrated them, the ivory decoration on caskets and mirrors, widely disseminated the ritual precepts. Any man who wished to be admitted to courtly gatherings had to conform to them. He was expected to choose a lady and to serve her. King Edward III of England in the bloom of his youth wished to become the model of chivalry of his day. He was married and the queen had given him beautiful children. She possessed all the virtues of the perfect spouse and it was a very good marriage. But one day Edward visited the castle of the Lady Salisbury whose husband, his vassal, had been captured in his service and was held prisoner. The king solicited the lady's favor and for an evening, before his escort, played the role of the captive heart, of triumphant but unattainable love. "Honor and Loyalty forbade him to place his affections so falsely, to dishonor such a noble lady and the noble knight her husband. Yet Love was so persuasive that it prevailed and vanquished Honor and Loyalty." Perhaps it was for his chosen lady that he founded the order of the Knights of the Garter, commanded the festival, and invented the device.

Through festival and play, courtly love permitted an escape from established order and an inversion of natural relationships. Adulterous as a matter of principle, it took its first revenge on conjugal constraints. In feudal society marriage was designed to extend the fame and fortune of a house. It was a matter which the elders of the two lines settled unemotionally, paying no heed to the stirrings of the heart. They drew up the terms of the exchange, of the acquisition of the wife who was to become the keeper of the future lord's abode, the mistress of his servants, and the mother of his children. Above all, she had to be rich, and of good stock, and faithful. The laws of society provided the direst penalties for the adulterous wife and for whomever attempted to steal her. But they granted full liberty to men. In every castle, unmarried maidens gratified the knights errant of courtly romance. Courtly love was consequently something more than sexual divagation. It was choice. It accomplished what the marriage contract forbade. Yet the lover did not choose a maid but another's wife. He did not take her by force, he won her—dangerously, gradually overcoming her resistance. He waited for her to yield, to grant him her favor. In conducting his conquest he followed a minutely wrought strategy which had every appearance of being a ritualized transposition of hunting techniques, tournaments, and laying siege to a fortress. The myths of amorous pursuit quickly developed into a chase through the forest. The chosen lady was a tower to be assailed.

But such strategy placed the knight in a state of bondage. Here again courtly love reversed normal relationships. In real life, the lord entirely dominated his wife. In the game of love, he served his lady, bowed before her whims, submitted to the tests she asked of him. He lived kneeling at her feet, in a position of devotion reminiscent of the attitudes governing the subordination of the retainer to his lord in military society. Courtly vocabulary and behavior as a whole was based on the patterns and rites of vassalage, on the form and content of the idea of allegiance. A lover had to be loyal to his lady just as the vassal to his lord. He pledged his faith and would under no circumstances betray it; it was not a tie that could be broken. He showed proof of valor, fought for her, and by successive victories in arms advanced in her esteem. Lastly, he had to surround her with thoughtful care, court her, in other words, continue to serve her, just as the vassals gathered around their lord in feudal times. But, like the vassals, a lover expected that one day his services would bring him reward and allow him to earn subsequent gifts.

On that plane, the game of love sublimated and transposed the sexual impulse. Not that it claimed to be totally disincarnate. By the thirteenth century, the attempts of the Church to bridle courtesy had succeeded in bringing forth a few poems which diverted the amorous process from its carnal intent and transferred it to mysticism. That religious and abstract transmutation culminated in the *dolce stil nuovo* toward 1300. But in ordinary courtly rites, love was kept alive by the hope of an ultimate victory which would bring the lady to surrender herself, fully, a secret perilous triumph over the major taboo and the chastisement awaiting adulterous embrace. While the waiting lasted, however, and it was advisable if it could last for a very long time, desire had to be content with very little. It was important for a lover who wished to conquer his chosen one to be capable of self-control. Of all the trials imposed by his love, that which most clearly symbolized the need for the agreed time limit was "the test" acclaimed in the songs of the troubadours: the lady would order her knight to lie beside her in common nakedness and yet master his desire. Love was strengthened by such discipline and the imperfect joys of moderate caressing. The amorous spark did not unite bodies but hearts. And when Edward beheld Jane of Salisbury he began to "think." The clerks in the service of the feudal princes had sought the adornments of a psychology of terrestrial love in Ovid. Furthermore, precisely when the rules of courtesy began to prevail in Western chivalry, Marian worship invaded Latin Christendom. As their conquests progressed, the spiritualization of the sexual instinct and the transference of feminine values into piety became mutually enriched. The Virgin soon assumed the bearing of the ideal lady, Our Lady, whom each had to serve with love. Elegant, gracious, attractive images of her were in much demand. So as better to strike the hearts of sinners, fourteenth-century Madonnas wore their hair beautifully combed and ornamented like courtly princesses, and the straying reverie of certain mystics sometimes ventured into the contemplation of their bodily charms. Conversely, the chosen lady expected tokens of devotion from her lover, lauds with metaphors borrowed from the songs of mystic love. The reflections of a form of piety which had become a matter of the heart enhanced the joys of worldly society.

Courtly love nevertheless remained a game, a secret amusement, kept up by knowing winks, discreetly dissembling in misleading guises. It was masked beneath the esotericism of the *trobar clus,* of symbolical gestures, of mottoes with a double meaning, of a language which the initiated alone could decipher. In essence and in expressive form, it was a complete flight from the real, like festival. It was an exciting interlude, but utterly vain, never involving the true personality. And if worldly personages happened to be caught at their own game, there was plenty of literature to undeceive them and to provide an effective antidote to the songs of courtly love. The satires and parodies which jerked one back to reason and nature were as successful as the amorous lyrics. Acquaintance with these books, Jean de Meung's sequel to the first *Roman de la rose,* which carried allegory to a lucid glorification of physical love, the account of the Wife of Bath in the *Canterbury Tales,* the merry anecdotes in the *Decameron,* prevented the knights from identifying themselves with the characters they impersonated. They wavered between two worlds. Yet the real world required no adornment. It was the world of festival, illusion, and amorous fancy that artists were commissioned to portray.

Courtly love was born of a vision and nourished by it. When Edward III entered the chamber of the Lady Salisbury, "each beheld her in wonder and the king could not help gazing at her. Then a bright spark sent by mistress Venus through Cupid, the god of love, struck him at the heart and its effect lasted long. After he had looked at her for some time, he went to lean at a window and fell into deep thought." In order to catch the eye and to retain it, it was important to embellish one's body and face. The art of chivalry in the fourteenth century first of all offered a poetics of the garment. One went to a festival in costume. Whoever failed to don the adornment which removed pleasure from the everyday and, by their sumptuousness and futility demonstrated a concerted will for waste, was refused admittance. In the miniatures of the *Très riches heures,* the decorative profusion of the copes and mantles vies in imagination with the ornamental crowns scintillating above the castles. Furthermore, since the festival represented the game of courtesy and was conducted as a formal conversation between the two sexes, it was advisable for the men and the women to wear different attire. It was in the aristocratic circles of the fourteenth century that ladies' clothes achieved singularity. This was asserted in the way dress underlined the attractions of the body, becoming an instrument of erotic display, without being strictly molded to a physical shape. Clothes acted as a decoy. They showed or failed to show, heightening body enticements. Vestimentary art drew inspiration from the lines and colors of the stained glass windows in Paris and effected a similar transmutation into the unreal. In playing the game of the fête, the individual had to conquer nature, go beyond, rise above it by artifice, by padding and folds, horns, and tails, which those elegant ladies roused by exhortations to penitence sometimes hastened to burn on the pyre at another festival, a mystic one, in an auto-da-fé of self-denial. Not unlike the illuminators who placed snatches of true nature amid the nonchalant arabesques in the margins of the psalters, the artists who designed the court wear for the festivals sheathed the half-glimpsed fragments of physical reality in the fictitious framework of a dream architecture. They worked for the lyrical illusion.

Amorous ritual made way for other visions nevertheless. The ways of courtesy in fact obliged the lady, as one of her pledges, to allow her paramour to glimpse her naked from afar, briefly, in a flash. The lover's mind would be haunted by the true picture of the body of his chosen one. On the other hand, the organization of public rejoicing reserved quite a large amount of space in its live tableaux for the female body stripped of all its finery, although a tenacious reticence continued to forbid the portrayal of the female nude in courtly art. Liturgical art had already begun to celebrate the glories of the human body, but it was celebrated according to "nature," in the sense attributed to the word by sacred thinkers, by means of the perfect forms, unsullied by sin, which had been bestowed by divine reason. Cathedral sculpture organized these pictures of perfection within two main scenes, the creation of man and woman and the Resurrection of the dead. In both, the flesh was displayed in all its beauty, before original sin, or in the resplendent freedom of the Day of Judgment. Since the end of the thirteenth century, the image-cutters had consistently treated the human body with tenderness, mindful of charms experienced. Gradually the idea matched its sensible appearances. Eve, and those resurrected from the dead, assumed adolescent graces. Yet *gula* and *voluptas,* living flesh avid for pleasure, still lurked in the shadows of forbidden delights on the edges of the large decorative groups where the artist was always less supervised and where symbolic portrayals of nameless desires were placed. These were represented by a woman's bare body. Or a woman consumed by the flames of hell: in the Arena chapel, Giotto slipped the first sensual nude of European painting in among the devils. Other images, less crushed by guilt, may have been lost. But on the whole it seems as if secular culture remained unbending in that respect throughout the fourteenth century. For princes and knights, the trimmings of courtly festival continued to conceal female lust. And when sculptors or painters dared to show a naked woman, they felt there was no alternative but to depict her as guilty. They could not escape a kind of uneasiness, prevalent in the overnervous angular outlines of the *danses macabres,* which induced them to lend the bodies a hint of perversity. In the Gothic world, or all the forms of reconciled nature, those of the female body were the last to discard sin and to blossom out in earthly gladness.

Italy again was the land of that flowering. The vestiges of classical art revealed bodies which were not masked by the guile of ornament, but on the contrary exhibited a remorseless nudity. In that country where the universities, no longer under ecclesiastical control, dared to explore dead bodies through dissection, at the risk of inconveniencing them later, the day came when the sculptors took to looking at Roman reliefs and the debris of ungarnished statues and to consider them as models. In their handling of the Creation and the Last Judgment, they drew inspiration from nature as it was. But in Parisian painting, the only body to emerge in the serene purity of an antique torso, at the very end of the century, was that of one raised from the dead, a man, Lazarus. The painters of Lombardy, which was a land of chivalry and courtesy, later carried their daring to the point of showing the bare body of triumphant Venus surrounded by that same glory which hitherto had surrounded the image of God then the image of the Virgin Mary; they were able to show noblemen kneeling before her in adoration, receiving the sparks of carnal love as Saint Francis had received the stigmata —one feels that a twinge of conscience caused their hands to tremble. It was in Tuscany, at the dawn of the quattrocento, in a grave Roman key and for a patrician aristocracy, that a stoic Christianity offered a release from the anxiety and the guilty shivers of erotic festival, that female flesh appeared in its fullness for the first time, in bronze and marble. Woman was not resurrected here, she was born. She brought new man the tranquil pleasure of her body.

Possessing the world first of all meant imposing one's law. Fourteenth-century culture led to the prince, who by his rule ensured the rule of justice and peace. The profane aspect of European art, which depended for its major works on princely commissions, primarily glorified power. It did so by pursuing the forms of feudal tradition. For centuries, Western representations of authority had been inseparable from the image of a soldier, the knight. The lord, who held the power to command and the power to punish in his hands, had above all to be a leader in war, and therefore lived on horseback. In a world in which every nobleman imagined he was Saint George, equestrian figures crowded the courts and even in Italy, where Rome had implanted other symbols of majesty, puffing croups in the battles of Uccello and the frescoes of the Schifanoia Palace and the Tea Palace were to enhance knightly virtue for a long time to come. But also, ever since the beginning of the feudal era, a lord's pride in his estate, founded on war, had been revealed to all by a tower. The tower, a fortified keep, provided the nucleus for all military action, the place where the troops were assembled, a last refuge for defense. Near the fortress were the high courts of justice. The tower only occasionally served as a residence; virile, upright like a standard, it was first and foremost a symbol of might.

And so it remained throughout the fourteenth century. Every man of importance erected a tower while he set about ordering a tomb. Consequently princely art was castral. After Charles V had stemmed the revolt of Stephen Marcel and shown the citizens of Paris that their attempts to control the authority of the kings of France were vain, he build the Bastille—just as William the Conqueror had built the Tower of London three centuries earlier. In Ferrara, a marquis constructed the so-called Rebels' Tower with the stones retrieved from the ruined palaces of the various opponents he had just crushed. In the calendar of the *Très riches heures,* each of the landscapes was arranged to form a kind of case around one of the castles of Duke John of Berry. Such walls were admittedly eminently functional. War reigned everywhere in the fourteenth century; its most effective episodes were not the engagements in the open country but the capture of fortresses, by seige or by treachery. More than ever walls had strategic value. Yet, though the sovereign ruled from within a castle, though he accomplished his principal duties there, the old duties of observing the liturgy, the new duties of intellectual patronage, it was not solely for reasons of security. The natural place for the prince's chapel and his books was behind the powerful ramparts which demonstrated his strength. Charles V accordingly installed his "library" in one of the towers of the Louvre. In Karlstein, a whole network of crenellated circles surrounded the imperial abode. In Avignon, the papacy, which had just passed into the hands of the French prelates, undertook the construction of a palace. The old building erected by Benedict XII, a former monk, was an austere cloister in the Cistercian manner. But Clement VI was fond of show. He enlarged the dwelling, placing a great courtyard in the center, which he fitted out for parades. At the top of a grand staircase designed for the processions were ornate arches beneath which the Holy Father might show himself on formal occasions. However, the place remained firmly closed on the outside, like a brandished fist. Not only because mercenary troops, whose captains vowed with a grin that one day they would go and rob the pope's gold, prowled threateningly up and down the Rhône, but because the sovereign pontiff, much to the horror of the mystics, wished to be regarded as a prince of this world, and the mightiest. The palace in Avignon—like the old Louvre, like the castle of Bellver, built for the king of Majorca—possessed a central space bordered by loggias for festive celebrations. But it gripped the sovereign's person in a crown of solid authority. Clement VI relieved the austerity of the walls with a few pinnacles, even so, and decorated small apartments for himself in one of the towers.

The princes of the fourteenth century were anxious that certain cheerful elements should be introduced into the citadels that demonstrated their rule. They achieved this in two ways. Although their abodes had to look like forts, they ought at least to be comfortable. The growing role assumed by noble women in aristocratic life and social display since the twelfth century had gradually drawn the knights away from the rough pleasures of combat and hunting. They had learned to put off their armor. And in the fourteenth century they learned to extend the joys of living, even in the evening, in winter, by candlelight at the fireside. The prince, as the flower of chivalry and therefore the model of courtesy, was expected to prepare rooms in his home conducive to quiet conversation and amorous entertainment. Next to the old hall where the warriors gathered and the master administered justice, all the new or renovated castles provided a few small chambers with fireplaces, hung with tapestries for ornamentation and warmth. It was in the fourteenth century that the royal castle began to be converted into a hotel. Saint-Paul, Charles V's favorite residence in Paris, had several pleasant outbuildings scattered in its grounds for the various amusements of life.

The second addition was decorative. Even war required adornment, which it found in festival. War was probably the most exciting event of all and the knights attended in splendid array. Shreds of silk, many colored tunics, gold belts, and broken jewelry strewed the battlefields of the fourteenth century. And the first duty of court artists was to set off the harnesses. When the French barons met in Flanders in 1386 with the intention of invading England, they sought "to embellish and adorn their ships and vessels and blazon them with their arms and ensigns." The duke of Burgundy had entrusted the decoration of his ship to his fine artist, Melchior Broederlam. Froissart added that "the painters did only too well; they earned whatever they asked, when they were to be found at all. The banners and standards of scarlet silk were so handsome one marvels to think of them, the masts were painted from top to toe and several were covered with fine gold leaf so as better to show off wealth and power. Below, they made the heraldic bearings of the lords to whom the ships belonged." As the ceremony of war was intended to glitter with all possible trimmings and ostentatious trinkets, it seemed equally necessary for the tower to be decorated too. It was accordingly topped with bristling flamboyant plumes like a helmet. The wrought gold of the shrines transposed into stone betrayed the sinuous manner which imparted the escapist dreams of courtly life. The Gothic arabesque indulged in one of its wildest fantasies under the rooftops of the castle of Mehun-sur-Yèvre, built to the orders of John of Berry. The upper stories of the duke's castle, the symbol of feudal power, boasted the luxuriant ornamentation of rood screens and the margins of the books of hours amid the flurry of standards and pennants—lost in the idleness of fancy and chivalrous largesse.

Another conception of authority had begun to occupy the European mind, however, more civil and more austere, deriving from Roman law. Far more men reflected on politics. The new attention paid to the mechanisms of power arose because of the growth of the states and the improvement of their organs. The principalities were obliged to employ better educated officials, who had acquired the habit of reasoning in the universities. They also held national assemblies at which the representatives of the higher estates were expected to give their opinions on important affairs and to discuss the public good. The first lineaments of a civic spirit made their appearance in Europe in the fourteenth century, while the number of men capable of an abstract idea of power increased. It was because the professional intellectuals had also begun to turn their minds toward the problems of government. Political science sprang from the profane area of knowledge which the doctrine of William of Occam had laid wide open to experience and rational deduction. This scientific trend of thought had originally developed in connection with the central clashes in medieval political life: the old conflict between emperor and pope, the two powers which had been interdependent since Charlemagne and alike claimed universal rule. The struggle had been brought to a close in the middle of the thirteenth century by the total victory of the Holy See. But the triumph of Rome entertained the controversies over the bases of civil power. While the papal jurists used all the ingenuity of scholasticism to complete a doctrine of theocracy for the purposes of pontifical authority, the legists of the king of France, Philip the Fair, turned to Roman law for arguments against the exacerbated claims of Pope Boniface VIII. Their theories coincided with those of the Ghibellines in Italy who exalted the idea of empire in Dante's *De monarchia.* In the late thirteenth century, the quarrel rebounded. The transference of the papacy to Avignon made its concessions to the temporal world even plainer. A king of Germany traveled to Italy to appropriate the diadem. A whole section of the

Franciscan order opposed the pope on the definition of poverty. It was then that the two works which remained the tutors of political thought throughout the fourteenth century were produced.

When the Franciscan, William of Occam, who was pursued for heterodoxy by the Avignon curia and sought refuge with the emperor, wrote his *Dialogus,* he again applied the central principle of his method by separating the sacred from the profane. He strictly divided Church and state, attributing the monopoly of political action to the latter. The pope, he asserted, "could not deprive men of liberties which had been granted by God or by nature." Acceptance of nature beside God as a reputed source of law signified the radical secularization of legal thinking and legal science. But another book, the *Defensor pacis,* published a little earlier by two teachers of the university of Paris, Marsilio of Padua and John of Jandun, was far more violently aggressive and revolutionary and deliberately attacked the powers of the Church. The Church had robbed its temporal rights from the prince. It was wrong to imagine that there could be such a thing as an independent spiritual power; there was no spirit outside the body, nothing spiritual outside the laity. Any special authority of the Church was a matter of usurpation—it had to be made subject to the state. But how had the state obtained its power? The old feudal tradition would have replied: by the sword, in the victorious wars waged by the ancestors of the prince. The teaching of the doctors of the cathedral schools replied: from God, who delegated the powers of kings. And the popes added: through the intermediary of Saint Peter. The *Defensor pacis,* with unexpected daring, replied: from the people. From the "majority of the citizens who promulgate the law."

People, freedom, citizens, law, majority, such words—soon to be echoed by virtue, order, happiness—sounded like the maxims on Roman inscriptions. Marsilio of Padua had first read them in Livy. And if they were still accompanied by the clash of arms, those arms were wielded by lictors and legionaries, not by crusaders. These ideas spread. Petrarch enriched them with his knowledge of the classics, and in the third quarter of the fourteenth century, the king of France, Charles V, sought to appear as a wise sovereign. It was made known to the people that he reflected on books in his chamber, that he lived surrounded by learned men, that in winter he "often read the fine stories of the Holy Scriptures or the deeds of the Romans or the moralities of the philosophers until dinner." Aristotle's *Politics* was translated for him; the *Songe du verger* constructed a theory of royal sovereignty exercised for the benefit of the *res publica,* guided by the counsel of moderate prudent men. "When you can withdraw from the care and the deep thought you devote to your people in general and to public affairs, in secret read or have read some good piece of writing or doctrine": the king no longer led the fray himself, he appointed a commander-in-chief. This was the clerk's revenge on the knight, but it was taken by a secularized clerk, aware of the "deeds of the Romans."

New attributes and new symbolical figures were needed for a power which claimed to be natural and said it rested in the people: the horse, as always—provided it was that of Constantine or Marcus Aurelius. No longer the tower. Ancient Rome now proposed other means of honoring the sovereign and establishing his authority. Some of these had previously been exhumed from the past by the artists of southern Italy in praise of the emperor Frederick II. When Pope Boniface VIII, by his promise of indulgences, attracted the Christian people as a whole to what had once been imperial Rome and to the apostolic See, for the Jubilee of 1300, he invited the best Italian artists to set similar emblems around his throne. He had his stone statue placed in the cities conquered in his name. The new image of majesty now resided in the triumphant figure of the living prince, in his effigy. The human likenesses which replaced the figures of the prophets and the apostles or the queen of Sheba in church doorways, or which dominated the reclining figures on the tombs, were portrayals of the great estate owners and their households in fitting splendor. The statue of the emperor Henry VII consequently appeared at a very early date in the apse of the cathedral of Pisa. Not far away, his four counsellors mounted guard beside his tomb. Charles V had himself shown with his wife and his male children on the new staircase of the Louvre. At the entrance to the Charles bridge in Prague, the kings of Bohemia held sway. And Queen Isabel of Bavaria bestowed her graces and bodily charms on the great fireplace of the palace at Poitiers.

Opposite the statue of the emperor in Pisa stood another figure, that of an abstract power, not a lady, almost a goddess: the statue of the city. It was incumbent upon the urban republics to enhance the civil face of authority, since their jurists had discerned its features in the laws of ancient Rome. The most advanced republics, in central Italy, enjoyed evoking their Roman origin. In their capacity as sworn associations of citizens equal in theory and acting as magistrates in turn, they conducted a vigorous and readily aggressive military policy, but entrusted its execution to hired mercenaries. Order, conducive to trade and general prosperity, was based in their opinion on concord, freedom, mutual fidelity, and a common love of the city. Men had to be united if the renown of their city was to spread. That renown could be observed in the monumental building undertaken at common expense and assigned to craftsmen chosen by competition. These collective enterprises designed to enhance prestige kept a few of the military symbols of power. The steeples of the collegiate churches and the belfries of the municipal buildings soaring to the sky in northern Europe, thrust squarely and solidly into the ground and gradually accepting the arabesque at their summits, were keeps, like those of the princely castles. The civic palaces of the Tuscan cities, the dwellings of the *podestàs,* the delegates of imperial power, were actually Roman houses commuted into fortresses with inner courtyards, and towers erected to vertiginous heights. All the patrician families wished to build similar towers of their own. Again, it was thought fitting to honor the victorious *condottieri* by portraying them as soldiers. Their statues peopled the squares and the walls of the communal halls with a helmeted cavalry force. However, at least one sector of the new urban art rejected such warlike emblems. Beneath the municipal tower and near the new loggias flowed civic fountains, the springs of peace. The nine paladins from the imagery of chivalry still adorned the fountain of Nuremberg, decorated in the last quarter of the century, whereas long before Nicola Pisano had placed the elements of a new iconography of civicism on the fountain ordered in 1278 by the municipality of Perugia. Here, too, the patriarchs, saints, signs of the zodiac, symbols of the months, and the liberal arts owe their origin to cathedral scholastics; but nearby one sees the she-wolf weaning Romulus and Remus and the twin statues of Perugia and Rome, *caput mundi.* A few years later the sculpture on the base of the bell tower in Florence praised work and good government, the guardians of order and peace.

The first Italian frescoes to glorify urban authority have been entirely lost. Nothing remains of the horoscope of the city of Padua which Giotto represented on the municipal palace in a faithful transcription of a program worked out scientifically by a university professor. The earliest of all such celebrations surviving today was executed by Ambrogio Lorenzetti between 1337 and 1339 for the Sienese Republic. It still stands as the most complete and the richest in expression. The municipality had previously asked Simone Martini to decorate the outside of the civic palace with scenes from Roman history. In order to aid the magistrates to keep to the right path, it also wished the images of the virtues they should observe and the consequences of their political acts to be permanently within sight and accordingly decided to submit the two conflicting allegories of Good and Bad Government to their consideration. The task of adorning the council hall with a convincing painting of the Aristotelian concepts proposed by school rhetoric fell to Ambrogio. At that time lay thinking still needed a go-between, an allegory, in order to rise to abstract ideas. Ideas needed to be given a human shape, a face, garments, insignia, and to be brought alive if they were to achieve their effect. Dismal troops of allegorical figures consequently traverse the didactic poems of the fourteenth century. They appear in all the theatricals designed to convey an acceptable picture of a conceptual theory. Wearing similar dress, they rub shoulders with the figures of the saints, overcrowding an entire province of profane painting.

In the Siena council hall, Bad Government is shown as a prince of Evil, escorted by the powers of Confusion, Disorder, Avarice, Vainglory, and

Fury, trampling Justice beneath his feet. The triumph of Good Government develops as a contrast. He rules in majesty, bearing the civil attributes of a sovereign. He is bearded like the emperors, and the she-wolf at his feet weans Romulus and Remus. A guard of knights with raised lances surrounds him. In his glory, he occupies the place of the Eternal Father judging the righteous and the wicked: on his left are the chained prisoners, the enemies of the commune, all the dangerous troublemakers reduced to bondage by his victory; on his right, the serene theory of the twenty-four council members. Like the triumphant portrayals of Saint Thomas in Dominican imagery, he reigns assisted by a council of allegorical figures, this time the nine cardinal virtues, not the nine paladins. Dominating in the sky, though in the distance, are the three theological virtues. Seated around his throne, wearing lesser crowns but in the attitude of the kings forming the court of the vicars of God in the symbolical images of imperial rulers, are the six virtues of earthly life, Strength and Magnanimity, Temperance and Prudence, Justice, and lastly, admirably idle, Peace. Further along, on the same throne, shown in the same hieratic frontality, Justice reappears, inspired by Wisdom. She punishes the wicked, crowns the righteous and, commutative, distributes worldly possessions in equity. For the lordly community which had commissioned the fresco was composed of those who had waxed fat and who regarded well-earned gain as legitimate. The two cords plaited by Concord as a symbol of agreement hang from her even scales and on meeting unite the body of magistrates by the same ties of friendship. Thus the concept as a whole takes shape.

On the other hand, it was through the reality of things experienced and perceived in everyday life that the virtues had their effects on town and country. A view of the world as it is consequently fills the lower section. Ambrogio Lorenzetti did not surround it with the symbolical frame of chapel architecture. He put it on the stage of a theater because politics were not bound by the liturgy. A whole people labor serenely to earn the riches they deserve. Their toil, depicted with minute exactitude, amasses the goods needed for the security which will allow the people to advance in peace. Yet the vulgar striving of peasants and merchants ended with the joys of the nobility, with idle tasks, with a swarm of dancing maidens, with the courtly ride, hunting the hawk. What finally emerges from that allegory of civic power, however, is one of the most magnificent representations of sensible nature. The first true landscape painted in the West.

Overrun by soldiers, decimated by plagues, Europe nevertheless experienced one of its greatest periods of song in the fourteenth century. The songs were frequently pastoral and rustic and always springlike. They were composed for gardens. Girls danced to their rhythms in the meadows. And the round of maidens with their gowns strewn with flowers introduced the grace of the nearby grasslands into the Siena of Lorenzetti's mineral cubist universe. Worldly joy found true fulfillment in nature, in the air of the fields and the woods, and the art it brought forth covered the walls of the closed rooms and the pages of books with a semblance of rural delights. The dreams it proposed strayed into the familiar countryside and the forests.

Chivalrous culture had sprung from a world which knew virtually nothing of the town. The great fortunes rested on the land and on peasant labor. The princes traveled constantly from estate to estate and held formal court in the open air. We know that Saint Louis liked to sit under an oak to administer justice, and the voluptuous exhilaration which fourteenth-century knights derived from war was largely due to the fact that the art of combat developed like an outdoor sport. The fray was led through the vineyards, on the edge of the woods, and amid the smells of newly trodden earth. The battles began in the dew, and warmed up as the sun rose. So when the tower unbuckled its belt of fortified walls and made ready to harbor the sweetnesses of life, it immediately opened on to a garden. The pope in Avignon had his orchard within the palace precincts, Karlstein stood far from Prague and Windsor far from London. In Paris, Charles V purchased gardens in the Marais to construct Saint-Paul because the old palace in the Cité and even the Louvre were too far away from greenery. The rich merchants also wished to own an estate outside the city walls so as to live in rural leisure, like noblemen. Since Western civilization had set the figure of the feudal lord at the center of its ideal of earthly happiness, it could no longer escape the enticements of rustic revelry, although urban customs, work, and tastes came more and more into their own. But as it turned out, such frolics had already been praised by Virgil. Incipient humanism consequently began to extol bucolic joys and glorify the happiness of pastoral life, encouraging its adepts to flee the adulterated luxury of the courts for the simplicity of country pleasures. It too established orderly sites for idle conversation in remote spots. The merry company of the *Decameron* did not meet in Florence and Petrarch fled Avignon for La Fontaine de Vaucluse. Among men of the world everything, even religious attitudes, tended to be aired outside. In courtly romance, the only characters who bore a Christian message were the hermits who had retreated into sylvan solitude along with the wizards. Perhaps nowhere offered a better meeting place for the optimism of chivalry and its God than virgin nature. For the Christian who set aside the liturgy because he wished to attain pure love, God, said Meister Eckhart, "glows in all things, because for him all things have the taste of God, and he sees his image everywhere." Mystic illumination transported the soul to the center of an orchard, surrounded with walls but filled with flowers, birds, and bubbling springs. The Church of the cathedrals had crowned the Virgin. It had presented her to the people as a queen amid a court of angels and the liturgical magnificence of power. The fourteenth century brought her closer to mankind. Admittedly it thrust her into the redeeming sorrow of men prostrate before the corpse of their dead God but it also made her into the image of a happy woman. The exulting Virgin of the Visitation, the Nativity, and the Childhood of Christ presides among bouquets of flowers and the very garlands which Joan of Arc and her companions went to hang on elf-haunted trees in the evenings. Seated on the grass in the garden, she rules like the queen of reconciled nature.

When the monks and the priests of the liturgical age spoke of nature, they referred to the abstract idea of perfection beyond the reach of the senses. For them, nature was the conceptual form which revealed the substance of God, not the transient fictitious aspects which sight, hearing, and smell could perceive. Not the hazardous and disordered appearances of the world, but what had been the Garden of Paradise for Adam before his sin; a universe of peace, measure, and virtue, obeying divine reason and escaping the upheavals and the decadence later introduced along with the powers of desire and death. They viewed *natura* as the opposite of *gula* and *voluptas,* or erring physical nature, rebelling against the commandments of God, recalcitrant and therefore condemned, despicable, unworthy of notice. In the twelfth and thirteenth centuries the idea intellectuals formed of nature was spiritual, not carnal. To pierce its mysteries it was best to proceed by rational analysis, from deduction to deduction, from abstraction to abstraction, until one reached divine reason. Their physics remained conceptual, which is why their thought had such a hearty welcome in store for Aristotle.

The point of departure of Aristotelian physics was certainly observation. Yet, by an approach not at all unlike the methods of scholastic logic, processes of thought tended to rise from the particular, the accidental, to the most general. Science consequently pressed deeper than the surface in order to attain the substance beyond the shifting changing world, the support and cause of all the effects that had been noted. It reached those forms by three successive stages of abstraction, physical, mathematical, then metaphysical. In Aristotle, physics, or the science of what still constituted change, was strictly separated from mathematics, or the knowledge of what had become stable when abstraction attained the highest level at which movement was eliminated. Once his philosophy had been revealed by the Arabic translators, the professors and students of arts at the university of Paris took it up with enthusiasm. They allowed themselves to be won over by a complete, hierarchical, perfectly rational cosmology and a symmetrical related science of man as a microcosm. This conceptualization of the universe suitably clarified a natural world which was regarded by intellectuals as shaping divine reason. Dominated by men who scorned the flesh, who said that it was tainted with sin, who denied direct observation and experience and who nourished their thirst for knowledge on syllogism and pure analysis, Gothic art, like Romanesque art, was accordingly abstract. It did not portray a tree but the idea of a tree; nor did it portray God, who had no appearance, only the idea of God.

Yet God had been made flesh. In cathedral art, the representation of the essence of created beings slowly approached a rendering of appearances. Lettuce leaves, strawberry plants, and vine shoots could soon be identified among the flora adorning the capitals. The gradual propagation of the new Christianity—preached by Saint Francis—which, with an optimism reflecting the joys of chivalry, was bent on reinstating the carnal world, brother Sun and other creatures, did a great deal toward luring the attention of educated men back to concrete matters. The many Minorite friars in the university of Paris and at the court of Saint Louis were highly influential. They spoke of a visible Nature which was no longer sinful and toward which one could turn one's gaze. At the same time a certain mistrust of Aristotle's system, in which certain cracks had begun to appear, arose within the school itself. Scholastic logic had been forged in order to bring out the contradictions in the classical authors and to solve them. It soon discovered that Aristotle's cosmology did not exactly agree with other systems, such as Ptolemy's, revealed by the translations of the *Almagest*. To reduce these discrepancies, to decide between the conflicting views, there was no alternative but to consider the world. In the thirteenth century the astronomers of Merton College in Oxford and at the university of Paris were the first scientists in the West to have deliberate recourse to experience.

But there was another drawback to Aristotle's system, far more serious. It did not agree with Christian dogma. By making man the prisoner of the cosmos, it denied his freedom. By proposing the idea of eternal matter, it failed to accommodate either creation or the end of time. The commentary of Averroës had spotlighted all that was irreducible to Christianity in the *Physics:* this, together with Averroism, was formally condemned in 1277 by the bishop of Paris, Stephen Tempier. Such intellectual policing, rejecting a comfortable theory which gave a straightforward answer to everything, thrust the world back into mystery and stimulated scientists to undertake research. In the Oxford schools Franciscan teachers were already following new paths. Robert Grosseteste, who opposed Aristotle by proposing light as the common substance of the universe, made it possible to conceive of a created world no longer hermetically sealed, no longer closed, which could be returned to infinity. Since light could have gushed forth and could be extinguished, the world could have begun on a specific day and could end on a specific day. The chief merit of his system was to provide a method. Since the universe was regarded as light, it was advisable to set down the laws of optics in order to understand the structures of the physical world. And optical laws depended on geometry and arithmetic. Mathematical science was consequently linked with physical science. The entire mystics of numbers taken up by Neoplatonism might make a legitimate contribution toward explaining the world, and the new system in any case was an invitation to measure the universe. The exact sciences made great strides along these lines after 1280. Aristotle's system attributed only conceptual qualities to the four elements. The scholars of Oxford and Paris sought to give those qualities quantitative values. And since light was a flowing, dynamic force, their meditations on movement led them to propose a mathematics of change, as against Greek mathematics based on repose. Finally, the new doctrine restored full value to the eye, and placed accurate vision, direct scrutiny, in the vanguard of research. Thus science became lucid. When in the late thirteenth century another Franciscan from Oxford, William of Occam, filled the breach opened by the challenge of Aristotelianism and persuaded the schoolmen that all conceptual knowledge was illusory, that attaining the substance of things was beyond the powers of the human intellect, which could only grasp the attributes and the accidents by sensory experience, he restored the essential value of the contemplation of visible nature. The intellectual movement which culminated in Occamism in the trecento and died with it pulled nature away from the abstract and back to the concrete and reinstated appearances. Allied with Franciscan gladness and the pleasures of the courts, it stimulated artists to open their eyes.

And to see the world in all its diversity. Chivalrous society, which had begun to alternate with the ecclesiastical elite in directing the creation of works of art, was naturally curious and fond of observing things. It had a liking for the bizarre. Exoticism opened one of its doors of escape. The knight, by virtue of his condition, sought adventure and delighted in exploring unknown territories. The crusade had been an excuse for wonderful journeys. In passing, most crusaders had cast a tourist's glance at the regions of the eastern Mediterranean. And the literature taking shape for knightly audiences immediately conjured up far-off lands. The pine and the olive tree figured in the early epics both as a reminder and as an incentive for new departures. The accounts of real voyages competed with the tales which wove a world of fable and make-believe around the courtly quest. The mirrors of the world, the books of marvels, the treasure books, the bestiaries, the lapidaries written in the vernacular gave minute descriptions of unknown creatures for the circles of the great lords. Unlike the dragons and the unicorns, such animals at least existed. To amuse themselves, but also out of a desire to possess the entire world, all princes in the fourteenth century assembled collections of strange articles which the traders brought back from the far corners of the earth. And the menageries they kept in their gardens housed live monkeys and leopards.

Knightly curiosity, however, was also directed toward familiar nearby nature which had a mystery of its own and was rich in material for exciting discoveries. The hunt was a conquest, and a daily one, a means whereby man could appropriate creation and subject it to his power. Out on horseback, men gained direct and very exact knowledge of wild beasts and their habits and lairs. Some of them, inspired by the emperor, Frederick II, set down the sum of their experiences in treatises. Along with amorous songs and accounts of distant expeditions, books on hunting were the first literary works composed by the knights. They contained the first natural histories and were immensely successful. Their readers enjoyed finding a faithful picture of the animals and plants observed on the beat adorning the margins of their psalters and the "hedges" of the books of hours. The painters showed them mingling with the images of fabulous beasts, intertwined in the straying arabesques of dream vegetation.

The culture of chivalry demanded an exact but fragmentary portrayal of reality. It expected to be shown objects which would be immediately identified by their distinguishing features, but in isolation, knit into a web of memories or poetic fancy. At courtly festivals the nobility did not stage nature as a show. The ornamental materials used included a selection of single elements linked together in gratuitous embroidery, dotting the unreal setting, the gold or the red- and blue-checked ground of the stained glass windows, which served as a back-cloth to the rites. Occamist physics replaced the coherent unity of a conceptual universe with a scattering of multiple phenomena. It had destroyed Aristotle's solid space, filling the emptiness of the world with the clutter of a collector's hoard, and dreamed only of infusing the separate pieces with the impetus contained in the movements of the mathematical theory then being constructed by the Parisian master, Buridan, in the very way the sinuosities of the *caroles* whisked along the flowered hats and the ardor of the joust caught up the shimmering steeds in a whirlwind. So it was not the influence of the Oxford mathematicians, though they happened to have discovered optics, that enabled painters to evolve the rules of perspective. Nature as represented in the illustrations of chivalrous joy was not structured according to reckoning as the Romanesque basilicas and the cathedrals had been. Its space broke up into the discontinuity of a multitude of sharp, lucid glances. The first attempts to build a rational landscape were Italian, not Parisian.

In Italy, the leading wing of Franciscanism professed poverty of spirit and cast anathema on scientific research. The universities on the whole remained unaffected by Occamism and went on commenting on Aristotle and Averroës. They lingered over the older philosophy until the overwhelming message of Plato made its belated appearance in Florence. All the scientific conquests of the fourteenth century, if not those of the physicians, were consequently conducted outside of the schools. The leading thinkers, the prelates and the preaching friars who enabled the urban elite to accede to academic knowledge and who drew up the iconographical programs for decorative undertakings, proposed the image of a conceptual universe, single and entire, coordinated in all its parts. Yet it was in Italy that the artistic idiom, drawing fresh inspiration from the roots of classical painting, had discovered the old illusionist techniques earlier than anywhere else. The grand theatrical art displaying civil majesty and the imitation of Jesus Christ required a simple symbolical setting, a few elementary signals to guide the dramatic action staged. Like Romanesque art and Byzantine painting it consequently made use of an abstract vocabulary. It set up ideas of trees, rocks, constructions, and thrones around its figures. But since it was now a matter of a theater, the properties of the set had to be arranged within a closed space marked out by a frame but not allowed to clash unrealistically with the convincing renderings of the actors. The material plasticity of the figures of God and the saints in Giotto's vast play gave them the weight and the physical presence of statues. But it was also important to provide a certain depth of field. Giotto made no attempt to surround them with an atmosphere or to pierce the wall behind them on to a receding landscape. He endeavored to use the tricks of nascent perspective to create the impression that the symbolical objects localizing the tale possessed three dimensions. The transference, inseparable from theatrical expression, then replacing liturgical expression, forbade an abrupt intrusion of realism. On the other hand, in a quasi-Aristotelian abstraction of accident and movement, it pleaded the respect of optical laws. These figures pointed the way to illusionism.

Giotto was far from seeking veracity. Yet, not many years after his death, Boccaccio praised him for his skill in portraying the real: "Nature can produce nothing he has not painted equally like and even identical with it; as a result men are often mistaken on seeing the things he did, taking the painting for the truth." The truth Boccaccio meant was not transcendental, however, and by nature he referred to the appearances of the world. For in the meantime Italian patrons had also begun to investigate the nature of things and henceforth expected art to offer them a truthful version of reality.

At this point it is important to take into account the influence of a frame of mind, which could not be called bourgeois without betraying its profound motivations, shared by all whose work had enabled them to grow rich and to fill positions of authority in the urban fiefs, and by the practitioners of medicine, law, and public management. Such dignitaries had not attended the universities. But the exercise of their profession had allowed them to acquire a visual acuity indispensable for gauging the quality of the countless articles in the *mercatura* at first sight. Their ubiquitous business transactions obliged them to form a careful and exact overall view of the world. They had a feeling for figures and knew that the word *ratio* also meant a bookkeeping operation. They wished the scenes that were painted to give a more faithful reflection of the real world while maintaining the coherence, unity, and depth of the theatrical field. The allegories of Good Government are concepts and remain part of scenic abstraction. But, lower down, at the level of profane curiosity, for a merchant aristocracy of traders in cloths and spices and money-handlers, precisely when Giovanni Villani was using statistical methods to describe the city of Florence, the first rationally constructed landscape appeared in Siena. It provided a model, which inspired Lombard artists after the upheavals of the plague and, once transported from Milan to Paris, allowed the Limburg brothers, the heirs of the fragmentary but more carnal realism of the imagery of chivalry, to give an honest rendering of nature. Nature was no longer a labyrinth, a mesh of interstices through which one might slip, lose oneself in mystery, proceed from conquest to conquest, from surprise to surprise, until one touched the simulacrum of heaven swathing it like a piece of drapery. By playing on the thickness of the atmosphere, the light cut deeply across the theatrical backcloth, attracting the discontinuous glances cast on things into a unity which nonetheless had no bounds.

Paris receded into the background at the dawning of what historians of European culture have called the Renaissance. Avignon and Rome too. The avant-garde of the new art was established in Florence and Flanders. By a political hazard: the Roman papacy had been undermined in the chaos of the schism; family feuds, riots, and the foreign war had dislocated and dispersed the court of the Valois. The accidental transference had not released artistic activities from the supervision of noble patronage, however, which had governed it throughout the fourteenth century. At that time, the most prosperous cities in the world covered Tuscany and Flanders. But when the art of courtesy had flourished, Paris, Avignon, and Milan had been major crossroads for trade and the most densely populated cities of their day. Like the Limburg brothers, Jan van Eyck was a court painter, a duke's valet. The other commissions he accepted were for businessmen who were also in the service of a prince and prided themselves on such privileges, imitating their master's taste. If Flemish art, which up to then had been provincial, suddenly took up its position on the advanced front of pictorial conquest, it was because the royal princes who had inherited the glory and fortune of the kings of France, the dukes of Burgundy, had set themselves up in Flanders, held court there, and assembled the best artists who could no longer find employment in Paris. The great Florentine century began when the disorders introduced in the urban aristocracy by the great deaths had been offset and when the patrician elite had once again become a stable society, a group of heirs raised in a cultured atmosphere of knightly inspiration; Florence became the focus of new art precisely when the republic was being imperceptibly transformed into a principality, when administration slid into the hands of a tyrant whose sons later endeavored to represent as the most magnificent of patrons. In Bruges and in Tuscany, the priests held as much power in 1420 as they had held before. But not more. Art remained the reflection of the ideal of the prince. The geographical transference was not a break, though it checked the attempts at Gothic synthesis. The two divergent trends it followed soon developed to form a vivid contrast.

In the circles of the dukes of Burgundy, in Dijon, then in the Netherlands, the sculptors outstripped the painters in audaciousness. In Florence too. Just as, about a hundred years earlier, Nicola Pisano had opened the trail for Giotto. But all the experiments culminated in painting, in Van Eyck and Masaccio. Van Eyck carried the analytical vision of Occamism to its utmost acuity, attentive to the singularity of each object. Yet, in the wake of the Limburg brothers, he succeeded in assembling his manifold observations and in uniting the diversity of visible appearances in a world which owed its coherency to the luminous principle of the Oxford theologians. Light, the breath of the Holy Spirit, the illumination of the mystics of Groenendael, which the painters of Cologne had already attempted to establish within the closed garden of the Virgin Mary, dispelled the mists of chivalrous escape. The play of the enveloping shadows, the changing reflection between mirrors and precious stones within the space of secluded rooms, the iridescence created in the open air when light pervades the atmosphere, gave truth and unity to the spectacle of the real. Whereas Masaccio, to express a stoic Christianity dissatisfied with reverie and mystic illumination, a Christianity of austerity, equilibrium, and self-control, returned to the majesty of Giotto. He discarded the superfluities of the arabesque, did not linger over the accidents of phenomena or the modulations of light. In his country, the architects who appreciated uncluttered masses and the dignity of bare stone, not only measured objects but space as well, or rather emptiness, arranging it with geometric simplicity. Like them, like Donatello, whose prophets express every human torment, Masaccio endowed *virtus,* as understood in Roman literature by the humanists, with the monumentality of the statues of the Empire. For him, painting was quite definitely *cosa mentale* [a thing of the mind]. And the reality he portrayed, as opposed to the view of Van Eyck, was the abstract world of Aristotelian concepts. His art showed a logical universe set out with rational clarity, itself measure and calculation.

Yet Van Eyck's Occamism and Masaccio's peripateticism converged in a common sense of human greatness. Both placed man at the center of their works. New man: Adam and Eve. For Van Eyck, the body of Eve was the visual discovery and acquaintance with the delights of sensible nature. His hills are converted into caressing shadows, his vegetation into a wonderful landscape even more persuasive than that of the *Adoration of the Lamb.* And Masaccio's woeful pair offer to religious meditation the spectacle of man crucified on his own destiny instead of Jesus nailed to the cross.

At that moment in the history of the arts, however, the real novelty still lay elsewhere. Jan van Eyck worked to commissions. He had produced the portraits of canons, princely prelates, and the financial magnates who directed the branches of the great Florentine firms in Bruges. One day he decided to paint a picture of his wife. Not as a queen, as Eve or as the Holy Virgin. But true to life. She was not a princess. Her image had no value except for its author. That day the court painter attained his independence. He had won the right to create freely, for sheer pleasure. At the same time, in Florence, while Ghiberti was preparing to write the *Commentaries* on his work, just as Caesar wrote about his victories, Masaccio placed his own image among those of the apostles in the *Tribute*. A man's face. The other face of the freedom of the artist.

ILLUSTRATIONS

1

Raoul Glaber wrote just before the middle of the eleventh century. All about him he perceived the stirrings of progress. He was a monk: for him such progress could only be spiritual. All the buildings recently constructed and those still emerging from the earth seemed to be spinning the robes of purity in which Christendom, reconciled with its God, would at last be clad. For us, such a flowering was obviously one of the first consequences of growth. Those walls were raised by armies of quarrymen, carters, stone cutters, and masons. In return for money. The men who shifted the huge bulk of materials to fashion dwelling-places for God were not peasants under forced labor or donors offering their grief to Christ, but professionals, workmen demanding a wage, as the chroniclers who attributed the origin of a fair number of these constructions to the chance (hence miraculous) discovery of a treasure were well aware. Bishop Arnoul of Orléans wished to have his church built rapidly: "One day when the masons were testing the firmness of the ground to choose the site for the foundations of the basilica, they came across a large quantity of gold" which they remitted to the prelate; it was reported that an earlier priest had hidden the reserve there when the original cathedral was constructed so as to provide for future renovations. But in actual fact the religious communities simply put into circulation part of the gold and silver accumulated in their treasures or brought back by the knights campaigning on the confines of Islam. The greater part of the wealth drained by the works on Cluny is known to have come from Spain. It was thanks to the first great financial undertaking of new Europe that the masterpieces of Romanesque art came into being.

The riches went mainly to the monasteries. It was there that most building was done. The first to benefit was that great family, solidly established and prosperous, plentifully endowed with land and with trusty servants, formed by every Benedictine community. Its abode communicated with the outside world. At the threshold were dependencies where the pilgrims were housed; nearby were the servants' lodgings; there the lessees deposited the fruit of their labor from the estates and the product of the rent, piling up reserves of food in the stores. Yet few ecclesiastics ventured into that area of contact with the perils of the age. Usually the friars lived in seclusion, cut off from the rest by a wall which they refrained from crossing. The monastic space was inward and closed as a matter of principle.

The Cloister

Surrounded on all sides by the communal buildings—hall, refectory, dormitory—the cloister lay at the heart of that closed universe (fig. 5). An island of nature, but one that had been rectified, separated from its wicked environment, a place where air, sun, trees, birds, and running waters recovered the freshness and innocence of the first days of the world. The design of the inner courtyard expressed its participation in perfections which the earth has not known since the fall of Adam. Square, laid out according to the four cardinal points and the four elements of created matter, the cloister wrenched a piece of the cosmos from the disorder which naturally threatened it and reestablished it in harmonious proportions. To those who had chosen to withdraw there, the cloister spoke the accomplished, finished tongue of the other world.

Within the community dwelling, that preserved space, entered very rarely even by the lord protector, the only spot not intended for a specific purpose, was a place where one meditated on the mysteries of God, where one advanced in knowledge. The head of the community assembled the monks there for the evening sermon, when time was devoted to properly academic exercises, to the perusal and the slow rumination of texts in the intervals between the psalms. Thus the teaching of the architecture and the decoration became extended to the image. Painted on the pages of the book given to each monk at the beginning of Lent to be read and reread aloud for a year, the image associated itself with the words (fig. 10). Painting instructed too. Accompanying the text, it furnished visual equivalences for each phrase, verse, and sequence, deepening the awareness of the meaning and easing the transition from one of the multiple shifting interpretations to the next, bringing the Holy Scriptures into touch with the spectacle of the world.

The Powers of Evil

The function of the images carved on the capitals in the cloister was different. They were mainly a warning, a reminder of the hostile forces waylaying man, setting snares where he trod, barring his path, endeavoring to lead him astray, to thwart his progress toward salvation. It was unadvisable for the soul to be lulled into tranquillity: the cloister was not an inviolate asylum. The soul should remain alert, alive to dangers because God's omnipotence was challenged by an opponent determined to resist him—Satan, the devil, the Enemy.

Neither imperial art nor classical art had portrayed the devil. Monastic art brought him into the front of the picture. Accommodating the beliefs which the Carolingian clerics had attempted to stamp out, the Christianity upheld by the monks annexed a whole folklore of funerary symbols and admitted the invasion of a nocturnal universe. The conventual precincts themselves were known to be haunted by devils. In order to outwit them, Cluniac custom prescribed that a light should always be kept in the dormitory. But that faint glimmer failed to prevent them from appearing "at night when the bell rang for matins." Raoul Glaber saw Satan three times. His was no ordinary mind, nor was he abnormally credulous. One wonders who, at Cluny, did not experience similar encounters.

To the monks who attempted to overcome their dread and to describe what they had glimpsed, the devil had not appeared in the alluring guises acknowledged by the more sophisticated psychology of the thirteenth century (fig. 35). He did not captivate, he roused and persecuted. He was a nightmarish fiend. Exact coincidences associate Raoul Glaber's vision with the clawing, dishevelled silhouettes on the capitals of Saint-Benoît-sur-Loire or Saulieu, dissembling behind the enticing articles they brandish, and almost always women. To portray the Enemy, sculptors and painters used two styles. The first was linear and sinuous, stemming directly from a type of barbaric ornamentation, and seemingly suited to the peoples of the Western seas, to Ireland, England, and Scandinavia. In those regions which had known only the reflection of the revival of classicism imposed by the emperors, Roman traditions were lacking. Christianity had inserted itself in the myths and stylistic forms of native customs without dislodging them. On the porches of the wooden churches of Norway, as in the miniatures of the workshops of Winchester, Satan took up his natural position amid the sylvan enchantments of witchcraft and legend (fig. 3), whereas in the cloisters of Catalonia, Castile, or Rouergue, the image of evil was incorporated in the structured forms of antique fable. The hunting scenes in a totally different spirit which decorated the sides of the sarcophagi of the Late Empire served to inspire the struggles of which the human soul was now the theater. Centaurs and chimeras chased one another in and out of scrolls of tidy flora. The artists of those provinces also sought to give shape to eerier phantasms, the winged creatures invented in the East, embroidered on the splendid cloths protecting the relics, the bewitching sirens, in which two perverse natures, closely related, were joined, that of woman and that of the monstrous beasts wallowing in the slime of the marshlands (fig. 7).

The Sanctuary

At one of the cloister arches which communicated with the dormitory, since the friars had to perform the service in the middle of the night, stood the last stronghold against temptation: the church (fig. 16)—a major spot designed for the primary function of the monastery, common prayer, but also for individual worship. "After the divine service," prescribes the Rule of Saint Benedict, "all the brethren shall go out in deep silence and with due reverence for God: thus if one brother wishes to pray there alone, let him not be prevented by the importunity of others. And, if at other times, a monk desires to worship privately, let him simply enter and pray." Few of the conventual buildings erected in the eleventh century still survive today. They were fragile, as were the palaces of the greatest lords. But the churches remain.

The actual construction of the church, making it solid, superb, with fine matching stones, was the first and the last task, so that the liturgical act might be unfolded in full magnificence. Above all, so that the very body of the structure might contain the major signs used in the art of building, a parallel to the art of music, to render the ordering of the universe discernible. Through painting and sculpture one attained only a reflection of the invisible, whereas the church set out to procure its utmost significance. It was a building which could cooperate in the revelation of the divine, like the sequences of the liturgy and the analysis of the Scriptures. Its duty was to assemble a group of symbols which, imperceptibly, would imbue the hearts of those whose prayers it enshrined. And in so doing, in offering a total representation of the cosmos and man the microcosm, in other words of creation as a whole, it showed God himself, who had not wished to be dissimilar from what he had created.

The church gave that image by the way it was established in space. Turned toward the sunrise, it welcomed the first streaks of daybreak arriving to dispel nocturnal anxieties, the light which the liturgical cycle greeted with praise of the Eternal Father each morning in the chill of the early dawn. It thus stood opposite hope and resurrection and, by its position in respect to the four cardinal points, guided the procession of men toward the unfurling of the glory of the Second Coming. Its plan, too, was symbolical, although doubtless determined to a very great extent by the requirements of the liturgy. The parallel aisles, the flights of stairs, the horseshoe deambulatories, the exits offered by the transepts were laid out to facilitate the performance of the ceremonies, the movement of pilgrims toward the relics, the coming and going of the monks from the cloister buildings to the place of prayer (fig. 2). The church was a functional building first and foremost. In structure it matched the internal dynamics of the exercises of collective prayer it was called upon to house. But it was also a sign. The crossing forming the frame of the basilical plan and the inflexions of the chevet suggested the cross. On a deeper plane they offered an image of man. Of carnal man; of God, who had created man in his own likeness; of the Son of Man, crucified, in whom the two natures, temporal and spiritual, were joined. The bays of the transept held the outspread arms, the apse sheltered the head, while the choir occupied the crucial point. The central space of the crossing was square, as was the cloister, and portrayed the four elements of the terrestrial universe. But, like the baptisteries and the palatine chapels, that square was the starting point of an ascension. The word of God was its instrument. The crossing of the transept often contained the symbolical images of the four evangelists carved on the stays at the four corners, supporting the roof. The whole was crowned with a dome, that is to say the circular image of celestial perfection.

Lastly, the monument demonstrated the order of God through the arithmetical relations linking each of its elements with all the others (fig. 6). The fundamental ideas of knowledge were expressed by numbers. For the initiated belonging to the High Church, four meant the figure of the world, five the figure of man. Ten, the sum of all the numbers, which indicated the perfect according to Pythagoras, was the sign for God. The most complex monastic basilicas, Tournus or Saint-Benoît-sur-Loire, and the simplest priory churches in the country were constructed to a web of mathematical agreements. Those who built them wished them to be prophetic representations of divine harmony after the manner of Gregorian chant.

Vaults

The chief innovation of the architecture which flowered in southern Gaul, in the Cluniac empire, in the area where triumphing feudalism gradually stifled what remained of the Carolingian era, was the regular use of the vault. The builders of the previous period were not unacquainted with this technique, which must have been in use ever since the eighth century in the structures added to the Frankish basilicas with the development of the liturgy and the cult of relics. The porch and the chevet had become two-story buildings, the upper floor being reserved for important ceremonies. As a result it had proved necessary to replace the columns with pillars and the timber roofing with a vault at the entrance to the church and in the crypt (fig. 4). The nave of the basilical space, however, was still covered by rafters and remained so throughout the eleventh century in all the regions faithful to the imperial tradition, Germania, Lorraine, the Ile-de-France, Norman Neustria, and in Italy longer than anywhere else (fig. 2). The idea of completely vaulting the whole sanctuary may have taken shape in the monasteries of Catalonia. There, where the Carolingian manner finally merged with living Latin traditions, the cultural contribution of a province fertilized by the influence of Mozarabic Christendom and stimulated at about the year 1000 by an exceptionally plentiful inflow of gold took on full meaning. Oliba, the abbot of Ripoll and Cuxa, was doubtless responsible for the experiments which produced the church of Saint-Martin-du-Canigou, begun in 1001, and the remarkable ensemble of San Pedro de Roda, consecrated in 1022. Other very precocious innovations were tried out in Burgundy: at Tournus, at Saint-Bénigne in Dijon, above all at Cluny. On one church designed to replace the first oratory of the Cluniac community, work had been begun as early as 955; it was consecrated in 981, entirely covered by a stone vault.

Chronicles relate that the vaults of the new nave at Vézelay were erected toward 1135 to replace a timber structure which had been destroyed by fire. To imagine, however, that a mere concern for security could explain such a vast and difficult enterprise, all the gropings, the failures, the efforts to throw barrel vaults across the major naves, to compensate the thrusts by groined vaults over side aisles, to develop the tribunes, to balance the domes, would be grossly to underestimate the men who created the Romanesque style. The vault must be regarded as one of the cardinal elements of the idiom forged by the monks of the West at that period, an idiom which claimed to be the expression of the world, both natural and supernatural, and at the same time a quest, an initiation, an itinerary toward a more meaningful apprehension of invisible realities. At a time when the monastic church was extending its funerary duties and thereby earning the favor of the people, the Benedictine abbots may have sought to spread through the church as a whole the dark womblike atmosphere surrounding the burial rites, heralding the Resurrection, celebrated beneath the vaults of the crypt and in the porch. At all events, the substitution of stone roofs for wood clearly signified that even in its very materials the building strove to achieve that substantial unity which would make it better equipped to symbolize the universe, itself a total unity in the divine will. Also, though a secondary consideration, the vault improved the acoustic qualities of a building primarily intended to house choral singing. Lastly and above all, the vault introduced the circle into architectural rhythms, or rather the image of circular time, a perfect endless line, consequently the clearest mark of eternity, of that heaven to which the monastic church claimed to be the anteroom (fig. 8).

Cluny

It was at the turn of the eleventh century that monastic architecture, the most noble of the arts at that time, attained fulfillment in the new abbey buildings of Cluny. Almost nothing of the construction survives today. It was huge, conceived for a vast family: more than three hundred monks made up the community in the mother house when Abbot Hugh began work in 1088, eager for liturgical celebrations more magnificent still and consequently deeming Odilo's splendid second church too mean.

He saw things on a very grand scale: a building more than 180 meters long; tall pillars so that the monks, escaping from the discipline of the cloister as if from a prison, might expand their souls and accede, through choral ceremonies, to the perception of divine splendor. Since it was the image of heaven, the basilica would be vaulted. Yet it would be as luminous as the churches built in the imperial tradition.

The monk, Gunzo, who drew inspiration from Saint Peter, Saint Paul, and Saint Stephen in his conception of the plan, was reported to be an "admirable psalmist." He had in fact composed the sanctuary as the polyphonists later composed their motets and fugues. A unit figure of five Roman feet provided the basis for complex arithmetical combinations. These numerical relations expressed the ineffable. The number seven commanded the proportions of the apse. The great door rested on the progression of one, three, nine, and twenty-seven. Above all, the church included the series of perfect numbers of Isidore of Seville and the Pythagorean series of harmonic numbers, an eminently musical idea, considered as representing the universal order on which the entire equilibrium of the monument rested. The interlacing figures were intended to imprison the mind in order to attract it toward God: the abbey was dedicated to Saint Peter, the fisher of men. Abbot Hugo, according to his biographer, had imagined the monastery church as a vast net for capturing souls. His ardent wish was that it should be "inhabited by the glory of God" and be "the promenade of angels."

And therefore sumptuously adorned. We like bare walls in Romanesque churches, but we should remember that when they were new, they were covered with frescoes and more often than not with storified hangings (fig. 9). In the eleventh century the entire trade of Amalfi was based on the importation of oriental silks. Such materials were not yet available for personal adornment, except to kings and the greatest prelates when, on solemn occasions, each represented the glorious myths of the higher world before the assembled population (fig. 8). They clothed the walls. Yet within the monastic church, the most precious elements of figurative ornamentation were concentrated around the central spot for the performance of the liturgy. Around the altar, and, if the basilica housed them, around the relics.

Reliquaries

After the emperors had imposed the observances of the Roman church, a style of building which provided the model for the Romanesque chevet was disseminated far and wide. It derived from the two-story structure Pope Gregory the Great had built on the tomb of Saint Peter. Two altars were set exactly one above the other: the reliquary altar at ground level stood over the sepulcher; immediately above, in a space which the windows flooded with light, was the high altar, where the public ceremonies were performed. Following the same pattern, the chancels of the pilgrim churches were erected over a crypt. In Tournus and San Salvador of Leyre, the crypt matched the basilical plan: at Saint-Bénigne of Dijon, constructed under the abbot William of Volpiano, it espoused the round form of the *martyria* (fig. 4). Cohorts of pilgrims, guided by the monks, would proceed downwards, tiptoeing into those mysterious underground precincts at certain dates to see and touch the holy bodies, the healing powers and the powers of hope which, for the majority of men, were the true and perhaps the only divinities. Sometimes the relics were brought out of their retreat, in hard times, and paraded through the countryside, courting evil spells in order to break them. But their dwelling place was there, below ground. They lived ensconced among lamps. They reposed amid a treasure. All the riches of the world, silver, vermilion, coins brought back from distant lands, charms, old jewels once offered by kings, and gold, accumulated round them. At the heart of the piety and the unease of the eleventh century—at the heart of Romanesque art—lay the wrought-gold object which the entire monument encased: the shrine. Its usual form was that of a sarcophagus with sides often ornamented with discreet images in the figurative tradition of the imperial workshops. Often too, it was given the appearance of the physical fragment it contained. In southern Gaul, as a result, it became a statue.

The pilgrims of Conques, enthralled, approached a disturbing fetish, the apparition of Saint Foy in majesty, entirely sheathed in gold and gems. Such effigies brought alive the anthropomorphic gods which peasant peoples with no history had always venerated and in which, from their utter poverty, they placed their expectations. These "idols" shocked the master of the episcopal schools of Angers who saw them in 1013. Nurtured on imperial traditions, he had entered another Christendom neglectful of school discipline and possessing a liturgy conveniently adapted to local beliefs. The decoration of the crypts effectively seemed to "extend the ritual of adoration formerly devoted to the gods, or rather the devils." "Ignorant as I am," he wrote, "I thought it very perverse and contrary to Christian law when I glimpsed the statue of Saint Gerald for the first time, set on an altar, modeled exactly in the shape of a human face; to most of the peasants who admired it, it seemed to consider them with a perspicacious eye and by the reverberation of its gaze give a kindlier response to their prayers." The miracles of Saint Foy, however, calmed his fears and helped him, like so many others, to grow accustomed to the reappearance of statuary. It was to capture the religious instincts of the population that the abbey opened its doors to figures, setting them up first of all, like a jewel slightly larger than the rest, in the half-light of the crypts.

2
Façades

The façade of Saint-Denis and the cathedrals which followed in its train were demonstrations of the strength of everlasting life. The city of God was

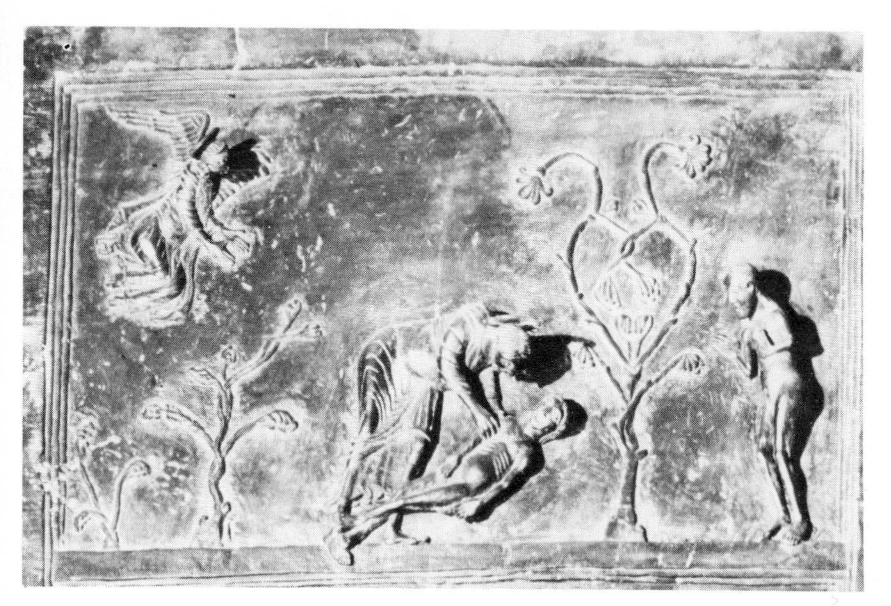

1. Genesis. Bronze doors by Bishop Bernward, upper left section. Hildesheim cathedral. 1015.

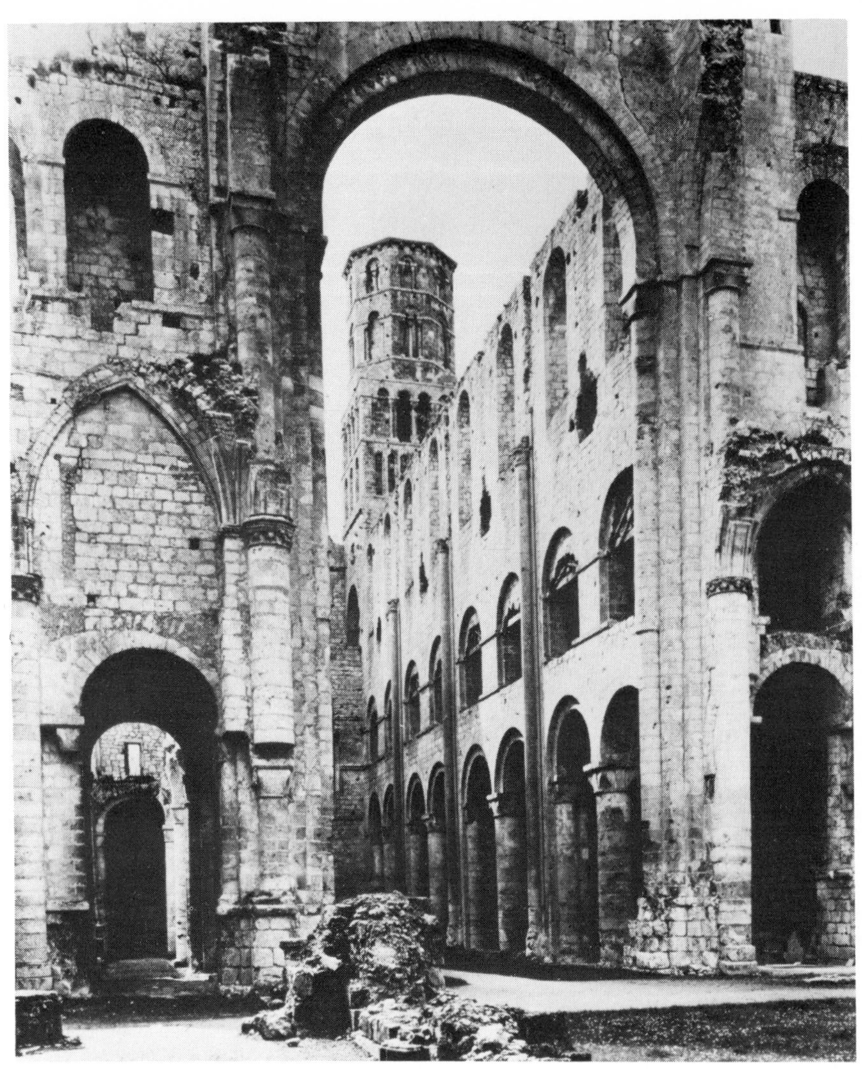

2. The church of the Benedictine abbey, Jumièges. 1040–67.

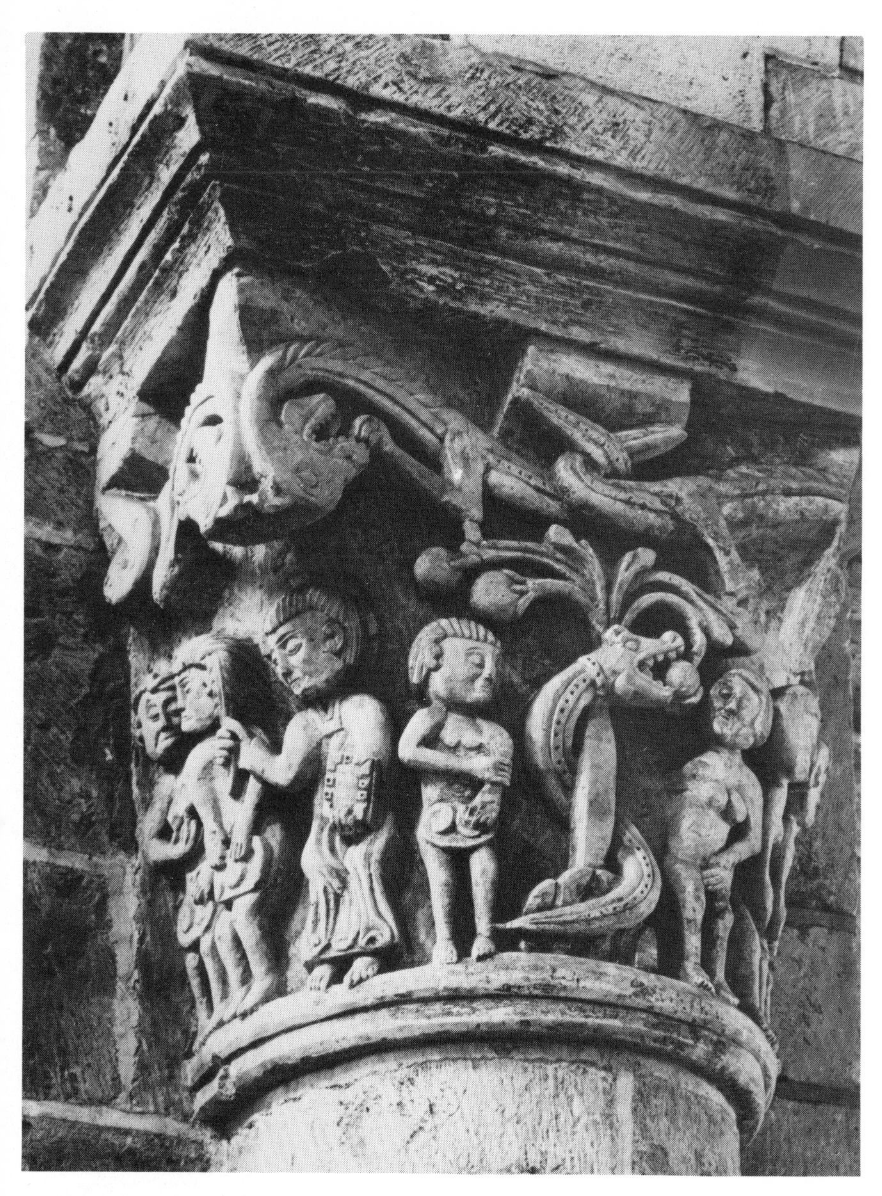

3. Adam's Sin. Capital, Saint-Benoît-sur-Loire.
Eleventh century.

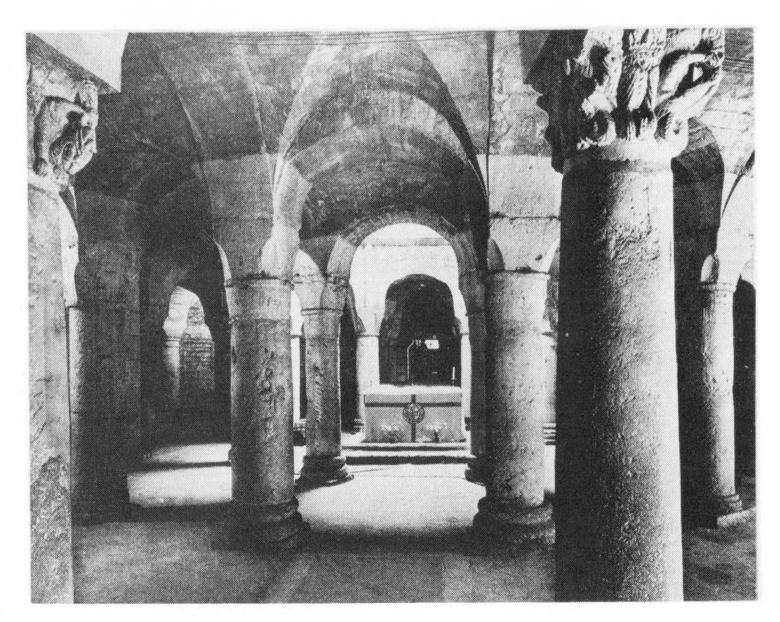

4. The crypt of the cathedral of Saint-Bénigne. Early eleventh century.

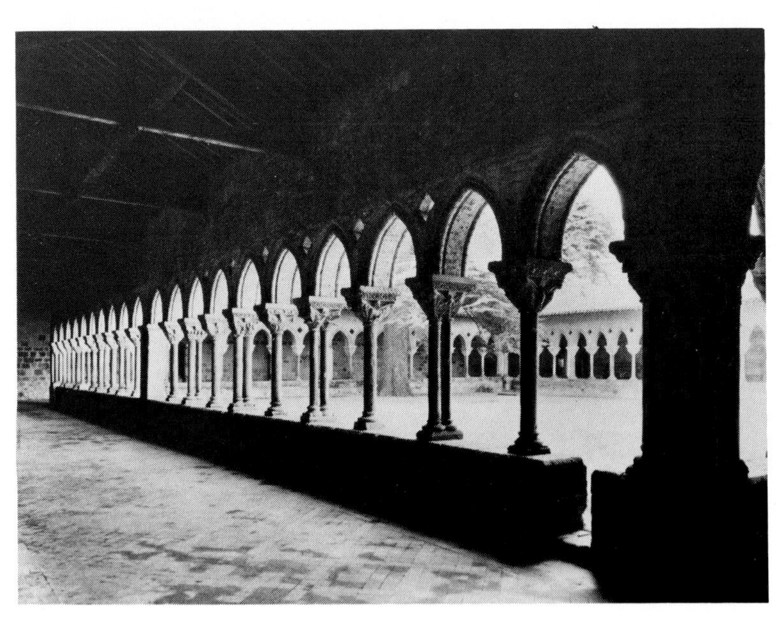

5. The cloister of the church of Saint-Pierre, Moissac. Completed in 1100.

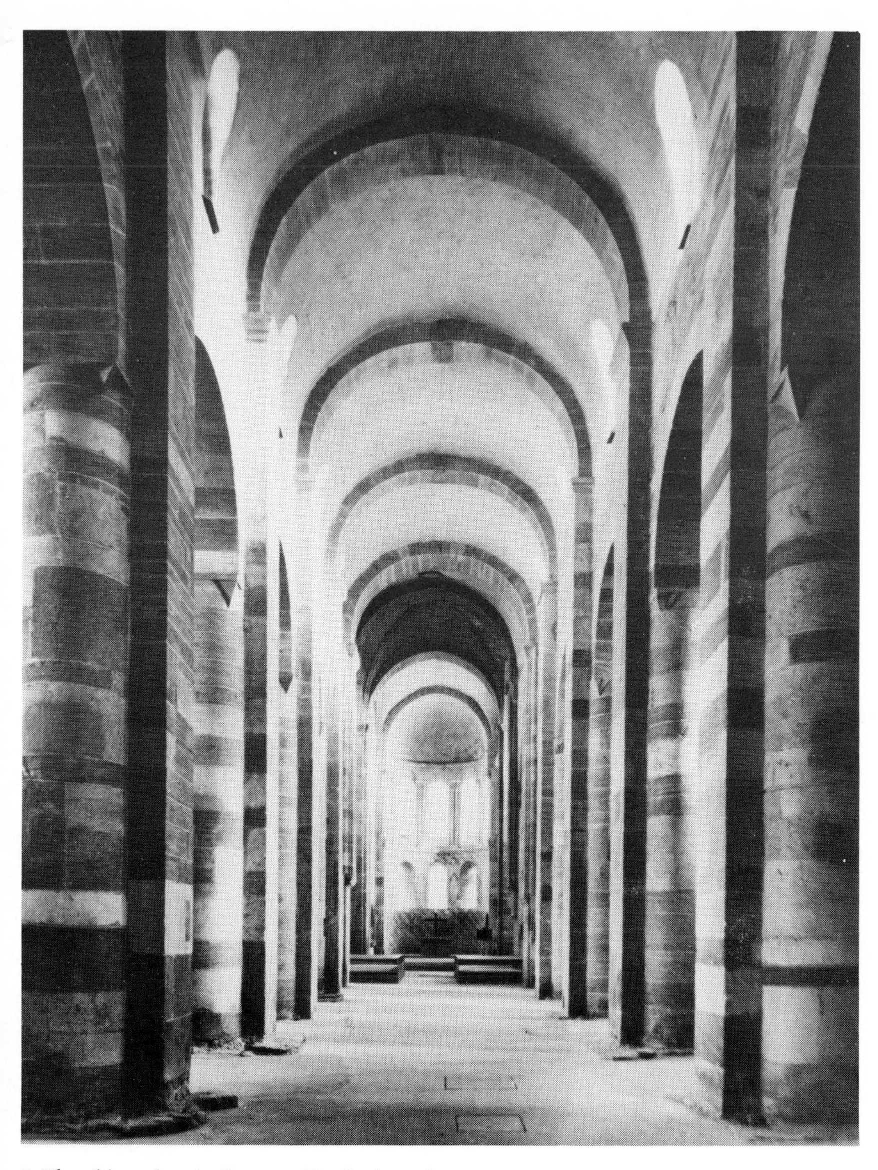

6. The abbey church, Payerne. Tenth through twelfth centuries.

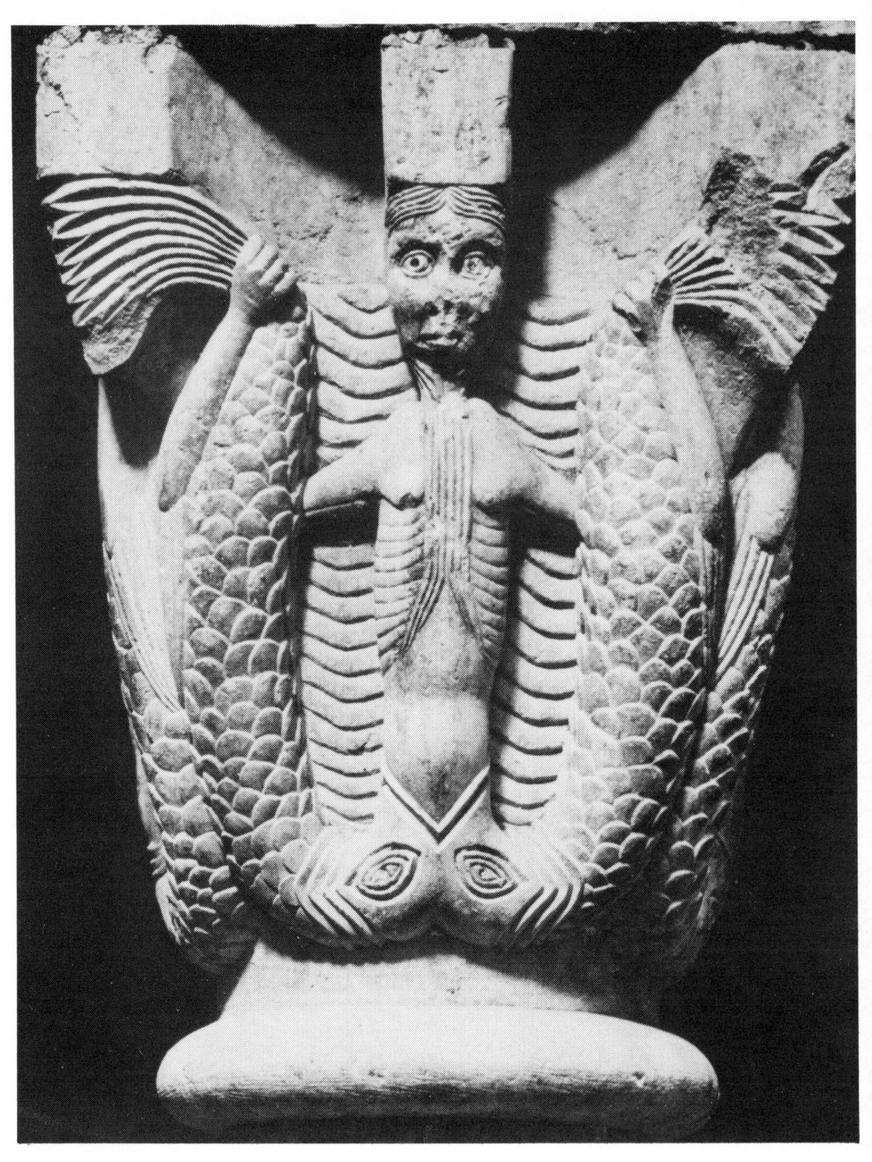

7. Cloister capital. Gerona, San Pedro de Galligans. Twelfth century.

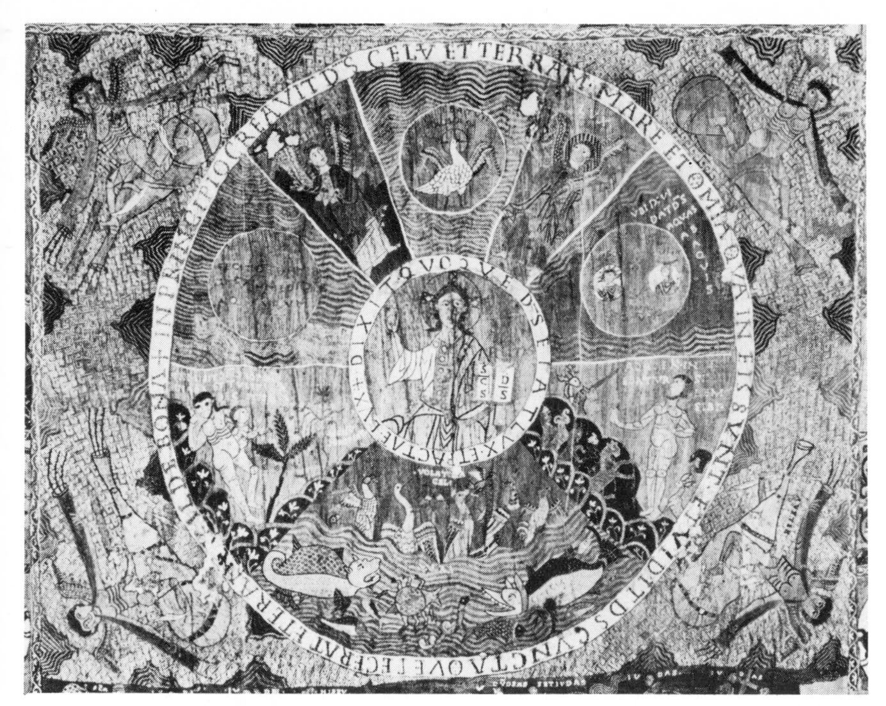

8. *The Creation* (detail). Tapestry from Gerona, treasure of Gerona cathedral. Ca. 1100.

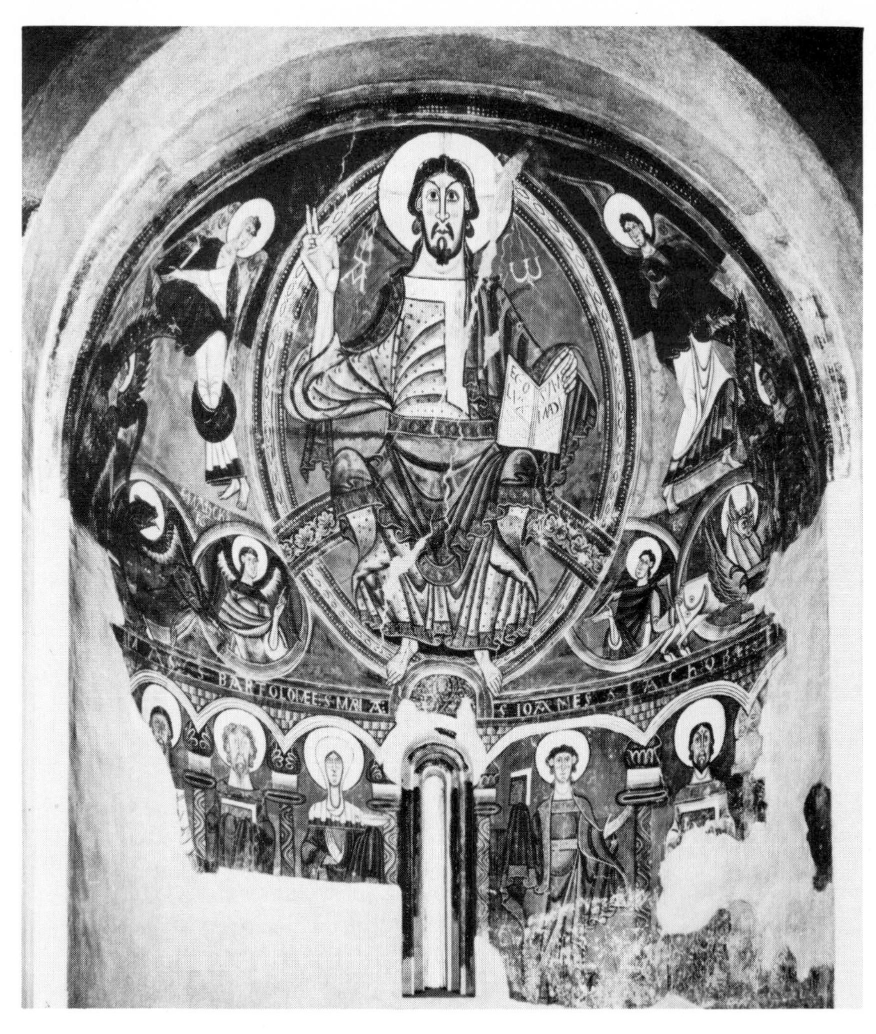

9. *Christ Pantocrator*. Fresco from San Clemente de Tahull. Barcelona, Museum of Catalan Art. 1123.

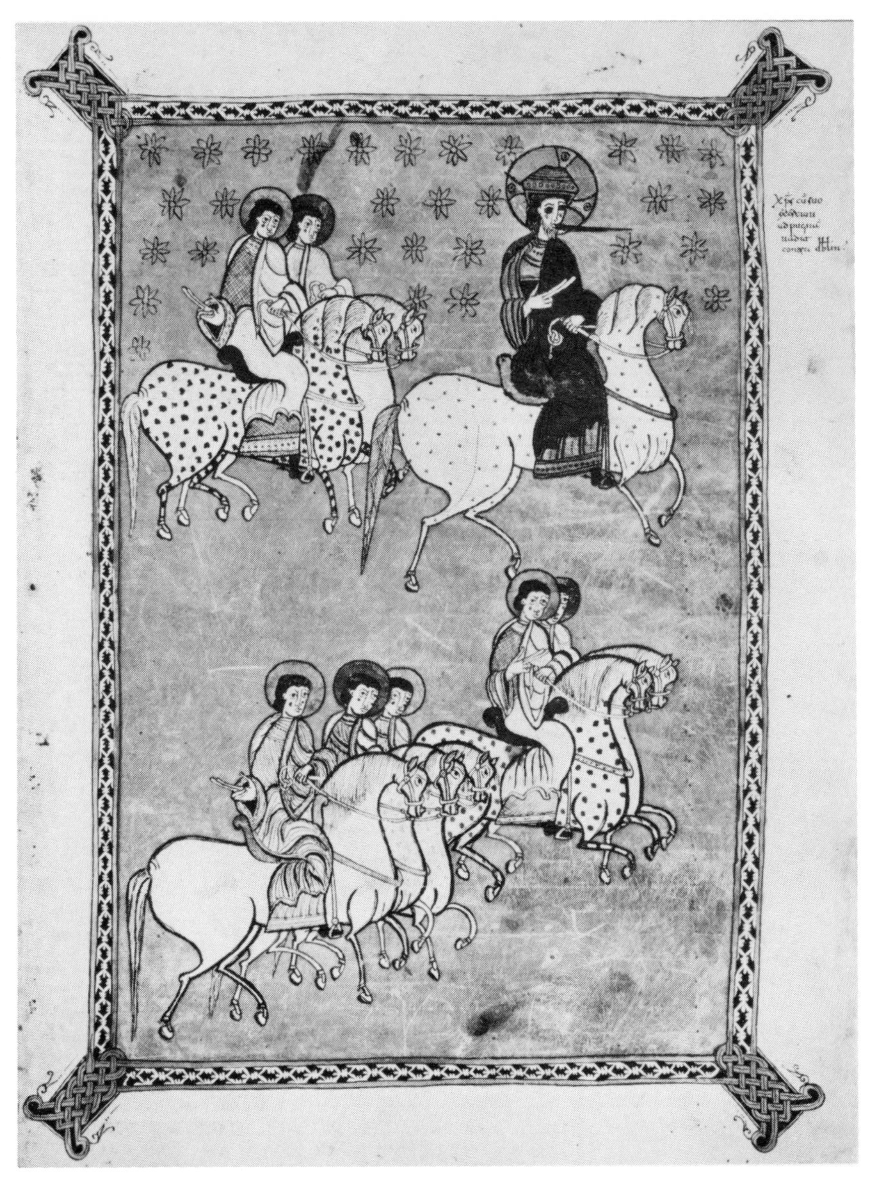

10. *The Horsemen.* Beatus of Liebana, *Commentaries on Revelation.* Soria, cathedral of Burgo de Osam. 1086.

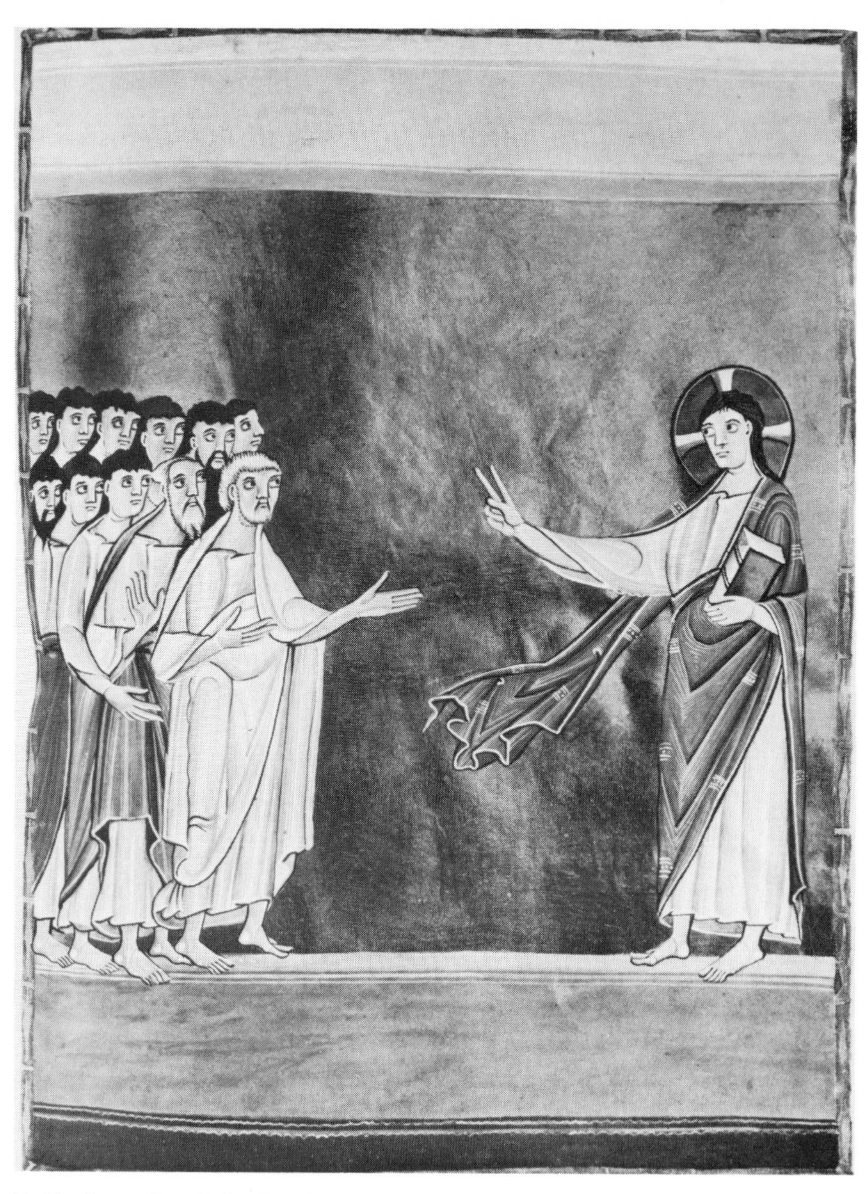

11. *The Farewell on Holy Thursday.* Pericopes belonging to Henry II. Munich Staatsbibliothek. Reichenau, ca. 1010.

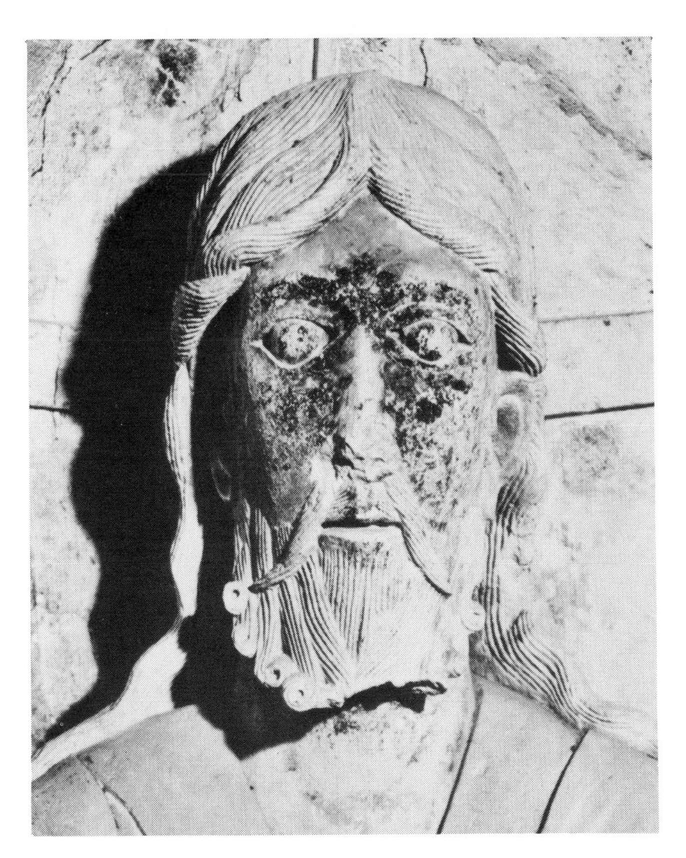

12. Christ. Detail of the doorway to the nave, church of Saint Mary Magdalen, Vézelay. Ca. 1120–50.

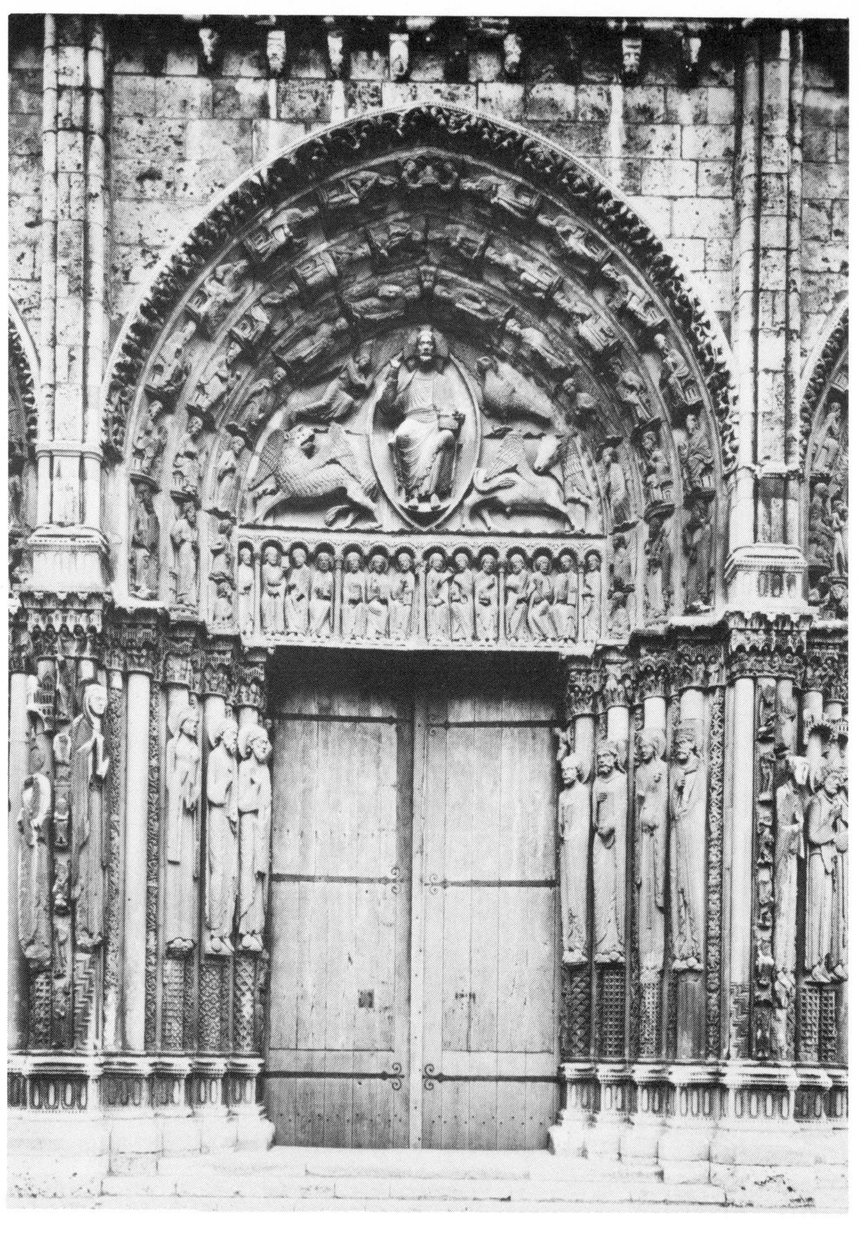

13. Royal doorway (or west door). Chartres cathedral. 1145–50.

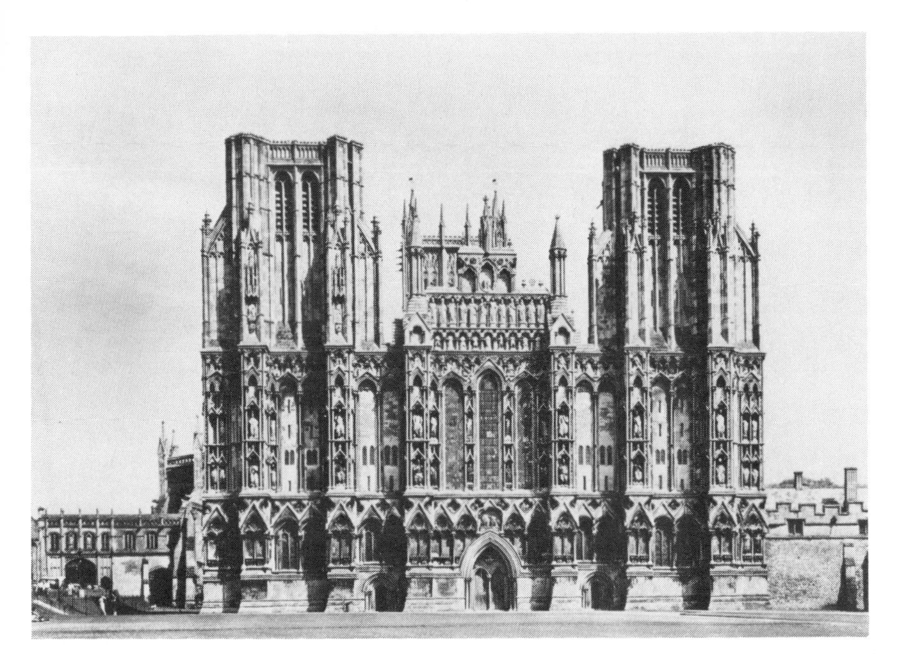

14. Wells cathedral, Somersetshire. 1220–39.

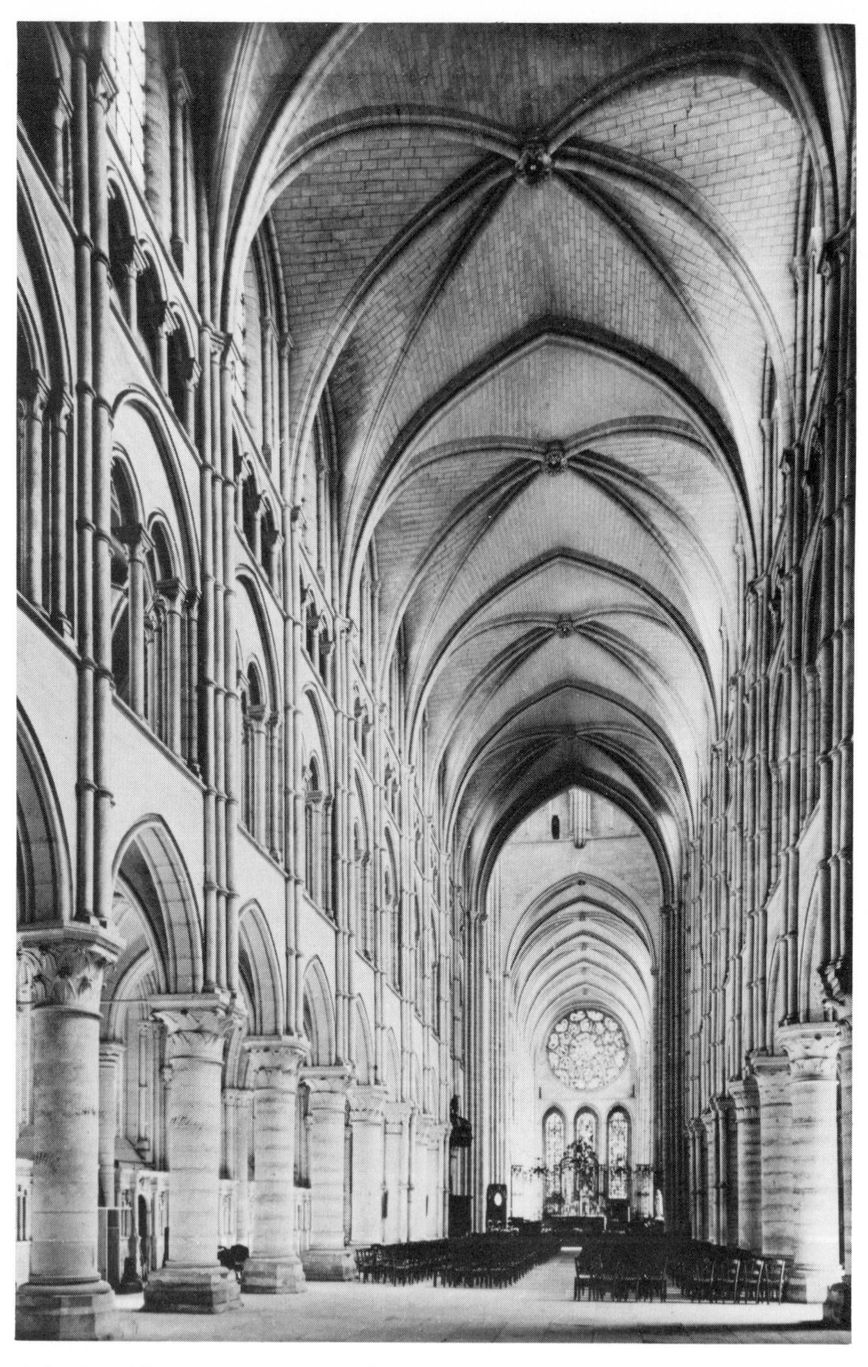

15. Interior of the nave of Notre-Dame of Laon.
Second half of the twelfth century.

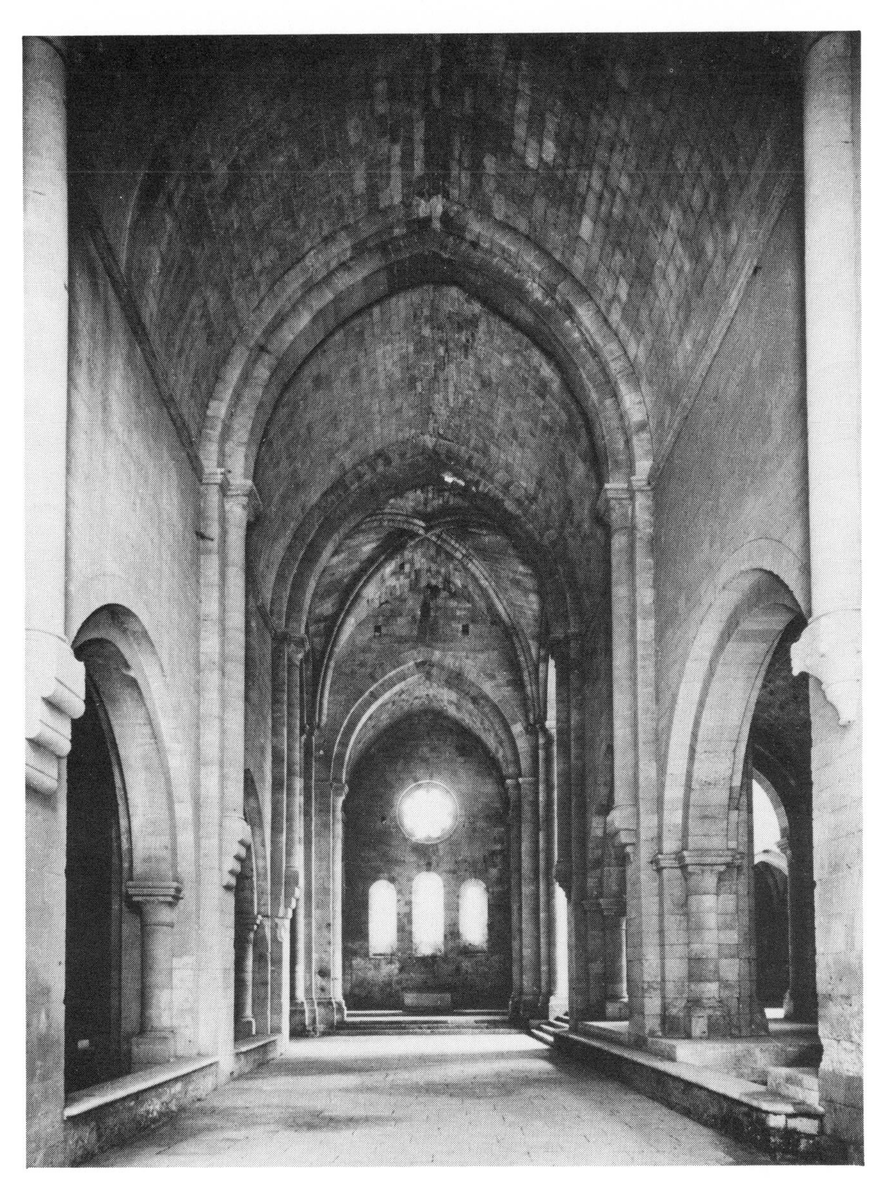

16. Interior of the nave of the abbey of Silvacane, Bouches-du-Rhône. Founded in 1147.

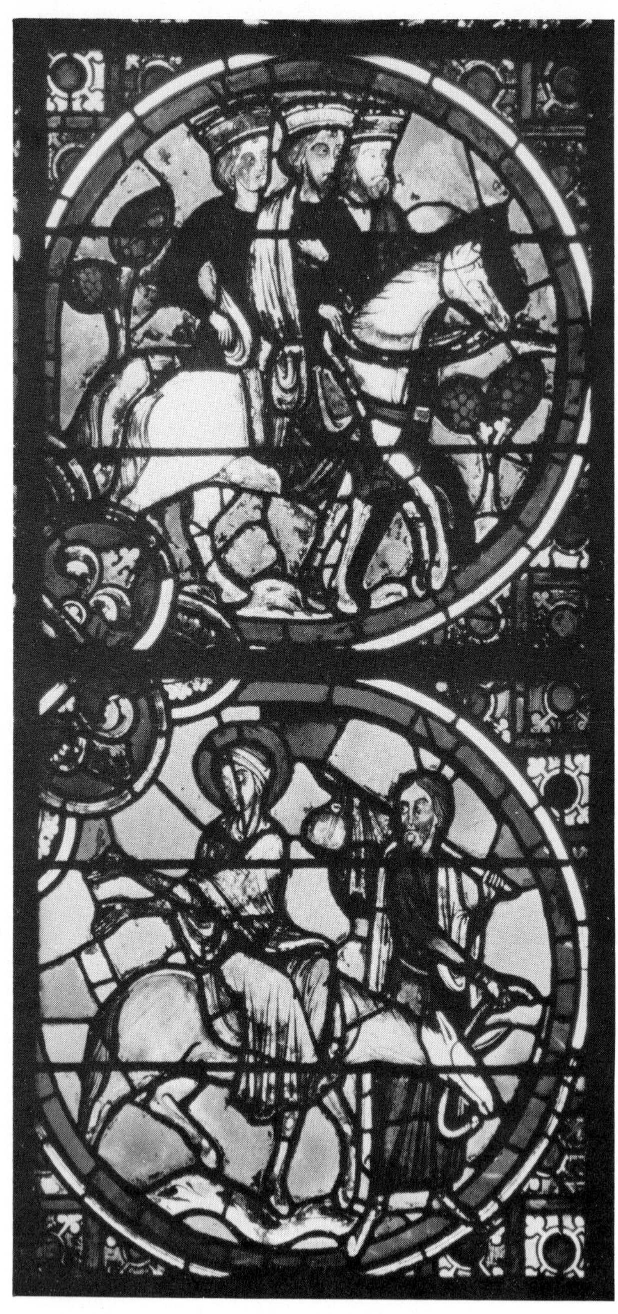

17. *The Magi and the Flight into Egypt.* Stained glass window of the apse, Notre-Dame of Laon. Ca. 1215.

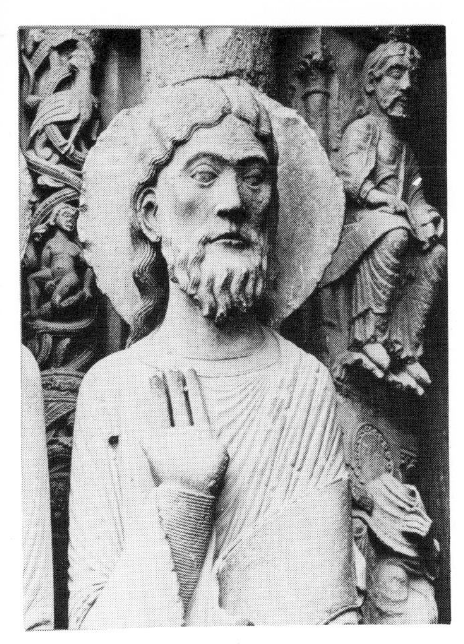

18. *A King of Judah.* Detail of a statue on the royal doorway, Chartres cathedral. 1145–50.

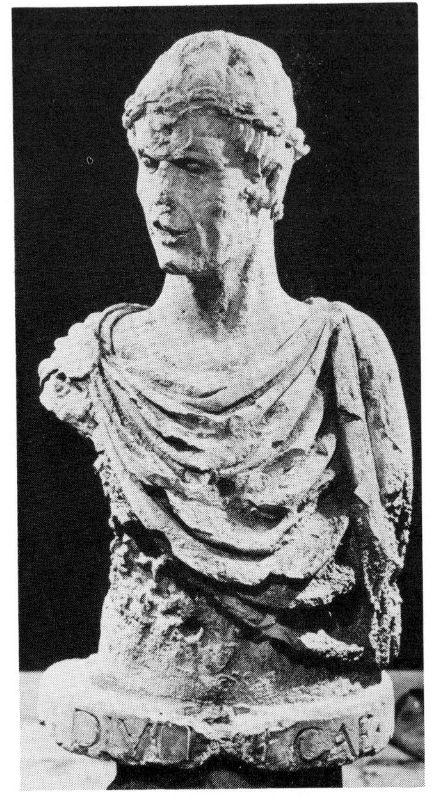

19. *Bust of Frederick II.* Barletta, Civic Museum. Mid-thirteenth century.

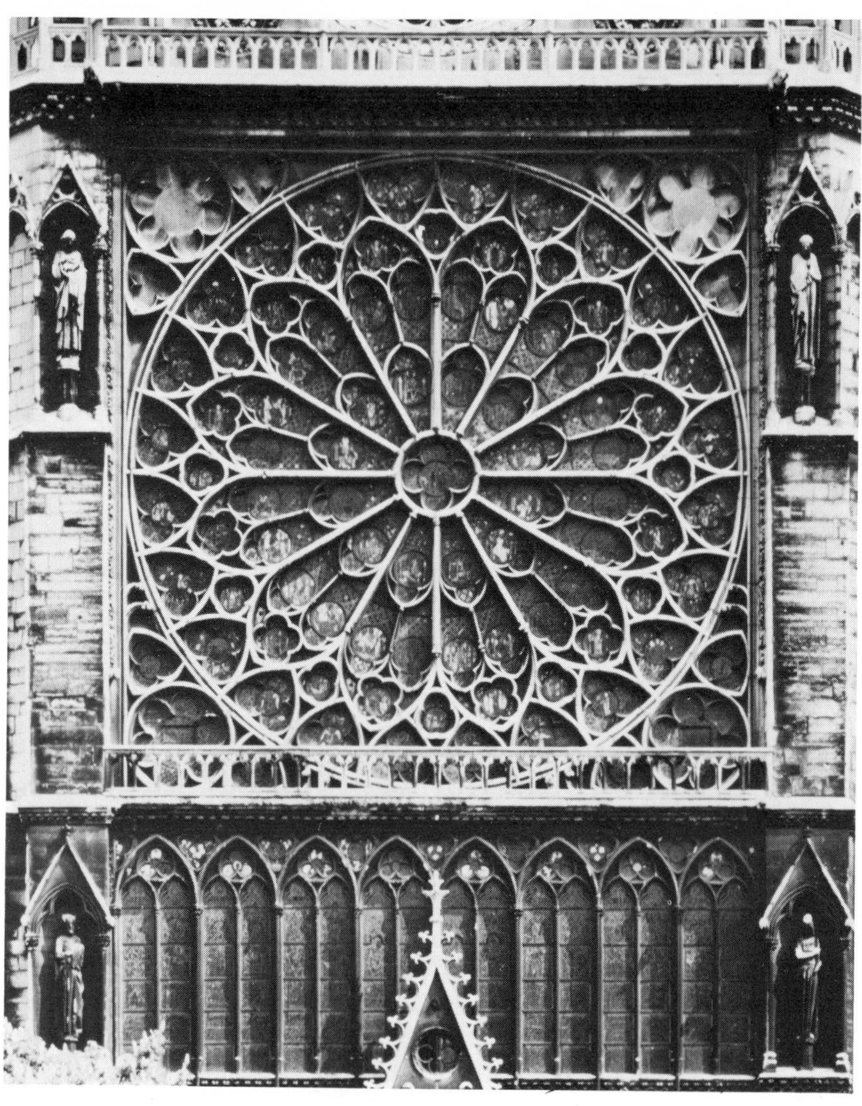

20. Exterior of the south rose window of the transept. Notre-Dame of Paris. Ca. 1270.

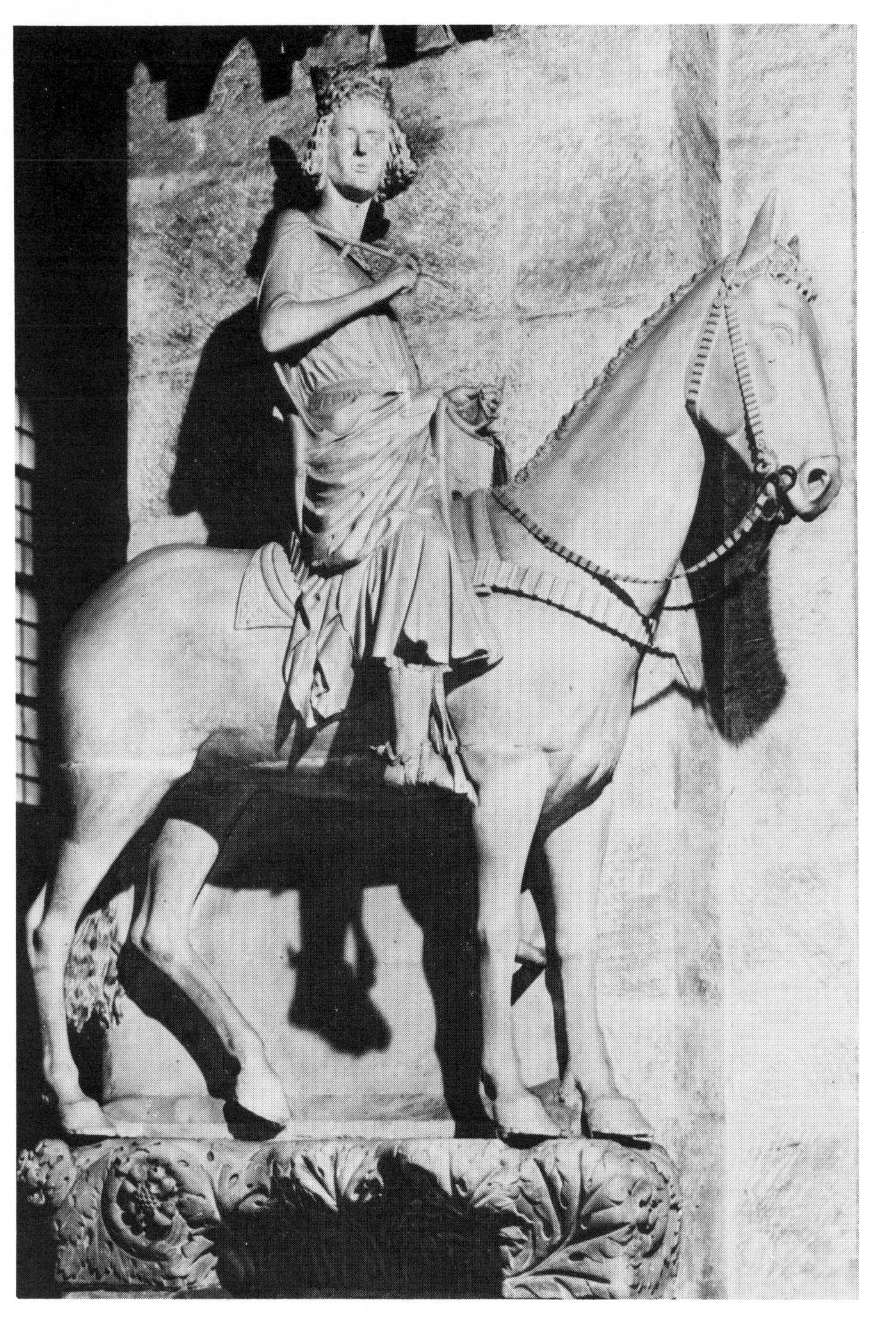

21. *The Knight of Bamberg*. Bamberg cathedral. Ca. 1235.

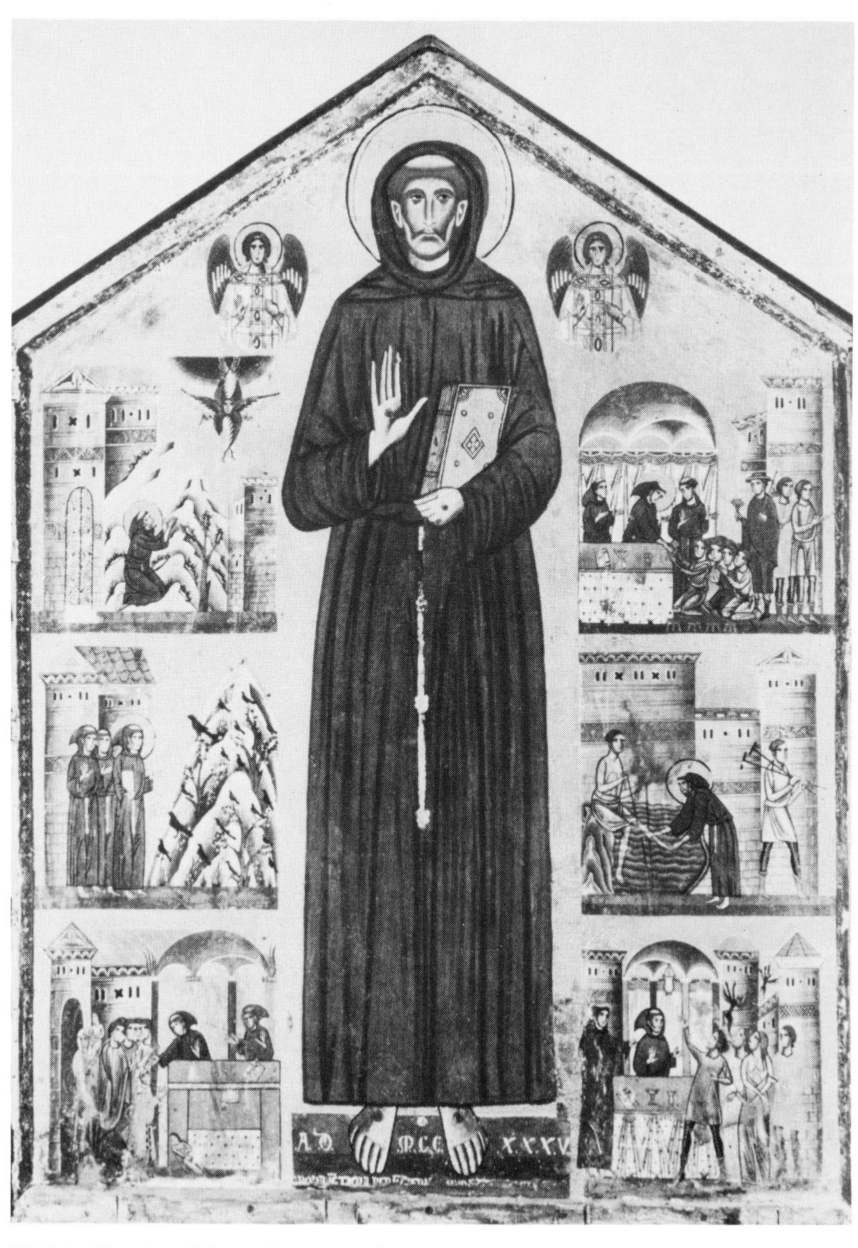

22. *Saint Francis and Scenes from His Life.* Bonaventura Berlinghieri (1228–74?). Pescia, Church of Saint Francis. 1235.

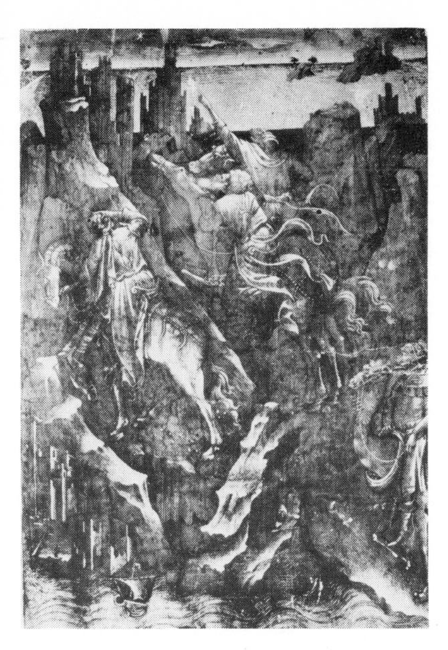

23. *The Ride of the Magi* (drawing). Lorenzo Monaco (ca. 1370–1424). Berlin-Dahlem, Staatliche Museen.

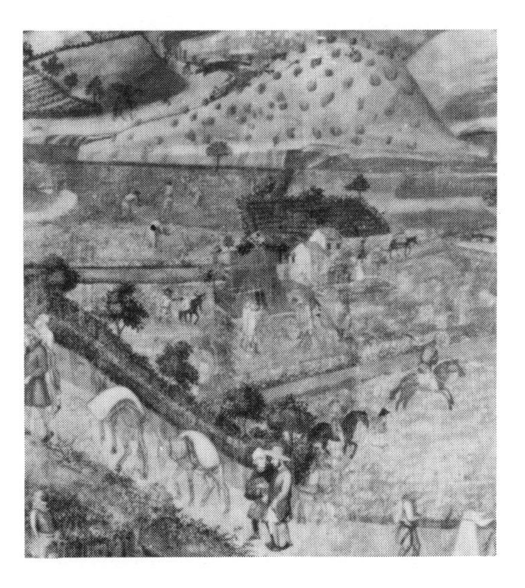

24. *The Effects of Good Government* (fresco detail). Ambrogio Lorenzetti (active 1324–48). Siena, Civic Palace. 1337–39.

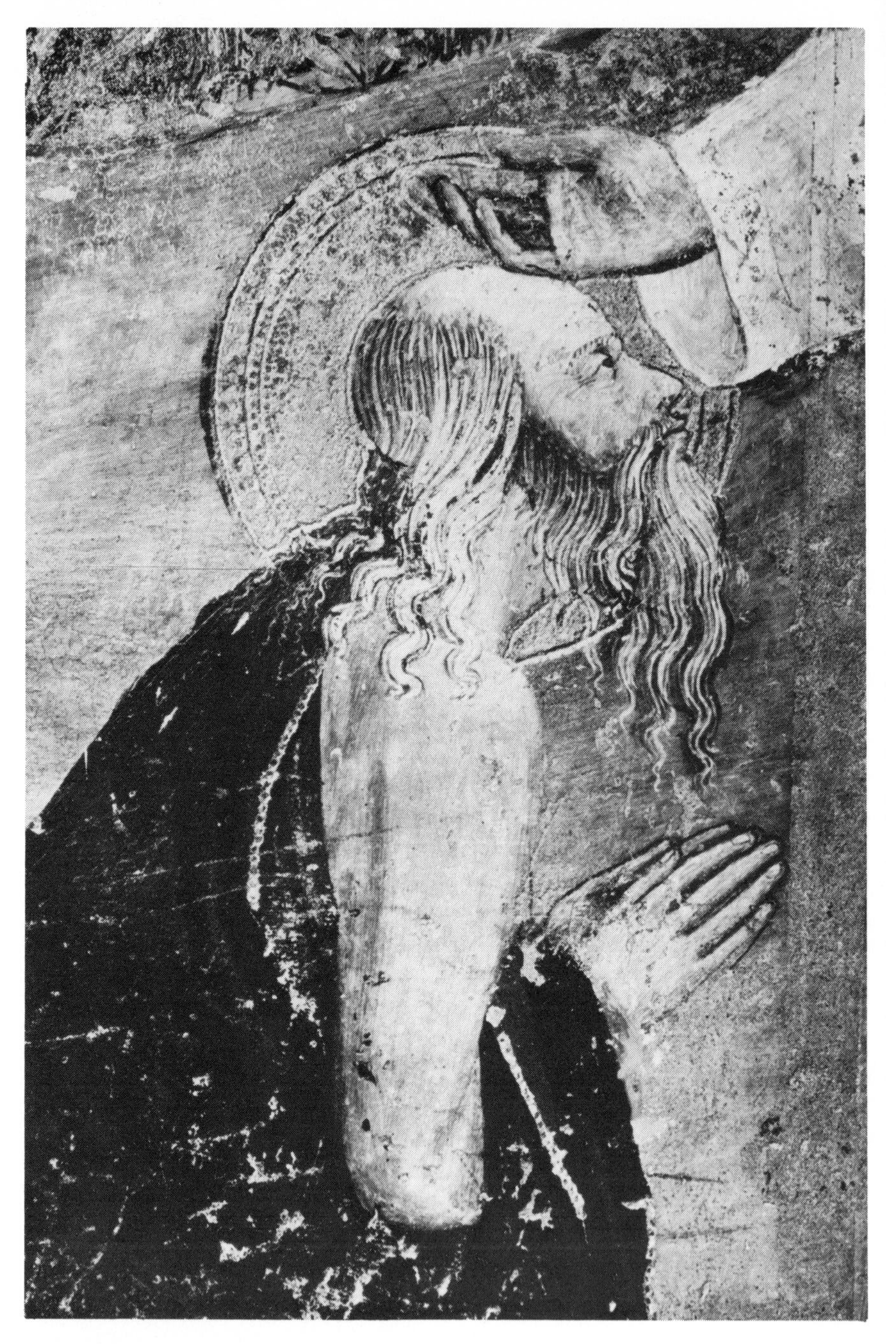

25. *The Vision of Saint John at Patmos* (fresco detail). Matteo Giovannetti of Viterbo (mid-fourteenth century). Avignon, Palace of the Popes, Saint John's Chapel. 1346–48.

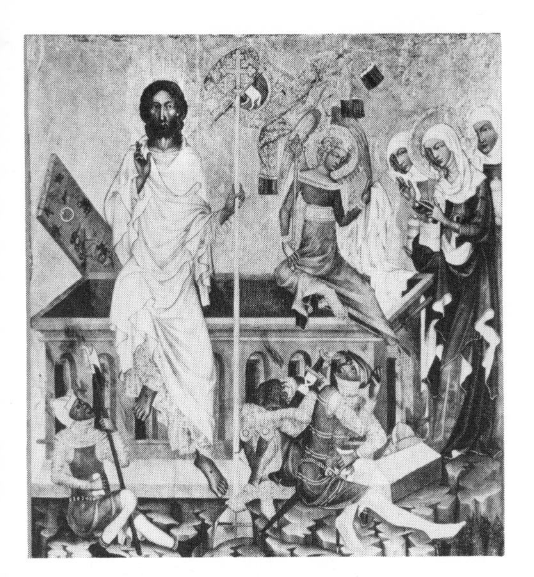

26. *The Resurrection.* Master of Vysebrod (mid-fourteenth century). Prague, National Gallery. Ca. 1350.

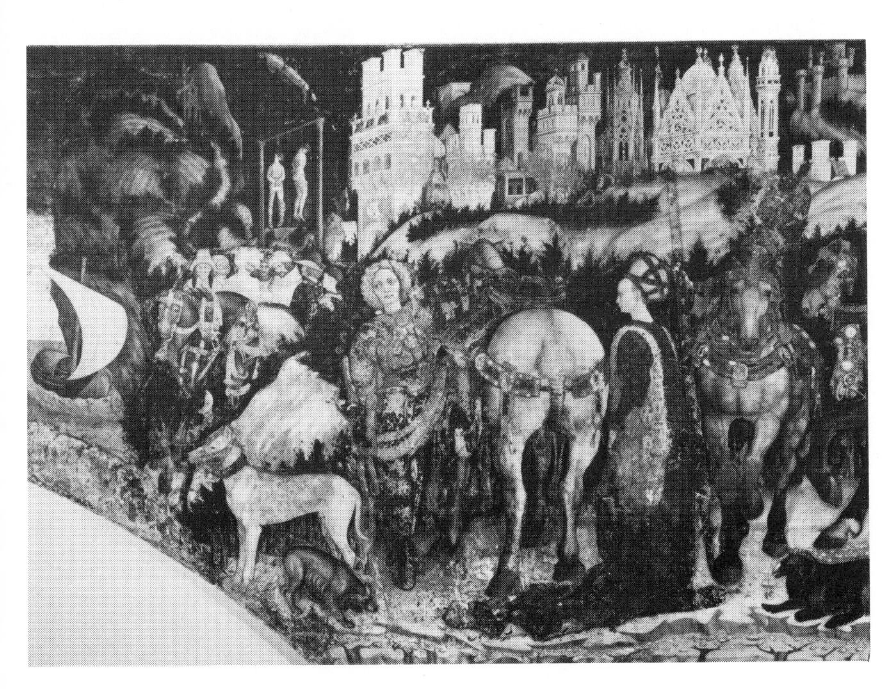

27. *The Legend of Saint George and the Princess* (fresco detail). Antonio Pisanello (1395–1455?). Verona, church of Saint Anastasia. Ca. 1435.

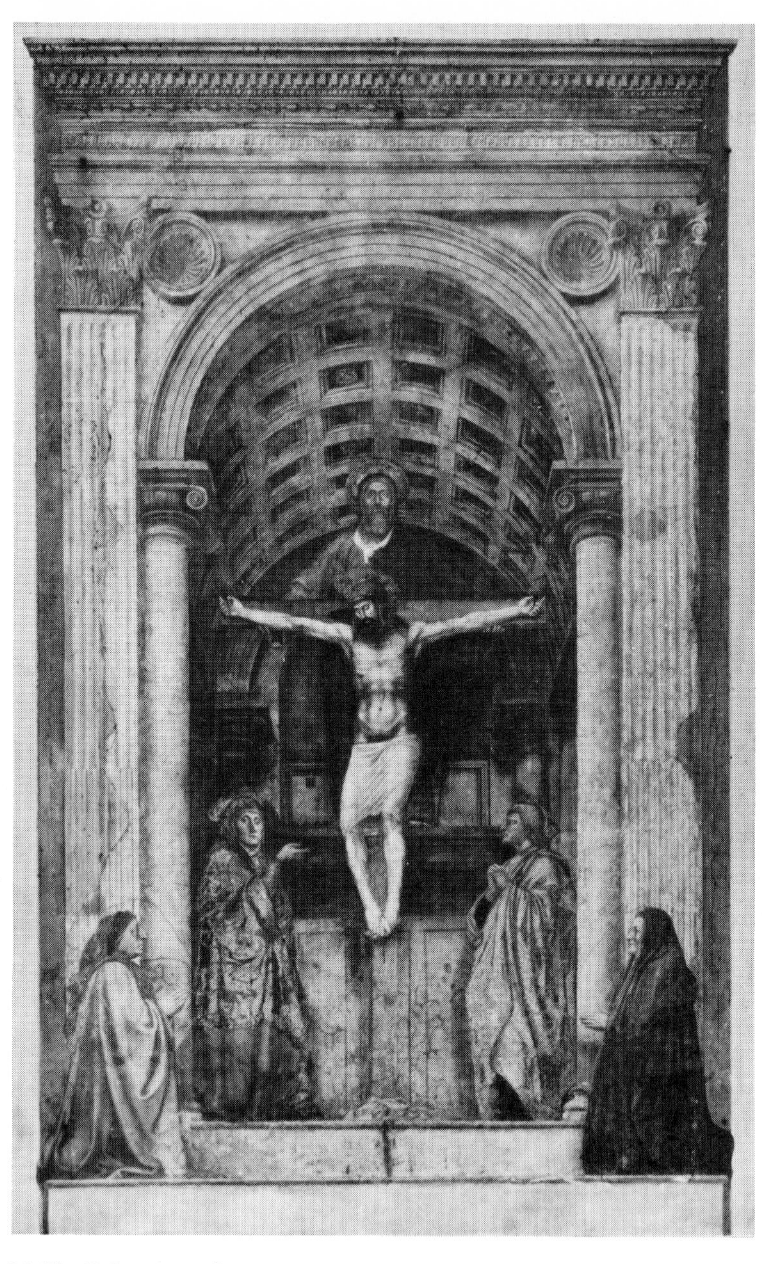

28. *The Holy Trinity* (fresco). Masaccio (1401–29). The lower section shows a skeleton on a sarcophagus. Florence, Santa Maria Novella. 1427.

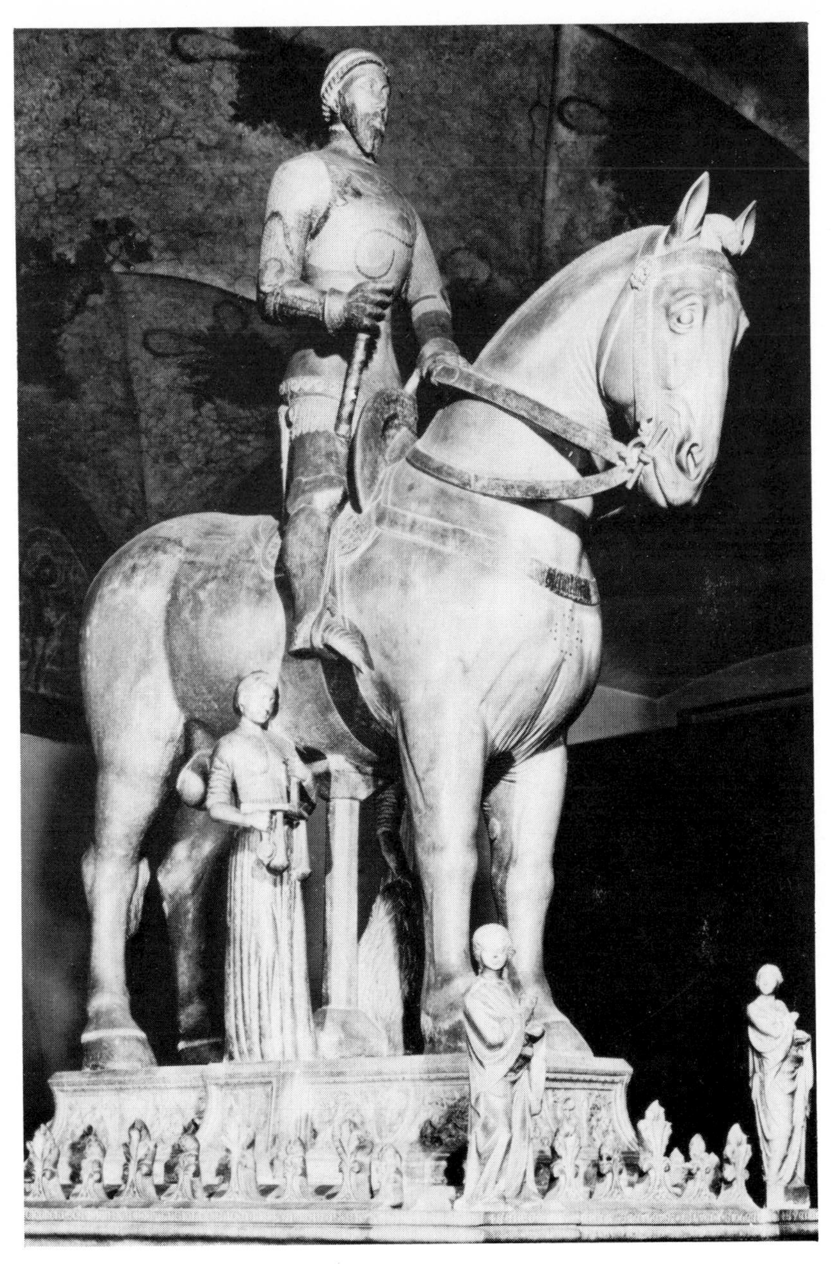

29. Marble tomb of Bernabò Visconti. Bonino da Campione (active 1357–88). Milan, Castello Sforzesco, Archaeological Museum. 1370.

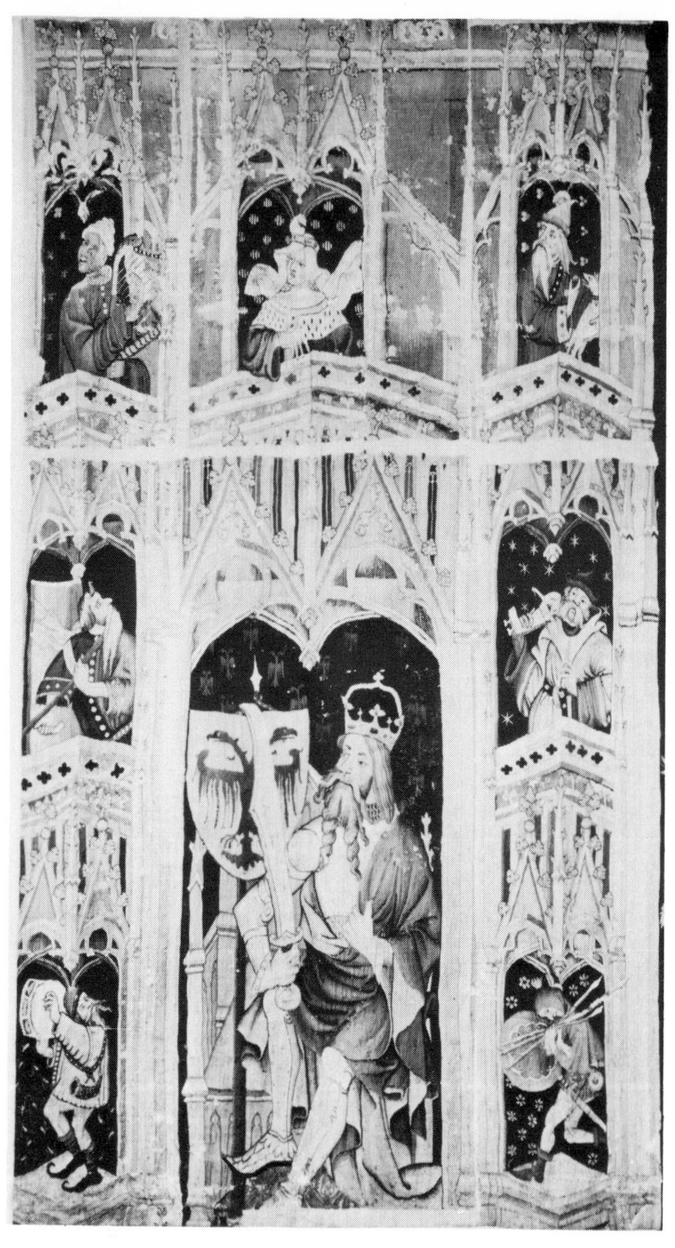

30. *Julius Caesar* (one of the pagan heroes from the *Tapestry of the Nine Paladins*). Nicholas Bataille (?). New York, The Cloisters. Ca. 1385.

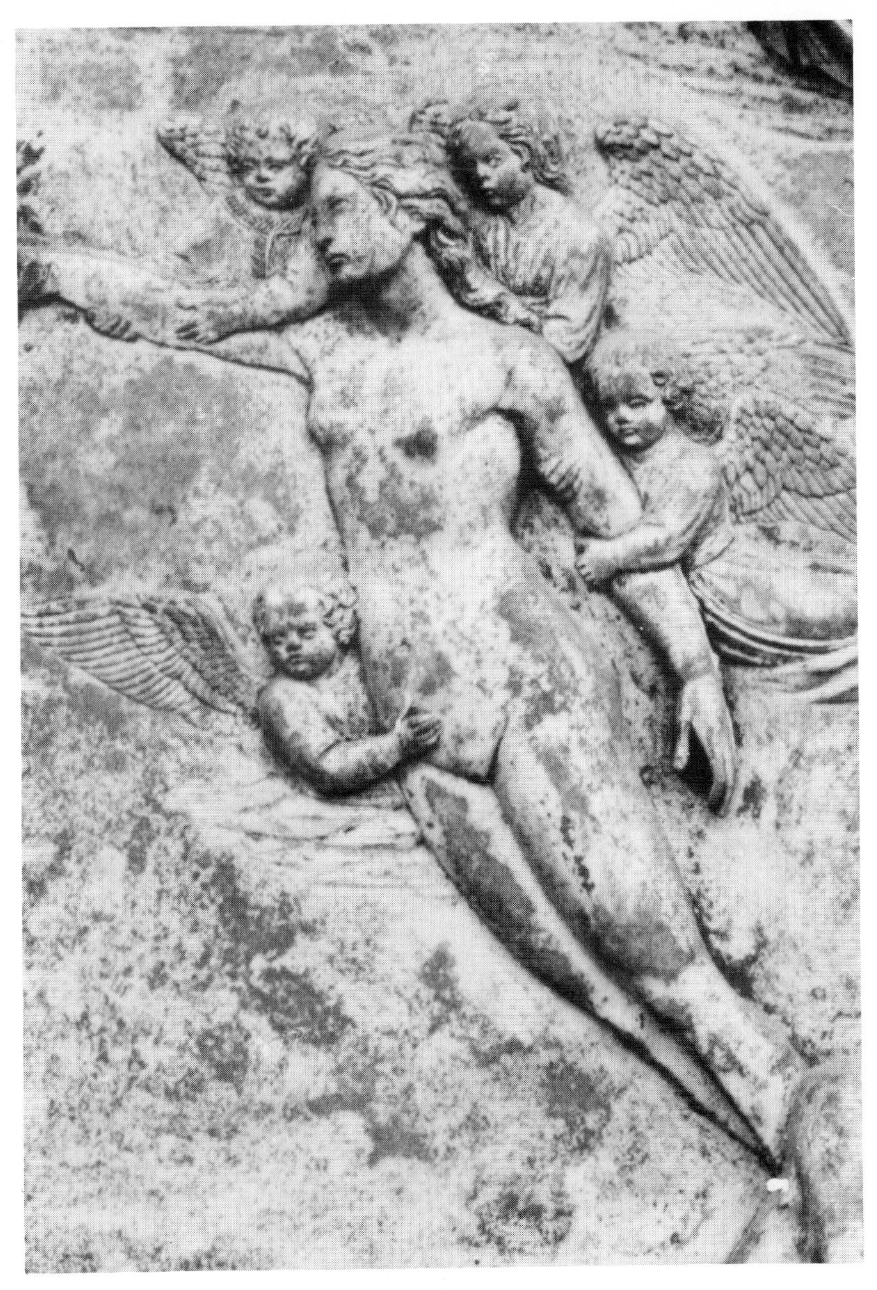

31. *The Creation of Eve* (fragment of a panel of the door of paradise). Lorenzo Ghiberti (1378–1455). Baptistery, Florence. 1425–47.

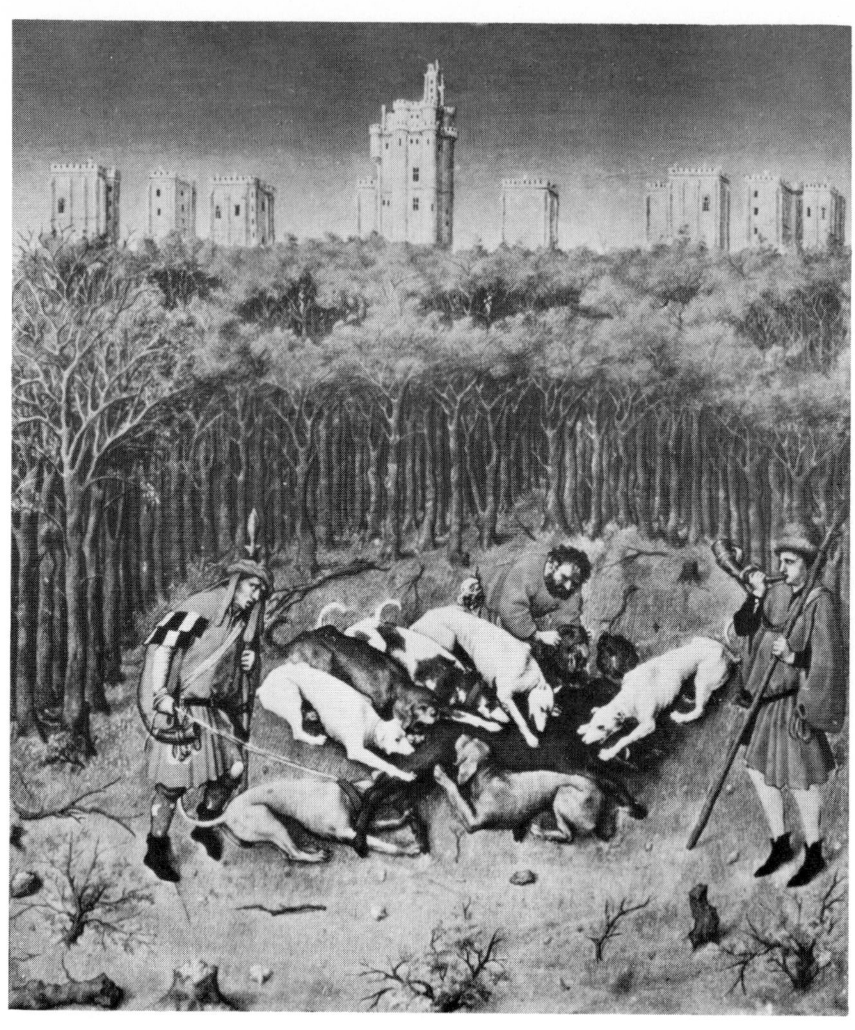

32. *December* (from the *Très riches heures* of the Duke of Berry). The Limburg brothers. Chantilly, Condé Museum. Ca. 1415.

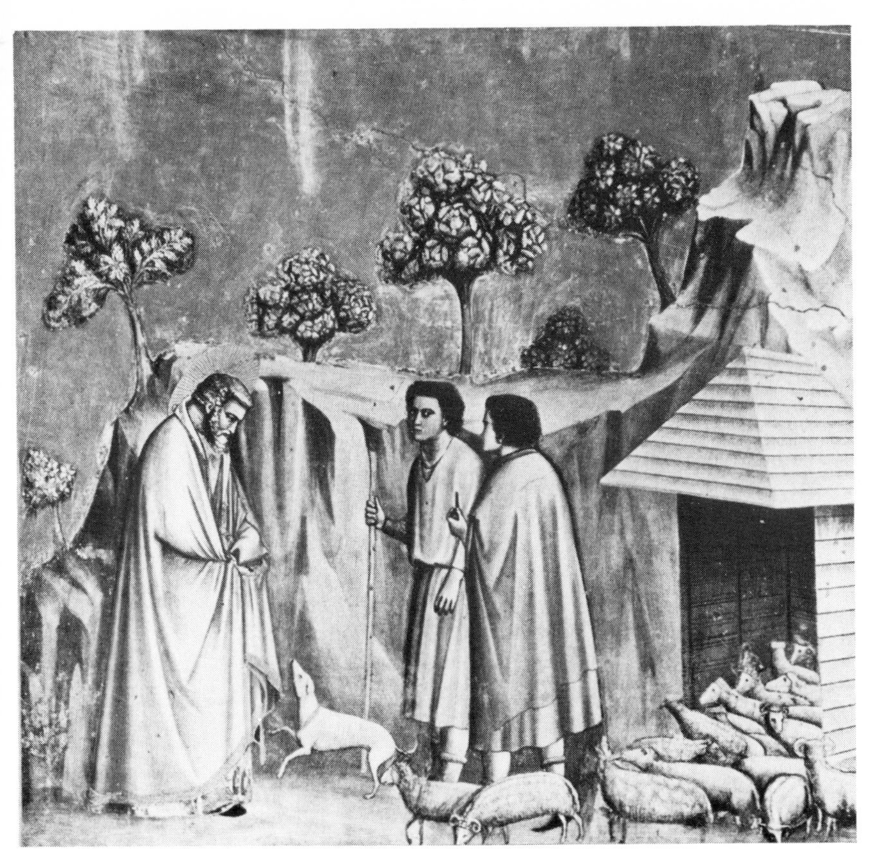

33. *Joachim among the Shepherds* (fresco). Giotto (ca. 1266–1337). Padua, Arena chapel (Scrovegni chapel). 1305–6.

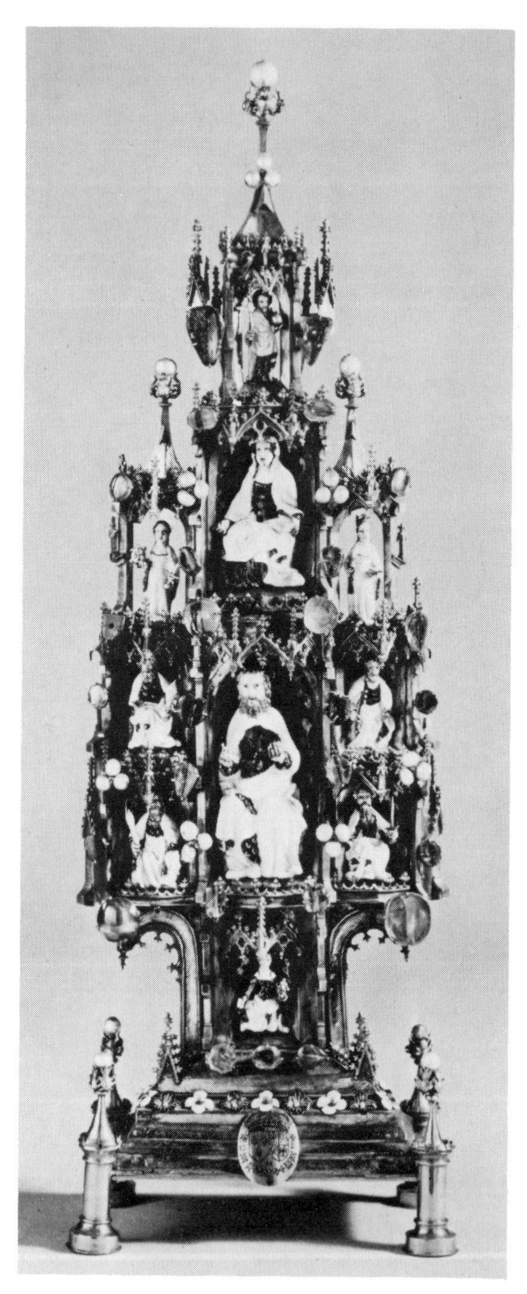

34. Reliquary of the chapel of the Order of the Holy Spirit. Paris, Louvre. France, early fifteenth century.

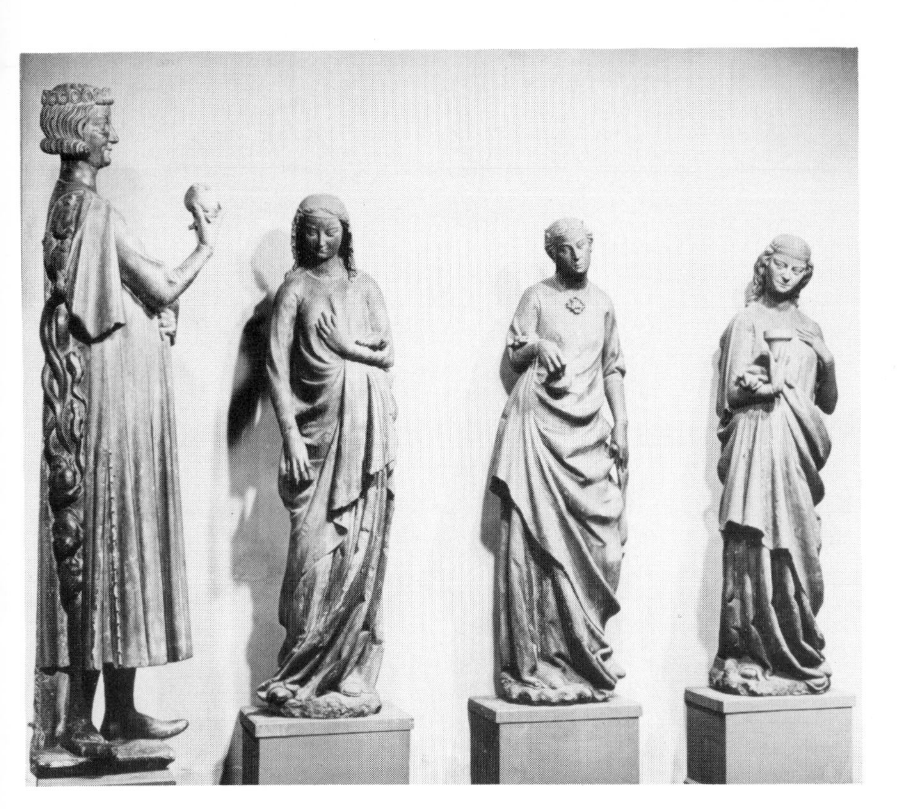

35. The Tempter, two foolish virgins, and a wise virgin. Statues from the façade of the cathedral. Strasbourg, Museum of Notre-Dame. Ca. 1280.

a refuge, a safe place where the heavenly militia kept victorious garrison. It was an impregnable fastness; the forces of evil and all the stirrings of corruption it set at naught were powerless to prevail against it. Its shape consequently resembled a castle, a dungeon of stone like those the barons erected along the Loire and the Seine at the end of the eleventh century. Sturdy and square, as they were, and vigorously upright, the front of the church occupied a commanding position. Like the crusade, which embraced the military calling of feudal society, it drew its followers along the road to salvation. The cohort of the kings of Judah, whose earthly sovereignty had been inherited by Jesus, welcomed the faithful at the entrance to a citadel (fig. 13).

In Neustria, very old architectural traditions offered the bases for such symbols of power. To build the forepart of his basilica, Suger took inspiration from the belfry porches of the Ile-de-France and was even more influenced by the façades of the Norman abbeys whose overlords had served William the Conqueror (fig. 2). In the Normandy of 1080, which launched helmeted warriors into every adventure, twin towers framed the entrance to the sanctuaries favored by the dukes, whence they gleaned the good priests, capable of reforming the English Church and keeping it in hand. The high walls erected at the threshold to the house of God in Ely and Wells, in vanquished England, came from the same stock (fig. 14).

When Suger incorporated the towers of the monasteries of Caen into the west wing of Saint-Denis, he introduced the structural principle of verticality which bore all the new episcopal churches skywards until the end of the Middle Ages. Yet the proportions of the antechurch he had conceived, the ordering of the three portals, the story for the upper chapel, the rose window lighting it, brought the monument down to the horizontal plane. The masters of works could henceforth give free rein to their imaginations in treating the relations between the two dimensions of the façade, the one soaring upwards on the ascending buttresses and pilasters and the other underlined by galleries and friezes. But the façade never lost its original appearance; it remained a vision of power and victory.

The City Church

Saint-Denis, which provided the model for Gothic structures, was an abbey church conceived for the performance of the monastic liturgy, built onto the cloister and communicating with it by means of the transept. It constituted the private oratory of a closed community, where the people were sometimes admitted but where they never failed to be intruders. The cathedral, on the other hand, was the sanctuary of the city, belonging both to the clergy and to the people; its bishop was the chosen representative, the minister. *Clerus et populus:* the cathedral, as an open church, had to accommodate the two sectors of Christian society. The ecclesiastical reform at the end of the eleventh century had in fact widened the distance separating the clergy from the faithful, and emphasized the superiority of the former over the latter. That was why the greater share of the space inside the cathedral was reserved for the clergy and why the building as a whole was primarily adapted to the requirements of their particular duties. Such requirements were not radically unlike those of the monasteries: here, too, the main activity of the cathedral clerics was to gather together in order to praise the glory of God. The bishop's church, like the monastic church, consequently organized its inner space around the choir, introducing corridors to ease the movement of the ritual processions (fig. 15). The people remained confined near the entrance or else, as in the basilicas of the pilgrim monasteries, installed above the side aisles, in the tribunes which looked on to the central nave. They were spectators. They attended the service but took no part.

The Cathedral Space

The inside arrangement of the cathedral differed from that of the monastic basilica for two main reasons. In the first place, the clergy was not cut off from the world. In the genuinely French countries, the reform had not thrust the cathedral clerics back into the strict community framework imposed by canonical rule during the Carolingian period. The canons formed a corpus, but a flexible one. They did not live together in a closed space. What was still called the "cloister" in the cities of France was a district near the sanctuary in which each member of the chapter possessed his own private house. The style was free: there was no community living therefore no transept. Since the vessel cutting perpendicularly across the central nave had lost its function, it became atrophied: it was still found in Notre-Dame in Paris but without external projections. As a result the cathedral space acquired greater unity within.

Again—even more decisive—the new theology of illumination took structural unity for granted (fig. 16). Light, which appeared both as God himself and as the agent of the union between the soul and God, reigned throughout the kingdom bounded symbolically by the cathedral walls. The inner volume of the church obeyed continuity as far as possible. Any interruption in the succession of the bays was avoided, any alteration between pillars and columns abandoned. The tribunes hindering the enlargement of the windows disappeared. Total unity was achieved in the Sainte-Chapelle, which was merely a shrine. But the five contiguous naves of the cathedral of Bourges achieved no less.

The Porches

"O thou who hast said: 'I am the door and he that enters by me shall be saved,' show us plainly to which dwelling thou art the door, at what moment and to whom thou shalt open it. . . . The house to which thou art the door is the heaven where thy father dwells." To the beseechings of the Cistercian friar, William of Saint-Thierry, the cathedral gave an answer. Jesus was the way, and the cathedral, the body of Christ, opened its doors on all sides (fig. 12). The transept now had no other function than to display to the north and the south of the building a porch as vast and as convincing as that turned toward the sunset. The entrances to the cathedral were amplified, each virtually becoming a complex monument in itself. The eye—lacking proper range and barely perceiving the decoration at the top because of the accumulation of houses in the towns without an esplanade—saw nothing else (fig. 13). Through its doors, the cathedral opened out on to the city—in order to teach it. The porches were schools where Latin was not spoken. Their task was to popularize the learning of the doctors, an educational assignment which warranted every expense, the colossal dilapidation of materials and work draining the fruit of the offertories, the taxes, and the many riches bishop and canons succeeded in wresting from the merchants of the town and the peasants of the surrounding countryside. Through its doors, the cathedral acknowledged its pastoral duties. It spread the true belief, strengthening and clarifying it within the center of studies it sheltered.

The earlier churches had allotted the forepart of the construction to funerary cults and placed the scene of the Last Judgment there. That representation still held a central position in the porches of the Gothic cathedrals but in a new arrangement bearing new significance. The Portal of Glory at Santiago de Compostela, carved by Master Matthew in 1188, is dominated by Christ the Judge. But he has been stripped of the compelling unreal quality possessed by all the Christs of the Return in Cluniac Aquitaine. He has been given body and spirit. But Jesus, surrounded by a choir of celestial musicians, has not yet descended to the level of the people. He appears as a priest, officiating in the divine liturgy, a king who has laid all the ornaments of his treasure about his throne, as for coronation ceremonies. In this case the objects are the relics of the Passion. Purifying cloths protect them; a cohort of attendant angels offers them to the view of the faithful as the earthly weapons of the victory of God, the instruments of common salvation.

In royal France, cathedral porches assembled the actors in the sacred drama in far greater numbers. They participated in a didactic production which sought to illustrate the entire Catholic dogma in all its complexity. Theatrical artifices had long been used to explain the meaning of capitulary liturgy. And those periodic performances for the people were now immobilized in stone. In the shows staged at Christmas the speakers who held the roles of Isaiah, Jeremiah, David, and Moses in turn declaimed the passages of the Bible heralding the incarnation (fig. 18). These paraliturgical dramas provided the prototypes for all the statues of the prophets, John the Baptist, Simeon, Elizabeth, the angel Gabriel, and the heroes of the Old Testament considered as prefiguring Christ: Adam, the image of the son of man, the shepherd Abel, Noah, Melchizedek who gave the bread and wine. Wishing to attain greater truth to life so as better to convince, those who prescribed the iconographical program broke the architectural frame which had surrounded the scenes of the sacred theater in the early stages. The wall had restrained them. Now they stood off from their backgrounds and moved forward toward the public, while the tympanum stretched up higher to allow the tale it expounded to develop along superimposed tiers. The entire population of actors grew more vivid and increased. In the various portals at Chartres, the statuary finally represents the whole of the Old and New Testaments, showing the creation of the world and also welcoming the interceding saints whose relics were kept in the sanctuary and whose individual virtues were held up as an example for sinners.

Incarnation

Very few pieces of the treasure of Saint-Denis remain today, and almost nothing of its sculpture. But Chartres, where the team of artists assembled by Suger probably arrived toward 1150, is intact: there, the royal portal blazes with the novelty of the art of France, a product of the upheavals wrought in the mental universe of churchmen at the dawn of the twelfth century (fig. 13). In the schools of Chartres, Laon, or Paris, they heard the most intrepid teachers in the West, whose lessons gradually released them from the unreal world in which the thought of their predecessors had evolved. The texts of Cicero, Ovid, or Seneca showed them man as a person, who loved, suffered, and strove in the face of adversity. At the very period when building commenced at Chartres, they practiced the analysis of the movements of the soul, a description of which had been introduced into the tales embroidered on classical themes, the Aeneid, or the Trojan war, to amuse the knights and their ladies. Lastly, and above all, the commentary on the Bible offered them a new image of God.

For those clerics and for the artists who gave shape to their ideas, beauty was what resembled God. Dazzled by the transcendence of the God of Moses, Isaac, and Jacob—the consuming fire, the glowing visage none could bear, with features invisible to the human eye—the monks of 1100 searched for symbolical equivalences not only for the world to come but also for the present world (fig. 10). For the new bishops, for the canons and the masters of the Ile-de-France, on the other hand, God the Creator was not the Father, the mystery, the idea which the human mind could not apprehend. The world was created *in principio,* that is to say, *in verbo,* by the Word, by the Son, by God incarnate for time everlasting. "Each created being," said

Honorius Augustodunensis, "is the shadow of the Truth and the Life"—that is to say, of Christ. Since Christ had existed on the first day, since his humanity had made him the artisan of all things, the world his reason brought forth from nothingness assumed human dimensions.

On the archings at Chartres, the God who fashions the body of Adam with his hand resembles his creation like a brother. Another man. The questioning which kept Christians prostrate before the mystery of the world and their own anxiety—which was the face of God?—found an answer in the science of the theologians of France: the face of God was a human one. To translate divine perfection, the artist no longer needed to retreat behind symbols. All he had to do was to open his eyes.

On the royal portal of Chartres, then at Le Mans, Saint-Loup-de-Naud, Bourges, the statues of the kings of the Old Testament and the apostles who joined them so as better to express the alliance between the two laws, are still fettered to the wall. Their proportions are those of the columns which engendered them (fig. 13). No apparent life, no hint of movement in their cylindrical bodies, narrow, rigid, motionless, sheathed in the grooves of robes with parallel pleats. But their faces are vividly alive. They have lost the symmetry which set them in the abstract universe of Gregorian sequences (fig. 18). In 1185, the master of Senlis no longer copied the models of the antiphonaries in order to portray the angels thronging around the sleeping body of the Virgin: he observed the flight of birds. After him, life flowed in from all sides, releasing the sculptured bodies from the armor of the column, lending them the flexibility of real postures, beneath the folds of their fine draperies stitched in Flanders.

Faces

The growing number of characters in the liturgical drama filling the theaters in the cathedral porches meant that each had to be distinguished. Certainly they bore their insignia, the special attributes given to each prophet, each precursor, each apostle in Christian iconography, but they also had to be endowed with personal features capable of conveying a specific psychological expression. The vocabulary of the literary works available to knights in the thirteenth century was extremely poor. Joinville abounded in eloquent portrayals of spirited combat and the motley glamor of courtly gatherings, but became tongue-tied when it was a matter of describing a character. In practical life at any rate, in the surveys carried out to ascertain the distribution of feudal rights or to settle points of usage and sometimes even before their confessors, the lords, great and small, gradually sharpened their analytical ability. As for the academic world, it was accustomed to introspection, which already offered a foothold for the morality of Abelard. All theology led to ethics. It involved the exploration of the soul, the classification of its capacities and its virtues. And as the intellectual system of the doctors was based on the principle of the unity of the universe, as it asserted the close cohesion of the three components of the human being—mind, soul, and body—it naturally considered that facial features faithfully translated individual dispositions. The scholastic approach, however, was bent on resolving the particularities of each individual through the forms common to his species. It proceeded by distinguishing kinds. More exactly, then, the faces of the statues represent types of men.

Workshops

Even in the cathedrals which were erected very rapidly, so many figures were carved that the work had to be spread over various workshops. It is not easy for art historians to discern how the teams of artists were structured and harder still to determine the share of work undertaken by each individual. Some were directed by the most brilliant artists, others by lesser lights. The finest sculptural groups were probably done under the control of very great masters of works in charge of the whole site, who coordinated the various parts of the program. It seems likely that at about 1250 John of Chelles personally supervised the execution of the Presentation in the Temple on the portal of the north crossing of Notre-Dame in Paris. The majority of the statues of the saints, apostles, and prophets which Master Gaucher placed in the great doorway at Reims between 1244 and 1252 can be attributed to the workshop of John of Orbais, the first of the architects to work on the cathedral. They are related to those on the north portal at Chartres but also and doubtless more closely to those arranged by the goldsmith, Nicholas of Verdun, between 1180 and 1205 at Klosterneuburg in Cologne on the shrine of the Magi, and in Tournai on the shrine of the Virgin. The outstanding figures, however, are Mary and Elizabeth in the group of the Visitation, the angel Gabriel, and certain prophets. The drapery swathing them is folded like the veils that wrap the goddesses of ancient Greece. Does this entitle us to imagine an immediate influence of Hellenic models after the crusade of 1204? The major innovation here certainly lies in the movement animating the body, releasing it from frontality and carrying it forward, like the Victories. The statues of the Virgin of the Annunciation and the Presentation, Solomon, the queen of Sheba and Philip Augustus were carved in the workshop of John Le Loup between 1228 and 1233. They are close to those of Amiens. But the work has gained expression, a dancing litheness and grace; the faces display a refinement and a variety of shades of meaning hitherto unknown.

The Knight

About 1237 the entire decoration of Reims was transplanted to Bamberg cathedral, constructed to the orders of Bishop Egbert, the brother-in-law of King Philip of France. The choir was dedicated to Saint George, the patron saint of chivalry. During the first half of the thirteenth century, the progress of the West had carried feudal society to fulfillment. The two dominating orders, churchmen and men of war, gathered around the king in whom priesthood and knighthood were joined. Governed by prelates possessing the highest culture, the art of the royal liturgies accordingly installed that equestrian figure in the cathedral (fig. 21). The knight of Bamberg has attained the age of accomplishment, the age when the head of the house took the government of his estate, the heritage of his ancestors, and the destiny of his line into his own hands, the age of all men and all women on the day of the resurrection of the dead. The figure is a manly one, that of the standard bearer of a male society. Like the knight of May, whose flowered gallop illustrates the renewal of nature, he sets out to conquer the world. He resembles Saint Louis, in other words, Christ.

The Virgin

History ill distinguishes the obscure forces that enabled the Virgin to supplant the martyrs and the confessors to whom each of the cathedrals of France had originally been dedicated and to become their one and only patron. Like the apostolic trend of the spiritual movements which preceded it by very little, like Carthusian hermitism, like the asceticism of Cîteaux and so many other models which had renewed religious representation since the end of the eleventh century, the irruption of Marian worship in the Gothic age may well have been one of the fruits of the expansion of Latin Christendom in the East. At that time the religion of Byzantium possessed more wealth and creative power than the religion of the monks of Gaul or Germania. In the East were the great sanctuaries of the Virgin. Embroidering on the few pages which speak of her in the Gospel and the Acts of the Apostles, Byzantine convents invented a succession of anecdotes and a complete iconography to tell the people the story of her life. It was there that the theme of the Dormition, the Sleep of the Virgin, originated, to be taken up by the sculptors of Senlis and Paris, as a further argument in support of the preaching of hope. Dwelling among thrones and dominations, the Mother of God brought the assurance of the Resurrection.

The Resurrection

Nothing is known of peasant death. But one perceives at any rate that noble society, which placed courage in the front rank of the virtues, was actually in the sway of fear. The knights recovered their valor in the great hall listening to the songs of the deeds of Roland and William of Orange. They trembled on the vessels which bore them to the Holy Land, they trembled on the day of battle, they trembled in the tournaments. All the progress achieved in armor and fortifications was due to that dread. It entirely governed the religion of the laity. One wonders how many men, on entering a church, kneeling before the cross, touching the relics, repeating the formulas, performing the ritual gestures, felt more than the need to fortify themselves against their terror of dying.

The religion portrayed by cathedral art was not the religion of the people but of a small elite of intellectuals. These men told themselves that Christ had conquered death. They denied death. At each break of day the beams of Easter morning lit up the sanctuary and fell upon the scene of mankind, redeemed, emerging from the grave as from a bad dream, illustrated on the registers of the tympanum. The faces of those raised from the dead are rid of the shadows of night, their eyes begin to open. They reject the shroud. They stretch their perfect bodies in the sun. They enter real life.

When the tombs of the prelates and the princes began to be decorated and images of the deceased represented inside the church, the cathedral clergy consequently only admitted them in transfiguration. The funerary effigies of Bishop Everard of Fouilloy at Amiens, of the Guelphic Duke Henry the Lion in Brunswick, and those carved for Saint Louis in Saint-Denis could just as easily have stood in the porches among the statues of the prophets. Their dress did not cover a corpse reclining on a funeral bed. Its folds sheathed an upright figure, prepared to receive the light of the beyond. Like King David or King Solomon, the expression on their faces was one of trust and fulfillment, unwrinkled and untainted, at peace. Saint Augustine wrote: "God was made man so that we might become like gods." Since the Christ of the Incarnation and the Resurrection bore all mortal men toward the Father, since death was but a passage and the tomb a place of germination where each carnal being made ready to open out in glory, cathedral art showed the body of the dead in the accomplished, timeless forms already bestowed upon them by faith.

Stained Glass Windows

Inside the cathedral, the stained glass window continued the teaching dispensed in the porch. The believer had crossed the threshold. He had risen one degree toward contemplation. Having become the son of God through the incarnation of Christ, he partook of his heritage, of illumination. He penetrated into that inbetween realm which, said Suger, existed neither in the bowels of the earth nor in the purity of the sky (fig. 15). God spoke to him with supernal clarity. Erecting the luxuriant decoration of tinted glass among so many windows was an immense undertaking. It proceeded apace but in a great variety of workshops, not all of equal worth. Often the composition lost its rigor and the outline its firmness, as in the Sainte-Chapelle. However, all these weaknesses melted away into the dazzling fairyland which dissipated scrutiny but held the feelings captive. Here the aesthetics of William of Auvergne found application: "Invisible beauty can be defined either by the figure or the position of the parts within the whole, or else by their color, or else by the two together, whether one sets them side by side or considers the relations of harmony referring one to the other"—colors chosen not to give the faithful translation of appearances but by virtue of the necessary relations they mutually entertain in the radiant body assembling them. Like the polyphony of Pérotin the Great, the stained glass windows achieved the agreement of an infinity of rhythms and countless discordant modulations. It enchanted the universe. It effected a transfiguration of the visible.

The stained glass of the lower windows was a narrative setting forth the subject-matter of a doctrinal argument in the same way as a master's lesson. The basic text—the kernel of the sentence—was illustrated in the central medallion. Around it, set side by side in counterpoint, the accessory figures of the Bible provided the answer and, through a process of complementary references, brought out the essential meaning in a progression from the literal to the mystic. Strictly coordinated by scholastic logic, the demonstrative image confirmed the close cohesion of dogma.

On the stained glass windows of the chancel in Saint-Denis, Suger had arranged allegorical scenes which could only be understood after a long itinerary through anagogical thought. But he had added clear illustrations of the story of Jesus. Evangelical iconography was given fuller rein in the windows of twelfth-century cathedrals than in the theaters in the doorways. It mentioned little of the public life of Christ and nothing of his miracles, drawing almost all its topics from the tales of his childhood and the Passion, in the liturgical readings of Christmas and Eastertime (fig. 17).

The Human Figure

In Bourges, ten low windows associate the apologetical scenes in a series of pairs so as to illustrate the basic coherences. A host of polychrome symbols compare the Passion and the Revelation, the New Alliance and the Last Judgment. Yet the bays up at the top of the cathedral show large silhouettes in isolation. The processions of prophets to the north and of apostles to the south frame the image of the Virgin-church around the chancel, again demonstrating the unity of history, of dogma, and the concordance of the Old and New Testaments, this time in monumental simplicity. At Chartres, the same prophets, amid the saints, bear the Apostles on their shoulders. Each day, the first gleams of dawn establish those watchers in light above carnal darkness. The colored profusion submerging the episodes of the Gospel and the complex figures of the analogies in the lower stories of the building has been tempered here. The tinted glass offers sovereign figures of men.

Men who had lived on the earth. Most of them were the saints whose reliquaries were housed in the cathedral, and at that time all the booty from the East came to swell the collection of sacred remains. Amiens had received part of the head of Saint John the Baptist in 1206 and dedicated a stained glass window to him. He had another in the Sainte-Chapelle where the back of his skull was venerated. There was a stained glass window to Saint Anne in Chartres, and one to Saint Thomas à Becket in Sens. The princes had paid for the adornments with their alms. Ferdinand of Castile had donated stained glass windows to Saint James in Chartres and to Saint Louis in Saint-Denis. They marked these offerings with their armorial bearings. Even the effigies of donors began to take up their position among the prophets. In the windows of Reims, the archbishop Henry of Braisne wished the façade of his metropolitan cathedral and that of the seven cathedrals in the province to be visible beneath the images of Christ, the Virgin, and the Apostles. Symbolical emblems identified these sanctuaries with the seven churches of Asia Minor, and the seven angels in Revelation, that heard the message of Christ. Then the prelate himself appeared with his suffragans gathered about him as at a feudal court. By the middle of the thirteenth century, in the upper windows of the cathedral and on the façade, in the gallery of the kings, the figure of man had begun to invade the celestial sphere.

Rose Windows

In the structures of the Gothic cathedral, the circle lost the importance it had held in the Romanesque church. Now it was the straight line that came into its own, the vector of history, the unerring projection of the luminous beam representing the creative act and divine grace, the impulse of rational dynamics, scholastic research, and all the progress of the times, shooting directly to the mark (fig. 15). Only the rose windows, the symbols of the fullness of creation, which reduced the circulation of light, flowing out from its ineffable center then returning to converge on it once more, to a single principle, still espoused the closed curve traveled by the stars in their firmament.

The art of stained glass culminated in these windows. Simultaneously they radiated the significance of the cosmic cycles, of time resolved into eternity, and of the mystery of God, God as light, Christ as the sun. God appears on the south rose of Notre-Dame in Paris within the circle of the prophets, apostles, and saints (fig. 20). He is resplendent on the rose of the Sainte Chapelle among the elders and the musicians of Revelation. Roses again portray the Virgin, the figure of the Church. They demonstrate the identity of Aristotle's concentric universe and the spouting effusions of Robert Grosseteste in a whirlwind of spheres. Lastly, the rose was the image of love. It represented the sparkling focus of divine love which consumed all desire. But it could also be seen as the symbol of the itineraries of the soul followed in the secret circles of worship already forming on the fringe of Catholic discipline. Or yet again as the labyrinth which guided profane love from ordeal to ordeal toward its goal.

When, about 1225, Guillaume de Lorris put into verse a sum of courtly ethics, in which "the art of love was quite enclosed," he entitled his poem: *Roman de la rose.* There the rose symbolized the ideal which the perfect knight ardently wished to pluck. In Jean de Meung's very long sequel to the *Roman* produced about forty years later, the allegories have been stripped of their mundane affectation and brought back to nature. The love of man for woman, the desire which the rose excites, emerges from the myths and the sport of courtesy, leaving the scene of dissolution. The rose becomes the image of a victory over death: Nature's victory, or God's victory. And also the victory of man, for men cooperated in creation. Joy and the will to live must be seen aflame in the blaze of the Gothic rose.

Italian Resistance

In the thirteenth century the art of France forced its way into Italy. The agents of the intrusion were the papacy, which regarded university aesthetics as the most effective rendering of Catholic theology, and the religious orders in its service, first the Cistercians, then the mendicants. But French influence was soon checked. It came up against two solid cultural traditions, two thick deposits successively formed in the course of the ages by imperial Rome and by Byzantium.

The Germanic invasions had unfurled over Italian territory, repressing figurative art and imposing the manner of jewelers and engravers, inspired by the monsters and barbaric geometry ornamenting their buckles and belt plaques. Quite a large section of Italy, however, had never let itself be put down or integrated into the empire of Charlemagne. Latium had never been more than a protected fringe; Venice and the entire south had slipped its grasp. Those regions remained united with the East by the sea, by ties which the retreat of Berber piracy had helped to strengthen since the tenth century. For that reason, when building began on Notre-Dame in Paris, the decoration chosen by the doges of Venice for Saint Mark's and by the Norman kings of Sicily for the walls of their palaces, oratories, and neighboring cathedrals was Greek.

The Legacy of Byzantium

The Byzantine church was the abode of the divine. Its façades were unadorned. Aesthetic considerations were confined to the internal space which the glittering mosaics were intended to transfigure in the half-light and endow with the symbols of the invisible. The mosaics of Palermo, Monreale, and Venetia, as well as those which enhanced the baptistery of Florence, as late as 1250, and the monastery of the Quattro Coronati in Rome, opted for narrative, extending the new intonations of the iconography of the East in their accounts of the Gospel and the anecdotes of the Apocrypha.

The Suffering Christ

Setting mosaics was a very costly art and, as a result, soon declined in the Latin West, a region still indigent and wild. The paintings decorating walls and altar panels, not books, were the surrogate of that sumptuous manner. So, in Italy, painting was both Byzantine and narrative (fig. 11). It expounded the episodes of the life of Christ. The art of the doctors of the Church, cathedral art, offered an intelligent, rational view of Jesus. The people, whose anxiety was no longer soothed by the old liturgical rites and whose minds remained too simple to accompany their masters to the conclusions of their meditations, invented another, less aloof and even more fraternal—that which Peter Valdo had found in a translation of the Gospel, that which had been shown in the sermons of the heterodox preachers and which the crusaders had glimpsed in the East. In Byzantium, the same desire had been experienced by the Christian throngs far earlier. But the Eastern Church had been less strictly separated from the laity: its married priests lived in closer communication with their flocks; it had accepted that the spirit of God should be widely disseminated among all believers and that it should be its duty to welcome the forms of spirituality springing up spontaneously from popular awareness. Long before Roman Christendom it had taken care to annex the simple tales of the Gospel as part of its service and put them into pictures. Admittedly, it placed the dominating figure of the Pantocrator in its apses. The frescoes of the monastery of Mileseva in Serbia, painted toward 1230, the Virgin of the Annunciation, pure, upright, solitary, like the Virgin of Torcello, portray the perfect form God had assumed in order to be made flesh. But in another part of the church the painters show the Virgin of the Sorrows weeping on the wounded hand of her son, just as fifty years earlier in Nerezi on the first of the Pietàs.

The Franciscan Note

These images which drew the divine so close to the human condition were made known in the West by the fall of Constantinople and the booty brought back by its conquerors. But also by the trading routes leading into south Germany along the Danube; the traffickers of Germania ventured eastwards and their king maintained ties with the Byzantine court stronger than those of any other European sovereign. On the psalters and missals of Swabia, on the reliefs of Naumburg, the pathos of the scenes of the Passion betray the emotion of oriental Calvaries. Nowhere, however, did Byzantine imagery exert more influence than in Italy under the impact of the preaching of Saint Francis. Large wooden crucifixes were painted in Pisa and in the other Tuscan cities to be hung in the churches above the triumphal arch. In that position they proclaimed the victory of Christ before the gaze of the whole congregation and at the same time displayed the victory of the

Church, with features identical to those of the Virgin, in a medallion at the end of the right arm of the cross. But the faith of the poor charged the symbol with another meaning. What they beheld was the body of a man. They looked for visible signs of the torture which had washed them of their sins. One day Saint Francis with his own eyes had seen one of those figures turn its face toward him (fig. 22). He had heard it exhort him to explain to the people in a very simple way what his sacrifice had been and in what its redeeming worth consisted. When the rumor began to spread that Francis himself had received the stigmata of the Passion, the Tuscan crucifix became the emblem of physical suffering.

Toward 1200 the Pisan artists sometimes set superimposed scenes of the Deposition, the Entombment, the Visitation, and the Resurrection on either side of the figure of the Savior. But Giunta Pisano, who worked between 1236 and 1254, and Coppo di Marcovaldo, known between 1260 and 1276, concentrated their most moving effects on the actual body of Christ. They preceded Cimabue, who turned the crucifixion into the drama of the death of God. Yet painting was still a minor art. And in Italy, moreover, it was foreign. The mother country was Roman. It gloried in stone, whether sculpted or built. On Italian soil, the visual experience of ancient Rome raised the strongest barrier to the penetration of Gothic art.

The Resurrection of Rome

If thirteenth-century Italy failed to produce a work of art which could match Chartres, Reims, or Bamberg, though it was flourishing and borne along on the tide of prosperity soon to establish its rule over the European economy, it was because that part of Europe was not a state. It remained divided among several political factions. No sovereign was able to concentrate enough power into his own hands to put his riches to proper use, no court could rival that of the king of France, nor even that of the king of Germany. The authority which had formerly guaranteed the monarch's control and protection of the great cathedral and monastic churches was in disintegration. Admittedly, the pope had his see in Rome, from which he claimed to govern the whole of Christendom. The magisterium he assumed nevertheless remained spiritual. He was not yet in possession of the fiscal instrument that would have plentifully filled his coffers and enabled him to embark on artistic enterprises as outstanding as those of Saint Louis. Admittedly, the central part of the peninsula was under his direct control, but the pontifical agents came up against the freedom of the cities as well as all the feudal lords who flouted them from their *rocca*. As for the authority of the Lombard sovereigns, it had vanished into the magma of rights vainly claimed in Tuscany and the Po valley by the kings of Germania, who never succeeded in wresting more than lip service from those towns when they rode down from the Alps with their knights. The citizens yielded for a time, waiting until the plague and fevers had decimated the Teutonic host and its leader had returned home crestfallen, retaining nothing. Communal independence thrived in Lombardy, in the valley of the Arno, but parceled out the regalities and the wealth it secured. A hundred hostile republics vied for them. At that time there was only one firmly established state in Italy, one kingdom, that of the princes of Palermo. They amassed gold by the handful, and used it to deck out their houses and churches in sumptuous array. Yet the provinces under their rule actually belonged to the Eastern Empire, and Greek artists hung the gleaming tapestries of mosaics about their pomp and their prayers.

FREDERICK II

Everything changed in southern Italy when Sicily passed into the heritage of the Staufens and when Frederick II, emerging from adolescence, became the self-appointed successor of the Caesars. This was a political event which brought about a far-reaching aesthetic reversal at the only Italian court where the bounty of a prince could fittingly be displayed, by a determined return to Roman sources and the archaeological restoration of classical art. In Campania, throughout the twelfth century, fantastic animals, dragons, hippocampi, engendered in the patterns of Byzantine cloths, had coiled up on the ambones of the cathedrals. The new art did not oust them. It did not enter the churches. It began by applying itself to the monuments of civil power. In the Lombard provinces, Romanesque aesthetics had already thrust its roots to the core of Roman antiquity. Its religious buildings rejected the luminosity and soaring impulse of French cathedrals. Like the ancient temples they remained inward-looking, surrounded by their girdle of arches. The values of equilibrium predominated. The baptistery of Parma rose toward the sky, but in the shape of a cylinder, not a spire, and its statuary was attuned to that which represented the gods and the heroic deceased at the gates of Latin cities. But for Frederick II the sculpture of Rome was deliberately given new life.

The castle of Capua, built between 1234 and 1240, when the statuary of Reims and Bamberg was at its peak, exhibited astonishing busts in which antiquity appeared unadorned, no longer draped in the liturgical forms of the Romanesque. Those effigies of the emperor, his counsellors, and civic virtues might have stepped out of an excavation site (fig. 19). Soon they were imitated by the artists who worked on the decoration of religious buildings. In 1272, in Ravello, Nicola di Bartolomeo da Foggia, whose father had served Frederick II, carved a woman's face to adorn the pulpit of the cathedral. Was it the portrait of Sigilgaïda Rufolo? Or might it not rather have been an allegory of the Church? At all events, it was the very image of Rome, raised from the dead.

At that period it was some time since the great Tuscan cities had attained a level of wealth at least equal to that of the great princes. But the population fought against the local aristocracy, gradually eliminating it from power. Almost all the leaders of the commune, the master of the public finances, belonged to an unstable sector of businessmen who had recently emerged from mediocrity and whose cultural experience still rested on shaky foundations. Some of the newly rich were already sufficiently sure of their taste to purchase objects of art, of the finest, in distant lands—like the New York bankers and the Moscow merchants in 1900. Such articles included Byzantine ornaments or books from France. Their own cities could not yet provide craftsmen vigorous or cultivated enough to create the pieces which matched their new desires. Then came Nicola Pisano. Little is known of him other than his name and that he was born about 1210 and died in 1278. Perhaps he visited Campania and Romagna, perhaps not. But his stone figures of Moses no longer came down from Mount Sinai, they came from the Capitol. In 1260, the year when the cathedral of Reims was completed, the year when the third age of the world was about to begin according to Joachim of Fiore, the pulpit of the baptistery of Pisa, sculpted by Nicola, rose up like a stele. On the very doorstep of the Renaissance.

3
The Courtly Forest

Like the universe of the cathedrals, the universe of chivalry was one of rites and liturgies. The values of prowess, bounty, and courtesy were embodied in the fabulous deeds of King Arthur, Charlemagne, Godfrey of Bouillon. These characters with their exemplary virtues were caught within a dreamworld. Formerly they had lived among men. Yet they no longer belonged to history, they were a part of legend, and remembrance of their actions paid little heed to chronology. They existed outside time. Periodically, the ceremonial of life at court, the coronation festivities, the tournaments, and the pursuit of courtly love revived the pattern of their rites and for a moment, by symbolical portrayal, drew them back into duration. These games likewise placed them in a fictitious space lacking firm dimensions and boundaries. At the center of the myth lay dangerous adventure, errant quest. One and the other transported the heroes of chivalry and the live actors who momentarily held their roles into the indeterminate realms of a forest (fig. 32).

Of all the forms of created nature, the forest was the most conducive to the strayings of romantic fancy and the secret frolics of lovers. With its undefined edges, its impenetrable depths, its countless detours, it proposed a gradual initiation into mystery. It abolished all partitions between reality and charm. In the fourteenth century, the tapestries of greenery transformed the knightly halls into bowers. But the flexible shapes of sylvan decoration were also incorporated into the walls of buildings and the parchment of books, where they laid out the formless space of myth.

By about 1300, through the alms donated by prelates and princes, the outer vestment of the great cathedrals was complete. The pressures of the knightly way of life had triumphed over builders' logic, causing it to disappear behind a mask of ornamental wrappings designed to substitute the idle ritual of chivalry. In the central doorway at Reims, the traditional scene of the Virgin stands off from the walls altogether. It has rejected their stability. Here the upward movement of Gothic structures frees itself from tangible dimensions, stretches higher, vanishes into the luxuriance of truant leafy blooms mounting the gable arch. At the end of its flight, borne on angels' wings, the sun itself becomes a flower: as the natural forest might spring up, as light gushed forth according to the Franciscan cosmology of the Oxford schools. In the vaults at Tewkesbury, the central lantern of Ely cathedral, or the capitulary hall at Wells, the same impulse destroyed the compartmentalized rigor of thirteenth-century builders who had found their principles in the physics of Aristotle.

The illogical space of the forest, of knightly evasions into an imaginary world, of the expeditions of parties of young noblemen in quest of amorous encounters, a wife, an establishment, or merely fame, crowded the pages of illuminated books. English artists readily took up the fantastic idiom of Celtic and Saxon miniatures. In the "hedge" which proliferated around the text, their inventiveness knew no bounds, intertwining minute fragmentary observations from animal life amid a confused tracery of delirious geometry mingled with plant motifs. For in the forest the knights sometimes came across dragons, although more often than not they hunted deer and hinds.

In Paris, the logic of the preaching friars of the university exerted too much power for book illustrators to be able to venture as far. Composed under Dominican influence for the Belleville family toward 1325, the breviary decorated in the workshop of John Pucelle delivered up its clear margins to more disciplined vegetation, limited to the modulations of pure arabesques and reproducing the exact shapes of the foliage in the gardens and the woods. In the initials, the importance given to the abstractions of the letter was considerably reduced. What was essential was the scene, framed within a sober airy construction recalling the space of Giotto's great theater. Echoes of Italian experiments had already reached Paris through the growing trade in objects of art.

Whereas the patricians of Italian towns, even in Florence, were fond of the graces, adornments, and refinements of chivalrous, courtly life. They delighted in the Gothic calligraphy of Lorenzo Monaco, a Camaldolese monk who possessed the art of conferring a melting sweetness and exotic quality on Christian worship and the Christian drama. His hallucinated Magi, in a landscape bristling with towers and rocks, also depart for dreamlike realms (fig. 23).

Festival

In 1310, the court poet, James of Longuyon, composed the *Voeux du paon* [wishes of the peacock] in circonvoluted lines describing the procession of the nine paladins. Henceforth each lord, each young knight eager to advance in the practice of arms, as Froissart said, endeavored to emulate their behavior. Duke John of Berry ordered a series of hangings to reproduce their heroic figures, which already adorned one of the fireplaces of the palace of Bourges. This tapestry constructed an imaginary architecture of intertwining fronds with tiered niches devised for the alternate praise and exhibition of festival. Julius Caesar, one of the three pagan paladins, sits on the throne of empire. His Carolingian beard, his crown, the plate armor protecting him, place him in the perpetual present of courtly parade (fig. 30).

History itself became a series of displays: military festivals, battles treated as tournaments and tournaments ending in battles, where the victors, on the evening after the fray, waited upon their vanquished captives at table. The idiom of the art of the courts thus had no difficulty in amalgamating actual images and dream representations. All its themes, the descriptions of coronations, romances, or love songs, the scene of the Annunciation, and naturally that of the adoration of the Magi, even the portrayal of the Virgin of Humility or the Crucifixion, provided excuses to illustrate dress (fig. 26). Chivalrous culture clothed Mary, the saints, and all the heroes of its myths in a vestimentary splendor formerly conceded only to ecclesiastical and royal liturgy. Festival, above all, was the joy of adorning one's person, of casting off one's usual attire for the apparel of the unreal. By the end of the thirteenth century, high cathedral sculpture had begun to follow suit. In Strasbourg, the Tempter and the Virgins he was to lead astray have been won over to worldly pleasures (fig. 35). The artist has condemned them, letting reptiles stream over the Tempter's cloak, stamping perverse inflexions on the elegance of the mad Virgins. But he showed that elegance, nevertheless, as it was: shimmering and overwhelmingly alluring.

A hundred years later, in France, in the reign of Charles VI, royal devotional art as a whole had slid into fantasy, dream, and the lavishness of courtly culture. It joined in festival by the refinement of its ornamentation and in show by its remarkable staging. One reliquary mounts like a pyramid in a glitter of gold, vermillion, and precious stones, all its little figures assembled, God the Father, the Virgin queen, Jesus the Savior of the world and their escort of apostles and protecting women saints (fig. 34).

Anxiety

The lords of the court of France and of the courts of Nicosia, Windsor, or Naples danced on a volcano they called hell. Until they were giddy. They were clad in robes of gold, they mounted splendid steeds, and caressed fair damsels, but in fear and trembling. For they were only too aware that the world they embraced with open arms was one of darkness and awe, plagues, sufferings, the madness which turned kings into beasts, death and the unknown universe it revealed (fig. 27). That danger spurred them on toward greater refinements of pleasure. It also spurred them on toward the refinements of asceticism. The graces of the art of 1400 were a poor disguise for the deeper reaches of anxiety. It was anxiety which caused the tormentors of the martyrs to grin immoderately on the altar pieces recounting the lives of the saints and which in Barcelona also inspired Bernardo Martorell to stretch out the tortured body of Saint George in a tragic diagonal. Anxiety which wrung the hands of the holy women on the wounds of Christ in all the Depositions. Anxiety which explained the spell that the visions of Revelation exerted on the princes by showing them the fissures in creation. After 1373, Nicholas Bataille, the most renowned of Parisian tapestry makers, was employed by Duke Louis of Anjou to put the amazing imagination of the Apocalypse into images. This time highly distinguished calligraphy and perfect agreement of color had rid the subject of its disquieting power; the Beast joined the unicorns, and the paladins, Hector and Charlemagne, in an illustration of the rites of courtesy. Whereas a little earlier, on the walls of the chapel of the Virgin in Karlstein, for the emperor Charles IV, an unknown artist had painted utter fright, the crumbling of all, the great spider and nightmarish pallid faces spinning in a whirlwind.

God Dead

The crucifix dominated religious imagery, crushingly. In order to combat the heretical beliefs which proclaimed the advent of the reign of the Holy Spirit, also propagated by the Franciscan Spirituals, the Church had concentrated its dogmatic teaching on the mystery of the unity of God in three persons. It popularized the image of the Trinity but mingled it with Calvary: God the Father sits in majesty on the "throne of salvation," while the dove of the Holy Spirit touches the face of the Son whose cross the Father supports with his own hands. Such is the central theme treated by Masaccio in 1427 on one of the walls of Santa Maria Novella within the simulacrum of a chapel surmounting an admirable representation of a decaying corpse (fig. 28). The note of gravity is concentrated on the crucified Christ. The two donors kneel in the background at the edge of the scene; the expression on their faces sets them firmly outside the universe of eternity inhabited by the motionless divine figures, the Virgin and Saint John, but at least they are the same size. Endowed with the same monumental static presence, they are raised above the humility of men and borne, fortified by divine grace, into transcendence.

Yet Christ emerged triumphant from the tomb (fig. 26). To express the plenitude and the compelling force of the spirit of the Resurrection, an artist required a capacity which donors apparently rarely urged him to display. Old liturgical art had conveyed the yearnings for celestial joys. In the fourteenth century common piety found it hard to rise above and beyond the abyss of carnal death. Chapel art struck a sentimental note, externalizing human distress. Skillful in transposing dreams, it restored the visions of Revelation in all their grandeur, but was at pains to imagine heaven; most of its paradises were derisory.

Lazarus

One painter, however, managed to bestow invincible power upon the resurrected Christ, showing him as the hero of a victory over the hegemony of night: this was the unknown master of the Bohemian altar piece of Trebon. The counterpart of that figure, born of an ardent untamed Christianity soon to inspire the Hussite sects, may even be seen in another man raised from the dead, the Lazarus of the *Trés riches heures.* He was a real man, with a remarkable face and torso, as pure and solid as those of an antique bronze. To the aging John of Berry the Limburg brothers had brought hope coupled with the old optimism of chivalry and the humanist premises arriving from Italy. Knighthood and humanism alike set that hope on earth.

Such images could only flower at the extreme point of refinement of the civilization of 1400, in the startling conjunction of parade and wit, curiosity and elegance, attained by the Parisian court before it was shattered by the hazards of war. The tone adopted toward the mystery of death by the preachers and by the people who trembled at their words and also by the stoic austere Christians for whom Masaccio worked was one of dread or gravity. The ceremony was not a preparation for a return to mundane joys; it laid out a last feast around a body vowed to corruption: it was a farewell.

Survival

But the feast was at any rate designed to perpetuate the memory of the one who had died. It sought to immortalize his visage. It led to a monument, the tomb, in other words, the portrait. It was a means of survival. (fig. 29).

The perfection of the faces of thirteenth-century reclining figures had projected that survival into the beyond, into the glory of the Resurrection. But in the fourteenth century the living hoped that it might also remain a little while on earth, that a part of themselves might be fixed in an effigy which would be recognizable to all. If their graves were built before their death, they posed for the sculptors. When the latter had to portray a dead person, they tried to grasp his likeness from the mask used during the funeral procession. In Naples the artists who portrayed King Robert the Wise as he had been in life, on his throne, took the cast of the dead face and merely opened its eyes. Thus they offered a terrifying version of the sovereign in majesty, a distraught face suddenly emerging from the depths of night, the savage countenance of the Eternal Father found in the early Romanesque.

Uncompromisingly expressionistic, funerary portraiture quickly attained acute verisimilitude. This is easy to observe, in different keys, in the forbidding statues of all the dead knights, imprisoned in their helmets, the figures of the prince-bishops, those great birds of prey who entered the afterlife clenching their privileges in their fists. Yet the tomb makers also had to carve the images of deceased ladies. To do so, they resumed the elegant manner. Tiny angels bearing garlands gracefully attend the body of Ilaria, the young wife of the tyrant of Lucca; Jacopo della Quercia has let her rest in the serenity of her perfect beauty.

Power

By the fourteenth century feudal independence had died its day, caught in a stranglehold by the princes. The world seemed to have shrunk and the end of the Crusades confined the military enterprises of chivalry to Europe. A hundred years earlier, the young King Edward III of England would have set out for the East like his ancestor, Richard the Lionhearted, but instead he sought fame in looting France. Henceforth the thirst for heroic deeds was quenched by political maneuvering. Christendom had been broken up into states consisting of a few kingdoms, but also into minor principalities, and all those jealous republics formed by the urban communes in Italy and Germany. These states were in conflict. Discord was rife around thrones and municipal magistracies, aggravated by family feuds and rival factions. The whole of the West resounded with the noise of men at war throughout a century which witnessed an impressive advance in military techniques and the art of fortification. Princes and towns alike found refuge behind walls.

Towers

In stark contrast, the admirable outline of the castle of Mehun-sur-Yèvre, one of the pleasure resorts of Duke John of Berry, and the view of the church spires soaring up on the horizon of German towns, the admirable landscape constructed by Ambrogio Lorenzetti (fig. 24), and all the towers of the communal, patrician, or knightly palaces he rendered in exact profile, express the spirit which governed the evolution of military architecture in fourteenth-century Europe, asserting the will for power of the aristocracies.

Two languages: on the one hand the unreal space of courtly myth, the vertical flight of mystic ascension, the linear curve carrying composition into the scrolls of poetic reverie. And on the other, a rigorous marquetry offering the view of a compact universe, profound and solid. But also two cultures: the tower of the French prince and the belfries of the collegiate churches ended in play, masking the protective apparatus at the top beneath the flowered garb of festival. They made ready for the fabulous adventures which lured the knights of the Round Table into the heart of imaginary forests. Or donned the trimmings of luxuriant nature which for believers was a demonstration of the bounty God bestowed upon creation. They were the image of chivalrous prodigality and as such were arrayed in the gleaming treasure they were to spread all about. The towers of the patrician families of San Gimignano, the communal tower of Gubbio, the walls girding the residences of the tyrants in the cities of northern Italy hid that treasure jealously from neighboring covetousness. They were strong, firmly established, suspicious. They half-opened on to a few loggias to take the air, but rallied the family, the urban community, or the armed company of the lord of the estate for collective conquest, both economic and military, and competition. Their striving was to overcome rival wealth.

Civic Space

In the cities of Italy, money and the artistic activities it maintained forsook religious building to concentrate on creating a properly urban and civic area where the glory of the commune might be made manifest. In 1334, Giotto was given a general office in Florence in charge of the work on the cathedral and the supervision of the municipal palace and the bridges and walls. The belfry he conceived was closer to the spirit of the commune than to the Church; at its base, he glorified the virtues and the works of the citizens. The central element in the rebirth of town planning was twofold: a castle, and beside it, a square. The magistrate, like the kings, gave his judgment in a tower, which commanded an open stretch where the militia assembled as well as the audience eager to hear the harangue. The people of Gubbio locked their consuls inside a superb fortress, bordered at incalculable cost by a balcony which formed an esplanade not intended for trade: it was on that platform open to the Umbrian sky that the rites of civicism were performed. The Sienese resolved to moderate the plans for the vast cathedral dreamt of by their forefathers. But in the horseshoe piazza del Campo they erected a monumental ensemble offering the earliest example of urban arrangement in Christian Europe. The pivot was the Municipal Palace, on which building had been begun in 1298, topped by the Mangia. Although slender and extremely elegant, it was a military tower nevertheless, flying the warlike symbol of sovereignty above the city.

The Tyrant Hero

In the trecento, almost all the Italian communes bowed to the rule of a tyrant, who had established himself by force or had received his "lordship" from patrician clans weary of the concatenation of revenge, plots, and uprisings, and hoped that the peace conducive to trade might be recovered under single authority. Those rulers, great and small, more often than not owed their success to the worth of their *condotte,* the troop of mercenaries they employed. But they liked to picture themselves in the guise of the dictators of antiquity and already imagined they could hear the tales of their virtues being handed down through the centuries. The humanists, in the manner of ancient Rome, sang their praises. Nowhere at that time was fame more highly lauded. It was thus in Verona and Milan, both governed by the heads of old races long in the tooth, who lived like princes, enraptured by their own omnipotence, violent and shrewd. They were huntsmen and their valor in that knightly sport enhanced their prestige. For parades and for the tournaments in which they shone at the head of youth, they put on the armor of Roland or Lancelot and sought to legitimize their power by copying the deeds of gallant knights. But they could never die. The foundations of their power were too unstable. A generation was not enough for usurpation to be forgotten. The dead tyrant consequently needed to be transformed into a hero. When a Scaliger died, his sons first of all kept the event a secret, then set up his sarcophagus in Verona, in public, at the heart of the city he had vanquished. An equestrian effigy stands above the tomb: the emblem of political triumph. The gallop of jousting and the heady evenings after the conquest bear away the *signor* of the city for all eternity.

In Milan, behind the high altar of San Giovanni in Conca, Bernabò Visconti holds sway motionless on an unharnessed steed, escorted only by his virtues (fig. 29). It was not to prostrate himself in paradise that he had crossed death. It was to continue the fight and to remain the master in his city.

Princely Statues

When true political statuary reappeared in Italy, princely effigies surmounted triumphs, no longer corpses. The first, in Capua, were still abstract portrayals. In the second half of the fourteenth century, when all European rulers wanted to have their portraits carved in painted stone during their lifetimes, as Frederick of Hohenstaufen and Pope Boniface VIII had before, they wished to be shown to posterity in the awe of their sovereign empire. But they also wished their features to be immediately identifiable to all. Artists proceeded by adapting cathedral sculpture, which had long represented Christ the king; it was only of late that it had been inclined to clothe the bodies of God and the Apostles in all the ornamentation of worldly display, to achieve a more vivid rendering, to mold them in everyday attitudes, to draw them closer to the life of ordinary men. So it was enough if the image-cutters substituted the face of their master for the faces of the princes of the other world, giving it the likeness imparted by the figures of the deceased on the tombs. Many such portrayals adorned the palaces; many were also established on the façades of churches. Philip the Hardy ordered his praying figure for the portal of Champmol from Claus

Sluter. That of Duke Albert of Habsburg, carved between 1360 and 1380, rules in a triangular tabernacle at the top of one of the towers of Saint Stephen's in Vienna.

Queens

The new statuary had no difficulty in placing the stone sovereigns in the vicinity of the prophets, who no longer belonged to sacred art. But the kneeling figures of the princes' wives can never be confused with the saints. The impressive spirituality converging on Mary maintained a great distance between the Virgins and the representations of ordinary women. It was only with the overriding advance of secularization and the triumph of profane values at the approach of the fifteenth century that female effigies, radiant with their own beauty, could compare with the images of the Mother of God, in turn growing ever more charming. The artist who erected the statue of the queen of France, Isabel of Bavaria, rid the lithe alluring body of every hint of otherworldliness. The perfection he aimed at belonged only to the flesh and to terrestrial happiness. He dedicated his figure to womanhood.

Nudes

On the tympanum at Bourges, carved in 1275, the resurrected are borne along on a liberating breath of springtime. They burst forth like early blossoms between the slabs of their tombs. Here the image-cutters have dared to make room for an elegant stance and supple forms within the light of spiritual illumination. The first and decisive revelation is that the joy imparted by these gentle, polished, and triumphant nudes is pure. It adorns glorious bodies, delivered from evil and the torments of profane love.

It was the rediscovery of the forgotten vestiges of Greek and Roman art, however, that dispelled what still remained of the unease engendered by the religious and social taboos, the shrinking from bare flesh, the obsession with sin, the shudders of a guilty conscience. By the last years of the thirteenth century, motifs of classical intaglio, representing Hercules and Eros asleep under a tree, had been transposed to the base of the great door of the cathedral of Auxerre. The group expresses an awareness of physical beauty uncluttered by Christian mistrust. The new outlook gradually took clearer shape in central Italy. In that country, image-cutters and painters had been influenced by French modes throughout the trecento, but they lived on close terms with all that bore witness to ancient art. Beneath their draperies, the madonnas of Arnolfo di Cambio borrow their majestic forms from Roman matrons. In the late fourteenth century, certain drawings showed signs of more specific curiosity and research. One of these, now in the Louvre, attributed to Gentile da Fabriano, selects a perfectly classical figure of Venus from the ornamentation of a sarcophagus. Thus a new canon of the female body emerged. Although far more malleable and graceful than Latin marbles, it marked a considerable departure from the forms produced by the aesthetics of the troubadours and stylized at the Parisian courts. Less flexible, more carnal, it eluded the troubles of the heart. At the threshold of the cathedrals it found its place in the portrayals of the creation of Eve. The sculptor who decorated the Duomo of Orvieto under the direction of Lorenzo Maitani in the first third of the fourteenth century was perhaps acquainted with the great building sites in France. His Eve was brought into being in the delights of French gardens but he has endowed her with the fullness and strength of antique reliefs.

The Female Body

About 1400 the hand of the artists in the service of Duke John of Berry allied classical distinction, arriving from Italy, and daintiness of line. Hence the unrestrained nakedness of Adam and Eve employed by the Limburg brothers in the *Jardin de paradis* of the *Très riches heures,* to enhance the joy of being free to live and to enjoy life. In his collections the duke kept a medal to the glory of the emperor Constantine; on the reverse it showed paganism in the guise of a young woman at the foot of a fountain of life surmounted by a cross. The body is stripped of the deceptive wrappings of courtly ornament. But the slender limbs, the tiny breasts, the fertile stomach, lend her the mannered elegance of Gothic courts where the sinuosities of the arabesque were required of the female body in obedience to the ritual of courtesy. Whereas for Jacopo della Quercia, the Eve of the Temptation signified power, not grace. What he glorified in her body was the rustic sturdiness of mother goddesses.

At that time Ghiberti was working on the door to the baptistery in Florence (fig. 31). He portrayed the creation of woman. Here the flight of angels which until then had borne only one carnal body to heaven, the Virgin of the Assumption, supports the soaring figure of Eve. She is saved at last, justified. Confirmed. She belongs to purity and splendor. Her beauty ascends toward divine light, victorious over all remorse.

INDEX